THE MORALITY OF WAR

second edition

THE MORALITY OF WAR

SECOND EDITION **BRIAN OREND**

broadview press

LIBRARY AND ARCHIVES CANADA CATALOGUING IN PUBLICATION

Orend, Brian, 1971–, author
The morality of war / Brian Orend. — Second edition.

Includes bibliographical references and index.
ISBN 978-1-55481-095-6 (pbk.)

1. War—Moral and ethical aspects. 2. War (International law) 3. Just war doctrine. I. Title.

U22.O723 2013 172'.42 C2013-904833-2

BROADVIEW PRESS is an independent, international publishing house, incorporated in 1985.

We welcome comments and suggestions regarding any aspect of our publications—please feel free to contact us at the addresses below or at broadview@broadviewpress.com.

NORTH AMERICA
Post Office Box 1243
Peterborough, Ontario
Canada K9J 7H5

2215 Kenmore Ave.
Buffalo, New York, USA 14207
TEL: (705) 743-8990
FAX: (705) 743-8353

customerservice@broadviewpress.com

UK, EUROPE, CENTRAL ASIA, MIDDLE EAST, AFRICA, INDIA, AND SOUTHEAST ASIA
Eurospan Group, 3 Henrietta St., London WC2E 8LU, United Kingdom
TEL: 44 (0) 1767 604972 FAX: 44 (0) 1767 601640
eurospan@turpin-distribution.com

AUSTRALIA AND NEW ZEALAND
NewSouth Books
c/o TL Distribution, 15–23 Helles Ave.,
Moorebank, NSW, Australia 2170
TEL: (02) 8778 9999 FAX: (02) 8778 9944
orders@tldistribution.com.au

www.broadviewpress.com

Broadview Press acknowledges the financial support of the Government of Canada through the Canada Book Fund for our publishing activities.

Edited by Robert M. Martin
Typesetting by Em Dash Design

This book is printed on paper containing 100% post-consumer fiber.

Printed in Canada

CONTENTS

For Michael

ACKNOWLEDGMENTS

I'm lucky to have a second edition of this book, and grateful to everyone at Broadview for the opportunity, and their confidence. Special thanks to: Stephen Latta, for the original idea and all the support and backing; Bob Martin, for great editing; Lisa Brawn for an amazing cover design; and Allison LaSorda, Tara Lowes, and Leslie Dema, and all the promotion people as well.

This book has taken me on quite the journey! Thanks to the militaries of the following countries for invitations, and acknowledgments, connected with it: Australia; Britain; Canada; France; Germany; and Holland. But I owe deepest thanks to the US military: for its use of this book (in spite of some of my criticisms); for its commitment to the ethical education of its service people; and for the many opportunities to address their soldiers and officers over the years. No country is more dedicated to debating these ideas than America. Special thanks to: the Army, especially the USMA at West Point (and Dan Zupan and Dave Barnes); the CGSC at Fort Leavenworth, (and Larry Dabeck, Sean Wead, and Ted Ihrke); the Air Force, and its striking USAFA at Colorado Springs; and lastly but specially the Navy, especially the USNA at Annapolis, the Stockdale Center, as well as to fellow just war theorists Martin Cook and George Lucas.

Thanks so much to those closest to me, my family and friends, and especially: my son, Sam, who's just getting old enough to ask smart questions about these issues; and Jennifer McWhirter, for all the things we've been able to share.

This edition is dedicated to Michael Walzer. I still remember the otherwise unremarkable afternoon when I happened across the second edition (☺) to his landmark study *Just and Unjust Wars*. It was 1995, and I was a young grad student simply browsing the shelves at Columbia University's old bookstore. I bought the book, devoured it, and it truly transformed the entire arc of my academic career. I wish everyone such an exciting experience. One of the deepest things Michael ever taught me was that one always writes within a tradition of thought, whether one likes it or not. Trained as a philosopher, I resisted this, preferring to be charmed instead by the image of Descartes, alone by the fireside, spinning existence out of the privacy of his own mind. But Michael was right, and even dear Descartes drew heavily on the thinking of others. I've since learned to embrace and appreciate my membership within the just war tradition—one of the longest-lived traditions of thought in all politics—and see myself as being a fellow-builder of this vitally important theory. Here's to its on-going development, and to Michael, for everything you've done for me. Cheers!

Brian Orend, May 2013

INTRODUCTION

"In War: Resolution
In Defeat: Defiance
In Victory: Magnanimity
In Peace: Goodwill"
—WINSTON CHURCHILL[1]

Imagine that you are the President of the United States, and it's the morning of September 11, 2001. You are enjoying a public relations session, reading to school children in Florida. Up rushes a Secret Service Agent, who whispers into your ear about the attacks in New York, Washington, and Pennsylvania. You close your eyes, briefly, and your mind reels. This is the absolute last thing you ever wanted to happen "on your watch." The full weight—the incredible responsibility—of the presidency suddenly seems to push you down, as if into the ground. You finish your session with the children politely, but your thoughts are detached, obsessing instead on the questions of what you should do, and whether more attacks are coming...

Well, what would *you* do? Your country has just experienced the most dramatic strikes against it since Pearl Harbor. Indeed, these attacks seem deliberately modeled after that explosive "Day of Infamy" in 1941. The attacks on the World Trade Center were terrorist acts, deliberately killing random civilians with the motive of spreading fear throughout the American people. But the strike on the Pentagon seems to be more a classical act of war, deliberately striking an official military target.[2] Put them together and you've got a powerful case that your country is under attack by a deadly force with malevolent intent: armed self-defense seems the order of the day.

But is it? Are you letting your anger, and desire for revenge, affect your judgment? What about your fear and uncertainty? How do you find out about who did this—and how do you know that you can trust that source of knowledge? How do you balance the views of those "hawkish" advisors urging a muscular military response and the views of those "doves" saying that terrorism is best dealt with by using "methods short of war" and not the armed forces? Do you project an angry and forceful exterior so as to convey strength, or do you rather remain measured and cautious, so you won't panic your people? Do you strike now—to prevent possible further attacks—or wait for more evidence and a cooler head?

How might your private beliefs mix with your public responsibilities here? Say you are an intensely religious person... a pacifist by faith. Should you let your *personal* attitudes affect your *official* choices, which will impact around the world? (For, even though you *are* the president, you're still merely one imperfect person representing over 300 million diverse Americans.) Say, by contrast, that you're a cynic, thinking it's "a dog-eat-dog world" out there. Will you let that cynicism rule your deliberations, on grounds that "we've got to get them before they get us again"? Finally, what if you're a moralist, and you are completely outraged by this huge injustice dealt to your country by the attackers? Should you turn that outrage outward, using military force like a flaming sword, crusading on behalf of righteousness?

These are all difficult questions—they push different buttons—and only one person had to confront them for real that day. We should, to an extent, empathize with those who have to make such seemingly impossible decisions. On the other hand, we must still insist that such decision-makers *explain* their choices to us—their fellow citizens—and enumerate their reasons for doing, and ordering, what they do. For warfare, in all its forms, is damn serious business. Its very gravity, its deep degree of consequence, its enormous cost, and its profound impact on people's lives, demand that we reflect intelligently upon its nature and the choices surrounding it.

War should be understood as an *actual, intentional,* and *widespread* armed conflict between political communities. Thus, a fisticuffs between individual persons does not count as a war, nor does a gang fight, nor does a family feud on the order of the Hatfields versus the McCoys. War is a phenomenon which occurs only between political communities, defined as those entities which either are states or intend to become states (in order to allow for civil war). Classical war is international war, a war between different states, like the two World Wars. But just as present—and apparently growing in incidence[3]—is war within a state between rival groups or communities, like the American Civil War or the on-going civil strife in Syria. I suppose that certain political pressure groups, like terrorist organizations, might also be considered "political communities," in that they are associations of people with a political purpose and, indeed, many of them aspire to statehood (or, at least, to influence the development of statehood in certain lands).

What's statehood? Most people follow Max Weber's distinction between nation and state. A *nation* is a collection of people which thinks of itself as a unique and separate group, usually because they have many important things in common, such as ethnicity, language, culture, historical experience, a set of ideals and values, habitat, cuisine, fashion, and so on. The *state,* by contrast, refers—much more narrowly—to the machinery of government which organizes life in a given territory.[4] Thus, we can distinguish between the American state and the American people, or between the government of France and the French nation. At the same time, you've probably heard the term "nation-state." Indeed, people often use "nation" and "state" interchangeably—but we'll need to keep them conceptually distinct for our purposes. "Nation-state" refers to the relatively recent phenomenon wherein a nation wants its own state, and moves to form one. This started out as a very European trend—an Italian state for the Italian nation, a German state for the German people, etc., but it has spread throughout the world. Note that in some countries—such as America, Australia, and Canada—the state actually presides over many nations, and you hear of "multi-national societies." Most societies with heavy immigration are multi-national. Multi-national countries are sometimes prone to civil wars between the different groups. This has been especially true of central Africa in recent years,[5] as different peoples struggle over control of the one state, or else move to separate themselves from the existing arrangement (itself often having been put in place by distant imperial powers insensitive to local differences between groups or ethnicities). All these distinctions will come in handy as we proceed. For now, we note how central nationalism, and the issue of statehood, are to the essence of warfare. Indeed, I would argue that *all warfare is precisely, and ultimately, a struggle between groups over governance.* War is a violent way for determining who gets to say what goes on in a given territory, for example, regarding: who gets power; who gets wealth and resources; whose ideals prevail; who is a member and who is not; which laws get made; where the border rests; how much tax is levied; and so on. War is the ultimate means for deciding these issues if a peaceful process, or resolution, can't be found.

The mere threat of war, and the presence of mutual disdain between political communities, do not suffice as indicators of war. The conflict of arms must be actual, and not merely latent, for it to count as war. Further, the actual armed conflict must be both intentional and widespread: isolated clashes between rogue officers, or border patrols, do not count as actions of war. The onset of war requires a conscious commitment, and a significant mobilization, on the part of the belligerents in question. There's no real war, so to speak, until the fighters intend to go to war and until they do so with a heavy quantum of force. (Most social scientists don't define an armed struggle between groups as a war unless and until there are 1,000 battlefield deaths.[6])

Let us here cite the views of the one and only (so-called) "philosopher of war," Carl von Clausewitz. Clausewitz, a Prussian officer who saw battlefield action against Napoleon, famously suggested that war is "the continuation of policy by other means." Surely, as a description, this conception is both powerful and plausible: war is about governance, using violence instead of peaceful measures to resolve policy (i.e., the principles by which government organizes life in a land). This notion fits in nicely with Clausewitz's own general definition of war as "an act of violence intended to compel our opponent to fulfill our will." War, he says, is like a duel, but on "an extensive scale."[7] As Michael Gelven has more recently written, war is intrinsically vast, communal (or political), and violent.[8] It is a widespread and deliberate armed conflict between political communities, motivated by a sharp disagreement over governance. In fact, we might say that Clausewitz was right, but not quite deep enough: it's not just that war is the continuation of policy by other means; it's that war is about the very thing which creates policy—i.e., governance itself. War is the intentional use of mass force to resolve disputes over governance. War is, indeed, governance by bludgeon. Ultimately, war is profoundly anthropological: it's about which group of people gets to determine what goes on in a given territory.

War is a brutal and ugly enterprise. Yet it remains central to human history and social change. These two facts together might seem paradoxical and inexplicable, or they might reveal deeply disturbing facets of the human character. What is certainly true, in any event, is that war and its threat continue to be driving forces in our lives. Recent events graphically demonstrate this proposition, whether we think of the 9–11 attacks, the counter-attack on Afghanistan, the overthrow of Iraq's Saddam Hussein, the Darfur crisis in Sudan, the intervention in Libya, the non-intervention in Syria, or the on-going (perpetual?) "War on Terror."

War's violent nature, and controversial social effects, raise troubling moral questions for any thoughtful person. Is war always wrong? Might there be situations when it can be a justified, or even a smart, thing to do? Will war always be part of human experience, or can we do something to make it disappear? Is there a fair and sensible way to wage war, or is it all hopeless, savage slaughter? When wars end, how should post-war reconstruction proceed, and who should be in charge? What are our rights, and responsibilities, when our own society makes the move to go to war?

This book will explore all these questions and more. It is designed to be an introduction to the ethics of war and peace which is clear, comprehensive, and informed by modern history and current events. It guides the reader through all the controversies and competing values, and it discusses in detail cases ranging from World War II to the Persian Gulf War, from Vietnam and 9/11 to the overthrows of both Saddam Hussein and Muammar Gaddafi. This text, it is hoped, will offer a very strong foundation, on war's essential moral questions, to any interested and reflective reader.

The book is split up into two sections, and it does recommend a particular way of best understanding these issues. This way is framed by current international law and just war theory. This way is, in my view, both the most important and influential perspective in today's world, as well as the most solidly grounded ethically. Hence the extended first section on this perspective. *Just war theory is a connected body of ideas and values which considers when war can be ethically justified.* It offers a set of moral rules which societies should follow during the beginning, middle, and end of war. We will examine and explain these rules in depth in the first section. It is especially important to do so, since so many of these rules have made their way into the international laws of armed conflict, contained in such famous documents as the United Nations Charter and the Hague and Geneva Conventions.[9] This is not, however, a dusty book devoted to pains-taking analysis of such laws; it is, rather, a "big picture" book centrally focused on the more important ethical principles behind these laws and how such principles apply to, and shed light on, actual cases of armed conflict.

Just war theory's core premise is that, sometimes, countries can be morally justified in going to war. Pacifism, by contrast, is best understood as the view that war is never morally justified. Realism, the third big perspective on this issue, disagrees with both pacifism and just war theory by suggesting that war's got nothing to do with morality: it is all about naked self-interest, survival, and the pursuit of power over one's rivals. Almost all opinions regarding war's morality can be slotted into one of these three fundamental attitudes, based on these definitions.

Realism and pacifism are examined and evaluated in the book's second section and, where appropriate, I do describe the historical context and delve behind each body of thought. While, in the end, I do argue for and endorse just war theory, I strive to be fair and charitable both to realism and pacifism. They each have something substantial to contribute to the debate. In the final analysis, though, I believe that realism and pacifism should be, on the whole, rejected as somewhat extreme doctrines, whereas just war theory appeals as occupying the sensible middle ground. This is not to say that just war theory is perfect or fully satisfying. It is neither of these things, and it probably needs constant redevelopment in light of new events, ideas, and technology, but it remains more satisfying than the alternatives. Just war theory is, so to speak, the least-worst theory in this regard.

This text—the second edition, I'm very happy to say—has a number of distinctive features which commend it to the reader. First, it is completely up-to-date, and analyzes the latest issues, such as: terrorism and preventive defense against it; armed humanitarian intervention (AHI); and cyber-warfare. Second, it also examines the latest cases, such as: the 2011 AHI in Libya; and the nearly ended efforts at post-war reconstruction in Iraq and Afghanistan. Third, the book includes an appendix offering lists of (and websites for finding) the most important laws of armed conflict. (There is also, in each chapter's endnotes, a comprehensive list of further sources.) Fourth, this book connects just war theory to deeper issues of ethics and politics, such as human rights protection. Too often, just war theory has been portrayed as a somewhat quaint, peculiar, self-standing structure at the margins of applied ethics—instead of as being a consistent, important, and integral part of a human rights-based approach to some of the most pressing political issues of our time. This is to say, I view just war theory as a set of rules designed to protect human rights as best they can be, amid the rough-and-tumble circumstances of war.[10]

This book goes well beyond conventional treatments of just war theory by examining: 1) its main rivals—realism and pacifism—in detail; 2) both just war theory's history and its current concepts and applications; 3) the interconnections between the various just war rules and categories, and the meaning of the international laws reflecting them; 4) new demands for international authorization for resorting to force; 5) supreme emergencies, including genocide; 6) the fast-gelling "R2P" doctrine (commanding the "Responsibility to Protect" people in the face of so-called "mass atrocity crimes" [MACs]); 7) cyber-warfare and other EMTs (i.e., Emerging Military Technologies, including drones); 8) the controversial growth of for-profit "private military companies" (PMCs); 9) the justice of peace settlements, occupations, and post-war reconstruction; and 10) the complex issue of how governments should treat their own citizens—be they civilians or soldiers—during wartime. This last issue concerns topics such as civil liberties and anti-terrorist legislation, and it only strengthens the profound connection between just war theory and political philosophy more broadly: what do we want our society to be, and to strive to achieve, even as we go about defending it from dangerous attacks and determined opponents?

Notes

1 Winston Churchill, *The Gathering Storm* (Boston: Houghton Mifflin, 1948), xi-xii. [Volume 1 of his six-volume *History of the Second World War*.]

2 Der Spiegel, *Inside 9/11: What Really Happened* (New York: St. Martin's, 2002); US Congress, *The 9/11 Commission Report* (New York: W.W. Norton, 2011).

3 Kalevi J. Holsti, *The State, War, and the State of War* (Cambridge: Cambridge UP, 1996).

4 Max Weber, *General Economic History* (London: Dover, 2003).

5 Gérard Prunier, *Africa's World War* (Oxford: Oxford UP, 2008).

6 Christopher Gelpi et al., *Paying the Human Costs of War* (Princeton, NJ: Princeton UP, 2009).

7 Carl von Clausewitz, *On War*, trans. Anatol Rapoport (Harmondsworth, England: Penguin, 1995), 100–02.

8 Michael Gelven, *War and Existence* (Philadelphia, PA: Penn State UP, 1994).

9 Adam Roberts and Richard Guelff, eds., *Documents on The Laws of War*, 3rd ed. (Oxford: Oxford UP, 2000).

10 Brian Orend, *Human Rights: Concept and Context* (Peterborough, ON: Broadview, 2002).

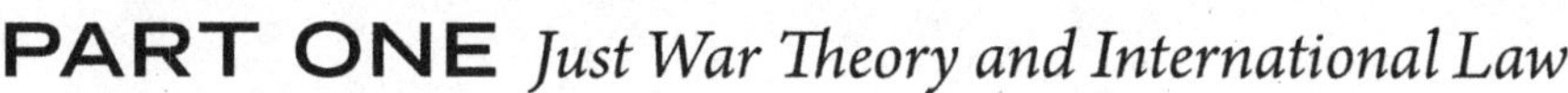

PART ONE *Just War Theory and International Law*

1 A SWEEPING HISTORY OF JUST WAR THEORY

"Some political theories die and go to heaven; some, I hope, die and go to hell. But some have a long life in this world..." —MICHAEL WALZER[1]

People have wrestled with the ethics of war and peace since the beginning of human history, and not just in Western civilization but world-wide. Almost all major civilizations—from the ancient Egyptians to the Aztecs, from Babylon to India, from China to medieval Europe and contemporary America—have featured quite colorful beliefs about acceptable reasons for going to war, and permissible means of fighting it.

Nearly all the major religious documents—from the Bible to the Bhagavad Gita, from the Book of Tao to the Koran—refer to warfare and moralize about it.[2] The Old Testament, for instance, is filled with fierce battles. Yahweh and the prophets repeatedly permit, or even command, the Israelites to go to war against their enemies. Sometimes the commands seem quite blood-thirsty, other times restraint in fighting is urged.[3] Jesus, by contrast, fills the New Testament with words and actions which seem at least anti-war and are, perhaps, pure pacifism. The Prince of Peace, as Christians know him, once famously commanded Peter to put away his sword.[4] In the ancient Sanskrit epic *The Mahabharata*, a spirited debate erupts between five brothers, focused on whether the suffering created by war can ever be justified.[5] Sun Tzu's *The Art of War*—from ancient Chinese civilization, yet often taught in today's Western business schools—details various kinds of battle, and the strategies required for victory. Yet it, too, includes a kind of ethic: of fighting only smartly and with honor, and not with rage, blunder, and blood-lust.[6] So, in a way, the ethics of war is everywhere, and is as old as the hills.[7]

One of just war theory's credits is that, over time, it has developed probably the most comprehensive consideration of the ethics of war and peace. So, even though just war theory first developed in the West—and, more narrowly, among Roman lawyers and then Catholic theologians—it genuinely deserves universal attention. The fact that just war theory has had such impact on international law—which is truly global—only emphasizes how important it is for anyone wanting to think incisively about the ethics of war and peace.[8] Just war theory, as we mentioned in the Introduction, is a coherent set of concepts and values which enables moral judgment in wartime. Traditionally, it's split into two categories: *jus ad bellum* (i.e., when it's just to start war) and *jus in bello* (i.e., how it's just to fight war, after it has begun). International law, by contrast, refers generally to treaties freely agreed to by sovereign states, wherein they promise to behave in a way detailed by the treaty. Treaties are like international contracts—solemn promises of behavior—between countries. And so the concepts and values first originating in the moral philosophy of just war theory have, over the centuries, made their way into binding treaties regulating state conduct during war—treaties we collectively refer to as "the laws of armed conflict."[9]

The purpose of this opening chapter is to sketch out the history of just war theory itself: *who* contributes *what*, and then *when* and *why*. Above all: what's the context here? Which events and personalities are crucial? Which mistakes get made, and strengths endure? What are the trends and cycles, discussions and debates? Where did we come from in this regard, and where are we heading? It must be stressed, however, that all that can be offered in one chapter is but a sweeping sketch. This book is not mainly a history book. It is a book about the ethics of war and peace *in our time*. So, while whole books could be written about the topics in each of the following paragraphs, it is not our goal to know every little detail and personality in the very long history of just war theory. The goal, rather, is to hit the high points and, above all, to set the context for the concepts which are going to be detailed in subsequent chapters.

1. The Greco-Romans

So where does just war theory specifically come from, and why should we care? Paul Christopher credits ancient Greek philosopher Aristotle (384–322 BCE) with being the coiner of the term "just war."[10] This concept was in contrast to the older idea of a "holy war," as mandated by some Divinity and described in some of the religious texts mentioned above. Just war theory is, at heart, a *secular* concept—i.e., a way of thinking about war's rightness or wrongness without appealing to God or scripture. But we'll see that, historically, just war theory does come to be associated, for some time, with Christianity and, more narrowly, Catholicism.

Aristotle, and his teacher Plato (427–347 BCE), reflected on war's justice, no doubt spurred on by all the wars fought between Greeks and Persians and, indeed, amongst the Greek city-states themselves. Plato, for instance, grew up during the destructive Peloponnesian War between Athens and Sparta and it profoundly affected his life and thinking.[11] Aristotle thought it morally justified to go to war to prevent one's community from being attacked and enslaved by another. Just war theorists today agree that self-defense from aggressive attack is the most obvious *just cause* for war. More controversially, Aristotle thought it alright to go to war to gain an empire, provided: 1) this empire would benefit everybody, including the conquered; and 2) this empire would not become so large and rich that it would attract attackers and hence result in more wars. Most notoriously, and appallingly, Aristotle did allow warfare to gain slaves for one's community—providing that such slaves were "naturally servile" to begin with. Not a single just war theorist would today endorse these last two propositions but the empire issue retains real life. For example, does America now have an empire? Has it come by this empire justly? Have its many recent wars been those of defense or, rather, of expanding and fortifying its dominion?[12]

After the Greeks came the Romans, and they clearly did have an empire. The shattering success of Rome upon the battlefield provoked thought amongst such luminaries as the senators Cato and Cicero and the emperors Julius Caesar and Marcus Aurelius. Cicero (106–43 BCE) probably developed the deepest reflections on war among them, and probably deserves credit for co-founding just war theory with Augustine (still to come) and, perhaps to a lesser extent, Aristotle. James Turner Johnson's observation—that just war theory is, in its origins, a synthesis of Greco-Roman and Christian values—rings true.[13] Cicero endorsed wars of self-defense, and was not immune to the allure of empire. Crafty lawyer he was, though, by framing his support for imperial expansion with the rhetoric of defense: defense of Rome's honor or glory might call for wars of empire whereas defense of Rome's safety strictly might not. But Cicero rejected wars for gaining slave labor. He was also a stickler for procedure. And so, to Aristotle's primordial just cause requirement for a decent war, Cicero added the rules of *proper authority* and *public declaration*.

So often did the Romans find themselves in battle—almost annually—that they developed a formal procedure for going to war. Rome would first send a diplomatic party (ambassadors and their aids) to the target city or rival empire, announce the problem, and demand rectification. The party would return to Rome and wait for one month. If nothing satisfying happened, the party would return to the enemy and threaten war. If they did not get an immediate, positive reply, the party would return to Rome and inform the Senate (seen as the proper authority for deciding war). If the Senate voted for war, the party would return to the enemy, read aloud the Senate's public declaration of hostilities, and then symbolically throw a sharp-pointed javelin into the enemy's soil. The party would then, obviously, quickly evacuate before the Roman army invaded and—more often than not—destroyed. There are, in this procedure, some shades of the later rule of war only as a last resort: the military had to hold off until the political procedure had worked itself out to the end. Cicero also insisted on vague rules of right conduct in fighting, too. He commented repeatedly on the need for restraint in battle, and advocated loudly and effectively that soldiers surrendering to Rome deserved to be protected rather than slaughtered. Those who refused to surrender, however, deserved a different fate in Cicero's eyes.[14]

2. Early Christianity and Augustine

Church father Augustine (354–430 CE) is often credited with inventing just war theory all by himself. This is a huge exaggeration which downplays the Greco-Roman contribution, which we've just seen is substantial. Indeed, Augustine wasn't even the first Christian thinker to consider the justice of war: Tertullian (160–230 CE); Origen (185–255 CE); Lactantius (260–340 CE); and Augustine's mentor Ambrose (340–397 CE) all made contributions. Indeed, Ambrose added content to Cicero's vague *jus in bello* by stressing that soldiers should strive to display the classical virtues—courage, prudence, justice, and moderation—while fighting. More significantly, Ambrose added to the Greco-Roman rules of *jus ad bellum*—just cause, proper authority, public declaration, last resort—by saying that wars approved by God were also just. Augustine followed Ambrose in this regard; the result was a blurring of the line between *just* wars and *holy* wars, lasting about 1,000 years, and providing support for the pope-ordered Crusades—of Christianity against Islam—between approximately 1100 and 1300 CE.[15]

Taking all this in, it's very hard to conclude that Augustine was the sole founder of just war theory. He was, however, a very high-profile and influential proponent of the theory, and Christianity's subsequent triumph in Western civilization led later thinkers to want to identify a Christian, rather than a Greco-Roman pagan, as the founder. (If we have to put names and faces on the foundation of just war theory, it would probably be the triumvirate of Aristotle, Cicero, and Augustine. Traditions take some time to be created and congealed.) Now, Augustine did add to the theory in an original way. He insisted on the rule of *right intention*, both in *jus ad bellum* and *jus in bello*. Augustine wrote during a time when Christianity had become—thanks to the emperors Theodosius and Constantine—the official, state-sanctioned religion of the Roman Empire. How could one, consistently, be both a Christian and a public official of Rome—especially when the Empire was coming under increasing armed attack from non-believing barbarians? Christianity seems, after all, to imply love and non-violence whereas the responsibilities of Roman officials regularly involved deploying armed force to hold the Empire together and to keep "the heathen barbarians" out. Augustine wrestled greatly with this dilemma, and concluded that a just ruler might permissibly use force to protect the innocent (i.e., ordinary civilians) from aggressive attack. A Christian ruler has to show love for his own people, and is duty-bound to ensure their survival and well-being. But such a ruler must order war with only the greatest reluctance, and not with any pleasure, or hatred for the enemy, whatsoever. The right intention must be love for, and desire to protect, the endangered innocents. Soldiers executing this command of the ruler must likewise get no joy out of bloodlust and violence but, rather, should protect the innocents and fend off the guilty attackers with nothing but solemn duty as their mental focus. So, in addition to *objective* just causes, such as the defense of one's community from attack, there is the *subjective* requirement of being psychologically motivated strictly by love and duty alone. Augustine summarized his thoughts this way:

> The real evils in war are love of violence, revengeful cruelty, fierce and implacable enmity, wild resistance, and the lust of power, and such like; and it is generally to punish these things, when force is required to inflict the punishment, that, in obedience to God or some lawful authority, good men undertake wars.[16]

3. The Dark Ages and Holy Wars

The Roman Empire collapsed in Western Europe in the 400s CE, fragmenting in the face of repeated barbarian invasions. It had grown too large to govern efficiently, and too often its governors were corrupt and incompetent, lacking the skill and drive displayed by such original builders as Caesar and Augustus. It managed to endure in the Near East—as the re-styled Byzantine Empire—for over a thousand years more, but in the West the only institution to survive the collapse of Roman civilization was the Catholic Church. The western empire otherwise dissolved into a series of small ethnic groups, and tribe-like families, and many wars between them ensued.[17] Not much information survives from this period, and so we call it the Dark Ages. What little does survive tells us, sporadically, of an anarchical and bloody existence, a dirty and decrepit life. Europe took major steps back during the Dark Ages, which lasted from about 500–1000. At the same time, Islamic civilization in the Middle East and North Africa (MENA), and Eastern civilizations in China and India, flourished.[18]

During the Dark Ages' latter years, starting around 800, attempts were made by ambitious local warlords to consolidate their control over larger pieces of territory. Alfred did this in Britain and Charlemagne on the Continent. While not immediately successful, these efforts pointed the way towards the future: local tribal heads gradually winning control over larger and larger pieces of territory, declaring themselves champions of the people in the process. They re-established law and order, by force of arms, farm-by-farm and forest-by-forest. A handful of such warlords eventually became self-styled kings, monarchs of their realms. All the while, such warlords had to deal with the Church: its longevity; its substantial land holdings; its moral authority over its flock. Most warlords were eager to win the Church's approval, for it was a powerful ally and could provide their rule no better stamp of legitimacy. As a result, many European warlords heeded the call when the Church, between 1000–1300 CE, demanded a series of military crusades, against the encroachment of Islam into Europe. These Crusades were massive armed invasions of Muslim strongholds in Eastern Europe, and throughout the MENA.[19]

It is important to distinguish just war and holy war, especially since so many early Christian thinkers conflated the two. A holy war (*bellum sanctum*) is a war approved of—either commanded or permitted—by God. The approval is thought to come from sacred scripture itself or from religious authorities, such as the pope. Pope Urban II, in 1095, inaugurated the First Crusade by declaring "*Deus vult*!" (i.e., "God wills it!"). God was thought to "will it" so that Christians would retake Jerusalem from Islamic control and prepare it for Christ's second coming to Earth. The Christian conquest of that city did indeed happen in 1099. The Muslims, under Saladin, later took it back, and the Second and Third Crusades were thus motivated. The other main feature of a holy war (labeled a "*jihad*" in the Islamic tradition)[20] is that soldiers fighting on behalf of the cause are seen, thereby, to be cleansing their sins and paving their entry into Paradise. Salvation of self, so to speak, through mutilation of others. A just war (*bellum justum*), by contrast, is not thought to be sacred, merely moral. There is no pretense of having divine approval, rather merely good reasons (like self-defense, or protecting innocents) for fighting a war. And while soldiers fighting just wars might be thanked or even praised (e.g., on Remembrance or Veteran's Day), there is no claim that their participation in the war has guaranteed them membership in Heaven. We see, then, that there need be no necessary connection at all between doctrines of just war and those of holy war. But Dark Age Christians, especially those involved in the Crusades, did forge such a connection—and so *jus ad bellum* became, frankly, polluted with some dark religious dimensions, like self-righteousness, inflexibility, demonization of others, and fanaticism. It was to be a long time before such pollution was met with sufficient dilution, and today no just war theorist endorses the holy war concept as a good reason to go to war.[21]

While perhaps regressing on the *jus ad bellum* side, this era did manage big progress on the *jus in bello* front. Great specificity was added to Cicero's vague calls for moderation, Ambrose's insistence on fighting with virtue, and Augustine's command for purity of intention. Two papal edicts—the "Peace of God" of 989 and the "Truce of God" of 1027—combined with the decrees of the Second Lateran Council of 1139 and Gratian's *Decretum* of 1148 to form quite concrete and sensible rules of *jus in bello*. Non-combatants were specified—notably, women and children—and held to be ethically immune from attack or hostage-taking. (This rule of *non-combatant immunity* is today seen, widely, as *jus in bello*'s most important rule.) A whole range of new weapons were prohibited, including cross-bows and anything—swords and arrows especially—dipped in poison or pestilence. Attacks on food sources, like crops, were completely ruled out, and churches officially declared "sanctuary" from military, and indeed police, activity. The sources of these rules were the Bible, Augustine's writings, experience with the new weapons, and even aristocratic sporting tournaments (featuring jousting) and their customs regarding fair play, honorable conduct, and chivalry.[22]

4. Aquinas and Legitimacy

By the time of Thomas Aquinas (1225–74), we can properly speak of a reasonably settled and articulated "just war tradition," with many different people deploying the same concepts and values in aid of judging the same thing—in this case warfare—and often arriving at very similar conclusions. We have at this time clearly separate and quite developed categories of *jus ad bellum* and *jus in bello*. Under the former, we have rules of: just cause; right intention; public declaration by a proper authority; and not exactly "last resort" but something like "give the enemy a chance to make amends before fighting." Under the latter, we now have: non-combatant immunity; right intention; non-use of prohibited weapons; an obligation to accept offers of surrender without slaughter; and something like "behave with virtue and chivalry on the battlefield." This constitutes, over 1500 years, huge theoretical progress from Aristotle's quick and spare declarations regarding just cause.

Aquinas was a huge fan of Aristotle's and, to the existing set of rules, the Italian theologian added *proportionality* to each category. This was good Aristotelian sense: war should be a proportionate, or balanced, response to the grievance (i.e., the problem must really be so severe—like an armed invasion—that war can be considered a fitting response) and the quantum of force deployed should be appropriate to the objective at hand on the battlefield. Aquinas also invented something called the Doctrine of Double Effect (DDE), which has important applications within *jus in bello*, to be discussed in subsequent chapters. Aquinas was also a transitional figure on two issues. The first is the acceptability of holy war as a just cause. Aquinas notably backed off here, saying that defensive wars to protect Christians from death (or severe persecution) at the hands of non-Christians *might* be permissible but aggressive wars designed to coerce non-believers into Christianity *definitely* aren't. Jesus himself, after all, didn't create Christians by cracking skulls. The spotty record of the Crusades also prompted Aquinas to pour cold water on the holy war concept.

Unfortunately, the idea would still come and go, at least in the West, until Hugo Grotius's authoritative proclamations against holy wars in the early 1600s. Truly, even after that, holy-war-style rhetoric has been known to infect justifications of war to this very day.

Aquinas also marks a transition on the important issue of proper authority for declaring war. In Greece, the proper authority was the head of the (city-) state, whether dictator or elected assembly. In Rome it was (during the Republic) the Senate and (during the Empire) the Emperor. During the Dark Ages, it was the Pope. But in the run-up to Aquinas's life, there was a very fluid political situation in Europe. There was still the Pope and the Church, of course, but there was also the development of these tribal or national kings, like King John in England. Furthermore, some areas of Europe were essentially Greek-style city-states, for example Venice. There were also very wealthy trading enterprises, with their own private militias or armed security corps—some so powerful they dwarfed the armed forces of towns and other political associations. Also sporting private militias were aristocrats out to challenge the king, on the belief that their families were just as entitled to the throne. Aquinas, perhaps surprisingly, did not side with the Church. Not so surprisingly, he condemned the private militias and armed trading companies. He favored the non-proliferation of armies. Common sense told him: the more armies we've got, the more likely they'll step on each other's toes and start fighting, leading to bad consequences all around. Aquinas's middle-of-the-road solution was that only genuinely *political*—and not merely *mercantile*—associations could declare war, and the body which spoke for the political association was the one that: 1) was capable of ordering that society; and 2) demonstrated clear intentions to rule for the common good of all (as opposed to the private greed of some, such as ambitious barons, dukes, and earls). Essentially, then, Aquinas favored more central authority, such as a national king or prince, but still strongly advised such a ruler to heed the advice of the Church, what with its centuries of experience in developing and applying just war theory. In this sense, Aquinas sided with the rise of the modern nation-state.[23]

5. Vitoria and the Spanish Conquest

It is important to note that, from the start, just war theory has been applied to real world conflicts and has served not just to *legitimize* but also to *criticize* the conduct of the powers that be. Augustine, it's true, was mainly looking for a legitimation of state violence: he wanted to square public Roman control with his private Christian beliefs. But later thinkers realized that, when a state (or prince) fails to meet the standards of just war theory, then it (or he) must be morally criticized and urged to stop. For instance, in Spain in the early 1500s, numerous figures used just war theory to condemn Spain's aggressive invasion and colonization of parts of the New World. Spain was motivated neither by love nor by any kind of defense or protection, they said. The kingdom, delighted by Columbus's 1492 discoveries, became driven by greed and love of power and conquest, and the harsh treatment of the natives by the infamous "conquistadors" revealed this, and was a separate evil besides.[24]

Key figures involved in the debate over the justice of the Spanish Conquest were: Bartolemé de las Casas (1474–1566); Sepulveda (1490–1574); Francisco de Vitoria (1492–1546); Francisco Suarez (1548–1617); and Alberico Gentili (1552–1608). Sepulveda and Gentili tried to use just war concepts to justify the conquest, with Sepulveda even resurrecting Aristotle's old canard about natural slavery. De las Casas, by contrast, offered a clear, eloquent, and principled denial and critique. The entire faculty of the University of Salamanca, in 1520, bravely resolved in public that Spain's actions constituted an unjust war. It's important, indeed, to note that European colonialism and imperialism did not proceed with unanimous support. Vitoria's work has stood the test of time as the deepest theoretical contribution from this fertile period.[25]

Vitoria was the first to say clearly that even non-Christian communities have the rights implied by *jus ad bellum* (notably, a general right not to be attacked and enslaved). He rejected the concept of holy wars, and insisted on the secularism of just war theory. He helpfully suggested that all plausible just causes for going to war be subsumed under the one concept of "a wrong received." He thus banned both aggression and pre-emption (because the wrong had to be received before one could justly respond to it). On this latter point, he memorably commented: "It is quite unacceptable that a person should be killed for a sin he has yet to commit."[26] Vitoria did allow for armed humanitarian intervention as a kind of war of "other-defense." He actually justified the Spanish Conquest on this basis, at least in terms of just cause. He sharply criticized Spanish intentions of greed and power but did believe that the Conquest liberated the natives of the Americas from indigenous oppression and such brutal home-grown practices as human sacrifice and ritualized cannibalism. So self-defense and other-defense were, for Vitoria, the only just causes for going to war, and in either case it had to be defense from attack which already occurred and not from an imagined one merely suspected to come in the future.

One of the most important contributions made by Vitoria was his stress on the quality and objectivity of the evidence needed to support a decision to go to war. Vitoria strongly rejected the idea that the ultimate decision should rest with only one man—even the king—since any given man is so subject to strong emotions, subjective biases, and incomplete understandings. A just ruler must first invite counsel from groups of wise men: 1) learned in just war theory; and 2) who represent different opinions about the war action contemplated. A hawkish ruler surrounding himself only with "yes-men" is not being responsible and may find himself ordering, and then later accountable for, an ultimately unjustifiable war.[27]

6. Grotius and The Wars of Religion

Hugo Grotius (1583–1645) was similarly motivated by the imperial experience, in his case by the colonizing Dutch, particularly in the Caribbean Indies. His landmark work, *The Law of War and Peace*, was also driven by the terrible Wars of Religion—between Catholic and Protestant—then rocking Europe in the wake of the Protestant Reformation and the end of the Catholic Church's religious monopoly over Western Europe.[28] The savagery of the fighting in both the New World and the Old concentrated Grotius's mind powerfully, and he vowed to do what he could to bring warfare within the confines of law once more. One of his biting remarks in this regard was:

> Throughout the Christian world I have seen a lawlessness in warfare that even the barbarian races would think shameful. On trifling pretexts, or none at all, men rush to arms and when once arms are taken up, all respect for law, whether human or divine, is lost as though by some edict a fury had been let loose to commit every crime.[29]

Grotius's work—not so much original as pains-taking, comprehensive, and level-headed—is credited not only as being one of the landmark pieces of just war theory but also as one of the first productions of the laws of armed conflict. Grotius thus straddles the gap between morality and law, and he intoned that the very point of law is to realize the ideals of morality. Not surprisingly, given the Wars of Religion, Grotius was a relentless secularizer, echoing Vitoria's rejection of holy wars and essentially sealing the debate on that issue for the remainder of the just war tradition (though not, as we noted, in popular political culture). Religion is a matter of conscience and choice—or at least for each nation to decide for itself, he wrote—and so it cannot figure into any just cause for war. On just cause, Grotius essentially shared Vitoria's understanding of self- and other-defense. Grotius did go further, however, in specifying that it was allowable not merely to defend against aggression in the process of happening (whether against self or others) but also to punish past aggression which still stood uncorrected. Grotius, as a lawyer, was strongly in favor of concrete penalties for violations of principle, and so wars of punishment (as well as defense) figured into his system. He actually justified some of the colonial conquests as punishment for iniquitous (ungodly?!) practices on the part of the natives. He also contributed the criterion of *probability of success* to *jus ad bellum*: one should only go to war if one has a decent chance of winning. It is, I suppose, lamentable that the two just war giants from this period—Vitoria and Grotius—both supported European colonial conquests, viewing them as justified forms of other-defense or humanitarian intervention, designed to rescue innocents in another country. That's true, but they also both criticized the intentions of the European imperialists and so, in the end, took a rather dim view of colonialism or, at the least, viewed it as a mixed bag of crimes and benefits.[30]

We can see that, with Grotius, most of the general principles of modern just war theory became set. Disagreements about what the theory exactly implied in terms of each particular war, of course, remained—and just cause remained especially contentious, and does so to this day. But the essentials were all in place, and indeed a new focus for the theory developed: getting nation-states to agree to the general *moral* principles in exact, formal, written, *legal* treaties. Just three years after Grotius's death, the Treaty of Westphalia (1648) brought the Thirty Years War (the bloodiest of the Wars of Religion) to an end.[31] Often seen as the first piece of modern international law, Westphalia enshrined a form of tolerance over religion, with national signatories pledging not to go to war with each other in attempt at armed conversion. A principle of non-intervention in "the internal affairs" of other nations was generated, and just war theorists Samuel Pufendorf (1632–1704) and Emmerich Vattel (1714–67) solidified this trend by rejecting humanitarian intervention as a just cause for war. This strong interpretation of state sovereignty, and hostility to any foreign intervention in local affairs, was to endure almost to the end of the 1990s. The prevailing interpretation of just cause was thus: 1) defense of one's nation from foreign attack; 2) defense of another nation (especially one's ally or friend) from foreign attack; and 3) (possibly, depending on the theorist) pre-emptive attack. War as punishment was not generally accepted, and humanitarian interventions were largely prohibited. "Westphalian state sovereignty" reigned supreme.[32]

7. Locke, Kant, and the Revolutionary Era

Other prominent thinkers wrote in a just war vein in this era of Pufendorf and Vattel, for example John Locke (1632–1704) and Christian Wolff (1679–1754). But they failed to add much of originality to the theory. Increasingly, the just war tradition declined in prominence because it dealt with war between states whereas the issue increasingly at hand was the right to make a war of revolution within a state or empire. Here, of course, Locke had much of import to say and his writings partly inspired the American Revolution (1775–83) and, through it, the French Revolution (1789–1800).[33]

Now, the question of revolutionary war can logically be incorporated within just war theory. It is, after all, a form of war—indeed, a kind of civil war. As such, it would fall under the principles to be defended in Chapter 3. These principles, we'll see, revolve around the legitimacy (or moral adequacy) of the state in question. Locke remains the classical source for insisting that, to be legitimate (i.e., to have the right to rule), a government must respect the natural (or human) rights of all its individual citizens to: life, liberty, and property (Thomas Jefferson substituted for this last, the pursuit of happiness). A government which fails in this regard is illegitimate and, should it forcefully resist reform, it may be forcibly resisted and overthrown, paving the way for a rights-respecting regime which the people support and recognize as their government. Locke's work on violent revolution is perhaps the first clear linkage between *jus ad bellum* and human rights, a linkage which was to be cemented following World War II and which remains absolutely central today. But Locke did not think of himself as a just war theorist, nor did the tradition embrace him in return. This is unfortunate since Locke drew substantially on Aquinas and, indeed, venerable old Aristotle had much to say about revolutionary struggles. Perhaps Locke's staunch Protestantism prevented a complete connection to what then remained very much a Catholic or "scholastic" doctrine.[34]

This religious difference also prevented Immanuel Kant (1724–1804) from connecting his thought with the just war tradition. Indeed, Kant explicitly distanced himself from the tradition, even poked sarcastic fun at its classical figures. However, as I've shown elsewhere,[35] Kant's thoughts on war and peace shared much of the moral logic of just war theory as it existed in his day—with one big exception. This was the whole issue of *jus post bellum* (justice after war). More than any other thinker before him, Kant reflected intensively on the justice of peace treaties, of forcing regime change in a defeated society, of post-war reconstruction, and of what might be needed for longer-term peace between nations. In particular, Kant favored widespread internal regime change in the direction of rights realization, and thought some international policies—like diplomatic engagement, cultural linkages, and free trade—would help bring this about. Pro-rights societies, he predicted, would eventually band together to form a prosperous, peaceful federation of free nations. Their success, in turn, would spur other nations to change internally so as to join the club, and a kind of peaceful "cosmopolitan federation" would grow and grow.[36]

In my view, we can all but completely credit Kant for inventing *jus post bellum*. It's true that Vitoria did insist that justice after war had to be part of just war theory—but he failed to add content to this observation. It's also true that just war theorists stretching all the way back to Aristotle intoned that peace must be the sought-after goal in war. But this assertion is banality itself: *every war ends in peace*, including an unjust one. This is to say that even an aggressor aims at, and looks forward to, the peace at the end of a conflict. The real question is: *what kind of peace can justly be imposed via war*? And on that difficult issue, there was fundamental silence, or else sweeping vagueness, until Kant came along. Indeed, to this very day a rather large number of just war theorists completely ignore *jus post bellum*. But they can't do that and pretend they have a complete theory. We have Kant to thank for "priming the pump" of our thoughts on this issue, which is so vital to our own times. *Jus post bellum* will be discussed in detail in Chapters 6 and 7.

8. The Coming of Codification

It really is remarkable that it was not until the mid-1900s that just war theorists equal to the stature of Grotius, Pufendorf, and Vattel appeared. Many of the figures, in the 1750–1950 period evidently believed that the existing synthesis could not be much improved upon. And those who did clearly improve upon the status quo—like Locke and Kant—weren't recognized as card-carrying members of the tradition. There is another factor relevant in the explanation: after 1850, there is a veritable explosion in the number of international treaties and laws regulating armed conflict, in particular *jus in bello*. Grotius's dream of codification came true—200 years after his death. The period 1850–1914 was extremely fertile in this regard. I've no doubt that many of the diplomats, academics, and lawyers who worked on such treaties and codes would have made first-rate just war theorists. But the opportunity was ripe for them to engage in legal construction instead of theory-building, and so pragmatically they chose the former. This may have come at the price of anonymity but the gain was the world's first formal codes enshrining just war principles within law.

European powers, for their part, signed the Declaration of St. Petersburg in 1868, which prohibited certain bullets and projectiles, but the US Civil War was truly the major spark in this regard. The North (Union) forces—in 1863—issued very detailed instructions on proper ways to fight to its soldiers. These *jus in bello* rules were called the "Field Army Manual" or "Lieber's Code" after their author. The American Civil War also brought into stark relief moral issues of *jus ad bellum*—e.g., the justice of fighting a war to end slavery—as well as *jus post bellum* issues of proper post-war pacification and reconstruction of the vanquished enemy. In these manifold senses, this war remains a very relevant case for even the most contemporary just war theorist.[37]

The culmination of this nineteenth century move towards codification (i.e., translating moral principles into specific legal codes) was the Hague Conventions, drafted and proclaimed in ten different treaties between 1899 and 1907. Incredibly detailed, particularly with *jus in bello* rules, they stand today as living and active pieces of international law which are a credit to their authors. They are, in many ways, the complete realization of Grotius's dream.[38]

9. World War I and Collapse

Grotius could not, of course, have foreseen the scale and depth of World War I (1914–18), which shocked the conscience of the world and provided an ugly birth to the ultra-violent twentieth century. The war—begun as a struggle of imperial rivalries between Germany, Austria-Hungary, and Turkey on the one side and Britain, France, and Russia on the other—degenerated into a long and tragic slaughter. The human meat-grinder which was this war was halted only when America intervened, in 1917, on the side of Britain and France. It's fair to say that the bleak experience of World War I—causing 20 million deaths—made people very cynical about linking justice and warfare, and so once more just war theory fell into disuse. Indeed, even one of the popes declared just war theory out of date! There are three important exceptions to these general observations. The first is that many people strongly criticized the 1919 Treaty of Versailles as an unjust peace treaty. (But no one went on to articulate a general theory about what a just peace treaty fully should be. They contented themselves with particular observations, like "Germany was treated too harshly," "Britain and France extended their empires out of greed," "America simply let all this happen," and so on.) The second exception was that, with the post-war formation of the League of Nations, there was an attempt to change the emphasis within *jus ad bellum* rules away from self-defense ("unilateralism") towards collective security and mutual responsibility in the face of aggression ("multilateralism"). The final exception was that the chemical weapons deployment experienced in the trenches of Europe—on both sides—spurred the development and signing of a treaty, in 1925, banning the use of poisonous gas in wartime. But it must be admitted that these were all political and legal developments, and they went unaccompanied by any new major piece of just war theory at this time.[39]

10. Rebirth and World War II

The Kellogg-Briand Pact of 1928 was an ambitious piece of international law, designed to shrink radically the number of just causes for going to war, and to buttress the war-authorizing power of the multilateral League of Nations. We see, during this period, the first attempts at making the declaration of war an international responsibility and power. The rise of the fascist dictatorships, in the '30s, effectively gutted both these institutions, but it also resurrected interest in just war theory. Many Catholic scholars, and political leaders like Winston Churchill, explicitly used just war concepts to justify and generate public support for the war against Hitler's Nazis in Germany and Mussolini's fascists in Italy. Indeed, dissidents in Spain used just war theory to justify their civil war against Franco's fascists earlier in the 1930s.

While not invoking just war theory explicitly, Franklin D. Roosevelt harkened all the way back to Aristotle when he explained that America had to enter the war in 1941, as a matter of self-defense following Japan's Pearl Harbor attacks.[40]

By 1941, the world no longer dismissed just war theory as sterile and of use only to European scholars of the history of Catholicism. Systematic works appeared, including English-language works by John Ryan and John Ford.[41] Extensive effort was placed into the justification of the war on the part of the Allies. But this rebirth was not merely one-sided, superficial Allied propaganda. It was the just war community, after all, who first raised the questions and criticisms which still haunt historians today: should the Allies, especially Britain, have engaged in deliberate terror bombing of Germany's residential areas—and emphatically the purposeful razing of Dresden to the ground in 1945? Should America ever have used the atomic bomb on Japan? There were no clear laws on these unprecedented issues—and so thoughtful people turned back to just war theorists for answers, or at least guidelines. It's fair to say most just war theorists were critical of these Allied actions, and this criticism perhaps reached a highpoint after the war when Elizabeth Anscombe wrote a much-read pamphlet, "War and Murder," criticizing Oxford University's decision to award an honorary doctorate to Harry S. Truman, the US President who had ordered the nuking of Hiroshima and Nagasaki.[42]

World War II, and its immediate aftermath, had profound impacts upon just war theory. Grotius's emphasis on proper punishment found ready application in the Nuremberg and Tokyo war crimes tribunals, the first in modern history.[43] The 1945 Charter of the United Nations (UN) rigorously addressed *jus ad bellum*, placing even more emphasis on collective security and international authorization than the League of Nations did—but realistically allowing for armed self-defense as well. Echoes of voices of the University of Salamanca faculty could be heard in the set-up of the UN's Trusteeship Council, an institutionalized process for aiding the gradual end to European colonialism, especially in Africa and Asia. But the clearest impact on, and expression of, just war theory resided in the 1948 Convention Banning Genocide, and the landmark 1949 Geneva Conventions, which are devoted to *jus in bello*, especially regarding the specification of "benevolent quarantine" for prisoners of war. These are two of the most important laws of armed conflict to this day.[44]

The main impetus for these legal reforms was the Holocaust and its horrors, which also inspired the 1948 Universal Declaration of Human Rights.[45] This was a moment of great significance for just war theory, because now theorists saw that the new moral basis for the age was destined to be human rights—the proper treatment of individual persons—and so they got to work interpreting traditional just war theory in light of human rights. This took some doing, and it wasn't done in a clearly satisfying way until perhaps the 1970s. But the move was made and it probably saved just war theory from ethical oblivion. In other words, and at long last, the just war tradition essentially had to welcome John Locke in from the cold, and forcefully and fully deal with core issues of state legitimacy, human rights, and—above all—the deep connection between the two, and how armed force may be required to defend them. This linkage is one of the most vital, and still challenging, to this day—as aspects of this book will demonstrate.

11. Our Time

11.1. THE 1960S: EARLY COLD WAR AND NUCLEAR DETERRENCE

The onset of the nuclear age posed new problems for just war theory, and attention focused on the morality of atomic weapons and of nuclear deterrence—i.e., of the threat to use such weapons second so that the enemy won't use theirs first. This was especially the case in the 1950s and early 1960s, and then again during the 1980s when Ronald Reagan was US President. But America's experience during the Vietnam War, 1955–75, sparked the biggest development in just war theory at least since World War II and perhaps even stretching all the way back to the Spanish Conquest. It's important to note that, historically, it tends to be the questionable wars—the Spanish Conquest, the Wars of Religion, Vietnam—which provoke the most soul-searching, and thus the biggest developmental spurts in just war theory. Some might wish to include on that list America's 2003 invasion of Iraq.

The center of action, in just war theory, moved at this time firmly out of the Catholic Church and into the corridors of international law and power, as well as into the groves of academe and even the streets of non-violent protest. English-language works, especially by Americans, now became the "must-read" contributions to the theory—and it has stayed that way since, though of course one cannot discount the contributions of others, such as Australians, British, Canadians, Europeans, and Israelis. (Israel's many post-1948 wars have sparked keen interest there in just war theory.[46]) In the 1960s, the work of Ian Brownlie, Joseph McKenna, William O'Brien, Robert Osgood, Paul Ramsey, and Robert Tucker stood out very prominently.[47]

11.2. THE 1970S: VIETNAM, AND WALZER'S *JUST AND UNJUST WARS*

In the 1970s, literally scores of important articles appeared, such as those published in the distinguished journal *Philosophy and Public Affairs* by R.B. Brandt, R.M. Hare, R.K. Fullinwider, David Luban, and Thomas Nagel. Vital books were written by Sydney Bailey, Yehuda Melzer, J.N. Moore, and Richard Wasserstrom.[48] But Michael Walzer's *Just and Unjust Wars*, of 1977, remains the breakthrough work of that decade, directly inspired by Vietnam. It's not much of an exaggeration to say this work has been to current just war theory what Grotius's *The Laws of War and*

Peace was to prior centuries. As such, it will be referred to throughout this work as well: there's simply no avoiding it. Even when it is disagreed with, Walzer's book remains the fundamental contemporary reference, which everyone "in the business" must read and understand. It is in Walzer's book, above all, that the cementing of human rights theory within the core propositions of just war theory occurs, and is offered some satisfying treatment. On the application side, Walzer's book is devoted to showing that World War II exemplifies just, but Vietnam unjust, wars.[49] In terms of the laws of armed conflict, so many treaties were signed in the '60s and '70s that the reader is simply directed to Appendix A for topics, listings, and locations. It was a tumultuous and therefore fertile time for just war theory. Just war theory grows in spurts, in reaction to war-ravaged events, and—as noted—especially in response to wars about which people are skeptical and critical.

The 1980s, 1990s, and forward have seen an explosion in the number of just war theorists, and important developments in the theory itself. In the '80s, nuclear deterrence was front and center, as Reagan's America stared down the USSR, and the Catholic Church got back in on the action, so to speak. In 1983, the US Catholic Bishops published a reflection on nuclear ethics which was high profile and influential, eliciting responses from European bishops, and academics and think-tanks world-wide. Also important was the topic of training new soldiers in ethics and international law. The US military in particular—stung by episodes of misconduct during Vietnam—invested large resources in the education of its soldiers and officers in just war theory. Other militaries followed suit. Walzer was a primary reference, as were new works by Sidney Axinn, Anthony Hartle, James Turner Johnson, Douglas Lackey, John Langan, Robert Phillips, Jim Sterba, and Jenny Teichman. (Johnson deserves special mention as probably the most learned historian of the tradition.) The morality of indirect (but still armed) American intervention in such Latin American countries as Nicaragua—highlighted by the Iran-Contra scandal—was also very topical in the 1980s, with proponents justifying the controversial moves as part of the larger chess game of defeating the USSR. Sometimes such figures justified the Cold War struggle between America and Russia in realist terms as a fight for survival between utterly opposed enemies; other times they made explicit appeals to morality, urging the need to destroy "the evil empire" and its godless, rights-violating system of police-state communism.[50]

11.3. THE 1990S: HUMANITARIAN INTERVENTION, AND THE NEW "R2P" DOCTRINE

In the 1990s, following the end of the Cold War and America's triumph in it, just war theorists returned to issues of collective security and the vigor of the United Nations, which the Cold War in many ways had sapped and frustrated. The 1991 Persian Gulf War generated a big just war literature—indeed, US President George

Bush Sr. argued for the war using just war language[51]—as did the nasty civil wars and severe humanitarian crises ranging from Bosnia to Somalia, from Rwanda to Kosovo. We will detail each of these wars later in this text. The ethics of humanitarian intervention became the largest just war issue in the 1990s, and it generated deep critical thought about whether the old defenses by Grotius, Pufendorf, and Vattel for non-intervention in local affairs, were mistaken. Perhaps, instead, renewed attention to the pro-humanitarian intervention doctrine of, say, Vitoria was more in order. The catastrophic consequences of the failure to intervene in Rwanda—800,000 people slaughtered, in an attempted genocide, in the spring of 1994[52]—put some clear pro-intervention flavor back into many just war works, and resulted in pro-intervention policies on the ground later on in Bosnia (1995), Kosovo (1999), and Libya (2011). Indeed, far from Westphalian state sovereignty, there has emerged since the '90s the so-called *"R2P Doctrine,"* short for "Responsibility to Protect."[53] We will detail the full content of this doctrine in Chapter 3. For now, we note how the humanitarian crises in the '90s provoked a revolution within just war doctrine and, through it, international law, allowing today for a much more expansive use of force on behalf of victimized innocents, wherever they may be.[54]

11.4. OTHER '90S DEVELOPMENTS: SWEEPING SANCTIONS AND THE ICC

Intervention was the big *jus ad bellum* issue of the '90s; the big *jus in bello* issue was the set of sweeping sanctions slapped on Iraq following its defeat in the Persian Gulf War by America. Did the sanctions violate the principle of discrimination, wrongfully inflicting serious harm on millions of innocent civilians?[55] We'll consider this issue in detail in Chapter 4. Prominent just war pieces were penned this decade by: Paul Christopher, Jean Bethke Elshtain, G.S. Davis, Michael Ignatieff, and Richard Regan.[56] The major reform in the laws of armed conflict was the 1998 Treaty of Rome, which created the first permanent and international war crimes tribunal—the International Criminal Court (ICC)—set up to judge war crimes committed anytime, anywhere, by anybody. Grotius the punisher would've been pleased.[57]

11.5. AFTER 9/11

This brings us to the very present, and of course we're not far enough removed to make good judgments about which works will last and which issues will endure the most. Scores of smart people are actively creating important pieces of writing, and others are crafting vital military and foreign policies on the ground. Clearly, though, the 9/11 terrorist attacks on the United States, in 2001, dramatically impacted the debate, and raised questions in particular about just wars against non-state actors. The subsequent 2003 invasion of Iraq created heated debate about *the justice of preemptive war* and/or preventive strikes. This is one issue around which there is very little consensus amongst just war theorists, stretching all the way back to its origins:

may you justly strike another before he strikes you, if you sincerely believe he is just about to do so? Or is it as Vitoria says, that you cannot punish someone for a sin they have yet to commit? These are big issues for Chapter 3.

An even deeper issue is whether, as some have argued, the laws of war and just war theory must be completely re-thought in the "Age of Terror." Why might this be? Well, the laws of armed conflict and just war theory have generally been constructed assuming that state governments, and their armed forces, are the main belligerents. But 9/11 revealed that so-called "non-state actors," such as terrorist groups, can now pose state-scale levels of threat and destruction. Are new principles needed to handle such "*asymmetrical warfare*"? Or do we have the tools already to evaluate the so-called "War on Terror"? And what of other non-state actors using force, such as so-called private military companies (or PMCs)?[58]

An emerging theoretical issue of *jus in bello*, which has caught on like wild-fire in the past decade, attracting the attention of some of today's most talented moral philosophers,[59] concerns *the moral status of the ordinary soldier*. Must s/he always obey commands? Should s/he refuse to fight a war s/he believes unjust? What is the true connection between the *jus ad bellum* issue of whether a war is just or not and the particular *jus in bello* controversies surrounding: 1) who is a proper target; and 2) what may soldiers do on behalf of the countries for which they fight?

The difficult and multi-faceted occupations of Iraq and Afghanistan—now just about to end—raise profound issues of *jus post bellum*. Just war theorists are increasingly coming around to the importance of this topic,[60] which Walzer himself has recently called one of the two most vital for the theory's future. The other is the *jus in bello* issue of *soldiers striving to carve out a risk-free fighting environment for themselves via technology*, perhaps off-loading their own risks upon powerless civilians. (Think here of the long-range, high-altitude bombing of Kosovo and Serbia in 1999, or, more obviously, the use of unmanned, weaponized "drones" over the MENA today.)[61] I might add a few more issues to Walzer's list of the most consequential current topics. The first concerns *the ethics of detaining and torturing suspected terrorists* to gain information thought needed to prevent future terrorist attacks. The second would be *the justice of overthrowing governments* and setting out, right from the start, to forcibly reconstruct their societies along better, more pro-human rights, lines. And the third: the so-called EMTs ("*Emerging Military Technologies*"), especially cyber-warfare, which form the focus of Chapter 5.[62]

12. Conclusion

It might seem strange—in this sweeping but still substantial history of just war theory—that no mention has been made of realism or pacifism. This was deliberate, since the focus was on just war theory and, to a lesser extent, the laws of armed conflict. But of course the other two doctrines have their own robust histories, and at times these histories have impacted on just war theory. This is true of realism in particular. Realism has been the main rival to just war theory, in terms of affecting the behavior of those with the war power. Pacifism is principled, and it has had its own kind of influence through time, but pragmatically no nation-state or empire has ever based its foreign policy on pacifism. The only exceptions to this might be old, isolated religious communities and conquered nations engaging in non-violent (or, at least, non-warring) resistance.[63]

Which has had more influence on foreign policy: realism or just war theory? The answer is that there is a kind of cycle, and at times realism is on the ascendant and at others just war theory. Walzer, in 2002, wrote an article entitled "The Triumph of Just War Theory." He clearly believes just war theory is ascendant in the post-Cold War era.[64] Perhaps this fact is connected with American hegemony during this era and America's self-image as an ethical force in world history, concerned with fighting only just wars. (There is some irony in traditionally Catholic just war theory living and thriving perhaps most strongly in historically Protestant America.) But perhaps that's not relevant. Perhaps it's more a fact—just like with Rome and Spain in their days—that the most powerful nation just naturally asks itself the most questions about the justice of its influence and its frequent resort to force. There is something substantial to Walzer's claim, no doubt. Recent armed conflicts have indeed been justified by vocal moral appeals to just war concepts like humanitarian intervention and self-defense. Other people have criticized the exact same wars using just war rules like right intention, proper authority, last resort, and proportionality. Scholars like Martin Cook, George R. Lucas, Jr., and Alex Bellamy have all shown the continued utility and impressive resilience of just war theory, even in light of brand new technology and drastically changing circumstances.[65]

But perhaps the triumph of just war theory is already fading. The post-9/11 world does, after all, concern itself mightily with national security. Some have suggested the on-going War on Terror is the next Cold War; the original Cold War (approximately 1946–91) was obviously a time of realism triumphant, what with the balance of nuclear terror and the cold-blooded chess game of geopolitical struggle between communism and capitalism. Only time will tell, of course. Other commentators view the recent wars not as isolated conflicts to be evaluated one-at-a-time with the tools of just war theory. They view them, rather, as parts of a larger, over-all strategy—an empire-building strategy—by the United States, as it seeks (in arch-realist fashion) to protect itself and to extend its domain, values, economy, and influence as far and as deeply as it possibly can. And America has done so—and is still doing so—in part to check the rise of potential future rivals, notably China (but also such others as Germany and Russia, and countries/movements in the MENA committed to doctrines, such as radical Islamic extremism, seen to be at odds with American interests).[66]

More will be said about the specific histories of realism and pacifism, and their competition with just war theory, in Part Two. For the moment, now that we've completed our sketch of the history of just war theory—and laid down some context of people and places, of wars and peaces—we must turn to the conceptual task of understanding the rules and values of present-day just war theory, and then applying such to recent cases of armed conflict.

Notes

1 Michael Walzer, "The Triumph of Just War Theory" in his *Arguing About War* (New Haven, CT: Yale UP, 2004), 3.

2 Paul Christopher, *The Ethics of War and Peace* (Englewood Cliffs, NJ: Prentice Hall, 1994), 8–16; Terry Nardin, *The Ethics of War and Peace: Religious and Secular Perspectives* (Princeton NJ: Princeton UP, 1998); John Kelsay, *Islam and War* (London: John Knox, 1993); Steven J. Rosen, *Holy War: Violence and the Bhagavad Gita* (Bombay: Deepak, 2004).

3 See, e.g., Deuteronomy 20, Joshua, or the Chronicles.

4 Matthew 26:52; John 18:10.

5 John D. Smith, ed. and trans., *The Mahabharata* (New York: Penguin, 2009).

6 Sun Tzu, *The Art of War*, trans. Samuel B. Griffith (New York: Oxford UP, 1963).

7 Gregory Reichberg et al., eds., *The Ethics of War: Classic and Contemporary Readings* (London: Wiley-Blackwell, 2006).

8 Alexander Gillespie, *History of the Laws of War*, 3rd ed. (London: Hart, 2011); Stephen Neff, *War and The Law of Nations* (Cambridge: Cambridge UP, 2008).

9 W. Michael Reisman and Chris T. Antoniou, eds. *The Laws of War* (New York: Vintage, 1994); Adam Roberts & Richard Guelff, eds., *Documentation on the Laws of War*, 3rd ed. (Oxford: Oxford UP, 2000); Gary D. Solis, *The Law of Armed Conflict* (Cambridge: Cambridge UP, 2010).

10 Christopher, *Ethics*, 10–11, citing Aristotle's *Politics* [1256b, 25].

11 Donald Kagan, *The Peloponnesian War* (New York: Penguin, 2004).

12 Christopher, *Ethics*, 7–13; Niall Ferguson, *Colossus* (New York: Basic, 2004); Michael Hardt and Antonio Negri, *Multitude: War and Democracy in the Age of Empire* (New York: Penguin, 2004); Ivan Eland, *The Empire Has No Clothes* (Oakland, CA: The Independent Institute, 2005).

13 James Turner Johnson, *The Quest for Peace* (Princeton NJ: Princeton UP, 1987), 45.

14 Cicero, *De Re Publica*, 3, XXIII, trans. Clinton Walker Keyes (New York: Putnam, 1928), 211–15; Christopher, *Ethics*, 13–16.

15 John Eppstein, *The Catholic Tradition of the Law of Nations* (Washington, DC: CAIP, 1935); Christopher, *Ethics*, 17–29; Jonathan Riley-Smith, ed., *The Oxford History of the Crusades* (Oxford: Oxford UP, 1999).

16 Herbert A. Deane, *The Political and Social Ideas of St. Augustine* (New York: Columbia UP, 1963); Christopher, *Ethics*, 30–48; quote from Augustine, *The City of God*, trans. Robert Dyson (Cambridge: Cambridge UP, 1998), 1:21.

17 Christopher Kelly, *The Roman Empire* (Oxford: Oxford UP, 2006).

18 Fern Braudel, *History of Civilization* (New York: Penguin, 1995).

19 Barbara H. Rosenwein, *A Short History of the Middle Ages* (Peterborough, ON: Broadview, 2002); John France, *Western Warfare in the Age of the Crusades, 1000–1300* (London: University College of London, 1999).

20 Alia Brahimi, *Jihad and Just War in the War on Terror* (Oxford: Oxford UP, 2010).

21 As a result, just war theorists tend to be very skeptical of any politician today making use of pro-war rhetoric which seems to skate on the edge between just war and holy war. See also: Riley-Smith, ed., *Oxford History*; James Turner Johnson, *The Holy War Idea in Western and Islamic Traditions* (Philadelphia, PA: Penn State UP, 1997); John Kelsay and James Turner Johnson, *Just War and Jihad* (New York: Greenwood, 1991).

22 Peter Temes, *The Just War* (New York: Ivan Dee, 2003); Christopher, *Ethics*, 49–52; Paul Robinson, *Military Honour and The Conduct of War from Ancient Greece to Iraq* (New York: Routledge, 2006).

23 Frederick H. Russell, *The Just War in the Middle Ages* (Cambridge: Cambridge UP, 1975); Aquinas, *Summa Theologiae* 2–2, Qs 40 and 64; Joan D. Tooke, *The Just War in Aquinas and Grotius* (London: SPCK, 1975).

24 Matthew Restall, *Seven Myths of the Spanish Conquest* (Oxford: Oxford UP, 2004).

25 James Turner Johnson, *Ideology, Reason and The Limitation of War* (Princeton NJ: Princeton UP, 1975); James Turner Johnson, *The Just War Tradition and The Restraint of War* (Princeton NJ: Princeton UP, 1981); Juan Ginés de Sepulveda, *Democrates Alter*, trans. Stafford Poole, in *Contemporary Civilization Reader*, 6th ed. (New York: American Heritage, 1997), 39–51; Bartolomé de las Casas, *In Defence of the Indians*, trans. Stafford Poole (Chicago: Northern Illinois UP, 1992).

26 Francisco de Vitoria, *Political Writings*, ed. Anthony Pagden and Jeremy Lawrence (Cambridge: Cambridge UP, 1991), 315–16.

27 Christopher, *Ethics*, 58–67.

28 Andrew Cunningham and Ole Peter Grell, *The Four Horsemen of the Apocalypse* (Cambridge: Cambridge UP, 2001).

29 Hugo Grotius, *The Law of War and Peace*, trans. by Louise Ropes Loomis (Roslyn, NY: W.J. Black Inc., 1949), 10–11.

30 Richard Tuck, *The Rights of War and Peace* (Oxford: Oxford UP, 1999); Christopher, *Ethics*, 70–110; David B. Abernethy, *The Dynamics of Global Dominance: European Overseas Empire, 1415–1989* (New Haven, CT: Yale UP, 2001).

31 Peter H. Wilson, *The Thirty Years War* (Cambridge, MA: Harvard UP, 2009).

32 David Boucher, *Political Theories of International Relations* (Oxford: Oxford UP, 1998); A. Cassese, *International Law*, 2nd ed. (Oxford: Oxford UP, 2005).

33 Tuck, *Rights*, 166–96; John Locke, *Two Treatises of Civil Government* (Cambridge: Cambridge UP, 1988); Bernard Bailyn, *The Ideological Origins of the American Revolution* (Cambridge, MA: Harvard UP, 1992); William Doyle, *The Oxford History of the French Revolution* (Oxford: Oxford UP, 1990).

34 Tuck, *Rights*, 169–99; Richard H. Cox, *Locke on War and Peace* (New York: Rowman Littlefield, 1983).

35 Brian Orend, *War and International Justice: A Kantian Perspective* (Waterloo, ON: Wilfrid Laurier UP, 2000).

36 Immanuel Kant, *Political Writings*, trans. Hugh Bar Nisbet, ed. Hans Reiss (Cambridge: Cambridge UP, 1995); Immanuel Kant, *Perpetual Peace*, trans. Ian Johnston, ed. Brian Orend (Peterborough, ON: Broadview, forthcoming 2014).

37 David Kennedy, *Of War and Law* (Princeton NJ: Princeton UP, 2006); James M. McPherson, *Battle Cry of Freedom: The Civil War Era* (Oxford: Oxford UP, 2003).

38 Reisman and Antoniou, eds. *Laws*; Michael Byers, *War Law* (Washington, DC: Atlantic, 2009); Lydia de Beer, *The Hague Conventions* (The Hague: International Courts Association, 2011).

39 John Keegan, *The First World War* (New York: Vintage, 2000); Manfred Franz Boemeke, ed. *The Treaty of Versailles* (Cambridge: Cambridge UP, 1998); Margaret MacMillan, *Paris 1919* (Toronto: Random House, 2003); Reisman and Antoniou, eds., *Laws*.

40 John Keegan, *The Second World War* (New York: Vintage, 1990).

41 John Kenneth Ryan, *Modern War and Basic Ethics* (Milwaukee, WN: Bruce, 1940); John C. Ford, "The Morality of Obliteration Bombing," *Theological Studies* 5 (1944): 261–309.

42 Gertrude Elizabeth Margaret Ancombe, "War and Murder" in Richard A. Wasserstrom, ed. *War and Morality* (Belmont, CA: Wadsworth, 1970), 41–53.

43 Joseph E. Persico, *Nuremberg: Infamy on Trial* (New York: Penguin, 1995); Timothy P. Maga, *Judgment at Tokyo* (Lexington, KY: U of Kentucky P, 2001).

44 Fred L. Borch III and Gary D. Solis, eds. *Geneva Conventions* (New York: Caplan, 2010); Geoffrey Best, *War and Law Since 1945* (Oxford: Clarendon, 1994).

45 Martin Gilbert, *The Holocaust* (New York: Henry Holt, 1987); Brian Orend, *Human Rights: Concept and Context* (Peterborough, ON: Broadview, 2002).

46 Ahron Bregman, *Israel's Wars* (London: Routledge, 2010).

47 Ian Brownlie, *International Law and the Use of Force by States* (Oxford: Clarendon, 1963); Joseph C. McKenna, "Ethics and War: A Catholic View," *American Political Science Review* 54 (1960): 647–58; William Vincent O'Brien, *The Law of Limited International Conflict* (Washington, DC: Georgetown UP, 1965); Robert E. Osgood and Robert W. Tucker, *Force, Order and Justice* (Baltimore: Johns Hopkins UP, 1967); Robert W. Tucker, *The Just War* (Baltimore: Johns Hopkins UP, 1960); Paul Ramsey, *The Just War* (New York: Scribners Sons, 1968); Paul Ramsey, *War and The Christian Conscience* (Durham, NC: Duke UP, 1961).

48 Sydney Dawson Bailey, *Prohibitions and Restraints in War* (Oxford: Oxford UP, 1972); John Norton Moore, *Law and Civil War in the Modern World* (Baltimore: Johns Hopkins UP, 1974); Yehuda Melzer, *Concepts of Just War* (Jerusalem: Hebrew University, 1975); Richard A. Wasserstrom, ed. *War and Morality* (Belmont, CA: Wadsworth, 1970).

49 Michael Walzer, *Just and Unjust Wars* (New York: Basic, 1977). [4th edition, 2006.]

50 Sidney Axinn, *A Moral Military* (Philadelphia, PA: Temple University Press, 1989); Anthony E. Hartle, *Moral Issues in Military Decision-Making* (Kansas City: U of Kansas P, 1989); James Turner Johnson, *Can Modern War Be Just?* (New Haven, CT: Yale UP, 1984); Douglas P. Lackey, *The Ethics of War and Peace* (Englewood Cliffs, NJ: Prentice Hall, 1989); John Langan and William V. O'Brien, eds., *The Nuclear Dilemma and the Just War Tradition* (Lexington, MA: Lexington, 1986); Robert L. Phillips, *War and Justice* (Oklahoma City: U of

Oklahoma P, 1984); James P. Sterba, *The Ethics of War and Nuclear Deterrence* (Belmont, CA: Wadsworth, 1985); Jenny Teichman, *Pacifism and The Just War* (Oxford: Blackwell, 1986); Martin Walker, *The Cold War: A History* (New York: Henry Holt, 1995).

51 Jean Bethke Elshtain, ed., *But Was It Just? Reflections on the Morality of the Persian Gulf War* (New York: Doubleday, 1992), 12–13.

52 Gérard Prunier, *The Rwanda Crisis: History of a Genocide* (New York: Columbia UP, 1995).

53 The International Commission on Intervention and State Sovereignty, *Report: The Responsibility to Protect* (Ottawa, ON: International Development Research Centre, 2002).

54 Alex J. Bellamy, *Responsibility to Protect* (London: Polity, 2009); Gareth Evans, *The Responsibility to Protect: Ending Mass Atrocity Crimes Once and For All* (Washington, DC: Brookings Institute, 2009); Nikolas Gvosdev, *R2P: Sovereignty and Intervention After Libya* (London: World Politics Review, 2011).

55 Geoff L. Simons, *The Scourging of Iraq* 2nd ed. (London: Palgrave Macmillan, 1998).

56 Paul Christopher, *The Ethics of War and Peace* (Englewood Cliffs, NJ: Prentice Hall, 1994); Jean Bethke Elshtain, ed. *Just War Theory* (Oxford: Blackwell, 1992); Michael Ignatieff, *Blood and Belonging* (Toronto: Viking, 1994); Michael Ignatieff, *The Warrior's Honor* (New York: Doubleday, 1997); Michael Ignatieff, *Virtual War* (Toronto: Viking, 2000); Richard J. Regan, *Just War: Principles and Cases* (Washington, DC: Catholic UP of America, 1996).

57 William A. Schabas, *An Introduction to the International Criminal Court* (Cambridge: Cambridge UP, 2001); G. Simpson, *Law, War and Crime* (Oxford: Polity, 2007).

58 Jean Bethke Elshtain, *Just War Against Terror* (New York: Basic Books, 2003); Eric A. Heinze and Brent J. Steele, eds., *Ethics, Authority and War: Non-State Actors and the Just War Tradition* (London: Palgrave Macmillan, 2009); Kateri Carmola, *Private Security Companies and New Wars* (London: Routledge, 2011).

59 David Rodin, *War and Self-Defence* (Oxford: Clarendon, 2005); Jeff McMahan, *Killing in War* (Oxford: Oxford UP, 2009); Seth Lazar & Cécile Fabre, *National Defence* (Oxford: Oxford UP, forthcoming 2013); David Rodin & Henry Shue, eds., *Just and Unjust Warriors* (Oxford: Oxford UP, 2008).

60 Larry May and Andrew Forcehimes, *Morality, Jus Post Bellum and International Law* (Cambridge: Cambridge UP, 2012).

61 Walzer, "Triumph," 17–18; Peter W. Singer, *Wired for War* (New York: Penguin, 2009).

62 Jeffrey Carr, *Inside Cyber Warfare* (London: O'Reilly, 2010).

63 Peter Ackerman and Jack DuVall, *A Force More Powerful* (New York: St. Martin's, 2000).

64 Walzer, "Triumph," 18–19.

65 George R. Lucas, Jr. "Postmodern War," *Journal of Military Ethics* (2010): 288–300; Martin L. Cook, *The Moral Warrior* (Albany, NY: SUNY, 2004); Alex J. Bellamy, *Just Wars: From Cicero to Iraq* (Cambridge: Polity, 2007).

66 Niall Ferguson, *Colossus: The Rise and Fall of the American Empire* (New York: Penguin, 2005).

Jus ad Bellum #1
RESISTING AGGRESSION

"[N]o just war can be waged except for the purpose of punishment or repelling enemies." —CICERO[1]

The core proposition of just war theory, uniting all its theorists, is this: *sometimes, it is at least morally permissible for a political community to go to war.* This is to say that there can be such a thing as a morally justified war; and World War II, on the part of the Allies, is often trotted out as the definitive modern example. Some even refer to this conflict as "The Good War."[2]

The goal of just war theory is to restrain both the incidence and destructiveness of warfare. Just war theory seeks to minimize *the reasons* for which it is permissible to fight, and seeks to restrain and limit *the means* with which communities may fight. Just war theory is NOT pro-war. It is, rather, a doctrine deeply aware of war's frightful dangers and brutal inhumanities. It seeks, accordingly, to reduce those dangers, and purge those inhumanities, by insisting that belligerents respect human rights to the extent possible during the grim circumstances of war.

While there are disagreements between just war theorists—no tradition or discipline generates unanimity—the clear majority endorse some version of the following principles. There is thought to be a fundamental division between the ethics of resorting to force—or in Latin "*jus ad bellum*" (literally "the justice *of* war") and the ethics of conduct during armed conflict (or "*jus in bello*," literally "justice *in* war"). Most just war theorists insist that *jus ad bellum* and *jus in bello* are, in a salient sense, separate. The notion is that a war can be begun for just reasons, yet prosecuted in an unjust fashion. (For instance, while World War II is called "The Good War" in terms of its cause—fighting against fascist aggression—many still raise critical doubts about some Allied tactics, notably the use of atomic weapons.) Similarly, though perhaps much less commonly, a war begun for unjust reasons might (conceivably) still be fought with strict adherence to *jus in bello*. The categories are at least logically or conceptually distinct, and so we must consider them separately, each with their own rules and considerations. For example, the *jus ad bellum* criteria are thought to be the preserve and responsibility of political leaders whereas the *jus in bello* criteria are thought to be the province and responsibility of military commanders, officers, and soldiers. Ultimately in this book, I am going to argue that there is a robust connection between *jus ad bellum* and *jus in bello*. This defies tradition.[3] Even so, I admit that the two categories can be focused upon one and then the other (without admitting they are literally separate). And so that is what we shall do.

A state resorts to war justly only if it satisfies each of six major rules: just cause, right intention, public declaration by proper authority, last resort, probability of success, and proportionality.

1. Just Cause

International law allows countries to defend themselves with force if they are victimized by an armed attack; it also allows them to so defend other countries should they be attacked. These entitlements commonly get referred to, respectively, as "self-defense from aggression" and "other-defense from aggression" (also called a "war of law enforcement" or "collective security"). These are the two most elemental just causes for war in international law and just war theory. No other kinds of warfare are allowed by international law unless explicitly authorized and endorsed—beforehand—by the United Nations' Security Council (UNSC).

The UNSC is empowered by the UN Charter to try to keep war from breaking out. Its decisions, or "resolutions," are binding on all UN member countries. It has five permanent members, who can veto any resolution. These are: America; Britain; China; France; and Russia. It also features 10 non-permanent members, who hold rotating two year terms and can propose, and vote on, resolutions—but can never veto them. This means that there are 15 UNSC members at any given time; and a resolution on war and peace, to pass, must enjoy majority support with no vetoes.[4]

Article 51 of the UN Charter calls the right of self-defense an "inherent right" (in French, a "*droit naturel*"—natural right). Note that what is being defended against is *aggression* and aggression is an armed attack against another country *who is a member of the UN*. A bit more on the "armed attack" part: suppose that you are a small country, C, next to a big neighbor, N. In response to domestic lobby groups, the government of N decides to close its border to your forestry exports (trees, lumber, etc.). You are devastated, because your forestry sector is your economy's biggest; your economy is going to suffer big-time (lost trade, layoffs, plant shutdowns, a recession). This is pretty tough treatment by N against C: it's not nice; it's completely un-diplomatic; and it might even violate a trade treaty. But international law, and just war theory, insist that—rough as it may be—it's not treatment severe enough to merit warfare in response. It is only when the tough treatment in question is coupled with physical violence that we can begin to contemplate armed conflict. This makes clear sense: in interpersonal life, e.g., we don't think getting fired is a sufficient reason to retaliate with violence, even if the firing sharply harms our interests. The loss—the danger—is merely economic. But most of us *do* think that, when someone physically attacks us (or those we love) with severe violence, we may employ physical force in response, seeking to resist the attacker, to force him to stop, and to protect ourselves or others from even deeper hurt. So for an international act to count as aggression, it must not merely be objectionable or even clearly damaging to a country's interests. It must, at the same time, involve the infliction of serious, direct physical force. Almost always in international affairs, this involves the deployment of a country's armed forces—by land, sea, air, or space—into the territory and against the people or government of another country. The classic example of international aggression is when one country uses its armed forces to launch an invasion into another country, with the objective being military, political, and economic conquest, such as Nazi Germany did to Poland in 1939 or Iraq did to Kuwait in 1990.

International law only stipulates that aggression is wrong and punishable with war in response; it does not explain why. Similarly, international law only dictates that states have the right not to be aggressed against; it fails to explain why.[5] It is the job of just war theory to fill in these gaps and offer a satisfying rationale. Let's start with the issue of state rights. Why do states—like the government of the USA—have rights? Which rights do they have? What are the underlying principles here?

1.1. STATE RIGHTS AND HUMAN RIGHTS

The purpose of the state, in our era, is to do its part realizing the human rights of its people. That is the state's reason-for-being and, if a state fails in that regard, its people have no reason to obey it and stick with the social contract. This is absolutely foundational: to believe otherwise is to reject any moral role for the state, and view it purely through the prism of power, a bleak view that offers only fear as a reason to obey the state. This is not, however, a mature and fitting conception of political life for grown human beings: they have the right to participate in their own governance—since it so deeply affects their lives—and they need a moral reason to do so. There's no better one than that such participation will help them realize their own human rights, which is to say their own vital human needs. So state rights are authorized and delimited by the human rights of individuals, much as Locke had speculated.[6]

Human rights are core entitlements we all have to those things we both vitally need as human beings and which we can reasonably demand from other people and the social institutions we share. Which things are these? As I have argued elsewhere,[7] the most important set of human rights objects are "the foundational five": 1) physical security (i.e., your very life and freedom from violent threats to it); 2) material subsistence; 3) personal freedom; 4) elemental equality (i.e., non-discrimination); and 5) social recognition as a person and rights-holder. These are the essential elements we all require to live minimally decent lives in the modern world. They are, as James Nickel says, "what we want, no matter what we want."[8] Whatever else we want out of life, we need the all-purpose means of security, subsistence, freedom, etc., which are required to pursue any such goals in the first place. Try becoming a software billionaire without your life; try becoming head of state without subsistence; indeed, try pursuing anything without the very freedom to do so. We each, therefore, have the most powerful reasons of self-interest to claim these foundational five objects as our most basic human rights. Such rights are, as John Rawls has declared, the very basis for moral and political legitimacy in our time.[9]

What does it mean to realize human rights, thus defined? Human rights are realized or respected when everyone *actually possesses* the objects of their human rights. Your human right to physical security, e.g., is satisfied or fulfilled when you actually enjoy life in a safe, secure social setting. If state rights are dependent upon, and delimited by, individual human rights, what does all this imply for state rights? It implies that states themselves must have rights to those objects genuinely needed to enable them to do their part in realizing the human rights of their people. Which objects are these? Though there are others,[10] generally we speak of political sovereignty and territorial integrity.

Political sovereignty is the right of a group of people to govern itself. This is to say the right of a community to make its own choices about how life gets organized in its land: the kinds of institutions it wants; the kind of laws it is willing to live by; the kind of culture, values, and traditions it wishes to impart to the next generation; and so forth. Fundamentally, political sovereignty is rooted: 1) negatively, in our disdain for aggressive foreign domination and slavery; and 2) positively, in the individual human rights to freedom and security possessed by everyone within that community.

It is a common human failing to tell other people what to do. It is a further failing to force other people to do what we want them to do, whether such "force" is through yelling, psychological manipulation, or flat-out physical violence. This is true between groups as well as persons. Usually, though, we think this wrong. Interpersonally, we call it coercion or bullying. Internationally, we call it aggression. In either case, it is a drive for dominance over others which fails to respect the right of other people to live freely-chosen, and thus fully human, lives. This core drive for dominance is, I believe, the basic cause of all unjust wars. The right of political sovereignty is designed to resist foreign dominance, by stipulating that a people freely grouped together politically has the right to its own political life and hence the entitlement not to be forced to succumb to the rule of others whom it does not recognize as legitimate rulers or, indeed, as part of its community at all.

Territorial integrity depends upon political sovereignty; the latter is logically and morally prior to the former. A state needs territory because its people all have to live somewhere, and it needs resources because human rights do not come for free.

For example, the human right to physical security implies the creation of law and order within a society, and that involves having a military and police force, and the construction and running of an effective judicial system—all of which absorb large resources. International law reflects these material needs by: enshrining a state's right to territorial integrity; and treating a state government as the "owner" of all the natural resources within that territory, and as the ultimate taxation authority within that land as well.

Political sovereignty and territorial integrity are tightly linked, and they are ultimately rooted in some of the deepest facets of human nature: 1) we prefer to live in groups; 2) we strongly prefer to govern ourselves; and 3) we vitally need land and resources. To protect these traits and values, international law endorses territorial integrity and political sovereignty as bedrock principles of how communities should interact.

Now, international law apparently extends these state rights to *all* member states of the UN, regardless of how unsavory some of these regimes might be. The UN—even though it has the authority, under its Charter, to kick out terrible regimes—has decided that it's better for everyone to be "inside the tent," so to speak, with no state left outside (for fear it might get even worse).[11] While there is some wisdom in this inclusive approach, it can also raise sharp moral questions, such as: why should we believe that horrible states have rights? If a state has rights in order to protect and realize the human rights of its own people, and that state uses its power instead to violate their human rights, why should we respect its "sovereignty" and the "integrity" of its territory? The very grounding of its state claims has evaporated! Granted, there might be good *strategic* reasons to lay off such a state—e.g., it's too powerful, or unpredictable—but it doesn't seem there's a *moral* case to view these states as having rights (which, after all, are moral entitlements). There has always been this tension in modern international law: do we recognize as legitimate a state or government merely because it has the most power in that society, or do we recognize it only if it also uses that power in a morally adequate way (at the least, by refraining from massively violating the human rights of its own people)?[12] The former way is the way of realism, and we shall discuss its nature and limitations in Chapter 8. Just war theory has always endorsed the latter, from at least the time of Aquinas. Only a morally fit—or, as I prefer to say, a minimally just government—has the right to go to war. It's inescapable, as I've said, that *all talk of justice regarding war must revolve ultimately around legitimate governance.*

1.2. MINIMAL JUSTICE AND STATE RIGHTS

Minimally just societies: 1) are generally recognized as such by their own people and the international community. The international community extends this recognition by allowing the society to enjoy membership in various international associations and events: e.g., the World Health Organization or the Olympics. Various countries also do things like send ambassadors to, and open embassies in, that society as well as enter into agreements with it, e.g., involving trade. The society is not shunned on a widespread basis nor is it the subject of pervasive official criticism or skepticism about its fitness to organize life in its community. The most obvious way for a people to show that it recognizes its own government as legitimate would be through majority endorsement in periodic, public, free, and fair elections. It's not the only way—simply the most obvious and verifiable. Another way would be the prevalence of peace and stability in the country: i.e., the absence of civil war, revolutionary activity, sustained and large violent protests against the government, and such. Crucially, though, this lack of internal conflict cannot be because of huge amounts of armed coercion on the part of the state against its people. There are, after all, ruthless police state dictatorships which impose social peace. So we must discern that the prevalence of social peace is not forced upon the people, rather, it is freely chosen by the people and hence indicative of their general acceptance of the political order.

Minimally just societies also: 2) avoid violating the rights of other countries. In particular, decent societies do not commit aggression against other states and nations. If they do so, they forfeit rights not to be resisted—with armed force if need be.

Finally, minimally just societies: 3) make every reasonable effort to satisfy the human rights of their own citizens. Why only "every reasonable effort" to satisfy and not, simply, "satisfies" these human rights? Well, we can't require perfection, since every society has human rights problems. We can only require serious efforts and sincere intentions. There are two general reasons why societies clearly fail to realize human rights: 1) they want to realize them, but simply lack the resources needed; or 2) they don't want to realize them, since they don't care about widespread human rights fulfillment. Only the second kind violate this third criterion, since they are regimes with wicked intentions and no desire to create minimally good lives for their people. Usually, such countries are governed by a malevolent minority, which hordes power and wealth, and discriminates against and/or cares not a whit for, the well-being of the majority. The governments in the first group require our assistance with human rights realization. Those in the second group do not deserve recognition as rights-bearing states with the authority to go to war.

It's fair to say that very many states around the world do satisfy these three criteria of minimal justice, and thus count as legitimate, rights-bearing states. So international law and just war theory line up here. But some states do not, and will not. Here is where international law and just war theory must part ways a little bit. The laws of armed conflict recognize a country as a rights-bearer if it is a member of the UN; nothing more being required. If you're a UN member state, and you're attacked with force, you have the legal right to go to war in response. Just war theory has, traditionally and by contrast, insisted that states show some moral fitness before being authorized with the war power. Why? Because what's so special about states, or UN membership? Why shower national governments with rights, if these governments lack basic moral legitimacy? Indeed, it seems paradoxical to suggest that an *immoral* form of governance has a *moral* right to arm and defend itself. Why privilege the governance of the nation-state (when other forms of governance are possible: e.g., cosmopolitan, or regional, or municipal) if the nation-state doesn't deserve it? The only way it deserves it is by earning it through its respect for, and empowerment of, the human rights of its own citizens and those of others. States which are like this truly *do* have moral value and are worth enabling and protecting.

Fundamentally, it's the difference between *legal* rights and *moral* rights. Legally, any UN member state has the right to go to war to resist aggression directed either against itself, or another UN member. But morally, only those states which are minimally just have rights to sovereignty, territory, and to resist aggression. So, most times just war theory and the laws of armed conflict run together and are mutually confirming: we'll see this throughout.[13] But other times they are not and I'm more concerned to defend and forward just war theory when that happens. Why? First, because just war theory *explains* its values whereas international law merely *asserts* them. Second, because international law (like all law) lags behind the times somewhat—especially concerning new technology and tactics—whereas our theories need not. Third, because international law is the product of state consensus, and sometimes consensus is wrong. Sometimes the laws of armed conflict enshrine a bad law, or fail to include a good law. Just war theory, better than any other, helps guide international law towards correction in this regard.

We'll say more about the role of human rights realization in the foundation for political legitimacy when we talk about the rule of proper authority. For now, we have what we need to progress on the just cause rule for going to war.

1.3. FORFEITURE AND THE MORAL CORE

Aggression is the focus in just cause, and aggression in the first instance is an armed attack which violates a state's rights and, in the deepest instance, is an armed attack which violates the human rights of people to live in security and freedom. It is a prominent feature of everything said so far that the commission of aggression causes a state to forfeit, or give up, its rights to territorial integrity and political sovereignty, rendering permissible a military response on the part of the victim and/or any third-party "vindicators" or law enforcers. Let us add more rigor and depth here—it's harder, but worth it—and flesh all these thoughts out as our "*Core Principle on Aggression*" (CPA):

> the commission of aggression by any aggressor A, against any victim V, entitles V—and/or any third-party vindicator T, acting on behalf of V—to

employ all necessary means to stop A, including lethal force, provided that such means do not themselves violate human rights.

This seems a complicated principle, but when it's broken down, we'll see that it's readily digestible and full of good sense. It stands at the foundation of everything which follows. Let's now understand the relevant agents A, V, and T as states, and let's consider first the reasons why V possesses such an entitlement to go to war: reasonableness; fairness; responsibility; and implicit entitlement.

First, it would be *unreasonable* to deny V permission to take effective measures to protect its people from serious harm, or lethal attack, at the hands of A. Simply put, it is not reasonable, given the kinds of creatures we are, and the kind of world in which we live, to expect a state charged with the responsibility to protect its citizens instead to capitulate utterly—to just roll over—in the face of aggression. Indeed, one of the core functions of a government is precisely to protect its people from foreign invasion and accompanying threats of slaughter or slavery.

The *fairness* argument stipulates that it would be not only unreasonable but unfair to deny V the permission to resist A with force, should A unjustly invade. Why? Because, in the absence of such measures, V will suffer substantial loss of life and liberty while A will actually gain whatever object it had in mind in attacking V. It seems clear that aggression, and rights-violation, ought not to be unfairly rewarded in this way, both in the particular case and for the sake of not eliciting more such behavior in the future.

Not only would denying V permission to resist forcibly the aggression of A be both unreasonable and unfair, it would also ignore the fundamental issue of who bears responsibility for the choice situation. It's the aggressor A who is responsible for placing V in a situation where V must choose between its rights and those of the aggressor A. (And this point ties neatly into the reasonableness claim, since it's only reasonable to expect V, in such a situation, to choose its own rights.) The aggressor A, if it does not wish to subject itself to the consequences of the resort to defensive force by V, can always cease and desist from its own aggression. Stop warring if you don't want to be warred upon. So if A does not cease and desist—if it keeps up its aggression—it's hardly in a position to cry foul should V decide to do the reasonable and fair thing and defend itself, and its citizens, with the needed force.

Finally, any victim V has the *implicit entitlement* to use whatever measures are necessary to realize the objects of its rights and those of its citizens. The relevant argument has the following form:

1. Minimally just states, as defined previously, have moral and legal rights to territorial integrity and political sovereignty.

2. These state rights entitle states to employ reliable measures necessary to secure the objects of these rights, and to protect them from severe, predictable threats to them, such as the violent aggression of others. (This follows as a matter of moral logic: if person P has the right R to object Q, and M is a means necessary to get and secure Q, then P must also have a right to M. Otherwise, to what extent could we speak of P's original right to Q?)

3. There is, presently, no reliable or effective international authority (or global government) which can guarantee to states the possession of the objects of their rights. States are, in the final analysis, on their own with regard to protecting their rights and the objects thereof.

4. Currently, the most effective and reliable form of self-help with regard to rights-protection—at least in the last resort against armed aggression—is the use of defensive armed force.

5. Thus, faced with armed violation of their rights (i.e., with aggression), states are entitled to employ armed force and war in order to punish the rights-violator, vindicate their own state rights, and protect the lives and human rights of their individual members. As Aristotle said, so long ago, the most fundamental just cause for going to war is self-defense: i.e., resisting foreign aggression against one's political community.

This brings us to the second core aspect of principle CPA: granted that V possesses entitlement to respond to A's aggression with armed force, how is V to do so without itself violating rights? There are two elements to note in response: 1) state A, through the commission of aggression against V, forfeits its state rights not to be attacked with lethal force in return; and 2) provided that V adheres strictly to the rules of *jus in bello* during its just war against A, it will succeed in offering the required "due care" owed to innocent civilians in both states, and thereby avoid violating their rights. It will therefore fully satisfy CPA. Let us deal with each one of these elements in turn.

Why and how does A forfeit its right, as a state, not to be subject to armed attack by committing aggression against V? A forfeits its rights because, as we just saw, the weight of reasons in the case indicates that no wrong is done to A in the event that victim V resists A's aggression with means of war. And the weight of reasons in this case must draw on those just offered in defense of V's entitlement to resort to force in the first place: it would be unreasonable, unfair, oblivious of responsibility, and at odds with implicit entitlement to declare that V does wrong in resisting A's aggression with armed force. And if V does no wrong in violently resisting A here, then A must fail to have moral rights that such not be done. It must thus have forfeited its rights.

Since A forfeits its state rights by committing aggression, this permits any third party T (or group of third-party states G) to intervene forcibly on behalf of victim V. This legitimacy of other-defense is grounded in the normative core of the victim's claim—namely, that the aggressor either stop or be stopped, regardless of who is the agent bringing about the stopping. Provided that the demonstrable aim is the protection of the victim and its citizens from rights-violation, armed resistance is permitted to any state willing to take on its associated burdens.

So V's (or T's, or G's) resisting A's aggression against V with armed force will not violate A's *state* rights because, by committing aggression, A has forfeited its state rights. But what of the *human* rights of the individual persons in both A and V (or T and G)? Why and how will launching a just war at the state level not violate these *individual* rights? These rights will not be violated, I submit, provided that V (or T, or G) fully adheres to the other criteria of *jus ad bellum* and *jus in bello,* which will be discussed subsequently. What this claim importantly asserts is that the principles of just war theory serve to fulfill the human rights of persons to the maximum extent that they can be fulfilled during warfare.

To sum up so far: a state has a just cause for resorting to war if, and only if: 1) it is the victim of aggression, or is coming to the aid of a victim of aggression; 2) it is a minimally just or legitimate state; and 3) its resort to armed force fulfills all aspects of the principle CPA. These three principles revolve, most centrally, around the value of protecting and defending minimally just communities and the lives and rights of their individual members. These are the very deepest ideas surrounding the core of just war theory in general, and those aspects of the international laws of armed conflict which have partially been derived from them.

Note how these principles—of reasonableness and fairness, of respect for life and rights, of responsibility for rights violation—themselves seem implied, at the most profound level, by the very meaning of a just society, and indeed by human civilization itself. The use of reason to inform action, and a value commitment to fair treatment, are all major objectives in a mature and just society, likewise the holding of everyone responsible for how they treat other people. Finally, respect for rights is truly one of the basic cements of civilization, and a decent and stable society must be committed to understanding, propounding, and protecting such rights and, above all, to ensuring that rights-holders actually enjoy secure possession of the objects of their rights. On this intensive reading of the just cause rule, then, *aggression attacks the very moral spine of human civilization itself.* Indeed it does; it reverts us to the laws of the jungle, from which our ancestors struggled so mightily to escape and evolve away from. This is why, if need be, aggression can be resisted with something as strong and dangerous as force of arms. Let's take it down from the clouds of abstraction and look at a recent concrete case.

1.4. THE 1991 PERSIAN GULF WAR

In August 1990, Iraq invaded Kuwait. This was a classic instance of a large, militaristic country aggressing against a smaller neighbor. Why did Saddam Hussein, then-dictator of Iraq, order this armed invasion and take-over of Kuwait? He had several reasons, none of them justified but most of them revolving around the fact he had just finished a miserable, destructive conflict with Iran. From 1980–88, Iran and Iraq slugged it out in a very expensive and bloody war with roots stretching way back in history. One million people lost their lives in the Iran-Iraq War, in which Saddam portrayed himself as the savior of moderate Muslims from the fury of radical Islam, which had just come to power in violent revolution in Iran in 1979. At the end of the war, Saddam was in a very difficult position. On the one hand, he was still in power in Iraq, and had prevented radical ayatollahs—religious extremists—from taking over his country. On the other, the war pushed him into enormous debt and he faced huge reconstruction costs. He asked both Kuwait and Saudi Arabia to forgive the debts he owed them, on grounds he "saved" them from being swept out of power by the ayatollahs. The two countries refused, and Saddam grew furious. His other big problem was that Iraq's military was restless—and huge. Having grown to over one million men during the long Iran-Iraq War, Iraq's military was disappointed that Saddam had called the war off against their despised enemy. Moreover, Iraq's military has long played important roles in various coups and revolutions within Iraq. Saddam thus feared armed revolt. So he hit upon a "solution": invade and conquer Kuwait. This would: occupy his army; cancel part of Iraq's debt; and give Iraq control over a lucrative asset it could use to help pay for reconstruction. And it might just scare Saudi Arabia into debt forgiveness as well. So the order was given, and then executed in the hot days of August, 1990.

None of these reasons, of course, justify Iraq's invasion—they merely explain it. War for any kind of economic gain is strictly ruled out, as is the old politician's trick of using war abroad to try to solve (or, at least, distract attention from) problems at home. Saddam did try to argue that Kuwait had been driving down the world price of oil—and thus Iraq's own revenues—by supplying too much oil to the world market. But, again, even if that were true—and it's not clear it was—that's an economic issue and thus not one where military force is an appropriate response. Remember back to our forestry example. Saddam then tried to suggest that—since the ancient Ottoman Empire used to administer both Iraq and Kuwait together—Kuwait "belonged to" Iraq anyway, as its "19th province." Not only was this not true, even if it were it would be like arguing today that, since Canada used to be part of the British Empire, it should once again today be run from the Mother of All Parliaments in London. Such an argument ignores everything which has happened between then and now—notably, how a new political community came into existence and came therefore to deserve separate protection. Saddam, finally, tried to argue that Kuwait was stealing Iraq's oil by "slant-drilling" underneath and across the border into Iraq's wells. This was, however, a lie; and, even if it were true, it would still just be an economic issue wherein demanding compensation would be appropriate but not armed invasion. Saddam's base motives of plunder, and pleasing his military, became undeniably clear when he authorized them, in the fall of 1990, to pillage Kuwait: raping women at will; stealing private property on a whim; crushing any Kuwaiti resistance; and wreaking havoc constantly. Amnesty International's December 1990 special report, on the behavior of Iraqi soldiers in Kuwait, makes for chilling—even revolting—reading in this regard.[14]

We know from what we've already established that this kind of freely-chosen, flagrant aggression causes a state to lose its usual right not to be subject to armed attack, either by the victim community or others coming to its aid. Kuwait's puny armed forces quickly succumbed during the August 1990 invasion. In the fall of 1990, the international community—led by America—generated a huge military build-up in neighboring Saudi Arabia (i.e., "Operation Desert Shield") and reflected on what to do.

Perhaps it might here be objected that the theory developed thus far claims that states forfeit rights against attack only when they unjustly attack other states which don't deserve it—i.e., states which are minimally just. While Iraq's attack against Kuwait was unjust—because of the political and economic motives—was Kuwait itself a minimally just state deserving of protection? Well, Kuwait was widely recognized as the legitimate government of that territory; indeed, it had membership in the UN. Kuwait was also, at that time, not involved in violating the rights of other states; unlike Iraq, Kuwait was not using its army to invade, pillage, and overthrow foreign governments. But was the Kuwaiti state seen as legitimate by its own people, and making every reasonable effort to satisfy the human rights of its own people? When regular elections are not held, it's harder to judge whether a people genuinely approves of its regime. Plus, the rights of women in many Muslim countries are often seen as not being as fully realized as they should. Does this mean the Kuwaiti regime was not legitimate? It certainly raises issues. But three points stand out: 1) there was un-coerced social peace in Kuwait prior to Iraq's invasion; 2) the Kuwait regime didn't attack and brutalize its own people the way the invading Iraqis did in the fall of 1990 (thus the Kuwaiti government had a much better claim to rule that society than Iraq did); and 3) the Kuwaiti regime no longer existed—i.e., had been overthrown by Saddam—when the West went to war in January, 1991, anyway. And most Western societies, including America, satisfy the criteria of minimal justice. The West went to war (in "Operation Desert Storm") to defend *the Kuwaiti people* from Iraqi conquest and brutalization, not so much to restore the old Kuwaiti *regime*. The old regime was restored, it's true, in the spring of 1991 after the war was quickly won by America and its allies. This does not mean the war was unjust. The war may not have had all desirable affects but the war was just (in its cause) as a war of other-defense against a country which committed aggression perhaps not the very second when it crossed Kuwait's borders but certainly did so the minute it unleashed its campaign of plunder and brutality against an un-armed Kuwaiti population.

Failure to resist such aggressive attacks rewards the aggressor and, as such, inappropriately structures incentives in favor of more aggression in international society. It also penalizes the victim, by doing nothing to reverse the effects of the aggression. By attacking the Kuwaiti people, Saddam's Iraq committed aggression. When it did so, it forfeited its right not to be attacked in response. There is very high consensus that this war was just in its cause, and indeed it was authorized by numerous UNSC resolutions and supported by a clear majority of just war theorists at the time.[15]

1.5. COMPARATIVE JUSTICE OF CAUSE?

So the only just cause, for resorting to war, is in response to aggression. The response may be two-fold: a war of self-defense on the part of the state victimized by aggression; and/or a war of other-defense, or "law enforcement," on the part of any other state coming to aid the victim. Walzer, for one, is adamant that there is no such thing as a war that is just on both sides. All things considered, he believes, the evidence can point in only one of two directions: either that, in a given war, one side is the unjust aggressor, the other the justified defender or that the war is unjust on both sides (a not infrequent occurrence in the real world). This "either/or" thinking sets Walzer apart from earlier just war thinkers, such as Vitoria, who suggested that it might be possible for all sides in a war to have some quantum of justice. Walzer disagrees with this graded or scalar approach, not only because the aggression/defense paradigm essentially forces him to—it seems silly to say a state is two-thirds of an aggressor—but also because he reasons that Vitoria's "comparative justice" conception confuses *jus ad bellum* with *jus in bello*. Vitoria included "comparative justice of cause" within his own account of *jus ad bellum* so as to mitigate the degree to which a state might pursue its otherwise just cause. Vitoria was afraid that a state with what we might call "100% Justice" on its side would be especially ferocious in its conduct of war. It would have a Crusading mentality and seek to obliterate the utterly unjust enemy. But Walzer contends, plausibly, that such mitigation can also be had from the distinct set of *jus in bello* rules. From the fact that just cause is defined by him in a binary way, it does not follow that a state satisfying its requirements is thereby justified in prosecuting its war effort however it likes. It must still confront and satisfy the rules of *jus in bello*, as contained for instance within the Hague and Geneva Conventions. More on the content of these rules in Chapters 4 and 5.[16]

I too am skeptical of the older comparative conception, not only for the sound reasons Walzer gives, but also because it simply seems wrong in particular cases. What, for instance, was the comparative justice of Nazi Germany's cause in World War II? I would claim that it was nil—that the Allies had complete justice on their side in that struggle, and that this cause was resisting brutal, unbridled Nazi aggression. But from the fact that the Allies were completely justified in terms of their cause, it does not mean they could do whatever they wanted to win—it only means they had a clear just cause to start fighting. Now for a crucial point: what about those who might say the Nazis had some claim for "*Lebensraum*" (i.e., "living room," more space and territory for the large and ever-growing German people) and that that was the small quantum of justice on their side? The vital reply: *from the fact that an actor in war claims his actions are just doesn't make it so*. The actor, much like an accused person in court, must show how his *subjective* understanding of his actions actually corresponds to *objectively* plausible moral and legal principles, based on inter-subjectively available, shareable, and discernible evidence. The point of just war theory, and the law of armed conflict, is precisely to serve as the objective principles in such a process, and not to serve as the speaking points, of rhetorical self-justification, for any deluded dictator bent on aggression.

What is compelling in the thinking behind comparative justice is that the evidence in wartime can be difficult to interpret, and we can predict the players are all going to interpret it in a way maximally advantageous to their own selfish interests. Some unscrupulous players will even lie, perhaps even fabricating phony evidence. All this has been known to happen in wartime, and even to be committed by societies we're inclined to believe are decent. There is, e.g., enormous controversy surrounding the evidence America enumerated in justification of its 2003 Iraq attack, and subsequent removal of Saddam's regime. Iraq's weapons of mass destruction (WMD), Saddam's alleged connections to al-Qaeda, Bush Jr's pre-9/11 interest in Saddam's removal, possible CIA manipulation of data, Saddam's own lying about his residual strength: all these aspects figure into the debate about the justice of the start of that war. More on that war later; for now, we cite the old verity that "truth is the first casualty of war." War can make people desperate, and desperately self-justifying. I don't think this means the truth is impossible to find through the impenetrable "fog of war"—we now know the WMD claims were false[17]—but I do agree that it means we must subject war justifications to the most rigorous research scrutiny, and accordingly there is a duty for war-seeking governments to disclose publicly the evidence and sources behind arguments supporting something as deadly and far-reaching as war. Failure to provide such—especially when arrogantly citing a "national security" need to keep such information secret—renders the resort to war unjust. In war, both consequences and procedures are important, and the latter does not evaporate in the face of the former. One can be legitimately outraged in the face of aggression, and take to the high road as a result, but one must always remain humble and truthful in the face of the evidence which proves such aggression. So, I don't believe in comparative justice but I do believe in critical, on-going examination of the evidence to determine who is the aggressor and who the defender—or whether, alternatively, it shows "a pox on both their houses": i.e., injustice all around.

1.6. APPEASEMENT?

Victims of aggression are, in Michael Walzer's mind anyway, "always justified in fighting." In fact, in most cases, "fighting is the morally preferred response." Why is this so, especially when we realize that many—perhaps most—cases of aggression involve a larger and more powerful state deploying its armed forces to coerce a less powerful state to make unjust concessions? Is not appeasement of the aggressor an understandable response from the victim, especially if that is its free collective choice? Is not neutrality, by third parties, a legitimate choice on their part, too? Walzer stresses that, ultimately, the decision to resist aggression, whether by the victim or by third party vindicators, can only be a free choice of the country in question. This follows from the right of political sovereignty. But he clearly articulates his preference in favor of resistance, especially by the victim. For resistance "confirms and enhances ... our common values [including] national pride, self-respect, freedom in policy-making," whereas appeasement "diminishes those values and leaves us all impoverished." Sometimes both appeasement and neutrality constitute "a failure to resist evil in the world." The unchallenged triumph of aggression is, Walzer asserts, "a greater evil" than war.[18]

By and large, I agree with this view on appeasement, yet sympathy arises in cases where small states are giving up simply to avoid the slaughter they would surely suffer if they fought back. Consider the difficulty of Edvard Beneš, the leader of Czechoslovakia in 1938–39. Hitler gave Beneš a stark choice: declare war against Nazi aggrandizement, and we'll slaughter you; or surrender and survive, but as part of the new Nazi empire. It's easy for us, with no stake in the decision, to say that Beneš still should've fought, instead of giving up to save lives and to prevent his small country from being utterly demolished by its huge, ferocious, well-armed neighbor.[19] Resistance, after all, can take several forms—whether a direct military response to the first act of aggression, or an indirect guerrilla campaign after the aggressor has been allowed a temporary win.

The decision not to resist directly probably will come at the cost of some national pride and, more seriously, moral integrity. Contrast with Beneš's choice the choice of Finland, scarcely a year later, to resist an invasion by Stalin's USSR.[20] The Finns, to this day, look back upon their armed resistance with pride whereas the Czechs have much more of a mixed attitude. But in both cases the short-term outcome was inevitable: victory and conquest by the overwhelming invading force.

National pride and moral integrity are important yet they remain abstract, unquantifiable things. Beneš obviously reflected on their cost but, on the other side of the ledger, were things that clearly could be counted: if the Czechs fought back, thousands of his people would die, infrastructure would be shattered, economic costs huge—and all merely to postpone the inevitable Nazi victory (at least at that time). I'm not saying the problem is insoluble, merely that it's difficult, and there are real costs no matter which option is chosen. While resistance is preferable because of the severe wrong of aggression, resistance can take several forms, and we have to respect people's free choices here—emphatically since it's their own lives and liberties on the line.[21]

2. Right Intention

Having finished (for now) with the many complexities of just cause, we turn to the other five rules co-constitutive of *jus ad bellum*. Let us begin with Augustine's obsession with right intention. It's commonly thought, by just war theorists, that it is not enough to have an objectively just cause for going to war (like resisting aggression); you must also have the proper subjective intention, or state of mind, for your act to be moral. Why? Consider an analogy from personal life: say a child Billy steals a bicycle. Ethically, he must return it. But most of us think it's better, morally, if Billy returns it because he is sincerely sorry (and not, say, because his parents order him or threaten him). His intentions and state of mind matter to our evaluation. Or suppose Sally drives through a red light, killing a pedestrian. We would evaluate that act very differently if we knew it wasn't an accident but, rather, hatred and score-settling that triggered the crash. Same physical act but different intention and thus a different moral evaluation: the latter is clearly much worse than the former. Legally, for instance, the intention marks the difference between first-degree murder and mere manslaughter. A comprehensive system of morality seems not only to require the proper external behavior but also internal reflection and the right attitude. It's more demanding to include right intention, true, but the whole point of morality is to demand a certain standard from people and the institutions they form.

Considering this rule's application to international affairs, Walzer observes soberly that "a pure good will [is] ... a political illusion." He also notes a vagueness in the just war tradition regarding whether this rule can be fulfilled only if there is purity of intention to secure the just cause, or whether it is possible to satisfy it, provided only that right intention is present amongst the mix of motives which usually animates state behavior. Walzer himself opts for the latter course: he believes it is possible, and meaningful, to criticize some of the non-moral motives which states can have in going to war while still endorsing the moral motive. But that motive *must* be present: Walzer concurs that right orientation towards just cause is a necessary aspect of the justice of resorting to war. This is to say that it must be part of a state's subjective intention in pursuing war that it secure and fulfill the objective reason which gives it justification for fighting.[22]

A related question, which Walzer doesn't answer, is this: must the moral motivation merely be present in the mix of motives, or need it be the main animating force in the mix? Consider, for example, the mix of motives that the Allied coalition, led by the United States, might have had in 1991 for launching the first Persian Gulf War against Iraq: the repulsion of Iraq from Kuwait; the punishment of Iraqi aggression; the desire to secure the oil supply of the Persian Gulf region (especially in neighboring Saudi Arabia); President Bush Sr.'s wish to demonstrate toughness in the run-up to the 1992 election; the desire by the United States to prove its superiority following the end of the Cold War with the Soviet Union; and the drive of the US military to test out its latest weaponry in real battlefield conditions, and perhaps to vanquish some disturbing ghosts left over from Vietnam. There are serious difficulties involved in discerning which motive dominates. Different parts of the American government, after all, might be seen as having had different intentions: which one would then count as the overall "dominant," or conclusive, one? Short-term aims might also have differed from medium- and long-term ones: which was definitive of *the* motivation? This makes it more plausible, though less interesting, to conclude that the moral motive need *only be real and present* amongst the various non-moral motives for this criterion to be fulfilled.[23]

Perhaps the difficulty in discerning correct motivation is one reason why just war theory's right intention rule is nowhere to be found in the international law of armed conflict. This is interesting, and in my view an unfortunate omission, for several reasons. First, it is clearly part of common moral discourse to speculate on, and judge, a state's resort to war based on its supposed motives. Both the first Iraq war (1991), and the second (2003), were labeled unjust by some people on grounds that America's motives supposedly revolved around oil, and/or imperialism, and/or chauvinism against Arabs and Muslims. Legal purists might object that an agent's *intentions* are a "mere" matter of ethics, whereas an agent's *conduct* is all that justice is, and can be, concerned with. But this fails to persuade. It is, for instance, part of justice systems the world over to include considerations of intention and motive when it comes to people on trial for such crimes as murder. Moreover, such trials also give indication as to how one might gain reliable knowledge of another's intent. *We know an agent's intent through his conduct.* Intentions can be, and ought to be, discerned through a reasoned examination of publicly-accessible evidence, relying on behavior, consideration of incentives, and explicit avowals of intent. Intentions are neither infinitely re-describable nor irreducibly private and mysterious. They are connected to patterns of evidence, as well as constrained by norms of logical coherence, and so right intention is not an empty criterion for moral judgment during war. Though difficult, it is possible to tell whether a state is prosecuting a war out of ethnic hatred, for example, as opposed to vindicating its right of self-defense. Dark motivations produce distinctive and noticeable results, such as torture, massacres, mass rapes, and large-scale displacements. We have the civil wars, in the 1990s, in the former Yugoslavia to offer as historical evidence. Or the recent violence in Sudan's Darfur region. Or the brutal set of inter-ethnic wars in Central Africa.[24]

Perhaps a deeper critical question can be raised here: can collective agents, like states, have intentions at all? Implicit here is a systematic analogy between the behavior of states and the behavior of individual persons. But does it make sense to speak of state "rights" and "intentions"? To refer to "crimes" which states commit against each other, like aggression, which should be "punished"? Of states acting for the right reasons, out of the proper motives? This is the so-called "domestic analogy."[25] This analogy, which also infuses international law, implies that one of the most useful ways to understand how states behave vis-à-vis each other is to liken such behavior to the way in which individuals behave vis-à-vis each other. It is important to note that this analogy need not involve any kind of "statism"—thinking of a state as its own unified, unitary kind of thing-unto-itself, somehow unrelated to the people who make it up. I've already said that states are merely political associations, and their rights are derived from, and delimited by, the human rights of their individual members. The domestic analogy, rather, draws its vitality from the sheer difficulty of speaking about the behavior of complex entities like states without employing simplifying assumptions—such as that they have a discernible identity, have intentions, face choices between alternatives, are thus responsible for their choices, and so on. It should also be emphasized that the domestic analogy is merely that: it is only generally persuasive and neither precludes the existence of important disanalogies nor commits us to a monolithic, naturalized, and homogenous conception of the state. The main point here is interpretive: we have always employed the domestic analogy in our moral and legal discourse about the ethics of war and peace; it is inherent in the deepest structure of our talk about morality and war; and we all understand what is meant by it. It is an irreplaceable aid to understanding in this regard.[26]

2.1. LINKING THE CATEGORIES AND CALLING YOUR SHOT

One interesting aspect of right intention is whether it should be part of the justice of the resort to war that a state commit itself, both publicly and in advance, to adhering to the other rules of war, contained in *jus in bello* (the justice of conduct in war) and *jus post bellum* (the justice of peace treaties ending war). The idea here, first proposed by Kant, is that a state should commit itself to certain rules of conduct, and appropriate war termination, as part of its original decision to begin the war.

Why? Because if it cannot so commit, it ought never to start the process. Unless a state pledges to fight in accord with the Hague and Geneva Conventions, and to terminate its war according to plausible principles, it should never involve itself in such morally serious business as warfare. This seems an important and forward-looking way in which one could, so to speak, run a bright red thread through each of the three just war categories, tying them into a coherent whole.[27] This addition is compelling not only because of the moral import of an agent's intent but, moreover, to ensure consistency of just behavior throughout all three phases of a military engagement. Thus, in addition to having one's subjective intentions (in going to war) be consistent with one's objectively just cause, one must also clearly and publicly commit, in advance of the war starting, to adhering to the other rules of just war theory.[28]

In other words, I propose we understand the three just war categories as ultimately linked. We can separate them out for the purpose of focusing in on various issues which different phases of war raise. But that just highlights things for the sake of analysis and perspective; it's not actually splitting the categories. I prefer to think of just war theory as forming one long action-guiding procedure, according to which each preceding step must be satisfied before setting on to the next one. This way of thinking stresses the value of each rule yet also properly emphasizes just cause as the crucial opening note, which sets the tone for everything which follows.

Another proposal I wish to make here is this: you have to call your shot, as in billiards. To tie it into the next rule: you have to declare publicly not merely your resort to war but your main reason for resorting to war. The reason this proposal is needed is to block the "scatter-shot" approach to justifying war, where you throw out every possible argument in favor of war, hoping some will stick in terms of persuading the public or attracting evidence which will stand the test of time and scrutiny. This addition is needed for both historical and conceptual reasons.

In recent history, the "scatter shot" approach has been prominent, particularly in terms of America's 2003 Iraq attack and forcible regime change. Such was justified, we were told, because: 1) Saddam had WMDs, some of which could be deployed within 45 minutes; 2) Saddam intended to give some of its WMDs to al-Qaeda, for use against America; 3) Saddam was actually involved with al-Qaeda in the 9/11 attacks; 4) Saddam needed to be overthrown as an act of humanitarian intervention on behalf of the Iraqi people; 5) Saddam posed a threat to regional security, especially regarding Israel and the Saudi oil fields; 6) Saddam's kicking out the UN weapons inspectors in 1998 violated the Persian Gulf War treaty, which specified possible violent consequences for doing so; and 7) Saddam needed to be overthrown so as to create forcibly the first Arab democracy, which would serve as a Trojan Horse for better values throughout the Islamic world.[29]

Now, there's nothing wrong with having multiple reasons for going to war if these multiple reasons are all real and backed with evidence. What is wrong is mixing strong ones with weak ones so as to create a false impression of an "overwhelming pro-war case." Even if you do have multiple reasons, you have the right intention issue of whether you can plausibly intend them all. Human attention, and intention, is finite and needs to be focused. In my view, you need to focus on your main reason for going to war, have your intentions disciplined accordingly, and be prepared to be judged for how well you called your shot. (This focus will also increase your probability of success, since achievement requires concentration and commitment, as opposed to running off in all directions.) This leads into the conceptual reason here: the scatter-shot approach is objectionable because war is such a serious and destructive business. You must know what you're doing. And the scatter-shot approach, frankly, conveys the impression you don't. You're just letting it all hang out, hoping at least some of it will gather the support you need. But to unleash the ravenous "dogs of war,"[30] you need clear proof of a rock-solid reason for doing so, such as self-defense from actual aggression.

3. Public Declaration of War by a Proper Authority

War must be declared publicly by a proper authority. Why a *public* declaration? To inform the target, or enemy, country that they now face war and its substantial hazards. This also gives the enemy one last chance, prior to hostilities commencing, to cease aggression and begin a process of atonement. Such entitlement to public notification is codified in the Hague Convention III, which mandates that signatory countries must not commence conflict without "previous and explicit warning, in the form either of a reasoned declaration of war or of an ultimatum with conditional declaration of war."[31] Public declaration also alerts one's *own* citizens to the government's intentions and plans. If state prerogatives in times of war are to be kept reasonably in line with the human rights of their members—which ground such state rights in the first place—we cannot lose sight of this just war criterion. The people must, in some public procedure, meaningfully consent to the launching of a war on their behalf.[32] More on the fuller meaning of this consent dimension later. For now, we continue to ask what "public" means. It means the declaration of war must be such that the target country, and one's own citizens, can reasonably be expected to be informed. Whether that's done through an official press conference, a formal speech, or a vote in an elected assembly, is not that material: any would seem to fulfill the meaning in question. Delivering an official notice of hostilities, say to the enemy country's ambassador, is in my view nice (so to speak) but not required. What would fail to meet the meaning of a genuinely public declaration would be: burying a war declaration within another piece of legislation; or being insincerely cryptic in one's language surrounding the military steps one is about to take; or, more plausibly and expectedly, to refuse to admit that a war is on when a *de facto* unleashing of armed force is already on display. Recall, from the Introduction, that war is an actual, intentional, and widespread armed conflict between political communities—wherein the ultimate objective is to force the other side to accept one's will regarding governance.

The public declaration and domestic consent critera need not preclude, or hamper the effectiveness of, rapid-fire responses to "blitzkrieg" attacks from dangerous aggressors. There are defensible procedures which can be put in place for just such reasons: for instance, empowering the executive branch of the national government to command the armed services to ensure rapid deployment, and then requiring legislative branch oversight and eventually approval (or not) of the executive's actions.

3.1. DIVISION OF WAR POWERS

Fundamental political issues arise when one considers which branch ought to be invested with the war power. The judicial branch is usually quite dis-empowered in this regard, with the executive and legislative branches enjoying—and often wrestling over—the vast majority of the war powers. America provides a compelling case study. On the face of it, Congress has the sole capacity to declare war. Yet the President also serves as Commander-in-Chief of the American forces. By convention, the President may deploy troops at will in all engagements short of war without Congressional approval. The precise definition of war can then become an important issue, as it did during Korea (1950–53) and Vietnam (1955–75). Executive orders to engage in "police actions" and "defensive operations" were issued, and some legislators argued angrily that war was being fought in violation of constitutional requirements for clear legislative endorsement. The War Powers Congressional Resolution of 1973 sought to clarify these issues, in particular by reasserting the authority of Congress.[33]

In practice today, the President enjoys enormous short-term *de facto* control over the armed forces, thanks to his role as Commander-in-Chief, which plugs him in directly to the military's chain of command. Congressional authorization of war thus suffers practical disadvantages, allowing the President at times to present Congress with a *fait accompli* for approval. More commonly in recent years—and emphatically since the 9/11 terrorist strikes—the President sought and got blanket authorization in advance of armed hostilities breaking out. There are some dangers with such a strategy. Yet Congress retains considerable medium- and long-term control over the armed forces, as it has within its powers sole final authority over military expenditures. The President may hold the whip of the war horse, so to speak, but ultimately Congress feeds it. This arrangement may represent a reasonable attempt to combine legitimate concerns—enabling effective rapid responses that warfare often demands with ultimately deeper insistences that war must have public, constitutional authorization.[34]

George R. Lucas, Jr. has recently argued that the public declaration/proper authority rule has important implications regarding mercenaries: i.e., soldiers-for-hire. Private, for-profit "security companies"—such as Academi, formerly known as Blackwater—are hard to square with the public use of force, and their deployment of violence in many instances raises issues of proper authority. Granted, sometimes these mercenaries can be contracted by constitutional governments to play roles supportive of national forces—thus implying some kind of ultimate public oversight—but Lucas and others such as Peter Singer are surely correct when they caution how, in principle, private mercenaries are generally inconsistent with this rule, and the utmost care and due diligence must be done prior to bringing any such forces "into the fold" of an otherwise justifiable action.[35]

Lucas has also argued more sweepingly in favor of this publicity condition. Like Sir Adrian Cadbury before him (regarding business ethics), and harkening all the way back to Kant, Lucas notes how the fulfillment of this rule almost serves as a guarantee of the fulfillment of all the other *jus ad bellum* rules, too. The notion is that, when confronted by the forceful court of public opinion, very few governments—in democratic countries, anyway—are going to be able to carry out a war without such actually being just, proportionate, the last resort, and so on. Publicity—i.e., transparency, open-ness, full reasoning offered, and seeking consent and authorization—is one of the most potent tools for ensuring overall justice during wartime decision-making.[36]

3.2. MINIMAL JUSTICE JUSTIFIED

Before leaving the domestic or national scene for consideration of the hot topic of international authorization of war, we need to reiterate and justify just war theory's standards on proper national authority. These differ slightly, we've seen, from international law's. In legal terms, the proper authority for declaring war must be the constitutionally authorized body of a UN member state. We pointed out previously the limitations of having a purely legal standard without a background moral theory which explains why and how political communities, and the governments which organize them, can be legitimate and proper. This background moral theory is a conception of minimal justice, itself founded ultimately on the value of protecting and forwarding everyone's human rights. What justifies just war theory in anchoring its precepts in human rights? And here's where we really run up against it: aren't these just Western values, ideological expressions of American imperialism—reflections of a Crusading mentality endemic to the Western mind? The answer is no. This accusation commits the "genetic fallacy," which is the rejection of an idea based on its origins instead of its merits, for example the Nazi resistance against teaching relativity theory in German schools because it was devised by a Jew, Albert Einstein. The idea of human rights did originate in the West, but it can't rationally be rejected on that basis alone. Indeed, the reason why it originated in the West was probably because the West needed it most: some of history's most gruesome human rights violations (like The Holocaust) occurred in the heart of Western Europe.

As for the merits, the concept of human rights has plenty going for it. It is genuinely *universal* in that everyone gets to claim human rights, and genuinely *beneficial* in that the things claimed—like "the foundational five" of security, subsistence, liberty, equality, and recognition—serve both objective human need and subjective human want. Whatever else you want, you *must* want the life and liberty needed to pursue them. Life requires subsistence and security; security requires recognition from others, and freedom from their domination; and liberty implies personal choice and the absence of brutal discrimination (i.e., equality). Everyone—not just Westerners—has overriding reason to believe in human rights and to work towards their realization. Human rights, perhaps alone among political concepts, genuinely acknowledge the worth of each individual human life and the importance of that life's value being protected against all the other people, forces, and institutions who might otherwise plot to use that life as a mere prop in their own projects.[37]

This might be one reason why human rights attract so much cross-cultural consensus—in moral commitment and in international, regional, and domestic human rights documents, protections, and procedures. For example—and note the overlap—becoming a member of the UN commits a state, under the Charter, to realizing human rights.[38] Of course, human rights still get violated, but that doesn't count against their universality because the universality is normative, not descriptive. It's about what we *should* believe and how we *should* act, and this cannot be dislodged or undermined by the behavior of rights-violators. They don't get to define justice, any more than thieves get to define property rights, or rapists bodily integrity. Indeed, isn't it odd (and noticeable) how often the accusation of "Western moral imperialism" is made by those who wish to violate human rights? Think of various outspoken governments in East Asia or the Islamic world: they stand to lose enormously by the spread of human rights, so they have huge incentive to resort to cultural chauvinism to stem the tide. But bad faith does not a good argument make.

Human rights, as a perspective on how society should be shaped, is : 1) thinner; 2) more accessible; and 3) more widely beneficial than rival doctrines on political legitimacy. It's thinner because it focuses only on the most elemental aspects of good social interaction, leaving everything above the baseline open to different commitments and to cultural and even personal preferences. It's not a comprehensive worldview the way communism was, or religion can be. This makes it more reasonable and accessible, as does the fact that the concept of human rights is pitched at every individual regardless of ethnicity, nation, religion, age, gender, or sexual orientation. The fact that human rights stand to benefit everyone also recommends the doctrine highly against those promising to benefit only, or disproportionately, the rich, or the workers, or the true believers, or white people, or Americans, or adult males, and so on.

A longer-term reason justifying these thoughts on legitimacy concerns the link between the satisfaction of human rights domestically with peaceful behavior internationally. Kant believed, and the recent researches of Michael Doyle support the notion, that rights-respecting societies don't go to war against each other.[39] There is, apparently, much empirical evidence substantiating this claim, otherwise known as the "democratic peace thesis." In any event, it makes clear conceptual sense: if a government does not care about the rights of its own people, how is it going to start caring about the rights of a foreign state and its citizens? If we look at history, we see that the embodiments of international aggression have, indeed, made horrible domestic regimes: Nazi Germany; Stalin's Russia; Hussein's Iraq. There is a clear connection here, and it probably runs quite simply like this: a rights-violator is a rights-violator. A group engaging in domestic rights-violation will not hesitate, if it can and if it wants, to violate rights internationally. That is why—and this is the profound conclusion—*we all have reason to be seriously concerned about rights-violating regimes wherever they are.* In fact, minimally just states have one further right as a consequence of these connections, and that is to do what they can, over the long term and in concert with others where needed, so that all states become human rights-respecting.[40]

Finally, consider a straightforward macro-comparison, regarding quality of life, in those societies which generally respect human rights versus that in those which don't. Where would you rather live: in a country like America, Canada, or Sweden or in a country like Iran, Cuba, and North Korea? Human rights respect does not make for a perfectly just society, but history clearly suggests it makes for a better, more enjoyable, life for the average person.[41]

All these powerful reasons—of self-interest, of autonomy, of accessibility and universality, of strong consensus, of good consequences, and connection to international peace—do not amount to "proof" of the "objective truth" of human rights. But such a proof is never forthcoming in moral and political life: skeptics holding such impossibly high standards can wait for Godot as long as they like. The rest of us realize that we've got to get on with the business of life and social organization, and here it is the weight of reasons which must be decisive, based on the judgment of sincere, sensible, and experienced persons. In the final analysis, you must have a theory of legitimate governance to talk comprehensively about the ethics of war and peace. It is my judgment that an appealing and sound theory of governance must integrate human rights. Ultimately, this is where the entire theory contained in this book rests: on the appeal of the idea of a minimally just, human rights-respecting society for everyone.[42]

3.3. INTERNATIONAL AUTHORIZATION?

We know, from our just cause discussions, that Article 51 of the UN Charter famously proclaims that, should an armed attack occur against a member state of the UN, both the victim and any vindicators have "inherent rights" (or "natural rights") to self-defense and other-defense. So, most international law experts agree that a UNSC vote is not needed to ground wars of self-defense, or other-defense, against obvious acts of cross-border aggression. That's clear. But what about wars where such is not the case: the aggression is not clear-cut; or the violence stays within borders and doesn't cross them (i.e., civil wars or humanitarian catastrophes); or, indeed, no aggression has even occurred yet (like in anticipatory attacks or "pre-emptive strikes")? Many international lawyers argue that, with these latter cases, UNSC authorization is absolutely necessary because: 1) they are not covered by the "inherent right" reference to self- and other-defense in the face of armed attack; 2) they are clearly more controversial than straightforward defense against an act of aggression which has already happened; and 3) the background ideals of the Charter include substantial UN and UNSC responsibilities for war and peace. (Indeed, the very first article of the UN Charter declares that one of the UN's core purposes is to "maintain international peace and security," and Articles 23–54 detail exhaustive procedures and powers for the UNSC to deploy in pursuit of this ideal.) So, a pro-UNSC vote for action in any of these controversial cases is a must.[43]

This was the position of most of the world in the run-up to America's 2003 Iraq attack. America was engaging in a pre-emptive strike (i.e., Iraqi aggression hadn't yet happened); and moreover this was a strike aiming to change forcibly the regime of a UN member. Thus, it needed a UNSC vote. It didn't get one, and so the war was illegal and unjust. The official American line was different. While the UNSC didn't vote explicitly in favor of "war" or an "American attack," it did demand Saddam resume UN weapons inspections or else face "serious consequences." Bush Jr. asserted that the war power was contained within the phrase "serious consequences" and so argued that UNSC authorization was in fact given. In any event, the Americans continued, the terms of the 1991 Persian Gulf War treaty (which was ratified by the UNSC in 1991) pledged Iraq to complete compliance with post-war measures, and also threatened a possible return to hostilities should complete compliance not be forthcoming. Since Saddam booted the UN weapons inspectors out of Iraq in 1998, he was in violation of that UNSC resolution, which contained this explicit warning of, and authorization for, armed force. Failing all that, America said, the Iraq attack was needed to defend America from future acts of terrorism, and self-defense is indeed recognized by the Charter as an "inherent right."[44]

So who was correct? It's not so clear if by "correct" you mean "has the best interpretation of international law." Believe it or not, both sides have serious and strong legal arguments; and it's not obviously the case that one side's arguments are better than the other's; and there's no overriding global legal authority to render a decision. Indeed I venture to say this is one of the reasons why international law is not completely satisfying in connection with *jus ad bellum*. Not only does it not directly deal with the hardest cases (such as pre-emptive attacks, terrorist strikes, humanitarian crises, and civil wars), but also its principles are not clear. Indeed, they are predictably vague because international law is the product of state consensus and it's very hard to get that on such controversial issues. The vagueness, in turn, allows for indeterminacy and for opposing sides to present strong arguments with little prospect of resolution. Thus, just war theory is stronger and more insightful on *jus ad bellum* than are the laws of armed conflict. (But note that the reverse is probably true in connection with *jus in bello*, where the detail of international law achieves incredible sophistication. See Chapter 4.) But if by "correct" you mean *morally* correct, then please consult the next chapter for an investigation into the justice of the Iraq attack, where I think answers can be had.

Should we buy into UN claims about its sweeping authority in connection with international peace and security, which gets asserted throughout the Charter (and other documents) in a very robust way? I personally believe that it is a very *desirable* thing to get UN authorization to go to war but I hesitate to say it's strictly *morally necessary*. On the one hand, requiring international authorization would represent one more barrier to overcome in any pro-war move, and so would make the resort to war more difficult. Isn't that a good thing? I guess so, but against that very point is that requiring international authorization might consume precious hours, days, and weeks, with the result being that the aggressor gets entrenched and becomes more difficult to resist and remove. We can easily imagine cases where the international community doesn't know enough, or care enough, about a local or regional war to get involved: so why give it final authority in that regard? Let's leave it to the people who do have their fundamental interests and rights actually at stake.

There's also the very fitness and legitimacy of the UN and the UNSC themselves to consider. At any given time, only 15 members are on the UNSC and, of those, only 5 hold vetoes and permanent seats. These five form the world's most exclusive club, and they are all rich, northern, nuclear powers, and all but one is Western. What gives such an exclusive club the right to legislate on war and peace for the world—especially in regions they know quite little about? Second, it's important not to succumb to naïve and romantic ideas about what the UN is, based on visions of what it might ideally become. The UN is not a world government; it is merely a voluntary association of states. It has, over the years, faced searing questions about its competence, efficiency, treatment and oversight of staff, and even over its integrity.[45] And the UNSC record authorizing wars and peacekeeping missions is spotty at best. While the UN has had real success—over Suez, over East Timor—it has had many controversies and failures, such as Cyprus and Congo. UN peace-keepers were so ineffective in Bosnia they were actually taken hostage by the Serbs; and, most notoriously, the UNSC failed to intervene at all in the genocidal civil war in Rwanda in the summer of 1994.[46] This, we might sharply ask, is the institution to which international lawyers would have us hand over ultimate authority on war and peace issues?

There is also the most important fact that, in spite of globalization, the state remains the crucial scene of political action in our lives. Recall that the UN is a voluntary association of states, and thus is ultimately their creature. The UN Charter itself enshrines state rights to political sovereignty and territorial integrity. And states remain, in terms of causal impact, the best poised to do serious harm to, or serious good for, their citizens. No wonder so many nations wish for their own state and why so much attention is paid to the legitimacy, or moral quality, of state structures. We still experience political life first and foremost as members of nation-states—Americans, Brazilians, Canadians, etc.—and only secondarily (or even less) as citizens of the globe. We strongly prefer to live in groups; and, while this fact never justifies shoddy treatment of other groups, it is a reality which must be accommodated by any plausible theory of international justice.[47]

My overall view on international authorization of war is this: it is certainly not required in straightforward cases of defense (whether of self or others) from actual aggression: no UNSC fiat could overturn those pre-existing rights of people. In more contested cases—humanitarian intervention and especially anticipatory attack involving regime change—the desirability of international authorization increases very considerably but might not even then, pending the details, strictly be required. I don't wish to be completely dismissive: at the very least, the UNSC always provides an on-going forum for countries to discuss and debate these issues and to present their cases for going to war on a formal basis, and that is always going to be worth something indeed.

4. Last Resort

Winston Churchill once said, memorably, that it was far better to "jaw jaw" than to "war war": i.e., to try to talk a problem over through diplomacy before fighting. Walzer concurs, observing that: "It is obvious that measures short of war are preferable to war itself." He continues: "One always wants to see diplomacy tried before the resort to war, so that we are sure that war is the last resort." In spite of this endorsement of the traditional last resort criterion, which is codified in Articles 2(4) and 33–40 of the UN Charter,[48] Walzer is quick with some helpful caveats. First, he points out that, strictly speaking, there is no such thing as a last resort. No matter how fearful the situation, there is always something else that can be tried—yet another round of diplomatic negotiations, for instance—prior to the resort to war. So it would be absurd, in this literal sense, to say that states may turn to war only as a last resort.[49] A second caveat concerns the fact that negotiations, threats, and economic sanctions are frequently offered as morally better means of international problem-solving than the use of force. At face value, this claim is indisputable: if a reasonable resolution to the crisis in question can be had through a credible and permissible threat, or through a negotiating session, or perhaps through sanctions, then surely that is preferable to running the sizable risks, and certain destruction, of war. Upon closer inspection, however, much depends on the nature of the particular act of aggression and the nature of the aggressive regime itself. Sometimes threats, diplomacy, and sanctions will not work. The incidents leading up to the 1991 Persian Gulf War are instructive: Saddam Hussein, in the face of all three, refused to be budged from his ill-gotten Kuwaiti gains.[50] Care must be taken that appeals to last resort do not end up rewarding aggression, by giving the aggressor extra time to entrench himself inside the victim. Finally, Albert Pierce and Lori Damrosch have pointed out that the leveling of systematic economic sanctions on an aggressor often violates the *jus in bello* principle of non-combatant immunity, since it is most often innocent civilians (often the poorest and most vulnerable) who bear the brunt of sweeping economic embargoes leveled on their country. In the absence of force directed against them, outlaw regimes always seem to find a way, within their own borders, to take care of themselves. The Hussein regime in Iraq, once more, offers lessons—surviving 12 years in the teeth of sweeping sanctions, which were then given up after the March 2003 US-led strike, which forcibly removed the regime from power. How much innocent civilian deprivation had to be endured while waiting for the sanctions "to do their job"—which they never did? I direct the reader to the relevant literature on the effects of the Iraqi sanctions in the 1990s.[51]

It seems much more plausible to contend not that war be the literal last resort—after all other imaginable means have been totally exhausted—but, rather, that states ought not to be hasty in their resort to force. There ought to be a strong presumption against the resort to force. Article 2(4) of the UN Charter is clear evidence of our deep commitment to such a presumption. It reads that all UN Members "shall refrain ... from the threat or use of force against ... any state."[52] But beyond this general principle, much depends on the concrete details of the actual situation in question. It is critically important, e.g., when the aggressor is mounting a swift and brutal invasion, to respond effectively before all is lost. It is also relevant to consider the nature of the territory of the victim of aggression; if it is a tiny country, like Israel, the need for a speedy and effective response against aggression will likely be much greater than that required by a country the size and strength of the United States. Any response from the international community is likewise relevant.

But attention must always be focused on the nature and severity of the aggressor and its actions, for frequently the international community is sluggish in mounting an effective response to aggression. The key question this criterion demands always be asked, and then answered in the affirmative, is this: is the proposed use of force reasonable, given the situation and the nature of the aggression?

5. Probability of Success

Probability of success is another *jus ad bellum* rule for which only general principles can be convincingly conveyed. Its prudential flavor explains this: probability of success is always a matter of circumstance, of taking reasonable options within the constraints and opportunities presented by the world. The traditional aim of this criterion—which, like right intention, is actually not contained within international law—is to bar lethal violence known in advance to be futile. As such, the principle is laudable and necessary for any comprehensive just war theory. Great care, however, needs to be exercised that this criterion, like last resort, does not amount to rewarding aggression, and especially that by larger and more powerful nations. This is so because smaller and weaker nations will face a comparatively greater task when it comes to fulfilling this criterion (which I think explains its absence from international law). And the calculation of expected probability of success for resorting to war is difficult. The vicissitudes of war are, as we know from history, sometimes among the most difficult phenomena to predict. Even when the odds seemed incredibly long, remarkable successes have sometimes, somehow, been achieved. Such are the stuff of military legend, like the ancient Greeks fending off the onslaught of Persians or perhaps even the American revolutionaries overthrowing the rule of the mighty lion of the British Empire. The lack of predictability, though, does not always turn out for the better. A notorious example is that the armies of Europe expected, in September 1914, to be home to celebrate Christmas.[53] Walzer also suggests that there are considerations of self-respect here, according to which victims of aggression ought to be permitted at least some resistance, should they decide on it, as an expression of their strong objection to the aggression and as an affirmation of their rights. It thus seems reasonable to judge that, given an act of aggression and given that the other *jus ad bellum* criteria are met, there is a presumption in favor of permitting some kind of armed response, even when the odds of military success (however defined) seem long. At the same time, this rule is not dormant: it remains important that communities contemplating war in response to aggression still consider whether such an extreme measure has any reasonable probability of success. That is the least, we might say, that they owe themselves.

6. Proportionality

Proportionality, codified at Articles 22–23 of the Hague Convention III, is one of the most contentious and challenging *jus ad bellum* criteria, ranking close to just cause itself. It mandates that a state considering a just war must weigh the expected universal (not just selfish national) benefits of doing so against the expected universal costs. Only if the projected benefits, in terms of securing the just cause, are at least equal to, and preferably greater than, such costs as casualties may the war action proceed. Walzer wrestles at length with the considerable difficulties presented by this otherwise sensible rule. On the one hand, the unchecked triumph of aggression is for him "a greater evil" than war. He also comments that "prudence can be, and has to be, accommodated within the argument for justice." On the other hand, Walzer comments on "the terrible presumption" behind the cost-benefit comparisons implicit in appeals to proportionality. He declares that "we have no way that even mimics mathematics" of making such proportionality judgments. He asks rhetorically: "How do we measure the value of a country's independence against the value of defeating an aggressive regime?"[54] In other words, how can we pretend to measure, on the same scale of value, the benefits of defeating aggression against the body count needed to achieve it? For example, it sounds ridiculous, totally without basis, to say things like: "My country's freedom from aggression is worth $300 million dollars and 245,000 casualties." The numbers appear completely arbitrary, and the comparison between an abstract, like independence, and a concrete, like cash or casualties, seems as ill-conceived as one between apples and oranges: they are simply different things.

The challenges of proportional "calculation" explode, in both number and complexity, as soon as one puts further thought to the question. What things actually count as costs and benefits in wartime? Only elements we can quantify, like the body count and economic expenditures? But usually we also want to appeal to qualitative elements, like the value of sovereignty and not enduring life as miserable slaves to some foreign invader. Is there a distinction between explicit and implicit costs, such as costs of mobilization on the one hand and, on the other, what else besides war we might have done with our time and treasure? Is there a difference between short-term and long-term benefits? Is it only the costs and benefits of prudence that matter, or do those of morality count as well? How to weigh the "universal" costs and benefits against each other when, usually during war, those who pay the costs are not the same group as those who enjoy the benefits, as when soldiers pay the present price for the future independence of their fellow citizens? The manifest, and manifold, difficulties involved in proportionality calculations cause vexation for just war theorists, and rightly so. The calculations needed are simply too complex and wide-ranging. It is wildly improbable that we could ever devise a completely satisfying set of cost-benefit formulae with regard to wartime action. Far better, I believe, to stick to a firm set of clear and universal rules to guide conduct, which is what the rest of just war theory strives to offer.

Walzer's final judgment on this issue, which seems sound, is that there is some truth in the proportionality maxim. But he insists that "it is a gross truth," an unrefined and imprecise truth, which can only point to obvious considerations of prudence and utility as limiting conditions on the pursuit of rights-respecting justice in wartime. Proportionality, at best, provides some checks and balances, some outside constraints, on the drive to secure a just cause. In other words—and with some irony—we know much better what disproportionality is than proportionality. We can usually recognize the former but, frankly, have trouble precisely defining the latter. We know when a war is a disproportionate—i.e., exaggerated, harmful, and inappropriate—response to a problem, just like we know that, within the context of a marriage, threatening divorce over a disagreement about what to have for dinner is disproportionate. Proportionality has, so to speak, negative content: it doesn't really positively add except to remind us that the problem in question has to be so severe (like unjust armed invasion) that war is, in fact, an appropriate response—and to suggest that the good to be gained from the war must be better than the substantial costs and evils we know war always brings in train.[55]

For some examples, Walzer says that, even though justice may have permitted otherwise, it was appropriate on grounds of proportionality that the United States did not go to war against the Soviet Union after the latter invaded Hungary in 1956, or Czechoslovakia in 1968. The real threat of a broad-based Cold War nuclear exchange between the superpowers was simply greater, and more universally fearful, than allowing Soviet expansion at the particular expense of the independence of these nations.[56] Slightly different, more obvious examples—deeper in history—include some of the old European wars sparked by marriage (or failure to marry) or failure to agree on who would succeed to the throne, or simply by some personal slight delivered to one monarch by another. None of these reasons balance with something as deadly as war as a "solution." To go even farther back, if the Trojan War really was fought over Helen—the woman "whose face launched a thousand ships"—then we can certainly ask questions of justice whether ordering all that fighting and killing was truly proportionate to the problem.[57]

7. Summary

This is a contemporary updating of the classical account of *jus ad bellum*. Any state, seeking to go to war against any other state, must show that its resort to armed force fulfills each of the six rules explained above: just cause; right intention; public declaration by a proper authority; last resort; probability of success; and proportionality. Failure to fulfill even one rule renders the resort to force unjust, and thus subject to criticism, resistance, and punishment. This allows us to appreciate just how demanding and stringent is just war theory. The laws of armed conflict make much the same claims, except that they: 1) do not endorse the rules of right intention and probability of success; 2) are more vague; and 3) are based on a looser conception of political legitimacy. Just war theory is thus even more demanding than international law, which is predictable since, quite often, morality sets itself a higher standard than law.

Since *jus ad bellum* is the province of those exercising the war power—often, but not always, heads of state, or the executive branch of government—it is their responsibility to ensure that its standards are fulfilled. By the same token, it is they who must answer for any *jus ad bellum* violations, for instance in war crimes trials after the war is over. As an illustration, consider that the Nazi high command (or what was left of it) was charged—among other things—with "crimes against peace" by the prosecutors during the Nuremberg war crimes trials after World War II. This is to say that they were accused—and many eventually convicted—of violating *jus ad bellum*, i.e., of committing aggression, of having waged an unjust war.[58]

The ultimate concepts and values underlying contemporary just war theory are the idea of a minimally just and therefore legitimate political community and the human rights of its individual citizens. It is for the sake of defending a minimally just state, and the human rights of its citizens, that we can morally contemplate the use of measures as forceful and destructive as those of war. We have this moral permission as a result of what aggression means—how it attacks the most basic values and possibilities of human civilization—and on the need to respond to it with effective resistance.

8. Case Study: World War II

Almost all just war theorists agree that World War II, on the part of the Allies, is the definitive modern example of a morally justified war, at least in connection with *jus ad bellum*. Let us briefly delve into this case, to see how the facts operate vis-à-vis the standards. For the sake of greater clarity and specificity, I shall focus mostly on the United States as the relevant actor. Of course, given the deep complexities of these real-world cases, attention cannot be paid to every element: the aim, in this section, is simply to give one application, of the six *jus ad bellum* rules, to a real and important historical case.[59]

Just Cause. Did the Allies, and particularly the US, have just cause in resorting to war between 1939 and 1941? It is clear that, in the European theater, Nazi Germany was the embodiment of precisely that kind of ultra-aggressive, totalitarian, outlaw state which just war theory holds up as the kind of threat against which the resort to armed self- and other-defense seems most plausibly grounded. Imperial Japan was likewise an ultra-aggressive totalitarian regime. Both of these powers were blatant aggressors: Nazi Germany first in Poland in 1939 and then in 1940 through the Low Countries into France; and Imperial Japan first in China in the mid-1930s and then also into Korea and the surrounding areas. There was no just cause whatsoever grounding the actions of these regimes: they were animated solely by desires for more territory, resources, power, glory—and even darker motives, related to their beliefs in their own ethnic superiority and their "racial destiny" to rule. Germany and Japan posed severe threats to the countries they invaded and, once they conquered these latter, subjected them to brutalizing rights-violative measures which still rank amongst the foulest in history. The commission of aggression caused both of these regimes to forfeit their state rights to non-interference and not to be attacked in return. So the Allies, as a matter of self- and other-defense, general rights-vindication and punishment for rights-violation, did no wrong—violated no rights—in responding with war. So the resort to war in 1939 by England and its Commonwealth, for instance, and in 1941 by the United States, was justifiable on this basis. Indeed, in the case of the United States, resort to war was made (explicitly) only after the Pearl Harbor aggression by Japan, and Germany's accompanying declaration of war on America. The moral requirement to defeat such regimes stands out as one of history's most compelling causes for resorting to force.

Right Intention. The Allies, in particular the United States, seemed to undertake World War II with the right intention, namely, the defense of their own nation and those of others, the defeat and punishment of aggression, and the repeal of its gains. Did the Allies display a reasonable commitment, prior to launching into war, to upholding the norms of *jus in bello* during its course and *jus post bellum* following its end? This is less clear, given the immense destruction that was eventually carried out during the war, and indeed is one of the reasons why I argued above that such ought to be newly incorporated into the right intention criterion. In fairness, the postwar actions and activities of the Allies—meaningful reconstruction of the defeated enemies, the Nuremberg and Far East War Crimes tribunals, and the formation of the UN—might, in retrospect, reveal some of the laudableness of their pro-rights intentions. In light of this conflicting data, perhaps all that can be said firmly, with regard to this criterion, is that the Allies really did seem to undertake the war with at least the proper *jus ad bellum* orientation of rights vindication.

Public declaration of war by a proper authority. Let us here take the case of the United States. America in 1941 was a minimally just society: widely recognized by the international community, with widespread and stable, uncoerced social peace domestically; it was not violating the rights of other societies; and it was seriously committed to the human rights of its citizens. America's explicit entry into the war, in 1941, was indeed declared through the appropriate constitutional channels, with both the executive and the legislative branches concurring. The declaration, on both Japan and Germany, was also publicly declared.

Last resort. It seems that the Allies did not hastily rush into war in the 1939–41 period. England and France, the major Allied powers in Western Europe, made a serious diplomatic effort to placate Hitler with the Munich accords in 1938. (Indeed, many people subsequently condemned these accords for appeasing an aggressor.) Hitler disregarded any such aspirations for peace; in fact, he used the Munich process as a bad-faith cloak with which he could legitimize his past actions and disguise his future ambitions. He then launched his ultra-aggressive attempt to conquer Europe on behalf of the Aryan race. Similarly, the Soviet Union signed the Molotov-Ribbentrop Pact of mutual non-aggression with Germany in 1939. The Soviet Union clearly wanted to avoid war. However, that pact was rendered asunder when Hitler, having conquered continental Western Europe, proceeded to turn his sights eastward in 1940–41. Indeed, it seems clear that, as of 1939–40 in Western Europe, and as of 1940–41 in Eastern Europe, there was no other feasible alternative to halting the aggression of Hitler than through the use of armed force. As such, the resort to war on the part of the Allies was not unreasonably quick.

It also seems that the United States' resort to war against Japan was not precipitate. After all, Japan had been committing aggression throughout East Asia, particularly in northern China and Korea, for several years prior to the outbreak of the Second World War. Secondly, Japan itself launched the armed attack on Pearl Harbor in 1941. Once Japan launched such a large-scale bombing raid, its intentions were clear and manifest: it wanted to fight the United States for supremacy in the Pacific region. America was not hasty in resorting to force in light of that attack.

Probability of success. This criterion is less clearly fulfilled in the case of Allied countries like Poland and France, and perhaps even England, but it seems that the United States clearly fulfilled it. Even though it was to fight enemies on opposite sides of the world at the same time, the United States could reasonably have foreseen, in 1941, that its manpower, industrial sophistication, and productive capacity, to say nothing of its military might, were second to none. It had every reason to believe, at the time, that it could eventually out-produce, out-fight, and overwhelm both of its enemies. And this would have been a strong argument even if those enemies were at the peak of their fighting capacity, which they were not: their earlier campaigns had drained huge military resources. With regard to Hitler, he was just beginning to be sucked into the endless morass of the campaign in Russia and was inordinately distracted, on the domestic front, by setting into motion the madness of the Holocaust. It was very predictable, in 1941, to see that Hitler, faced with the might of the Soviet Union on one front, and the nexus between Britain, her Commonwealth (notably Canada and Australia), and the United States on the other, was outmatched. He was sandwiched between huge powers. At the very least, it seems that the United States entered the European war with a considerable probability of success.

Proportionality. It is very important to consider the extent of Allied, and especially American, fulfillment of this category solely in terms of the time of the decision to resort to war. It is reasonable to contend that no one could have foreseen, in 1939–41, the full and total extent of the immense costs and casualties of World War II, much of which were tallied up in the final few months of the war in 1945. At the time, say, of the American entry, it was reasonable to suggest that the defeat of these two ultra-aggressive regimes was worth the projected prudential and moral costs of doing so.

In terms of Japan, it could've been foreseen that this would be a difficult and costly war, given the ferocity and resources of the enemy and the logistics involved in organizing fighting across the immense Pacific Ocean. But America had local allies in the Australians and Indonesians. It could count on sympathy and support from civilian populations in China and The Philippines, which were under the Japanese boot. The nub of the matter was this: what choice did America have, given the Pearl Harbor strike? Japan wanted and started that war, so it was indeed appropriate to respond with armed defense.

In Europe, given that Hitler was going to be so clearly outgunned on both fronts, it would have been reasonable to contend, at the time, that the military casualties in Europe would be absorbable, and that damage to the United States itself would probably be negligible. One thing that would have weighed on the conscience at the time, however, was the quite foreseeable fact that, given Europe's population density, there would be considerable civilian casualties from stepping up the war effort, and moving onto the continent itself to roll Hitler back within his own borders. As we have seen, there is no uncontroversial calculus for balancing foreseen but unintended civilian deaths and the great importance of defeating regimes the likes of Nazi Germany. But Walzer, for one, clearly believes proportionality was met, and he justifies himself thus:

> Nazism was an ultimate threat to everything decent in our lives, an ideology and a practice of political domination so murderous, so degrading even to those who might survive, that the consequences of its final victory in World War II were literally beyond calculation, immeasurably awful. We see it (and I don't use the term lightly) as evil objectified in the world, and in a form so potent and apparent that there never could have been anything to do but fight against it.[60]

Notes

1 Cicero, *De Re Publica*, (III, 23), trans. Richard J. Regan, in his *Just War: Principles and Cases* (Washington, DC: Georgetown UP, 1996), 16.

2 Michael Walzer, "World War II: Why Was This War Different?" *Philosophy and Public Affairs* (1971/72): 3–21.

3 Though I do believe one can detect, within the tradition, recent movement in the direction of inter-connection. See not only this work but also: David Rodin and Henry Shue, *Just and Unjust Warriors* (Oxford: Oxford UP, 2010); and Jeff McMahan, *Killing in War* (Oxford: Oxford UP, 2011).

4 United Nations, *Basic Facts about the United Nations* (New York: United Nations, 2011).

5 For sources on international law, see Appendix A.

6 John Locke, *Two Treatises on Civil Government* (Cambridge: Cambridge UP, 1988); Jan Narveson, *Respecting Persons in Theory and Practice* (Lanham, MD: Rowman and Littlefield, 2002).

7 Brian Orend, *Human Rights: Concept and Context* (Peterborough, ON: Broadview, 2002); Brian Orend, *Introduction to International Studies* (Oxford: Oxford UP, 2012).

8 James Nickel, *Making Sense of Human Rights* (Berkeley, CA: U of California P, 1987), 10–11.

9 Orend, *Human Rights*, passim; John Rawls, *The Law of Peoples* (Cambridge, MA: Harvard UP, 1999).

10 Brian Orend, *War and International Justice: A Kantian Perspective* (Waterloo, ON: Wilfrid Laurier UP, 2000), 89–126.

11 Thomas G. Weiss and Sam Daws, *The Oxford Handbook on the United Nations* (Oxford: Oxford UP, 2009).

12 Ian Brownlie, ed., *Basic Documents in International Law*, 4th ed. (Oxford: Oxford UP, 1995); Terry Nardin, *Law, Morality and the Relations of States* (Princeton, NJ: Princeton UP, 1983); Thomas W. Pogge, *Realizing Rawls* (Ithaca, NY: Cornell UP, 1989).

13 Regan, *Principles*; Terry Nardin, ed., *The Ethics of War and Peace: Religious and Secular Perspectives* (Princeton, NJ: Princeton UP, 1996); Michael Walzer, *Just and Unjust Wars*, 2nd ed. (New York: Basic Books, 1991).

14 Thabit Abdullah, *A Short History of Iraq* (Toronto: Pearson, 2003); Lawrence Freedman and Efraim Karsh, eds., *The Gulf Conflict, 1990–91* (Princeton, NJ: Princeton UP, 1993); Wolfgang F. Danspeckgruber and Carles R.H. Tripp, eds., *The Iraqi Aggression Against Kuwait* (Boulder, CO: Westview, 1996).

15 David E. Decosse, ed., *But Was It Just? Reflections on the Morality of the Persian Gulf War* (New York: Doubleday, 1992); James Turner Johnson and George Weigel, eds., *Just War and Gulf War* (Washington, DC: UP of America, 1991); Alan Geyer and Barbara G. Green, eds., *Lines in the Sand: Justice and the Gulf War* (Louisville, KY: John Know, 1992).

16 Walzer, *Wars*, 63–72; Francisco de Vitoria, *Political Writings*, ed. Anthony R. Pagden and Jeremy Lawrence (Cambridge: Cambridge UP, 1991).

17 Bob Woodward, *Plan of Attack* (New York: Simon and Schuster, 2004); US Congress, *The 9/11 Commission Report* (Washington, DC: United States Congress, 2004).

18 Walzer, *Wars*, 51, 67–72, and 233–38.

19 It must be noted that Beneš's decision was controversial among his own people. For more, see Edvard Beneš, *My War Memoirs* (London: Greenwood, 1971).

20 William R. Trotter, *A Frozen Hell* (Toronto: Algonquin, 1999).

21 Bruce S. Thornton, *The Wages of Appeasement* (Washington, DC: Encounter, 2011).

22 Walzer, *Wars*, xix.

23 Walzer, *Wars*, xix-xx.

24 Human Rights Watch, *Slaughter Among Neighbours* (New Haven, CT: Yale UP, 1995); Mahmood Mamdani, *Saviours and Survivors* (London: Pantheon, 2009); Gérard Prunier, *Africa's World War* (Oxford: Oxford UP, 2009).

25 Walzer, *Wars*, 58; Hidemi Suganami, *The Domestic Analogy and World Order Proposals* (Cambridge: Cambridge UP, 1989).

26 Chiara Bottici, *Men and States* (London: Palgrave Macmillan, 2009).

27 Thanks to Thomas Pogge for the image.

28 For more on this proposed addition to right intention, and the original Kant scholarship, see Orend, *Kantian Perspective*.

29 Woodward, *Plan*; Williamson Murray and Robert H. Scales, Jr., *The Iraq War* (Cambridge, MA: Harvard UP, 2003).

30 The origin of this much-used phrase is Act 3, Scene 1, of Shakespeare's *Julius Caesar*. Marc Antony is predicting the "fierce civil strife" that he believes will arise after Caesar's assassination:

> And Caesar's spirit, ranging for revenge,
> With Ate by his side come hot from hell,
> Shall in these confines with a monarch's voice
> Cry "Havoc," and let slip the dogs of war
> (Ate is the Greek goddess of discord and vengeance.)

Interestingly, the "blood and destruction" Antony anticipates exceed the normal results of well-regulated armed clashes: a medieval commander cries "Havoc!" to free the soldiers from normal discipline (lets slip—unleashes—the dogs of war—soldiers), and orders chaos—pillage and rape. See the discussion further on in this book of *jus in bello*—justice in war. (Another quotation from Shakespeare: "Do not cry havoc, where you should but hunt with modest warrant." [Coriolanus, III, 1]. See further discussion of "proportionality.")

31 Reisman and Antoniou, eds., *Laws*, 40.

32 Walzer, *Wars*, 34–40 and 138–43.

33 Max Hastings, *The Korean War* (New York: Simon & Schuster, 1998); George C. Herring, *America's Longest War: The United States and Vietnam, 1950–75*, 4th ed. (New York: McGraw Hill, 2001).

34 Louis Fisher, *Presidential War Power* (Lawrence, KS: U of Kansas P, 1995); and Regan, *Principles*, 20–47.

35 George R. Lucas, Jr., "PMCs: Internationalism and Military Interoperability," *International Journal of Applied Philosophy* (2009), 87–98; Peter W. Singer, *Corporate Warriors* (Ithaca, NY: Cornell UP, 2007).

36 Lucas, "PMCs," 87–98; Adrian Cadbury, *Corporate Governance and Chairmanship* (Oxford: Oxford UP, 2002); Immanuel Kant, *Political Writings*, trans. Hugh Bar Nisbet, ed. Hans Reiss (Cambridge: Cambridge UP, 1995).

37 Herbert Lionel Adolphus Hart, "Are There Any Natural Rights?" *Philosophical Review* (1955): 175–92; Alan Gewirth, *Human Rights* (Chicago: U of Chicago P, 1982); Henry Shue, *Basic*

Rights, 2nd ed. (Princeton, NJ: Princeton UP, 1996); Onora O'Neill, *Constructions of Reason* (Cambridge: Cambridge UP, 1989).

38 Brownlie, *Law,* 255–387.

39 Michael W. Doyle, "Kant, Liberal Legacies and Foreign Affairs," *Philosophy and Public Affairs* (1984): 204–35 and 323–53; and Michael E. Brown et al., eds., *Debating the Democratic Peace* (Cambridge, MA: MIT, 1996).

40 Kant, *Writings.*

41 I detail the pros and cons of justifying human rights versus their critics in Orend, *Human,* 67–100 and 155–90.

42 Orend, *Human.*

43 Reisman and Antoniou, eds., *Laws,* 3–35; Regan, *Principles,* 20–47 and 213–31.

44 Woodward, *Plan.*

45 Weiss and Daws, eds., *Oxford Handbook.*

46 Edward C. Luck, *United Nations' Security Council: Practice and Promise* (London: Routledge, 2006).

47 Michael Walzer, *Thick and Thin* (New Haven, CT: Yale UP, 1995).

48 Reisman and Antoniou, eds., *Laws,* 3–9.

49 Walzer, *Wars,* 84, xiv.

50 Walzer, *Wars,* xiii-xiv.

51 Walzer, *Wars,* xxv-xxxii; Albert C. Pierce, "Just War Principles and Economic Sanctions," *Ethics and International Affairs* (1996): 99–113; Lori Fisler Damrosch, "The Collective Enforcement of International Norms Through Economic Sanctions," *Ethics and International Affairs* (1994): 60–80; Geoff L. Simons, *The Scourging of Iraq,* 2nd ed. (New York: Macmillan, 1996); R. Clark, *The Impact of Sanctions on Iraq* (London: World View Forum, 1996) and Anthony Arnove and Ali Abunimah, eds. *Iraq Under Siege* (London: South End, 2000).

52 Regan, *Cases,* 214; and Reisman and Antoniou, eds., *Laws,* 5–9.

53 Walzer, *Wars,* 67–74.

54 Walzer, *Wars,* xv-xxi.

55 Thomas Hurka, "Proportionality and Necessity" in Larry May, ed., *War: Essays in Political Philosophy* (Cambridge: Cambridge UP, 2008), 127–44.

56 Walzer, *Wars,* xv-xxi.

57 Barry Strauss, *The Trojan War* (New York: Simon & Schuster, 2006).

58 Joseph E. Persico, *Nuremberg: Infamy on Trial* (New York: Penguin, 1995).

59 Alan John Percivale Taylor, *The Origins of the Second World War* (New York: Atheneum, 1962); John Keegan, *The Second World War* (New York: Vintage, 1990).

60 Walzer, *Wars,* 253.

3

Jus ad Bellum #2

NON-CLASSICAL WARS

"[T]he injustice of the opposing side ... lays on the wise man the duty of waging wars." —AUGUSTINE[1]

The classical account of *jus ad bellum*, developed last chapter, cannot be considered complete. For it deals solely with standard inter-state conflicts, like World War II or the Persian Gulf War, leaving out such important intra-state conflicts as civil wars. Furthermore, what happens when the aggressor is not another state, nor even a rival internal group striving to establish its own state but is, rather, something like a terrorist group? Finally, how is the so-called "aggression paradigm"—involving the binary struggle between attacker and defender—consistent with such things as anticipatory attack and humanitarian intervention? To respond meaningfully to such important issues—which seem, increasingly, to reflect the future face of war—we must amend the standard account of *jus ad bellum*. But we must stress, crucially, that *all the forthcoming amendments have to do with the just cause requirement.* All the other rules for a justified resort to force—right intention, proportionality, etc.—still hold straightforwardly for the four revisions which follow. The amendments are all in terms of *carefully expanding the just cause* for resorting to armed force beyond the classical scope of responding to interstate aggression. I should add that, in this chapter, we are squarely within just war theory; international law is profoundly unclear about these difficult cases beyond a general norm to get prior United Nations Security Council (UNSC) endorsement.[2]

1. Terrorism and 9/11

Because of September 11, 2001 ("9/11"), the world is wary of attacks by so-called "non-state actors," particularly terrorist groups. What's terrorism? Terrorism is a tactic; it is not itself an actual, full-blown "ism"—i.e., a coherent, developed political ideology with a systematic view of how social institutions should be structured.[3] There were radicals in the 1800s who referred to terrorism as a full-blown "ism"—some writing passionate, bizarre manifestos about random violence and the subversion of order—but they were mistaken. Terrorism is a tactic used in the service of some other "ism." In the case of the nineteenth century radicals it was anarchism: i.e., the idea of society without a coercive governing structure (like the state).[4] Terrorism, defined, is the use of violence—especially killing force—against civilians with the intent of spreading fear throughout a population, hoping that this widespread fear will advance a political objective. Crucial to terrorism is not just the deed itself but also what some have called "the propaganda of the deed." Since terrorists want to spread fear, it's vital that their deed not only be terrible but be so terrible that it gets covered by media, and word and image about the threat become widely disseminated throughout the population. The 9/11 attacks on America, e.g., were clearly motivated not just by the desire to kill civilians (over 3,000 of them) but also by the drive to maximize the propaganda value of the high-profile strikes. (Ditto for: a) the explosive "7/7" attacks in Europe (July 7, 2005), which struck such mass transport hubs as train stations and subways (killing at least 50)[5]; b) the April 2013 bombings of the Boston Marathon (killing at least 3 and injuring over 150); and c) the dramatic hostage taking, by al-Qaeda, of workers at a massive natural gas plant in remote eastern Algeria in January 2013. When the Algerian military responded with force, a bloody battle ensued, killing over 60.)

Though we might imagine cases where terrorism gets used by other "isms,"[6] most often it occurs historically in three contexts. The first is as a tool of authoritarian regimes to crush their own populations into submission: e.g., the dictatorship under Robespierre, during the French Revolution, established the "Reign of Terror" (the root source of the word "terrorism" in Western vocabularies). The Reign of Terror names the period, 1793–94, when "Enemies of the Revolution" were rounded up and, in a very deliberate, public, propagandistic way, given their own special "close shave" by Mme. La Guillotine. At the Terror's peak, Robespierre had 40,000 people guillotined in just one month.[7]

The second context is when terrorism gets used as a tool of extremist outsiders against representative regimes. In this context—which is where the 9/11 attacks fit—terrorism is a violent attempt to circumvent such democratic processes as rational persuasion, coalition- and consensus-building, the rule of law, and the will of the majority expressed in free elections. The terrorist seeks to short-circuit all these things and simply inflict his will on a population, probably because he knows his extreme beliefs would have no chance of achieving mainstream success. He can't persuade people, so he seeks to coerce them. The terrorist, in this sense, is actually much like a tyrant—but without the power and control the tyrant already has. The terrorist is a tyrant-in-waiting, and he dreams of becoming someone like Robespierre, who is able to radically transform all of society from the top-down through what he views as the cleansing power of violence. The personnel of al-Qaeda fit this mold precisely, with their desire to force Western governments—especially the USA—out of the Middle East and North Africa (MENA), so that they'd be free to overthrow local governments and establish extremist Islamic theocracies, blending "church" and state, throughout the region.[8]

The third common context of terrorism is as a tool in guerrilla warfare. Guerrilla warfare refers to the use, by at least one side, of irregular military tactics against the standard tactics, and regular forces, of the other side. Often, guerrilla warfare is resorted to by weaker forces against more powerful ones: the weaker side knows it will be crushed by the stronger should it engage the stronger in open, classical combat. Instead, the weaker side uses irregular tactics like surprise attacks, traps and ambushes, quick strikes followed by rapid disengagement and disappearance, assassinations, clandestine and camouflage operations, sabotage and even terrorism. Consider the recent insurgencies in Afghanistan and Iraq, following US invasions in 2001 and 2003, respectively. These invasions resulted in the quick overthrow of the ruling regimes. Groups opposed to US occupation, post-invasion, became insurgents (as they realized that directly engaging US forces in open warfare—in a so-called "set-piece battle," e.g.—would result in their own annihilation). So they refused to engage, instead: planting landmines in the road to blow up US soldiers as they drove by; launching ambush-style missile attacks on US helicopters when they were in the middle of loading and thus were "sitting ducks"; hiding among civilians and then blowing themselves up when US soldiers came close by on daily patrol; and so on. Now, such actions don't count as terrorism, because they target military forces. How can terrorism come into play in a guerrilla war? Well, the guerrillas might view it in their interests to spread terror throughout the civilian population—even if it is their own. Why? Consider again the American occupations of Afghanistan and Iraq throughout the 2000s. The Americans, and American-supported local governments, were in control. The insurgents opposed all this. Using terrorism, they believed, could challenge that control—making the authorities look ineffectual and incapable of ruling. So the insurgents randomly blew up civilians, striking especially during religious observances (when people's guards were down). The insurgents hoped that the people, scared and exhausted by the violence, would then push for political change, and the insurgent forces would step in to fill the gap left by the vacating Americans. That was their theory, anyway. And it shows the extreme extent to which ruthless insurgents can be willing to go: gladly killing their fellow citizens to advance their own partisan objectives of winning power for themselves.[9]

Whether terrorism as a tactic is consistent with any "ism" or "ocracy" is a difficult and delicate debate. Fortunately, I don't have to resolve it here. From just war theory's point of view, *terrorism is always an impermissible tactic*, since it involves the deliberate killing of innocent civilians—which right-thinking people view as murder. We'll talk more next chapter about just war theory's ban on deliberately killing innocents—what does it mean, what justifies it, what consequences does it have, and so on. For now, we merely diagnose terrorism for what it is and note how, clearly, it can pose a dangerous non-state threat to the existence and peace of legitimate states (especially in the second context).[10]

Terrorists are not the only non-state threats which states confront. Mercenaries, which used to be major threats in this regard, continue in some parts of the world to be of real concern. Mercenaries are soldiers who do not have a political objective, only a financial one: they offer their killing services to the highest bidder, and have no political objective of their own. They band together to form so-called "private military companies" (PMCs), and as such tend to be viewed very dimly by professional soldiers devoted instead to the public cause of defending their country from aggression.[11] Finally, in some parts of the world, Mafia-style criminal gangs, and/or drug cartels, can pose enough of a threat that the state(s) in that region respond with force that is war-like in scale and seriousness. Consider Colombia, in South America. For a long time, the government and the cocaine cartels have fought something very much like a war. But the cartels don't have a political or state-related objective: they only want to be left alone to profit from the drug trade. The government, however, is unwilling to let them, since cocaine is everywhere illegal. What has made their conflict war-like has been the scale and ferocity of the fighting, along with a combination of the weakness of the Colombian state and the strength and wealth of the cartels. In recent years, Mexico has come to experience similar levels of violence, related to drug and people trafficking, along the US border.[12]

Usually, non-state threats are best dealt with using so-called "measures short of war." Which ones are these? All the tools of domestic law enforcement: surveillance; information-gathering; investigation; "making a case"; infiltration; strong border controls; drug and crime "stings" and "busts"; a robust and effective police force; an efficient and non-corrupt legal system; and a sustained political commitment to weed out the threat.[13] Sometimes, however, these measures might not be enough, and the more extreme measures of war-fighting can be contemplated. This might happen when the state itself is weak, perhaps because it is generally under-resourced owing to the poverty of its people, or else owing to systematic corruption or inefficiencies in its own structure. Both are true of Colombia. The other possibility is that the non-state threat is abnormally well-endowed, and represents a genuine state-scale security threat, as in the case of the Colombian and Mexican drug cartels and the terrorist group al-Qaeda, which is—or, at least, was[14]—flush with the wealth of ex-Saudi billionaire Osama bin Laden. Al-Qaeda also received expert military training back in the 1980s, when America was keen to supply and educate the USSR's enemies during Russia's aggressive war against Afghanistan.[15]

There is very little amendment to the just cause rule which is required to deal with these threats. Why? Because there's nothing, in just war theory or international law, which says that aggression can be committed only by states. Aggression, recall, is the use of armed force in violation of a legitimate state's right to either territorial integrity or political sovereignty. And states have these rights insofar as they help realize the human rights of their people. Ultimately, then, *aggression is the violent violation of human rights.* So either states or non-state actors can commit aggression, which we've seen is what roots a morally justified resort to war.

Consider the 9/11 attacks, which were clear instances of aggression. They involved the use of armed force, first to hijack the planes and then to use the planes themselves as high-powered missiles. They violated America's right to territorial integrity, in so far as they were lethal attacks on American soil, having penetrated American airspace. And they violated America's right of political sovereignty, by attempting to force serious foreign policy changes upon a freely-choosing population. America, moreover, was in 2001 a legitimate state: by being widely recognized by the international community; by enjoying widespread, un-coerced social peace; by making serious efforts at the realization of its citizens' human rights; and by not—at that time—violating the rights of other states and peoples. So 9/11 was an act of aggression, very reminiscent of Pearl Harbor, just as it was obviously designed to be ("propaganda of the deed" and all). And aggression, we explained last chapter, justifies a defensive war in response.

The only "wiggle room" here, for any supporters of that attack, would be to argue that America violated the last condition of minimal justice by somehow violating the rights of foreign political communities and their citizens at that time. I suppose they would focus on Iraq, Saudi Arabia, and the Palestinians. But you can't just throw out accusations; you have to make a sustained and reasonable argument and have it backed by publicly accessible evidence.

America had a significant presence in Iraq in 2001. In fact, it enforced no-fly-zones (NFZ) in both the south and north of that country. It also supplied aid to humanitarian camps contained within the NFZ. But it was entitled to do so by the terms of the treaty ending the Persian Gulf War in 1991, to which Iraq agreed. More controversially, America still maintained sanctions on Iraq in 2001. While these hurt Iraq, they were being maintained to ensure full compliance with the 1991 treaty terms, and the Americans felt the treaty provisions regarding full disclosure of Iraq's program for developing weapons of mass destruction (WMD) were not being met. Legally, the Americans had the right to do this: it's clearly there in the 1991 treaty which Iraq signed. As for the privations which the sanctions created in Iraq, detailed comment will be made next chapter. For now, we note that Saddam's regime also contributed substantially to the sanctions-related deprivations suffered by the Iraqi people in the '90s. In fact, it benefited from them: the sanctions actually made Iraqis more dependent on Saddam's regime and, if he truly wanted the sanctions to stop, all he had to do was fully comply with UN and US demands. So to blame Iraqi civilian suffering—an admitted reality—solely or even mainly upon the US is not clear-cut. It is certainly nowhere so clear-cut as to justify mass murder in retaliation.[16]

How exactly did America's presence in Saudi Arabia violate that community's rights? America's military was there at the request of the Saudi Arabian government, and indeed had been so since the days of Desert Shield (against Iraq) in 1990. If the terrorists were then to argue that the Saudi government was and remains illegitimate, they'd have to tell us why. It's not a democracy, true, but: 1) we left open last chapter the possibility that non-democratic states might still be legitimate; 2) the Saudi government, in spite of its imperfections, is still widely recognized internationally; and 3) besides, if al-Qaeda had its preference, it would not institute a democracy in Saudi Arabia anyway—it would institute an Islamic theocracy (i.e. a union of "church" and state, based on a strict, extreme fundamentalist reading of the Koran). Would such a regime be consistent with human rights? It's hard to make that case, for such would probably deny freedom of belief and association to non-believers as well as radically curtail female access to such human rights as participation in governance, recognition as equals, elementary education, property ownership, and so forth. America's military presence in Saudi Arabia is found "offensive" to al-Qaeda because Americans are seen as non-believers "defiling" the Islamic holy land with their very presence (a religious, not a moral reason); and because America's presence there simply makes it harder for al-Qaeda to overthrow the Saudi regime and institute an Islamic theocracy there (a self-interested strategic reason, not a sincere, objective moral one).

Islamic extremists—like al-Qaeda and the Taliban, the radical ex-ruling party of Afghanistan—don't hate the West for its own sake. To them, Westerners are just infidels who refuse to believe the truth of the Koran: write-offs, so to speak, destined for Hell. What makes these extremists truly hate the West, especially America, is that America stands in the way of their ultimate goal: the overthrow of governments in traditional Arab lands throughout the MENA, and their replacement with strict Islamic theocracies *à la* the Taliban or Iran. They especially wish to do this in Saudi Arabia, since that is Islam's holy land. But America supports numerous Arab governments—Egypt, Kuwait, Pakistan, Saudi Arabia—and thus frustrates their goal. America also supports Israel, which the Islamic radicals view as being on traditional Arab land, too. So the extremists decided to commit large-scale terrorism against America, hoping such would create enough pain and fear among the American people that they would force the US government to withdraw from the MENA.[17]

This leaves America's "offensive" support for Israel, and the association in many Arab minds between that and the persecution of the Palestinians. The

Israeli-Palestinian problem is difficult, and can't easily be swept aside—or solved for that matter. (We will return to this conflict in detail in Chapter 7.) There seem to be serious issues of disenfranchisement and aspirations for statehood. But, in the first instance, it's Israel which has front-line responsibility, not America. Secondly, it's not as though Israelis have no claim to the disputed territory, either—which they, unlike their neighbors, have actually turned into a democracy with sincere commitments to human rights (at least for citizens).[18] To count as a systematic violation of human rights sufficient to justify armed attacks in response, it must be a directly, clearly culpable action, not indirect support for another country which has some controversial policies. And it must deal not merely with what your group wants, or schemes to get, but with the substance of vital human needs, i.e., human rights. All too often people inflate their mere preferences into the status of human rights claims because they know the language of human rights commands attention. But, as I've said, *just because you claim it, doesn't make it so*. You need a sober, non-religious argument—accessible to any reasonable person—which draws on real evidence and fits the definition of what a human right actually is. Without such an argument, proving America's mass human rights-violations (and not merely its preponderance of power and its policies which you don't like), you can't question America's status as a legitimate state. And if you can't question that, you cannot justly attack America out of the blue.

1.1 STATE SPONSORSHIP OF TERRORISM

A connected issue, of vital importance, concerns whether the non-state actor's aggression was itself "sponsored" by a state actor. If so, war is justified not only against the non-state threat but against the state sponsor as well. Aggression is, in this regard, a symmetrical relation: if Q commits aggression against R, and Q had substantial support from P in doing so, then P also aggressed against R. Consider again the 9/11 attacks. It immediately came to light, following the strikes, that al-Qaeda was receiving substantial and knowing support from the government of Afghanistan, known as the Taliban. The Taliban embodied strict Islamist principles—seeking to impose their own extremist reading of Islam upon their people—and found common cause with al-Qaeda's terrorist objectives, in particular the desire to spread radical Islamic theocracies throughout "traditional Arab lands." So the Taliban allowed al-Qaeda refuge within Afghanistan, knowing full well al-Qaeda was running terrorist training camps with the objective of committing terrorism around the world. In doing so, the Taliban made itself a legitimate target in the so-called "War on Terror" following the 9/11 attacks. Since al-Qaeda committed aggression, and the Taliban's Afghanistan made it possible for them to do so, it was a material part of their aggression—i.e., a co-conspirator, a material accomplice. The term most often applied to states that sponsor terrorism is that they are "rogue" or "outlaw" states: i.e., states disobedient of international law and moral custom in such a flagrant way that they become dangerous. America, along with 28 other countries, invaded Afghanistan in November 2001 and, within two months, routed the Taliban from power. Since early 2002, Afghanistan has been in a complex state of uneasy, sub-optimal post-conflict resolution, to which we shall return in Chapters 6 and 7.[19]

Care must be taken to show, however, that any suspected sponsorship is actually there. We can imagine cases, especially in the developing world, where states simply lack the resources to know everything that is going on within their territory. Some states might unwittingly be host to terrorists—as indeed America itself was, during the few weeks before 9/11. The implied duty for states here is one of good citizenship in the international community: actively co-operating in the identification of, and hunt for, terrorists; helping other states to weed out any of their terrorists; and being open and self-critical to the possibility that perhaps terrorists are located on one's own soil. Such are much-needed attitudes in furthering the legitimate aims of the war on terror. (A concrete recent example of such co-operation was shown in early 2013, when the government of Mali invited such countries as France and Canada to engage in strikes on violent splinter groups of al-Qaeda operating inside its borders, who were in fact attempting a coup.) It is only when there is an adamant refusal to co-operate, coupled with concrete evidence of a material link between that state and a terrorist group, that the state itself may be subjected to criticism and opposition, in extreme cases leading to armed resistance. "Material links" include: financing; the provision of weapons, intelligence and/or training; the knowing provision of safe harbor, residence, or citizenship; and any blending between the state's own resources and personnel with that of the terrorist association.[20]

2. Anticipatory Attack and Preventive War

This is a thorny issue much on people's minds since America's decision, in March 2003, to launch an ostensibly self-defensive attack on Saddam Hussein's regime in Iraq. To get theoretical grounding, let's consider Walzer's thoughts on this topic.

Walzer wants to walk a fine line between two extremes: denying that anticipatory attack by one state on another—or on a non-state actor—is ever justified; and supporting the doctrine of preventive war. A preventive war, as he defines it, is a war prosecuted in the present for the sake of maintaining the future balance of power, itself thought necessary for even longer-term peace and security. Such wars used to be very frequent in Europe, especially in the eighteenth century. The grounds most frequently offered for preventive war are utilitarian—i.e., we must war now to avoid future costs and/or gain future benefits. European powers used to do this to prevent any one power from getting too big and threatening. War was, so to speak, a way of taking powers down a peg or two, so they wouldn't cause an even bigger war down the road. Walzer believes, soberly, that the calculations required to morally ground preventive war are simply too fantastic to be plausible. *We just don't know that much about how the long-term future will unfold.* Furthermore, the danger to which preventive war is intended to respond is too distant and speculative. It simply doesn't seem to justify the certain deaths in the present to go to war based on speculation of what another country—say, China—might be like in roughly 30 years. If any kind of advance action is to be grounded at all, the danger aimed at must be *imminent*, not distant; it must be a threat which is *concrete*, not merely abstract.[21]

"Anticipatory attack" denotes an armed attack wherein you strike first, not out of aims for a distant, future balance-of-power but, rather, out of immediate aims to pre-empt an attack you know is coming against you in the very near future. This is "pre-emptive," as opposed to "preventive," war. (I prefer the term "anticipatory attack" to avoid any confusion between the two). A sufficient threat for justifying an anticipatory attack, Walzer suggests, is composed of three needed elements. The first is "a manifest intent to injure," revealed either through a bitter history of conflict between the communities in question (like the Arab-Israeli struggle) or through recent and explicit threats. Walzer suggests that the recipient of a justified anticipatory attack can only be "a determined enemy," one demonstrably committed to doing severe harm to one's political community. The second element of sufficient threat is "a degree of active preparation that makes the intent a positive danger." Mere malign intent, even given a conflict-ridden history and/or recent hostile declarations, is not enough to ground anticipatory strikes. There must also be a measurable military preparation on the part of the proposed recipient of the attack, such as its build-up of offensive forces along the border. Finally, the situation must be one "in which waiting, or doing anything other than fighting, greatly magnifies the risk [of being attacked]." Only under all three conditions is an anticipatory attack justified.

In general, Walzer suggests, "states may use military force in the face of threats of war, whenever the failure to do so would seriously risk their territorial integrity or political independence." Indeed, he goes so far as to contend that, should State X be faced with these three conditions involving Bellicose State (or Non-State) Actor Y, then Y has already committed aggression against X, and thus X has at least a just cause to launch an attack. We now see how, for Walzer, the actual deployment of force is not a strictly necessary condition for aggression to have occurred. It is no less a violation of state rights to pose "a serious risk" to the political sovereignty and territorial integrity of a legitimate state than it is to launch an armed invasion against it. Though there are obvious and substantial concerns to be raised here—with regard to loosening the concept of aggression—Walzer himself stresses that anticipatory attack can only be truly exceptional, and a very burdensome weight of justification is borne by the attacker to prove, with evidence, that the three general criteria really do hold in its case.[22]

The key here, in my view, is that the word "defense"—as in "defense from aggression"—can be construed either descriptively or normatively. Descriptive defense means you must wait to be, empirically, the second one to use force—that your use of force comes after that of the aggressor's. He takes his shot, and then you're entitled to take yours in reply—like the textbook cases of self-defense. Normative defense, by contrast, means that there might be circumstances where, empirically, one's use of force can come first against an aggressor. A just war is one which is *normatively* defensive—it defends people from aggression and seeks, in response, to resist and repeal it—whereas the tactics which may be employed, within the context of such a just war, may be either empirically defensive or offensive.

Aggression, after all, is universally defined by just war theorists and international law as the violation of state rights to territory and sovereignty. This violation occurs when a state, or non-state actor, obviously presents itself as a severe threat to another state and its people. And a state, or non-state actor, can present itself as such a threat in at least one of two ways: 1) by actually attacking a state without just cause; or 2) by posing a *credible, grave, and imminent threat*, based on compelling evidence, of launching such an aggressive attack. So a just war of self- or other-defense need not be wholly reactive: there is a bit of room here, I believe, for anticipatory attack as well.

The key notion, with regard to anticipatory attack, is that forcing states to wait for the actual attack, despite its evident and imminent coming, is not a reasonable insistence. This is especially the case if there are compelling, public grounds for believing that the coming attack is going to be of considerable force and destruction. *A state would be derelict in its duty to protect its members if it did not reserve the right to make well-grounded anticipatory attacks in this regard.* It is no less a violation of fundamental rights to deliberately pose a credible and imminent severe threat—i.e., a clear and present danger—to another person or state. Such interferes with the lives and liberties of states and peoples as readily as does an explicit and actual invasion because it leaves them just waiting for the oncoming attack. The coercive threat functions, and is intended to function, in the same manner as an actual attack: to bring about the unjust capitulation of the other country or person. From a just war point of view, the resort to arms by the victim is hence equally justified in either event.

Think of a personal case where an attacker breaks into your home with a gun and declares repeatedly his intention to kill and rob you. He then releases the safety switch on his gun, leaving him free to fire. It's not unjust in such a case, if one has a gun oneself, to fire at that point: the attacker has violated your space, declared terrible intentions, shows himself capable of realizing them, and then he takes the final step of just leaving you waiting for the hammer to fall. Given the potentially final consequences of waiting for that hammer, it seems quite reasonable for you to defend yourself. And it is clearly still defense, even though you're the one firing first. An even better analogy, representing the state more accurately, would be if a policeman happened upon the scene. Every police force I've heard of allows the policeman to fire at this point—and probably sooner, at the point when the attacker raises his gun towards you—in defense of your life. The cop, or you, fires first—but the moral damage and physical danger has first been committed by the attacker, rendering him open to being resisted. You're not creating the menacing conditions, after all: he is. You are defending yourself from what you have every reason to believe is a credible, grave, and imminent threat to your life and rights.

Jeff McMahan makes an important point here when he says that, even when we go to war in response to an attack which has already occurred, a prime objective in doing so is to prevent even further damage inflicted by the attacker. This suggests that the difference between reactive and anticipatory defense is not so rigid and black-and-white. When we see aggression, we move: 1) to punish it; 2) to resist it in the moment; and 3) to prevent further harm in the future. We can, moreover, plausibly say that all three are done in defense: defense of values and defense of lives.[23]

The just war tradition is, admittedly, seriously split on this issue. We know, from Chapter 1, that Vitoria disagrees with both Walzer and me here: the Spaniard insists you must wait for the actual attack before you may go to war to fend the attacker off and punish him. International law, for its part, seems to concur with Vitoria, at least in the absence of special permission from the UNSC. Most pre-9/11 writers and international lawyers would be in this camp, other than Walzer of course. Let's call this camp "strict defense purists." Many of the medieval writers, however, argued strongly in favor of the idea—inspired by Augustine—that "protection of the innocent" was a prime purpose of the state, and a just cause for war. And they concluded, upon reflection, that there could be rare occasions when a first military strike could be consistent with this principle. If you wait to receive the first strike, some of your civilians will die and you'll thus have failed in your duty to protect them. Post 9/11, and in the era of WMD, this view is gathering renewed attention.[24]

The American government, in its 2002 *National Security Strategy*, makes the case that—in light of modern terrorism and its objectives of spectacular, hard-to-predict instances of mass civilian slaughter—a responsible government must reserve the right to strike first if such will most likely prevent such instances from occurring. "The greater the threat," the document reads, "the greater the risk of inaction—and the more compelling the case for taking anticipatory action to defend ourselves, even if uncertainty remains as to the time and place of the enemy's attack. To forestall or prevent such hostile acts by our adversaries, the United States will, if necessary, act pre-emptively."[25]

It is vital to understand that these considerations do not lighten the load of a government making use of first strike. For such a government must then publicly justify its first strike in light of Walzer's three grounds for anticipatory attack and show, fundamentally, how such action is consistent with its function and duty of protecting its people.[26] All this amendment to just war theory does is refuse to rule out such strikes as a matter of conceptual stipulation or verbal fiat. It leaves it open to reasonable argument, and appeal to public evidence, whether such attacks might be morally justified in particular instances. Just war rules need to offer firm and clear guidance, yes, but to remain relevant over time some aspect of flexibility and openness to considering new situations is an absolute must.

2.1. AMERICA'S 2003 IRAQ ATTACK

Now let's examine an actual case of anticipatory attack: America and Britain's strike into Iraq in the spring of 2003.[27] There were many arguments trotted out in support of a pre-emptive strike on Iraq, prior to its launching on March 19, 2003. But the one most relevant, for our concern in this section, was that the regime in Iraq posed a clear and present danger to the United States. Why? The Bush Jr. Administration said that Iraq either harbored al-Qaeda terrorists, who carried off the 9/11 attacks, or at least possessed WMD, which it was willing to give to such terrorists (who, we know from 9/11, would not hesitate to use them). The moral structure of this argument is similar to that offered above, but it adds a further player that we must note with clarity, and some emphasis, in light of recent events. This player is that of the roaming terrorist organization, which moves from state to state, or which operates on a clandestine basis in a variety of states. The principle here seems to be that it is justified to perform a pre-emptive attack on a bellicose state either because: 1) its own actions fulfill Walzer's three criteria as outlined above; or 2) it harbors a terrorist organization which fulfills the three criteria; or 3) the mixture between the actions of the state offering sanctuary to the organization and the actions of the organization itself fulfill the three criteria. In the case of the 2003 attack, the final category seems to have been the one foremost in mind of the American war-planners and executors.

There was a history of recent armed hostility: both between Iraq and the United States and between al-Qaeda and the United States. Iraq and America (as well as the UK and others) clashed in the 1991 Persian Gulf War, and exchanged sporadic fire in connection with the NFZs enforced over Iraq between 1991 and 2003. Al-Qaeda attacked America in 2001, and America replied by invading Afghanistan a few weeks later and, according to some commentators, driving some al-Qaeda members out of that country and into Iraq. Throughout the 1990s, in fact, America had engaged, and been targeted by, Islamic terrorist organizations on a number of occasions and throughout a variety of Middle Eastern, African, and American locales. So, supporters of the 2003 pre-emptive strike could argue plausibly that the "bitter and determined enemy" condition of Walzer's was here obviously fulfilled, both with reference to Iraq and al-Qaeda. I agree. We know, however, that that is not enough: that there must be both indication of a political willingness of the bitter enemy to attack, and clear military indications that the bitter enemy is imminently about to attack, before an anticipatory strike can be justified in terms of just cause.

Here is where the issue of WMD clouds the picture. Essentially, the United States government argued that the military build-up condition was satisfied, in the spring of 2003, simply because Iraq had WMD. (Or so they thought.) In an era when weapons-which-can-kill-tens-of-thousands can be deployed within under an hour, how meaningful is it to have the military "build-up" criterion? Doesn't just *having them* count as satisfying that condition? The most plausible answer, I believe, must be no, otherwise we'd have to define all the major military powers as severely dangerous, as ticking time-bombs. What has to change is how we conceive of the military build-up, or offensive capacity, condition when it comes to WMD. The key here is not the raw fact of possessing these weapons, but the recent history regarding their use. It is relevant, e.g., to consider the fact that the Hussein regime in Iraq deployed chemical weapons at least twice in recent history: once against Iran in the middle 1980s, the other in 1988 against the Kurdish minority group within Iraq itself. Contrast that with the recent behavior of other powers who admittedly have such weapons, yet who have not used them. In the latter case it seems most plausible to infer, from their behavior, that such powers have such weapons for defensive and deterrent purposes, and are making a reasonably responsible use of them. The Hussein regime did not, and thus could be counted as a serious danger. This judgment is only underlined by considering that the Hussein regime had a record of recent international aggression—in 1990 into Kuwait—and also deliberately shot missiles into Israel's civilian population centers during the Persian Gulf War which followed. What this reasoning establishes is that the military build-up condition is to be understood as outlined above when it comes to conventional forces—i.e., as a literal build-up, usually along the border. But, when it comes to WMD, *mere possession* of such weapons can count as a severely threatening military capacity only when coupled with a recent history of: 1) using them; or 2) of having committed international aggression; or 3) of having deliberately targeted civilians during wartime.

We've now established our rule regarding WMD, but a large problem for America's pro-attack case is whether Iraq actually had them. We know, post-attack, that the UK and USA gave up looking, finding none. That's a stinging fact which reflects poorly on the war. There are also indications that the "evidence" in favor of Iraqi WMD possession was highly "massaged," raising sharp questions about the professionalism of the intelligence services ostensibly serving their heads of state to the best of their ability. Indeed, in December 2005, President Bush Jr. himself admitted in a public address that: "It is true that much of the intelligence turned out to be wrong."[28] Yet it's not all so badly lop-sided and scandalous. Iraq did, after all, actually have and use WMD in the 1980s—so why wouldn't they still have a few tucked away somewhere? The answer might be that the UN weapons inspection process—authorized by the peace treaty of the 1991 Persian Gulf War, and continuing throughout the '90s—actually succeeded in identifying and stripping Iraq of its WMD. There was obviously severe skepticism, by American intelligence, that the UN could've achieved such success. But that's allowing one's expectations to shape one's perception of the evidence, instead of the other way around. A further complication is that, apparently, Saddam was still on the record asserting Iraqi WMD possession. Why would he lie, if this wasn't true? One possible answer is that he still wanted to seem tough and dangerous in a very rough part of the world. Should we really be surprised to learn a man like Saddam might lie, or spread disinformation exaggerating his military strength? I don't think so: his miscalculation was in failing to realize how risky such posturing might turn out to be.

In any event, the main question is: *what was it reasonable* (for Bush Jr., of the USA, and Tony Blair, of the UK) *to believe in the spring of 2003*? And did they make serious efforts to inform these beliefs to the best of their ability? On the one hand, their intelligence services were advising them of Iraqi WMD possession. On the other, many participants within the decision-making process behind that war noted a marked rush to judgment—with pre-formed expectations slanting perceptions of evidence. But that's not what we mean when we talk about making an effort to inform your beliefs. Considering the stakes—not only war but an anticipatory attack involving violent regime change—I think here we must hold the actors to the very highest standards when it comes to clear evidence, reasonableness of belief, and effort at critically cross-checking beliefs and their sources. The decision to go to war, after all, is a decision in favor of deliberate mass killing, and an attempt to change the course of history for millions of people. Ethically, it is far too serious to be based on pre-formed expectations, impetuous judgment, and perhaps over-excited emotions—emotions like antagonism against Saddam and fear of future terrorist strikes. The standard with anticipatory attack is higher, not lower than that for a classical, reactive response to a prior act of aggression. The case, for this to be justified at all, must simply be impeccable.

This leaves the final issue of the bitter enemy displaying a political willingness to deploy an offensive military capacity on an imminent basis. Many critical questions can be raised here. Iraq seemed fairly docile following its humiliation in "Gulf War One," coupled with the strict post-war sanctions and NFZ. America and Britain argued that Iraq's refusal to submit itself to further UN weapons inspections not only violated the peace treaty of that first war, but also stood as evidence of Iraq's newfound determination either to hide its existing WMD and/or to construct new ones. Even if true, does this count as a growing political willingness to deploy WMD imminently? Here is where the reference to al-Qaeda came in: even if the Hussein regime was not itself willing to deploy such weapons, it was willing to supply them to the al-Qaeda terrorists who had fled Afghanistan following America's destruction of the Taliban government. Since we know, from 9/11, that al-Qaeda would eagerly be willing to use such weapons, what we have is essentially a conspiracy, by both a belligerent state and a belligerent terrorist organization, imminently to attack America, and with WMD no less.

The structure of this argument seems right, according to the criteria defended above. The real issue here, of course, is whether these normative criteria were actually fulfilled when the strike was launched in March 2003. In other words, the principles seem right, but was the evidence wrong—or, even worse, manipulated and exaggerated? We've just considered the question of Iraqi WMD possession. Now let's turn to the supposed "substantial connection" between al-Qaeda and the Hussein regime. The Bush Jr. Administration said it had evidence of a handful of sporadic meetings between low-level al-Qaeda and low-level Hussein regime officials. OK, but is such clear evidence of conspiracy? You'd think there'd be regular, high-level meetings. Some of these low-level people might have had personal, not political, reasons for meeting each other. Or, if they were political, they might have dealt with a range of issues—including a coup attempt against Saddam—that had nothing to do with America. Many Middle East experts have noted that al-Qaeda and Saddam would make for genuinely bizarre co-conspirators, since al-Qaeda are religious fanatics and Saddam's regime was a secular dictatorship in the style of Stalin. Indeed, Iraq fought a long war, in the 1980s, against Iran to resist any export of Iran's Islamic extremism. Saddam seemed to purge, rather than protect, any fundamentalists on his soil. Truly, given the aims of al-Qaeda to install radical Islamic governments throughout the Middle East—including Iraq—why on earth would Saddam give them WMD? They'd be much more likely to use such weapons against his own regime than on the USA. It just doesn't add up.

Mere acknowledgment that here were two dangerous organizations, in the same general region of the world, both with reason to loathe and perhaps attack America, does not add up to a strong and plausible connection of a conspiracy between them to do so in the very near future. Indeed, the US Congressional Commission on the 9/11 attacks, in June 2004, said it had no evidence of any connection between Saddam and al-Qaeda.[29]

To summarize: while the condition of the bitter, determined enemy was clearly satisfied in connection with the Spring 2003 attack, it is quite doubtful whether the other two conditions were satisfied—i.e., whether the enemy was both capable and imminently willing to launch an attack. Al-Qaeda seemed imminently willing, whereas Iraq—perhaps as a result of its own disinformation—imminently capable. Put the two together and you've got your case. *But it's precisely that putting together which is in deep and profound question,* alongside the reasonableness of the belief that

Iraq was actually capable in the first place. Until more information surfaces to the contrary, it seems that far too many questions and ambiguities remain to declare this cause of war justified. I believe, as I've mentioned, that the grounds for an anticipatory attack—even in the post-9/11 world—have to be *crystal clear,* in order that the permission not become so flexible as to allow for anything to get through. In my judgment, then, the 2003 Iraq attack was much better justified not as an anticipatory attack of pre-emptive self-defense but, rather, as an act of humanitarian intervention (of which we will say more below). As anticipation, the argument on the whole fails, satisfying only 1 of the 3 needed conditions.

All these questions and difficulties might seem to stretch beyond this particular case, and into the very principle of anticipatory attack. But I don't necessarily see why. It is, admittedly, much more difficult to ground a pre-emptive strike than it is to ground an empirically defensive maneuver. The bar is set much higher, and rightfully so, in order to reign in warfare and to limit the grounds for launching it. But the abstract analogies above suggest that it is not impossible; and even in relatively clearer instances of justified wars, there are always deep questions to ask about any interpretation of the empirical evidence cited and what it most plausibly shows. Think, for instance, of the right intention condition, or the probability of success condition. An empirically defensive justified war does not escape from these difficulties any more than an empirically offensive justified war does. The devil truly is in the details, and knowing what they show. But in either case it does not follow, from the fact that the details can be difficult to make out, that the principles which authorize force themselves get called into question. That is a separate matter which has to be dealt with at the level of principle alone.

3. Civil Wars

There are two main moral questions when it comes to civil war. The first is whether it can ever be just to fight one; the second is whether it can ever be just to intervene in somebody else's. The answers to both questions, however, revolve around the same issue: what counts as a minimally just and hence legitimate state.

3.1. MINIMALLY JUST POLITICAL COMMUNITIES

The issue of a minimally just political community, introduced last chapter, is of central importance to just war theory. The reason why we should limit ourselves to talking about "minimally just" political communities is two-fold. The first aspect is modesty: there is no perfectly or "maximally" just political community in existence. Some are better than others, of course, and some pass the threshold of minimal justice while others fail it. But no existing political community embodies the ideal; all are, in some ways, flawed or sub-optimal. As Kant once insightfully intoned, "out of the crooked timber of humanity, no straight thing was ever made."[30] The second relevant aspect to the "minimal justice" construction is that the political community in question must at least have that degree of moral value, otherwise it has no ethical reason to exist. From the fact that we humans live in groups, and have formed nation-states, it does not follow that we have to respect all such groupings and state structures. For such might be brutally exploitative, slavery-condoning, tyrannical, or war-mongering. The groupings we freely create, and the state structures we condone, have value only if they are minimally just. I have already suggested, last chapter, that a minimally just state: 1) is recognized as legitimate by its own people and most of the international community; 2) avoids violating the rights of other legitimate states; and 3) makes every reasonable effort at satisfying the human rights of its own citizens.

The most basic purpose of a national government is defense: defending its citizens from outside aggression by another state (or non-state actor), and also defending its citizens from predatory criminals residing within its borders. If a state is fundamentally incapable of being reasonably successful in this regard—i.e., of providing its citizens with security—then the social contract dissolves. There is no reason for the people to obey such a state and participate in it. Such a state must be radically transformed into a new one, or several, which can offer reasonable success in this regard, otherwise its people cannot count on living a life at all, much less a happy and enjoyable one. There simply must be a baseline of physical security, and freedom from severe and systemic violence, if there is to be a political community at all.

This quick reminder of the basics of the minimally just or legitimate state is essential to an understanding of the ethics of civil war (as indeed we've seen it is for war in general). For many, perhaps most, political communities today are, in fact, composites of many sub-groups and communities. Sometimes, group rivalry within the one state becomes so intense that fighting breaks out, either to control the one government shared in common, or else to secede and form a new state, out from under control of the old one. When, if ever, is it just to fight a civil war? One case would be when the central government fails any of the criteria of minimal justice. Any such government has no moral reason to exist, and so to resist its tyranny with force of arms is permissible.

3.2. BLUE VS. GREY: THE US CIVIL WAR

One case of a justified civil war was the North's war against the South, in America, from 1861 to 1865.[31] But the North represented the Union—the central government. So how does this case fit? For here it was the secessionist South which represented injustice. It did so because the South was the aggressor in the war, deliberately starting hostilities by bombing the federal Fort Sumter in South Carolina. Moreover, the South explicitly fought to form and preserve a mode of government which condoned slavery. Slavery is a massive social injustice, a grotesque and widespread violation of human rights—depriving slaves of freedom, basic equality, social recognition as persons, and, quite often, their very physical security. As such, the Confederate government of the South, led by Jefferson Davis, failed the criteria of minimal justice and had no moral value which would root a permissible defense against aggression. There has to be something there which has moral value for it to be permissible to go to war to gain and/or defend it. This is the key question in a civil war: *who has minimal justice on their side?* Is the central government minimally just, like the Union in the US Civil War, whereas the seceding state either is, or aims to become, unjust—as did the South? Or is the central government an oppressive tyranny, or a severe discriminator which respects the rights of one privileged group while violating those of another? In the latter two cases, the seceding group would have justice on its side provided that, should it win, it clearly commits to establishing a legitimate state. Unfortunately, new states have sometimes been known to engage in discriminatory human rights violations against hated minority groups within their new borders—especially if such minorities were part of the majority in the old state they formerly shared. Of course, if new states do this, they themselves fail the criteria of minimal justice, and their secessionist struggle is revealed to have been dark and tyrannical, not bright and liberating. In sum, the civil war, to be just, must be done either in defense of an existing minimally just state, or with the aim of escaping an illegitimate political structure and creating a new, legitimate one. This all supports the accuracy of our core conception of war as, ultimately, a massively violent struggle over the governance of a territory.[32]

3.3. WALKING AWAY? QUEBEC, CZECHOSLOVAKIA, AND THE SUDAN

Now, what if both sides have minimal justice on their side, which is to say we simply have two communities, formerly united, which now wish to separate? We can't pronounce this unjust. Preserving union, just for the sake of union, is not sufficiently serious to justify warfare. Borders, while possessing real value, are not sacrosanct and eternal. Communities, like people, do change and so political associations can change too, provided they each remain minimally just in their essential structurings. The compelling analogy here is to a "no-fault divorce" between a couple. Here we have no injustice—"no fault"—on the part of both sides; we simply have a case of both sides having changed, wanting something different for the future, and hence wanting to dissolve the current set of rules. This is totally fine but note that, like divorce, the separation agreement must be comprehensive and fair. These agreements, predictably, are complex—involving splitting of territory and assets (as well as debts), custody and support issues relating to any "dependents," and perhaps even support or "alimony" payments as well. When we think of splitting a country, new borders and territory are vital issues, as is access to water and farmable land.

Dividing the assets and liabilities of the old central government must be done fairly, and especially important for security and the avoidance of war is the dissolution of the old armed forces and the sound distribution of military assets.

Particularly sensitive is the treatment of "dependents." Take the case of Canada, which has contemplated these issues from time to time as Quebec separatism flares and then fades. If Quebec, which has a French-speaking majority, separates from Canada, what happens to the English-speaking minority concentrated in Montreal, and the Native or Aboriginal communities concentrated in the north of that province? The peaceful and just answer is that a negotiated settlement has to be arrived at, which might involve anything from Quebec giving land back to Canada to house these minorities or else Quebec keeping all its land but coming to arrangements with these groups to protect their human rights in an independent Quebec. The reason why this is such a sensitive issue is that, in European history anyway, the failure to resolve minority rights issues peacefully has sparked many a dreadful armed conflict.

There might also be issues of "international alimony" arising in such a split, say where one side agrees to let the other have a chunk of territory in exchange for a cash payment. Or perhaps a valuable resource deposit resides in the territory of one side—perhaps to keep it, that side must promise and deliver an on-going share of the profits to its ex-partner. Or perhaps one side, after secession, will be so poor that it cannot afford to ensure minimal justice for its citizens, which after all takes resources. In such an instance, a transfer payment would have to be required, until the poor side develops more and its economy gains the needed traction to generate rights-respecting resources.[33] These are all politically explosive issues, and fighting has often broken out in connection with them. But it doesn't have to—the recent split, in the early 1990s, between the Czech Republic and Slovakia (formerly together as Czechoslovakia) shows that new communities can be formed in ways that are peaceful and minimally just. Both sides, if you ask them, are quite proud, and justifiably so, of their "Velvet Divorce."[34]

While things can go well with such splits, often they don't. A very recent case concerns The Sudan in Africa. The Sudan contains a northern, mainly Arab and Muslim, population, and a southern, mainly black and Christian, population. The central government is controlled by the Arabs, and it has been—for at least the last 10 years—permitting radical Arab groups, or militias, to push the black Christians out of the Darfur province. This is called "*ethnic cleansing*": trying to drive out a whole, distinct people from a certain territory where they've been clearly established and living as a community (or even kill them off). Fighting has erupted between the groups, with casualties pegged at 300,000 and climbing. Following a referendum in January 2011, the southern region seceded and, in July of the same year, became a new independent country known as South Sudan. (The northern region still calls itself Sudan.) While this move to split was probably inevitable, and even desirable given the bloody violence, there will likely continue to be lingering disputes over precise border drawing, control of Darfur, and, especially, ownership disputes over the lucrative oil fields.[35]

3.4. PICKING SIDES AND INTERVENING

We now turn to the issue of justifying armed intervention in some other country's civil war. This seems justifiable only when there is an obvious injustice on one side of the civil war, and you are intervening on the side of justice. There must be substantial injustice at stake—no country, e.g., would've been justified in sending their army to bust up Czechoslovakia's "Velvet Divorce," or to slant the terms of that break-up to favor their own country. That would itself be aggression. But if there is substantial injustice at play in a civil war—either on the central government side, or on the secessionist/reformer side—then armed intervention on behalf of the just side is permissible, assuming that side has requested outside assistance. If it has, you are entitled to intervene. Moreover, you are entitled to try and win the war for your side. Walzer's notion—that you are only entitled to "counterbalance" or "neutralize" the unjust side's influence, and then "let local forces prevail"—is to me not operational.[36] It is not operational in the sense that the only objective which is coherent and action-guiding on the ground in war is seeking victory. Think of the general's point of view on the field of battle: how do you know when your forces have merely "offset" or "neutralized" the unjust side, versus when they have defeated them? Are you only supposed to knock out two-thirds of a division? Take only four-fifths of a valley, or city? Walzer's aim of counterbalance is simply too abstract actually to be acted upon. We are entitled to try to win the just wars we fight, not merely to enhance our odds or to neutralize certain countervailing forces. And winning a war means forcing the enemy to both surrender and accept decent terms of peace.

Intervening in a civil war will always remain controversial. There is a lingering, intuitive suspicion that "this is their struggle, let them fight it out and resolve it themselves." This attitude might be compelling when both sides in the war are unjust, or if both sides are just and are simply having difficulty negotiating a separation. But I don't share this hands-off attitude when one side is just, the other clearly unjust. In such a case, it is more important for justice to be served than it is for "local forces" to be balanced. What matters most in political life is justice, not washing one's hands of what is going on next door. More on this when we shortly discuss humanitarian intervention.

3.5. THE VIETNAM WAR

It's hard not to feel for the people of Vietnam, one of the most war-ravaged pieces of territory in the twentieth century. Formerly a French colony, Vietnam was conquered by Japan and occupied throughout World War II. France, during the peace settlement of that war, reclaimed Vietnam. But a focused, armed group of Vietnamese—who also happened to be communist—resisted this return to French control. They came to be called the Viet Minh, or Viet Cong, and they wanted an independent Vietnam. When they saw that they would not get their way, they started to fight. We can call what followed something like the French-Vietnam war, from 1945–54. (The French call it "The Indochina War.") It was an anti-colonial struggle, and it eventually split Vietnam between North and South, with the communists prevailing in the North and the French and their Vietnamese sympathizers in the South. The Vietnam War was thus a civil war—a brutally long one, with different phases—and one featuring extensive foreign intervention on both sides.[37]

In 1954, the Geneva Settlement was supposed to have ended the issue. It called for Vietnam to be temporarily split into North and South, with free elections to be held in 1956, and then for the temporary split to be dissolved, and re-unification begun, based on the election results. France would quit the country entirely, and there would be a new, unified, and independent Vietnam. On the basis of this deal, relative peace obtained for nearly two years.

What re-ignited war was the fact that the government of South Vietnam, led by Diem, betrayed its pledge to participate in the 1956 elections. In response, insurgents from the South, who identified with the North, tried forcibly to overthrow Diem: if Vietnam would not be unified by ballot, it would be so by bullet. What's interesting, though, is that France decided to leave anyway at this point, and the Diem regime begged for, and received, extensive American support to fill the gap: cash, weapons, military training, technology, and eventually US troops themselves.

The Americans got involved, under presidents Eisenhower and Kennedy, because of the Cold War with communism. China had experienced a communist revolution in 1949, and American decision-makers in the 1950s were terrified of a so-called "domino effect" of communism toppling government after government throughout Southeast Asia, as it had several years prior in Eastern Europe. They decided to "draw a line in the sand" at Vietnam, and, when the French got out, the Americans felt they had to go in. So began the American-Vietnam War, which lasted from 1956–73, though some would debate the starting point and argue for placing it as late as 1964, when the Tonkin Bay Resolution in effect officially declared war on North Vietnam. The battle lines were by now firmly drawn: on the one side, southern insurgents, North Vietnam, and, to an extent, communist China; on the other, the southern establishment (Diem and later others) and the United States.

Critics of the Vietnam War, like Walzer, argue that it was unjust for a number of reasons, but mainly two. First, America entered the war not out of any sincere concern for the Vietnamese people but rather for reasons of *realpolitik*. Its motivation for fighting had nothing to do with resisting aggression; rather, it had everything to do with this cynical Cold War chess game of preventing communism from expanding beyond the Soviet Union, Eastern Europe, and China. In just war terms, America failed right intention. Secondly, it has been established that it is unjust to intervene in somebody else's civil war unless you are intervening on behalf of the just side, and at its request. Well, the Diem government certainly did request American help, but many questions can be raised about whether it was a minimally just regime. First, it betrayed its pledge to the North, and the international community, to participate in the 1956 elections. The elections were meant to decide the future of the country: to fail to participate was bitter bad faith—violating a pledge and preventing voters from exercising political sovereignty. Second, Diem's regime had clear streaks of corruption, discrimination, and authoritarianism, showing lack of respect for human rights, especially those of non-Catholics. Part of this oppression might be explained by the pressure of the civil war, but most experts sensed a real disconnect between Diem and the South Vietnamese people, and they weren't surprised when he was assassinated in 1963, just days before JFK. After Diem, South Vietnam lurched unstably from regime to regime, and people like Walzer argue that this political instability showed that the people of South Vietnam simply didn't endorse American-supported governments. As Walzer puts it: "(T)he continuing dependence of the new regime on the US [was] damning evidence against it ... a government that receives economic and technical aid, military supply, strategic and tactical advice, and is still unable to reduce its subjects to obedience, is clearly an illegitimate government."[38] And armed intervention on behalf of an illegitimate government is not just.

The counter-argument, made by supporters of the war, is that America was indeed responding to an act of aggression: the South may have backed out of the election, but it was the Southern insurgents who first attacked the Southern government with the object of armed conquest in the name of communism. Secondly, there was clear evidence that the North, and China, were involved in creating the political instability in the South. Thus, you can't use that instability as evidence of the illegitimacy of the Southern regimes: it doesn't reflect the choices of the Southern people so much as pressure from outsiders. Indeed, the Americans could say they were merely "counter-invading" after the prior invasions of the North and China. Finally, the Diem regime might have been bad, but communism was a terrible form of government, which we all know now was complicit in massive human rights violations. Some of the most terrible mass slaughters of the twentieth century were perpetrated by communist regimes, like Stalin's purges in the 1930s, China's Cultural Revolution in the 1960s, and Cambodia's Khmer Rouge "Killing Fields" in the 1970s. Communists believe that only the mass (of workers) has worth, and that individuals themselves have no human rights.[39] What could be more just than trying to save the South Vietnamese from that?

Coming at a final judgment on Vietnam is difficult, since there are these competing considerations. Civil wars usually are more complicated to figure out than classical inter-state struggles. The cause of resisting communism was compelling, and the North and China were on the scene as early as the Americans were. On the other, the election betrayal was major, and Diem's legitimacy was deeply questionable. There's the almost inscrutable issue of popular support—with whom did the people of South Vietnam identify? There's some indication it was with the North. Indeed, Diem arguably betrayed the election pledge precisely because he feared a Northern victory. Furthermore, America absolutely pummeled the Viet Cong communists in the late 1960s with massive—maybe disproportionate—bombing raids, and over a half-million active US troops in the thin sliver that is Vietnam. It seems to me that the only way the Viet Cong could've survived such an incredible onslaught, from a superpower, was precisely because, as Walzer says, they came to enjoy the support of most of the Vietnamese people. This public support allowed the Viet Cong to engage in the covert attacks and guerrilla tactics that so frustrated conventional US forces: they would strike, and then melt back into villages, farms, and cities, where they were provided cover. Another relevant piece of information is this: after the US withdrew in 1973, it took the Viet Cong only one year to control all of Vietnam, and the communists remain firmly in control today, 40 years later. Such quick and enduring success seems possible only with considerable public support. One might say the alternative explanation is the sheer force the North Vietnamese, backed by China, brought to bear. It is a difficult call. My own judgment is that it was probably more the indigenous support factor, which itself was fueled more by furious anti-colonial sentiment than by any genuine pro-communist feeling. Don't forget that Vietnam had been a colony at that time for more than 100 years. They just wanted to be left alone.

This is not to say the current Vietnamese government is legitimate, for the people might not have known what they were getting into and may feel betrayed by the police state communism put into place in the unified Vietnam. Countries, like people, can make bad choices under pressure. But so long as those choices aren't so bad as to justify humanitarian intervention—to be discussed below—it seems they are free to make them outside of foreign intervention.

In sum, I'm saying that *the Vietnam War was unjust on both sides*: on the American side, owing to South Vietnamese popular support for the non-colonial side and, on the communist side, for aiming at the institution of communism in South Vietnam. The tragedy was that the non-colonial side was also the communist side, and so popular support—in a very pressured situation—had a severe downside. The people couldn't, at the time, get their non-colonial regime without it being communist. Is this like selling yourself into slavery? Perhaps quite so and, odd as it seems, that remains your own choice.

One quote from the Vietnam War which sheds light here is the infamous quip of an ordinary US soldier: "We had to destroy the village in order to save it." This line is often quoted as a kind of dark joke, or else to ridicule the pretensions and naivety of American imperialism. Instead, the quote captures precisely the cruel dilemma of that war: America went into Vietnam to save it from the imposition of communism, ostensibly a just cause. It turns out, however, that the communists had widespread public support—probably not so much because they were communists but because they were Vietnamese and the people were sick of foreign forces—French, Japanese, Americans—ruling them. Plus, the Diem alternative to communism had its own legitimacy issues. So the people sympathized with the communists—who were, admittedly, extremely aggressive and themselves foreign-supplied—and resisted. The ultimate result: destroyed villages all over. To call that kind of destruction just, you need crystal clear justification, not strength on some issues and weakness on others, as in this situation. *When there is no clear justified side, just war theory insists you pronounce the war questionable on both fronts.*

4. Armed Humanitarian Intervention: Rwanda and Somalia

The fourth, and final, revision to the classical account of *jus ad bellum* concerns armed humanitarian intervention (AHI), such as occurred in Kosovo in 1999 and Libya in 2011. This is a hotly disputed topic, and the body of international law is nowhere near as settled as it is when it comes to individual and collective self-defense. In general, there is a very strong presumption in international law—going back to Grotius, Pufendorf, and Vattel—against any outside interference with the domestic situation of any country, especially interference backed up with the force of arms. But it should be noted that a considerable number of such interventions have nevertheless been authorized by the UNSC, such as in Somalia in 1992–94, Libya in 2010–11, and, in a more complex fashion, in the former Yugoslavia in 1992–95. Recall that most international lawyers believe UNSC authorization is absolutely necessary prior to humanitarian intervention.[40]

AHI seems, at first, to pose a special problem for the prevailing aggression-based paradigm, since it involves armed intrusion in a country which has not committed aggression against another state. Moreover, such intervention is animated by moral and political ideals which may seem to lack universal endorsement, and thus raise the ugly specter of violent paternalism on the global stage: "Treat your people the way we think you should, or else feel our wrath."

The only kind of AHI which Walzer accepts is intervention designed to rescue citizens of a state from "acts that shock the moral conscience of mankind." He is willing to endorse AHI only in cases where the state in question is using military force to engage in wicked and widespread human rights violations. This is the key: I propose we think of such a state as an *"internal aggressor,"* since here too we have the use of rights-violating military force on display. We have a failure to meet the conditions of minimal justice, which in turn renders that state illegitimate and, as it were, attack-able. The International Commission on Intervention and State Sovereignty (ICISS), in its influential 2001 report, comments similarly that protection of a population is a key implication of, and responsibility within, the right to sovereignty. If a state cannot provide such—or, worse, if it itself becomes the threat—then it is actually consistent with the concept of sovereignty for others to go in, in order to protect that population.[41]

Walzer is keen, I think correctly, to stress the degree to which the armed human rights violations in question must be "massive" and "terrible," such as incidents of "massacre and enslavement," to ground armed intervention by a foreign power. As examples of justified interventions, Walzer cites Vietnam in Cambodia in the mid-1970s and the North Atlantic Treaty Organization (NATO) in the former Yugoslavia throughout the 1990s.[42] In the Cambodia case, for instance, the unbelievably brutal and bloody Khmer Rouge regime put into operation its "Killing Fields," murdering one million fellow Cambodians deemed to be enemies of the regime, which was attempting to forge an entirely new, severely socialist "utopia."[43] The unified government of Vietnam invaded and overthrew the regime, stopping the "Fields" and all the dislocation and refugees they were producing. In the case of the former Yugoslavia, the countries of NATO—led by America—bombed Serbia in 1995 to make it stop its involvement in massacres of Muslims in such cities as Sarajevo. The bombing is widely credited with forcing Serbia to sign the Dayton Accords, which ended the Bosnian civil war that developed out of Yugoslavia's collapse. (See below for the case study.) When the Serbian regime went back to its old nasty tricks—massacring and forcibly displacing tens of thousands of Muslims (and perhaps many more) in 1999 in Kosovo—NATO again attacked, this time much more aggressively, resulting in a change of regime in Serbia.[44]

Let's comment more on the extent of government brutality which needs to be actual before we can consider AHI. Faced with what we might call "run-of-the-mill" government insensitivity to some human rights claims (say, non-discrimination), citizens need to take it upon themselves to begin the kind of political activism and struggle needed to win such freedoms and benefits. Self-help is the order of the day; that's part of what we mean by political sovereignty and self-determination. Thus, it is only those truly terrible human rights violations which, in Walzer's words, "make talk of community or self-determination ... seem cynical and irrelevant" which justify AHI by a foreign power. In these extreme cases, it is precisely the incapacity for self-determination that draws foreigners in, and rightly so. Interestingly, Walzer believes that such humanitarian intervention is morally *obligatory,* whereas intervention in a secessionist struggle, or in a civil war, is merely *permissible.* I concur. This sense of obligation in the face of humanitarian catastrophe is clearly displayed when Walzer swears that: "People who initiate massacres lose their right to participate in the normal ... processes of domestic self-government. Their military defeat is morally necessary."[45]

Walzer is especially critical of those who, when confronted with such a grave and genuine humanitarian emergency, reason as follows: yes, there's a fire burning and fire-fighters are probably needed to put it out; but it's not *our* building, so there's no claim on our resources, much less our fire-fighters. Walzer's effective rejoinder: "[T]he price of sitting and watching is a kind of moral corruption that ... [we] must always resist." What about those who argue against intervention not so much out of a misplaced respect for whose turf it is but, rather, out of fears of intervening in a conflict they know little about—and of running the risk of making things worse? Walzer answers compellingly: "Of course, every fire has a complicated social, political and economic background. It would be nice to understand it all. But once the burning begins something less than full understanding is necessary: a will to put out the fire—to find fire-fighters, close by if possible, and give them the support they need." Fires like the ethnic cleansing and Muslim massacres in Bosnia in the mid-1990s, or the mass expulsion of Kosovars from Serbia in the late 1990s, require us to "see the fires for what they are: deliberately set, the work of arsonists, aimed to kill, terribly dangerous."[46]

What about those who urge non-intervention, even in such obvious humanitarian catastrophes, on grounds that such might be a slippery slope to imperial aggrandizement—to great powers meddling in vulnerable communities? Walzer's reply is that such might be a risk, but not one so real it justifies willful non-intervention in a clear humanitarian emergency. The moral balance—between certain massacre and possible imperialism—is obviously on the side of preventing, or stopping, the massacre. The risks of imperial tinkering are more distant and abstract than the closer and more palpable risks of watching people get murdered when one could have done something about it. The risk far greater than great power meddling or aggrandizement is the moral indifference that leads to non-intervention, even in spite of overwhelming evidence of a grievous and preventable humanitarian tragedy. Rwanda, of course, serves as the most searing and terrible example of this in recent history. In the spring of 1994, almost 800,000 people—again, *800,000 people,* in just one season—were slaughtered in an act of near-genocide, and the international community failed to respond effectively. Indeed, it hardly responded at all. Typically, everyone pointed the finger of responsibility and blame at everyone else. Most agree that it was a disgustingly horrible and deeply shameful event. Some wondered aloud whether, in light of Rwanda, we had actually learned the clearest lessons of The Holocaust.[47]

Perhaps a little bit more on Rwanda, in central Africa, would be insightful. Rwanda, during its colonial days under the rule of Belgium, was dominated by a minority group, the Tutsis. The majority group, the Hutus, resented being dominated and, when independence from Belgium came in 1959, the Hutus turned the tables and took control. Relations between the groups were always tense, and at times broke out into armed conflict between the Hutu-dominated Rwandan Army and the Tutsi-dominated rebel force, the Rwandan Patriotic Front (RPF). In 1993, after several years of fighting, a peace accord and power-sharing arrangement were achieved. Before they could be implemented, Hutu extremists formed private militias to carry out an audacious and murderous plan: not only to destroy the peace accords but to eliminate the Tutsis and even any moderate Hutus who supported peace with the Tutsis. They truly had genocide on their minds: to destroy the Tutsi people. The Hutu extremists seized power in a coup d'état in early 1994, killing the moderate Hutu leadership. While the UN did have a peacekeeping force already in Rwanda, as soon as some of its (Belgian) members were killed in the coup's early days, the UNSC ordered a complete withdrawal—in spite of the pleas of the peacekeeping unit's own commanding officer, Roméo Dallaire. He knew what was going to happen and presented the UN with evidence of a genocidal plot. But all Western troops left the country, taking their own nationals with them. They even closed their embassies. The Hutu extremists had free reign to execute their horrible plan and, by April, had killed about 800,000 people, both Tutsi and Hutu. Most were butchered brutally with machetes or shot at point-blank range with small guns. *Fully one-third of all Tutsis on earth were murdered.* France, alone amongst Western countries, re-intervened late in June and helped re-establish some sanity (though some say France allowed the perpetrators to leave the country as well). Then—then!—the UNSC voted to return "peacekeeping" forces back to Rwanda.[48]

So concerned has Walzer become over this threat of non-intervention—or even of withdrawing in the face of mass slaughter—that he has actually changed his views about what justice requires of an intervener in an humanitarian emergency. Whereas he used to believe that the goal of a justified intervener was "the in-and-out rule", he now believes more extensive obligations may be involved, and it's important to hear him out. The "in-and-out rule," designed precisely to mitigate the likelihood of great power meddling, called for interveners to focus on "rescue, not rule": to get in, rescue the people who need it, and get out as soon as the rescue has been secured. The goal was to make intervention as little like intervention as possible, thereby maximizing space for local self-determination. Now, however, Walzer believes that recent international experience demonstrates that interveners need to make a deeper commitment than simply "in-and-out," and they need to make it explicit even before they go in. On the limits of this deeper commitment, Walzer is vague, if not silent.[49] But its content, I believe, clearly involves some kind of post-intervention assistance in reconstructing the society that required rescue. The question ties into deep perplexities of post-war, or post-conflict, settlement and rehabilitation: we'll return to these vital issues in later chapters. This is all to say, importantly, that those who intervene face an additional burden when it comes to just cause: they must commit themselves, in meaningful fashion, to reasonable aid and assistance in the post-conflict situation. The ICISS puts it thus in its report: "to provide, particularly after a military intervention, full assistance with recovery, reconstruction and reconciliation, addressing the causes of the harm the intervention was designed to halt or avert."[50]

Note that post-conflict aid and reconstruction is premised on actually being able to aid and reconstruct, and this usually means being in a strong position at the end of the intervention. This is a vital point, in light of contemporary experience with humanitarian intervention: *if you go in, you must go in with the goal of winning.* We saw, in America's 1992–93 intervention in Somalia, that a very mild and limited intervention—aimed at separating belligerents and alleviating starvation—was perhaps doomed to fail from the start because the goal was not the military defeat of the culpable side, merely the separation of forces and the interdiction and arrest of one of that side's leaders. As soon as serious resistance was met, the US turned tail and ran.[51] The result? Somalia was no better off than before America intervened. So what did those US troops die for? Even worse, the Somali failure was almost certainly the real reason why America did not intervene in Rwanda a year later, to the loss and misery of staggering numbers of people. America feared another failure in Africa and thus didn't even risk it the second time around. Inserting a small armed force to try to keep the peace between rival factions does have a time and place—notably when the belligerents agree to be so separated—but that time and place is not during a humanitarian intervention. The side slaughtering the other needs to be defeated militarily. The size and strength of the intervening force should be adjusted accordingly, and the terms of engagement (i.e., instructions to soldiers) must be clear, and allow fighting forces to do what they do best and are actually trained to do: pursue victory, and force the other side either to surrender or be destroyed. As the ICISS puts it here, effective intervention demands "clear objectives, clear and unambiguous mandates at all times; and resources to match."[52]

There are some anti-imperialist thinkers who want to say that the interveners must also be freely invited into the country on behalf of the group they are intending to aid. I think this is mistaken, and naïve. Naïve, because it fails to grasp the brutalities under which the victims may be suffering: they may not have meaningful chances to articulate a clear communal petition to the international community while they are running, and fighting, for their lives. Mistaken, because their failure to make a formal request might prevent someone from going in, with the result being a terrible massacre and perhaps even worse. The anti-imperialist position is like saying a cop shouldn't intervene in a gang's brutal street attack on an innocent bystander until she formally requests his or her help. From the dreadful deeds alone, we can infer that the victims of massacre do indeed consent to any intervention on their behalf, at least in the absence of any explicit non-consent. No formal requirement of request seems reasonable here, given the gravity of the threat.

Finally, what of those who object to armed intervention, even in humanitarian catastrophes, on grounds that it is unclear who exactly should bear the duty of intervention? Walzer's reply: the duty to intervene forcibly in cases of humanitarian emergency is admittedly imperfect—it picks out no one specific country. The duty is, rather, borne at large by the international community. This does not, however, imply that only global agencies like the UN have the moral legitimacy to authorize and execute armed rescues in states which remain externally non-aggressive. Walzer submits, and I concur, that any state willing to take on the burdens of armed rescue is permitted to do so, provided of course that all the criteria for a just intervention, as here laid out, have been fulfilled. The imperfection of the duty to intervene has caused much of the controversy surrounding armed rescue, since a main temptation in favor of sitting on the sidelines has been a belief—sometimes sincere, sometimes otherwise—that another country, or regional grouping, is better placed to intervene. Walzer has recently grown more accommodating to the idea of experimenting with a global security force, for instance under UNSC auspices, that might one day have responsibility for such actions. Indeed, NATO has recently created a rapid reaction brigade to act in similar fashion within its jurisdiction, which is to say North America and now most of Europe including Turkey.[53] Until we have rapid reaction forces in regions around the world, or else under UNSC control, there seems little prospect for changing from what we already have: an imperfect situation wherein we must rely on our own moral responsiveness to move in, where needed, to rescue people from being massacred, enslaved, or displaced by their own government. And it is indefensible to suggest that failure to have intervened in one spot (e.g., in Tibet, or Rwanda, or—thus far—in Syria) implies that for the sake of some twisted concern for consistency we should fail to intervene everywhere else. The more appropriate response is to regret and condemn our past mistakes—our previous acts of weakness of will—and move ahead to rescue those who need it on a more reliable basis.[54]

4.1. R2P: LIBYA AND SYRIA

In 2000, the government of Canada—feeling its peace-keepers in Rwanda were betrayed by the UNSC—convened The International Commission on Intervention and State Sovereignty (ICISS) to try to better guide the UNSC regarding when it ought to authorize AHIs. The "responsibility to protect" (or "R2P") doctrine outlined in the ICISS' report, *The Duty to Protect*, asserts that:

1) All states have the responsibility to protect their own people from such "mass atrocity crimes" (MACs) as: genocide; war crimes; crimes against humanity; and ethnic cleansing.
2) If a state fails in this responsibility, then other states have the duty to step in: a) in the first instance, to aid and enable the state's capacity, if that's the issue; or b) to intervene with armed force, if the issue is (rather) the state itself turning murderously against its own people.[55]

Though R2P is considered only a new norm (or rule, or expectation), and not full-blown international law, some experts have argued that it is well on its way to becoming the latter. After all, in 2005, the UN General Assembly hosted a World Summit on this subject, and it issued a unanimous "*Outcome Document*" which clearly endorsed R2P. More to the point, the UNSC itself has endorsed the R2P in principle, on at least two occasions: once in 2006 following the World Summit; and, in 2011 when it authorized an AHI in Libya: a military action Canada participated in.[56]

Fighting broke out in Libya in late 2010 as part of the so-called "Arab Spring" uprising (This refers generally to sweeping anti-authoritarian, and pro-human rights, protests and changes which have been sweeping the MENA region since late 2010, with differential results in different countries).[57] The fighting in Libya eventually coalesced into two groups: those supportive of existing dictator Muammar Gaddafi; and those devoted to his overthrow. When Gaddafi's army turned violently against not only the rebel groups but un-armed civilians, and even whole towns deemed to be "enemies," NATO—as initially led by France and Italy, which have historical ties to Libya—sought authorization from the UNSC to intervene with armed force. In March 2011, the UNSC gave its approval—citing the R2P doctrine as rationale. From March-October, 2011, NATO forces provided aid to the rebels, and performed many direct strikes—especially air strikes—on their own against Gaddafi's forces. Canada and the United States were robust participants in this action, which ended when Gaddafi was killed in October. The NATO mandate ended in November, 2011, and Libya is currently in a state of post-conflict transition.[58]

The case of Libya stands in stark contrast to that of Syria, which also had fighting erupt between pro- and anti-government forces in the wake of the start of the Arab Spring in December 2010. This very bloody, on-going civil war—estimated casualties of over 90,000, (as of early 2013) and growing—has been raging domestically, with no AHI undertaken, or even contemplated, by NATO or the UN more broadly. Since the two situations seem so similar, when thus described, what accounts for the difference: AHI in one, nothing in the other (thus far)?[59] The reason seems to be that, in spite of their deep moral similarities, there are profound political and strategic differences between the two cases: the Libyan regime under Gaddafi had few if any allies in the region, whereas the Syrians have tight ties with Iran in particular and, to a lesser extent, are protected at the UNSC by favorable votes from Russia and China. Any military move into Syria thus risks a wider regional war, potentially involving such powerful and controversial states as Iran and Israel. Libya is also a wide-open, mainly desert, country, whereas Syria is tiny and densely-populated; and so an air-based intervention in the former was easily do-able (high probability of success), whereas any intervention in the latter would probably involve many civilian casualties and involve complex combat in dense urban environments: one of the least-favored fighting options (low probability of success). Finally, AHI in Libya allowed the West to show clear support for regime change in the Arab Spring and, having done that, the case for doing it again—in a far riskier environment—was much lessened. This is to say that Libyan AHI made Syrian AHI much less likely. Others have also noted how France and Italy were deeply interested in the Libyan oil supply (whereas Syria has none), and America had anti-terrorist scores to settle with Gaddafi going back to the 1980s.[60]

Now, these differential reasons raise important issues about the interplay between moral reasons and political or strategic reasons. We've seen from Rwanda that there is sad evidence that, when countries have only a moral reason to intervene, but no political or strategic one, then they probably won't. But where, in addition to moral reasons, they also have political and strategic reasons to intervene, then it's much more likely that they will (Libya and, below, Bosnia/Kosovo). This raises a vital question: *to what extent do moral considerations actually figure into decision-making during wartime at all?* We shall consider some possible answers in the forthcoming chapter on realism.

4.2. BACK TO IRAQ

Now, what of the prior declaration that the strongest justification for America's 2003 war of regime change on Iraq was as an act of AHI? The war was, after all, labeled "Operation Iraqi Freedom": freedom from the rights-violating brutalities of Saddam's unjust dictatorship. In light of the failure to locate Iraqi WMD, President Bush Jr. himself, in December 2005, boldly re-asserted this justification for the war, claiming: "(W)e are in Iraq today because our goal has always been more than the removal of a brutal dictator. It is to leave a free and democratic Iraq in his place."[61]

I do believe that this was the strongest reason available to America but that doesn't mean I believe the war was justified. Why? First, there's the requirement to call your shot, defended last chapter. Even if the most traction came from arguing humanitarian intervention, we all know this was not the main reason advanced in the run-up to the war in early 2003. The focus was on pre-emptive self-defense for America; and we effectively called that into question above. The fact that America's real reason in going to war was pre-emptive self-defense, I speculate, probably fueled things like the Abu-Ghraib prison tortures: the wrong reason attracted the wrong intention, and the perception of self-defense (as opposed to other-rescue) motivated and sharpened the treatment of those prisoners in violation of the principle of benevolent quarantine enshrined in *jus in bello* and the Geneva Conventions.[62] Had the real reason and motive behind the war been the rescue of the Iraqi people, such actions would probably not have occurred. It was the obsession with pre-emptive self-defense, and getting information about any forthcoming terrorist strikes, which produced them.

Second, even if I were to agree that the war was an act of AHI, all that does is satisfy the just cause criterion. But many criticisms can be made of the other *jus ad bellum* criteria—which *all* must be fulfilled—in this case. Questions can notably be raised regarding whether this war was a last resort, whether proper authorization occurred, whether it was a reasonable and proportionate response to the problem of Saddam's tyranny and, above all, whether the war was animated by the right intentions and had decent probability of success in achieving its aim. In terms of right intention, many have raised the issue of a Bush family animus against Saddam, and Iraq's role as a key world oil and gas supplier. Others have said, similarly to Walzer's criticism of American intentions during Vietnam, that the war was animated not so much by genuine concern for Iraqi well-being as it was by Iraq's potential strategic role serving as a Trojan Horse for more acceptable values against the new enemy in the New Cold War: militant extremist Islam. In terms of probability of success, the war did admittedly overthrow Saddam. But whether, as a result, it has substantially improved conditions of peace, security, and rights realization for ordinary Iraqis is, so far, not entirely in evidence.

It might even be wondered whether this was a fitting case of AHI after all. Saddam was a rights-violating tyrant, to be sure, but his regime was still recognized as the government of Iraq by most of the international community. So did his reign truly "shock the conscience of mankind," as Walzer insists we ask? Further, it's not clear that Saddam was violating the rights of other countries during the run-up to the invasion (though admittedly he had certainly done so in the past). The real problem with his regime, in 2003, concerned domestic human rights satisfaction. Here, serious violations must be noticed—no press or political freedoms, discrimination against non-Sunnis, and even rapes, kidnappings, and killings of political opponents. This might add up to a case that the Iraqi people were, in fact, "enslaved" by Saddam's regime. I admit it very well might; I'm no apologist for Saddam's Stalinesque hold on Iraq and the utter ruin which his long dictatorship brought to that society. At the same time, it does not seem as though Iraq in 2003 was comparable to the huge-scale massacres of Rwanda in 1994, or Khmer Rouge Cambodia in the 1970s: cases which stand out clearly as humanitarian emergencies needing quick and decisive stopping. It's a judgment call, I concede: my only purpose in raising this point is to stress that it *is* a judgment call, and not a crystal-clear observation with which any reasonable observer must agree. Usually, with AHI, I think we want to achieve that degree of overwhelming consensus before we authorize force. Obviously, there was no such consensus with Iraq.

I'm on the record, in this book, as declaring that regimes which fail the conditions of minimal justice are not legitimate and thus have no state rights, including the right not to be attacked and overthrown. It seems as though Saddam's regime violated the condition of making every reasonable effort at domestic human rights satisfaction: who doesn't pass that test, if he is allowed to pass? So I admit that Saddam's regime had no right not to be attacked. But one can have the right to do something which it's still not wise, or prudent, or smart, to do. My overall judgment is that it's deeply questionable whether America's going to war in 2003 was the best way not merely to remove Saddam but also to create pro-rights realization for the Iraqi people. I think the checkered post-war situation so far has revealed this. So, last resort and proportionality questions haunt this war, as does the matter of probability of success.

5. Summary

In this chapter we finished our look at *jus ad bellum* by examining cases not covered by the classical account, such as: civil and guerrilla wars; terrorism; anticipatory attacks; secessionist struggles; and humanitarian rescue. In each case, we detailed reasons for carefully expanding the standard just cause rule to allow for responsible military action. These reasons were, however, kept fundamentally consistent with the essence of just cause, which permits armed force only as resistance to aggression. We suggested, e.g., that a regime can commit "internal" aggression against its own people as readily as "external" aggression against foreigners. Non-state actors, like terrorists, can commit aggression, too. It might even, rarely, be consistent with the need to defend people from aggression to make the first strike. Justified military action can be taken in each of the non-standard cases, provided such meets the demanding criteria defended in this chapter, as well as the remaining *jus ad bellum* principles, such as right intention, proper authority, proportionality, and so on.

6. Case Study: Bosnia

To cap off this chapter, let's consider the West's, and particularly America's, intervention in the Bosnian civil war of 1992–95.[63] This was both intervention in somebody else's civil war, as well as an act of humanitarian rescue. Let's mirror last chapter's final case study by putting this complex, non-standard armed intervention to the test, not only in terms of just cause but of the full complement of *jus ad bellum* principles.

Bosnia was part of Yugoslavia. Conflict broke out in the region after the Cold War ended and communism collapsed in Eastern Europe, in 1989–91. As communists fell, new politicians struggled to influence the development of the post-communist era. Some of these leaders found that appealing to traditional ethnic, religious, and nationalist loyalties and identities made them powerful. Among the strongest of these new leaders was a Serb named Slobodan Milošević. Serbs traditionally were the dominant group in Yugoslavia, and they made moves to keep it that way in 1989–91. But the forces of nationalism, ethnicity, and religion drove the other groups in Yugoslavia—such as the Croats and Slovenes—to want their own separate states. So they broke away from Yugoslavia in 1991, and there were some battles between the new Croatia and Serb-dominated Yugoslavia. Then trouble erupted in Bosnia, a province right in the heart of the old Yugoslavia. Bosnia was unique in that it contained a mixture of three large ethnic groups: Croats, Serbs, and Muslims. Originally, it looked as though Bosnia might just split into three parts, with the Croat part joining the new Croatia, the Serb part remaining with Serb-dominated Yugoslavia and a Muslim-dominated part to retain the name "Bosnia." But the deal fell through, partly because of international pressure to stay together, but mainly because the Serbs backed out of the deal. The Serbian army—i.e., the old Yugoslav army—then moved into Bosnia to prevent the separation of Bosnian Croats and Bosnian Muslims. The Bosnian civil war was then on, between Croats (backed by Croatia), Serbs (backed by Serbia), and Muslims (on their own.)

Terrible battles ensued and a process of "ethnic cleansing" took place, according to which groups dominant in one area would, through armed coercion, drive minority groups out of that area—leaving them to go "where they belonged" and leaving behind only members of the dominant group. The result? The part of Bosnia beside Croatia became almost exclusively Croat and the part beside Serbia became almost exclusively Serbian. The Muslims were driven into a handful of cities, notably Tuzla, Srebrenica, and Sarajevo. The Serb army was very successful during this 1992–94 period, capturing 70% of Bosnia. Milošević, now president of Serbia proper, said he wanted to keep the new war gains as part of a "Greater Serbia" and he enjoyed very close ties with Bosnian Serb leaders, such as Radovan Karadžić.

Just Cause. The United Nations had tried early on to intervene in this process, to no positive effect. In 1991, it slapped an arms embargo on all of former Yugoslavia. Still the war raged. In 1992 UN peacekeepers arrived in Bosnia. They were, however, small in number and poorly armed. So poorly armed, in fact, that they were actually taken hostage by the Serb army several times, to be used as bargaining chips with the UN and sometimes as shields against enemy armed forces. Peace negotiations had begun as early as 1991, but the war was not to end until 1995.

America, frustrated at the UN's impotence—due in some measure to the influence of Russia, a traditional Serb ally—activated the old structure of NATO. America knew that would give them more control. America's just cause in going to war against Serbia and the Bosnian Serbians revolved around two concepts: the minimally just state and humanitarian intervention. In terms of the first, it was clear that Serbia did not have justice on its side. It was the one who sent in the army, first sparking the war. Moreover, Serbia's actions during the war showed that it would not impose a just peace. Serbia, under Milošević, had quickly grown into an ultra-nationalist, authoritarian regime. Like other such regimes in history, it wanted to aggressively increase its territory—into a "Greater Serbia"—and it also acted to purge its own territory of those not part of the "ideal" ethnic mold. Hence the ethnic cleansing, some of which produced mass graves of Muslim men—the first mass war graves in Europe since The Holocaust. (Admittedly, the other sides engaged in some ethnic cleansing practices as well.) In terms of the second cause, the Serbs showed repeated, and marked, violent aggression against the Bosnian Muslims in particular. Several times during the war, the Serb army deliberately shelled the Muslim-dominated cities, resulting in tens of thousands of civilian casualties. There were also the mass graves noted above, as well as Serb army rape campaigns against Bosnian Muslim women, and torture and starvation of Bosnian Muslim male prisoners of war (POWs), held in Serb concentration camps.

After a particularly bloody Serb shelling of Sarajevo in 1995, NATO under US command intensively bombed both Bosnian Serbia and Serbia itself. For two weeks, the bombs fell, forcing the Serbs to sign the Dayton Accords, which ended the war. These Accords forced the Serbs to give back land they had conquered, agree to some war crimes trials, and submit to constitutional re-structuring—but only in the Serb part of Bosnia, not Serbia itself. (The latter would happen 4–5 years later when Milošević returned to his ethnic cleansing ways in the Kosovo province of Serbia—this time against ethnic Albanians—forcing NATO into action again, and this time resulting in his overthrow. He was put on trial for war crimes at The Hague in Holland, but died (of natural causes) in prison in 2006, while awaiting the court's verdict.)

Right Intention. Recall that purity of motive is not required here, only that the moral motive actually be present. Whatever else America wanted in intervening, rescuing the Bosnian Muslims from slaughter was clearly on the agenda. Did America want to rub it in the face of Russia, Serbia's traditional ally? Did it want a successful intervention after the failures of Somalia and Rwanda? All these things might be true, but they don't imply failure to meet the condition. America's actions post-war also show that it had no ambitions for controlling Bosnia or Serbia—only preventing slaughter and trying to make institutional changes more conducive to peace.

Public Declaration by Proper Authority. America, a minimally just and legitimate state, publicly declared all its plans and intentions—e.g., to switch from the UN to NATO. The Dayton Accords were likewise fully public, and highly profiled. All America's acts were performed through its own appropriate domestic channels as well. But was America the proper authority? The answer seems to be yes—but only by default. The UN did get involved first, but its intervention was ineffective. The Europeans couldn't get their act together sufficiently to perform on their own, in spite of the fact that it was their own backyard. America was willing to act—at least eventually, when all the evidence of Serb misbehavior and atrocity piled up to the point where it demanded recognition. America then used the NATO infrastructure—which represented a union between North America and Europe working on a common problem—and other countries such as Canada and Britain joined the force. NATO and America may not have been the obvious choice but became the only one after the UN failed and the European initiative didn't materialize. We must recall Walzer's principle that, when it comes to humanitarian rescue, any state (or collection of such) may act, given the prime importance of saving people from slaughter.

Last Resort. If anything, America waited too long to act. The events in Bosnia burned warm and hot for nearly 4 years before decisive action was taken. So this criterion was met—and may show that, for AHIs anyway, certain requirements of speed and responsiveness are implied before all is lost. But, as traditionally stated, this rule was obviously satisfied: multiple negotiations were held; arms embargoes were tried; UN peacekeepers were tried; multiple threats and warnings were issued; and, finally, when the Sarajevo shelling showed the Serbs hadn't changed at all, it was war.

Probability of Success. Serbia might have been a regional power in the Balkans, but it was no match for the United States and NATO. Indeed, it only took two weeks of bombing to bring about surrender. America at the start could've counted on victory, especially since it had learned from Somalia that it had to intervene to win, not just to separate the factions as the UN had failingly attempted. I suppose longer term questions of "success" might be raised, since Milošević was left in power and another war against his side was necessary four years later regarding Kosovo. That's true, and it highlights the importance of how we should define "success." I think we should leave long-term success for consideration when we reflect on *jus post bellum*, justice after war. When it comes to aiming at success at the start of the war, we need only hold actors to reasonable foresight of the war and its immediate aftermath. In this sense, America could've readily foreseen a successful stop to the slaughter and cleansing, and being able to force a Serb surrender and signature on a reasonable peace agreement in the Dayton Accords.

Proportionality. When we see what Milošević was up to, we can agree with decision-makers at the time that it was proportional to use force. He and his Bosnian Serb cronies were up to aggression, ethnic cleansing, and growing and expanding an ultra-nationalist, authoritarian regime. After they conquered Bosnia, what would be next? The Serbian forces, moreover, conducted themselves with appalling violence—deliberately shelling civilians, starving POWs, and raping women in a systematic way to instill fear and to "reward" themselves. Such a force, morally, had to be stopped. And when it couldn't be stopped with all the other things they tried, it really does seem as if force was the only effective option left. And it turned out better, in the short and medium term, than what NATO dared hope for—only two weeks' worth of bombing, with minimal civilian casualties.

Notes

1 Augustine, *The City of God*, trans. David Knowles (Harmondsworth: Penguin, 1972), 862.

2 See Appendix A for international law sources.

3 Leon P. Baradat, *Political Ideologies*, 10th ed. (New York: Prentice Hall, 2008).

4 Mikhail Bakunin, *Statism and Anarchy*, trans. and ed. Marshall S. Schatz (Cambridge: Cambridge UP, 1990).

5 James P. Sterba, ed., *Terrorism and International Justice* (Oxford: Oxford UP, 2003); Der Spiegel Magazine, *Inside 9/11* (New York: St. Martin's, 2002); UK House of Commons, *Could 7/7 Have Been Prevented?* (London: Stationery Office, 2009).

6 Some believe, e.g., that the deliberate Allied bombing in 1945 of residential centers in Germany, and the atomic bombings of Japan, count as acts of terrorism. That would be democracy's use of terrorism to serve its ends. While that's controversial, if you look at the definition it's not totally empty, either. I suppose the issue is whether the intent was to terrorize or, rather, to gain revenge. More during the next chapter.

7 Mind you, in the end things turned out badly for Robespierre, getting the guillotine himself. Walter Laqueur, *The Age of Terrorism* (Boston: Little Brown, 1987); Walter Laqueur, *New Terrorism* (New York: Oxford UP, 1999).

8 Jane Corbin, *Al-Qaeda* (New York: Nation Books, 2002); Paul Berman, *Terror and Liberalism* (New York: W.W. Norton, 2003). Thanks to Judy Wubnig for discussions on this.

9 Thanks to an anonymous reviewer, and John Burbidge, for pushing me on this. See also Robert A. Pape's *Dying to Win: The Strategic Logic of Suicide Terrorism* (New York: Random House, 2005). To be crystal clear: as I'll suggest below, terrorism is always impermissible but that doesn't mean guerrilla warfare is always impermissible. It just rules out one tool that

guerrillas have been known to use. We can imagine scenarios where a powerful and unjust aggressor conquers a country and the most effective (indeed, perhaps the only realistic) means of resistance left to the justified victim community is irregular tactics. Such is fine, provided such remain *aimed at the unjust occupier's military forces and not at civilians.*

10 Jean Bethke Eshtain, *Just War Against Terror* (New York: Basic Books, 2003); Richard A. Falk, *The Great Terror War* (New York: Olive Branch, 2002).

11 Kateri Carmola, *Private Security Companies and New Wars* (London: Routledge, 2011).

12 Robin Kirk, *More Terrible Than Death* (Washington, DC: Public Affairs, 2009); David A. Shirk, *The Drug War in Mexico* (New York: Council on Foreign Relations, 2011).

13 Stephen C. Neff, *War and The Law of Nations* (Cambridge: Cambridge UP, 2005).

14 Until bin Laden's execution by US Navy SEALS, in Pakistan, in May, 2011. See Chuck Pfarrer, *Seal Target Geronimo* (New York: St. Martin's, 2012).

15 Rohan Gunaratna, *Inside al-Qaeda* (New York: Berkley Group, 2003); M. Scheuer, *Osama Bin Laden* (Oxford: Oxford UP, 2011).

16 T. Abdullah, *A Short History of Iraq* (Toronto: Pearson, 2003).

17 Gunaratna, *Inside*; Corbin, *Al-Qaeda.*

18 Journalists of Reuters, *The Israeli-Palestinian Conflict* (New York: Reuters, 2002).

19 Ahmed Rashid, *Taliban* (New Haven, CT: Yale UP, 2001); Michael T. Klare, *Rogue States and Nuclear Outlaws* (New York: Hill and Wang, 1996).

20 Daniel Byman, *Deadly Connections: States that Sponsor Terrorism* (Cambridge: Cambridge UP, 2005).

21 Michael Walzer, *Just and Unjust Wars,* 2nd ed. (New York: Basic, 1991), 74–80.

22 Walzer, *Wars,* 74–85.

23 Jeff McMahan, "Preventive War and the Killing of the Innocent" in David Rodin and Richard Sorabji, eds. *The Ethics of War* (London: Ashgate, 2006), 169–90.

24 Michael Ignatieff, *The Lesser Evil: Political Ethics in an Age of Terror* (Princeton: Princeton UP, 2004).

25 *The National Security Strategy of the United States of America.* September 2002, available at <www.whitehouse.gov/nsc/nss.pdf>, pg. 15.

26 So I agree with Ignatieff (Note 24) that the post-9/11 era is one where anticipatory attacks might be more permissible but I disagree with him when he says Walzer's criteria are out of date. I always hesitate to agree when people talk about the "dawn of a new age," etc., and the need for completely different principles. Such declarations are too often proven hasty and false. These principles have stood the test of time and can be incorporated into the new risk context.

27 Information for this section comes from: Williamson Murray and Robert H. Scales, Jr. *The Iraq War* (Cambridge, MA: Harvard UP, 2003); Scott Ritter, *War on Iraq* (New York: Profile, 2002); Bob Woodward, *Plan of Attack* (New York: Random House, 2004).

28 President George W. Bush, *Public Address,* 14 December 2005. See <www.whitehouse.gov>.

29 *The Congressional Commission Report on the Attacks of 9/11* (Washington, DC: US Congress, 2004). Bob Martin wisely notes that history has shown that the MENA is a region wherein the old principle of "my enemy's enemy must be my friend" regularly breaks down.

30 Immanuel Kant, *Perpetual Peace and Other Essays,* trans. Ted Humphrey (Indianapolis, IN: Hackett, 1983), 31–32; Isaiah Berlin, *The Crooked Timber of Humanity,* 2nd ed. (Princeton, NJ: Princeton UP, 1998).

31 James B. McPherson, *Battle Cry of Freedom* (Oxford: Oxford UP, 1988).
32 Allen Buchanan, *The Morality of Political Divorce* (Boulder, CO: Westview, 1991); Stephen Macedo and Allen Buchanan, eds., *Secession and Self-Determination* (New York: New York UP, 2003).
33 Brian Orend, *Michael Walzer on War and Justice* (Montreal: McGill-Queen's UP, 2000), 153–79; Michael Walzer, *Thick and Thin* (Notre Dame, IN: Notre Dame UP, 1994); the special 2000 issue on secession in the *Canadian Journal of Law and Jurisprudence*.
34 Robin E.H. Shepherd, *Czechoslovakia: The Velvet Divorce and Beyond* (New York: St. Martin's, 2000).
35 Richard Cockett, *Sudan: Darfur and the Failure of an African State* (New Haven, CT: Yale UP, 2010).
36 Walzer, *Wars*, 96–100.
37 Material for this section comes from: Stanley Karnow, *Vietnam: A History* (New York: Penguin, 1997); George C. Herring, *America's Longest War*, 4th ed. (New York: McGraw Hill, 2001); Richard J. Regan, *Just War* (Washington, DC: Georgetown UP, 1996), 136–50.
38 Walzer, *Wars*, 99.
39 Brian Orend, *Human Rights: Concept and Context* (Peterborough, ON: Broadview, 2002), 162–72; Stéphane Courtois et al., *The Black Book of Communism* (Cambridge, MA: Harvard UP, 1999); François Firet, *The Passing of an Illusion* (Chicago: U of Chicago P, 1999).
40 See Regan, *Just War*, 179–211 for more on Somalia and Bosnia from a just war perspective. For a detailed look at the international law regarding armed intervention, see: Simon Chesterman, *Just War or Just Peace? Humanitarian Intervention and International Law* (Oxford: Oxford UP, 2001). On the politics of humanitarian intervention, see: Nicholas J. Wheeler, *Saving Strangers* (Oxford: Oxford UP, 2003); Nicolaus Mills and Kira Brunner, eds., *The New Killing Fields* (New York: Basic Books, 2002); Martha Finnemore, *The Purpose of Intervention* (Ithaca, NY: Cornell UP, 2003); J.L. Holzgrefe and Robert O. Keohane, eds., *Humanitarian Intervention* (Cambridge: Cambridge UP, 2003); Stanley Hoffmann, ed., *The Ethics and Politics of Humanitarian Intervention* (Notre Dame, IN: Notre Dame UP, 1997).
41 The International Commission on Intervention and State Sovereignty, *Report: The Responsibility to Protect* (Ottawa: International Development Research Centre, 2001).
42 Walzer, *Wars*, 103–08.
43 Ben Kiernan, *The Pol Pot Regime* (New Haven, CT: Yale UP, 1998).
44 Wesley K. Clark, *Waging Modern War: Bosnia, Kosovo and the Future of Combat* (New York: Public Affairs, 2002); Tim Judah, *Kosovo: War and Revenge* (New Haven, CT: Yale UP, 2002).
45 Walzer, *Wars*, 103.
46 Michael Walzer, "Kosovo," *Dissent* (Summer 1999): 5–7; Brian Orend, "Crisis in Kosovo: A Just Use of Force?" *Politics* 19 (1999): 125–30.
47 Martin Gilbert, *The Holocaust* (New York: Henry Holt, 1987).
48 Gérard Prunier, *Rwanda: History of a Genocide* (New York: Columbia UP, 1995); Michael Barnett, *Eyewitness to a Genocide: The UN and Rwanda* (Ithaca, NY: Cornell UP, 2003); Linda Melvern, *A People Betrayed: The Role of the West in Rwanda's Genocide* (New York: Zed, 2000); Roméo Dallaire, *Shake Hands with the Devil* (New York: Random House, 2004).
49 Michael Walzer, "Preface to the Third Edition," in his *Just and Unjust Wars*, 3rd ed. (New York: Basic Books, 2000), xv.
50 ICISS, *Report*, xi.

51 Walter Clarke and Jeffrey Herbst, eds., *Learning from Somalia* (New York: Basic Books, 1997); Regan, *Just War*, 179–211.

52 ICISS, *Report*, 57–68.

53 <http://www.nato.int/cps/en/natolive/topics_50088.htm>.

54 Walzer, "Preface," xiii-xvi.

55 The International Commission on Intervention and State Sovereignty, *Report: The Responsibility to Protect* (Ottawa: International Development Research Centre, 2002).

56 Gareth Evans, *The Responsibility to Protect: Ending Mass Atrocity Crimes Once and for All* (Washington, DC: Brookings Institute, 2009).

57 Lin Noueihed and Alex Warren, *The Battle for the Arab Spring* (New Haven, CT: Yale UP, 2012); T. Weiss, *Humanitarian Intervention*, 2nd ed. (London: Polity, 2012).

58 Alex J. Bellamy, *Responsibility to Protect* (London: Polity, 2009); Nikolas Gvosdev, *R2P: Sovereignty and Intervention After Libya* (London: World Politics Review, 2011).

59 In early May 2013, Israel launched airstrikes into Syria, ostensibly to destroy some high-tech weapons destined for radicals committed to Israel's destruction. Further, allegations arose that the Syrian regime was now deploying outlawed chemical weapons—allegations which triggered stern threats from the USA about possible, more forceful, intervention.

60 Council on Foreign Relations, *Syria: The Crisis and Its Implications* (Washington, DC: United States Senate, 2012).

61 President George W. Bush, *Public Address*, 14 December 2005. See <www.whitehouse.gov>.

62 Walzer, *Wars*, 127–224.

63 Information for this case study comes from: David Rieff, *Slaughterhouse: Bosnia and the Failure of the West* (New York: Simon and Schuster, 1995); Human Rights Watch, *Slaughter Among Neighbours* (New Haven, CT: Yale UP, 1995); Richard Holbrooke, *To End a War* (New York: Modern Library, 1999); Clark, *Waging Modern War*, passim; Regan, *Just War*, 192–212.

4

Jus in Bello #1

JUST CONDUCT IN WAR

"The greatest difficulty in the right of nations has to do precisely with right during war; it is difficult even to form a concept of this or to think of law in this lawless state without contradicting oneself" —KANT[1]

"*Jus in bello*" is the Latin term just war theorists use to refer to justice *in* war—to right conduct in the midst of battle, after the war has started. Most just war theorists insist that *jus in bello* is an ethical category separate, in some sense, from *jus ad bellum*. Why? We have not finished our task of evaluating warfare once we have determined whether a community has resorted to war justly, using the principles developed in the last two chapters. For, even if a state has resorted to war justly, it may be prosecuting that war in an unjustified manner. It may be deploying immoral means in pursuit of its otherwise justified end. Just war theory insists on a *fundamental moral consistency between means and ends* with regard to wartime behavior.

Concern with consistency, however, is not the only, or even the main, reason behind our endorsement of separate rules regulating wartime conduct. Such rules are also required to limit warfare, to prevent it from spilling over into an ever-escalating, and increasingly destructive, experiment in total warfare. If just wars are limited wars, designed to secure their just causes with only proportionate force, the need for rules on wartime restraint is clear.

All that being said, and sincerely endorsed, I wish to reiterate my conviction that the so-called "separation" between *jus ad bellum* and *jus in bello* is mainly for focussing attention on different issues. It does not denote a complete split between the two, as if they had nothing to do with each other. Indeed, I assert that the three just war categories *must* morally be linked, with *jus ad bellum* setting the tone for all that follows. There is nothing more wrong, conceptually, than to adopt the "check list" approach to just war theory, as if all the rules and criteria were simply separate "boxes" to be checked off during the war, like ticking off the items on your grocery list as you buy them. The rules and criteria all presuppose shared values, such as: rejecting aggression; restraining warfare; and protecting the state rights of legitimate communities and the human rights of their individual residents. We'll actually see that we literally cannot make moral sense of some *jus in bello* rules—notably, proportionality—and probably the entire *jus post bellum* category without considering the just cause of the war to begin with.

The best metaphor—regarding just war theory as not segregated but, rather, as united into one long procedure with different phases—is probably something like surgery. You've got, quite literally, an opening phase, an operational phase, and a closing phase. Different phases raise different questions and concerns, and there needs to be well-founded and well-understood rules governing each. But everything is connected and substantially affected by what happened prior, and the ruling concern which started the whole process was why surgery was necessary in the first place.

As for the sewing up and the post-surgery rehabilitation, we have the future *jus post bellum* chapters. For now, we inaugurate the operational phase. We've diagnosed the need for surgery, have made our cut and gone in. We're in the thick of it: now what do we do? This is the topic of *jus in bello*.

We can distinguish profitably between external and internal *jus in bello* rules. The external rules concern how a state, in the midst of war, should conduct itself regarding the enemy state and its civilians (and/or the enemy non-state actor). The internal rules, by contrast, concern how a state, in the midst of war, should treat its own citizens, be they soldiers or civilians.

Before examining and explaining these rules, it is worth stressing how responsibility for fulfilling *jus in bello* differs from the responsibility inhering in *jus ad bellum*. Responsibility for the justice of resorting to war, we saw, rests on those key members of the governing party most centrally involved in the decision to go to war, particularly the head of state or anybody authorized with the war power. Responsibility for the conduct of war, by contrast, rests on the state's armed forces. In particular, responsibility for right conduct rests with those commanders, officers, and soldiers who command and control the lethal force set in motion by the political hierarchy. In general, anyone involved in formulating and executing military strategy during wartime bears responsibility for any violation of *jus in bello* standards. In most cases, such violation will constitute a war crime. Detailed discussion of war crimes trials will be reserved for Chapter 6.

1. The External Rules

1.1. DISCRIMINATION AND NON-COMBATANT IMMUNITY

The requirement of discrimination and non-combatant immunity is the most important *jus in bello* rule. It is also the most frequently, and stridently, codified rule within the international laws of armed conflict.[2] The substance of the rule is this: soldiers charged with the deployment of armed force may not do so indiscriminately; rather, they must exert every reasonable effort to discriminate between legitimate and illegitimate targets. How are soldiers to know which is which? *A legitimate target in wartime is anyone or anything engaged in harming.* All non-harming persons, or institutions, are thus ethically immune from direct and intentional attack by soldiers and their weapons systems. Since the soldiers of the enemy nation, for instance, are clearly engaged in harming, they may be directly targeted, as may their equipment, their supply routes, and even some of their civilian suppliers. Civilians not engaged in the military effort of their nation may not be targeted with lethal force. In general, as Michael Walzer asserts: "A legitimate act of war is one that does not violate the rights of the people against whom it is directed."[3] In response, we might ask: how is it that armed force directed against soldiers does not violate their rights, whereas that directed against civilians violates theirs? In the chaos of wartime, what exactly marks the difference?

One of the murkiest areas of Walzer's just war theory concerns the moral status of ordinary soldiers. His references to them exhibit, on the one hand, a humane sympathy for their "shared servitude" as "the pawns of war." On the other, his references occasionally display something like a glib callousness, as when he concurs with Napoleon's (in)famous remark that "soldiers are made to be killed."[4] How can soldiers be made to be killed when, as human beings, they enjoy human rights, to security among other things? The answer must be that soldiers do something which causes them to forfeit their rights, much as an outlaw country forfeits its state rights to non-interference when it commits aggression. One could be forgiven for inferring, from this principle, that only soldiers of an aggressor nation forfeit their rights, since they are the only ones engaged in the kind of rights-violating harm which grounds a violent, punitive response. Interestingly, and perhaps problematically, Walzer denies this. He believes that *all* soldiers forfeit their right not to be targeted with lethal force, whether they be of just or unjust nations, whether they be tools of aggression or instruments of defence.[5]

1.1.1. The Moral Equality of Soldiers?

Walzer's concept here, which is the widely accepted traditional view, is of "the moral equality of soldiers." The first "war right" of all soldiers is to kill enemy soldiers. We do not, and should not, make soldiers pay the price for the injustice of the wars they may be ordered—perhaps even conscripted—to fight. That is the logically and morally separate issue of *jus ad bellum*, for which we have already elaborated a theory of justice, focusing on the responsibilities of political leaders. But lawyers like the chief British prosecutor during the Nuremberg trials, and philosophers like Thomas Pogge and David Rodin, ask: why shouldn't we hold soldiers responsible for the justice of the wars they fight? If we held soldiers responsible in this regard, wouldn't that constitute an additional bar against aggressive war? Wouldn't that account for the fact that, even though the war was set in motion by others, soldiers remain its essential executors? Wouldn't such a move impose and highlight an important responsibility for soldiers, namely, to refuse to participate in the prosecution of aggressive war?[6]

Walzer experiences difficulty answering this argument fully. As an opening gambit, he contends that soldiers "are most likely to believe that their wars are just." But this alone cannot justify their actions, since their beliefs may not be well-grounded, especially considering the incentive they have to believe such justification in the first place. Walzer also says that soldiers rarely fail to fight, owing to "(t)heir routine habits of law-abidingness, their fear, their patriotism [and] their moral investment in the state."[7] But the fact that soldiers rarely fail to fight does not demonstrate that they are always justified in fighting, especially if the cause is unjust. Walzer next suggests that knowledge about the justice of the wars soldiers fight is "hard to come by." This is a truly surprising claim from a just war theorist who has tried to make such knowledge more accessible and comprehensible. Perhaps, then, this is a reference to the soldier's historical lack of education, as well as to government tendencies towards secrecy. Fair enough, but ignorance at best constitutes an excuse, and not a justification, for willfully fighting in an unjust war: it seems a stretch to assert that such ignorance can morally ground a "war right" to kill enemy soldiers deliberately. Walzer's subsequent move appeals to the authority of Vitoria, who suggested that if soldiers were allowed to pick and choose the wars they were willing to fight in, the result would be "grave peril" for their country.[8] (This argument has recently been endorsed by the Israeli government, which has found itself in Israeli courts being sued by a handful of its own soldiers, who do not want to fight in the on-going struggle with the Palestinians. Israel has a system of compulsory military service for all citizens.[9]) But this empirical generalization is speculative: why wouldn't the result actually be the preferred one, namely, that states would be seriously hampered only in their efforts to prosecute an aggressive war, which they couldn't justify to their soldiery?

Walzer then claims it is a plain fact of sociology that we do not blame soldiers for killing other soldiers in the midst of war. We blame soldiers only when they deliberately kill either civilians or surrendered enemy soldiers kept by them as disarmed prisoners of war (POWs). We extend to all soldiers, caught in the midst of battle, the right to deploy armed force on behalf of their own country. This is a true legal contention—equal belligerent rights seems established international law[10]—and while it is not an implausible moral one, the latter is not quite so obvious as Walzer suggests. Do we really believe that those soldiers who fought for Hitler, for example, were utterly blameless for their bit part in the execution of his mad aggression? No doubt, we tend to exonerate conscripts like The Hitler Youth in the closing days of the war, presuming they were far too young, gullible, and propagandized to have made a morally responsible choice. But what about those mature German soldiers—many of whom with prior war experience—who invaded Poland, or France, at the war's outset? It's not so clear to me that we do not blame them for fighting on behalf of their country. Indeed, today, even ex-soldiers, living abroad, who played very small roles in Hitler's army can, if found out, be stripped of their citizenship and deported back to Germany—even in spite of their very advanced age.[11]

Walzer stresses more generally the pervasive socialization of soldiers of any nation, their relative youth, their frequent conscription, and their usual background as members of underprivileged classes as grounds for not holding soldiers responsible for the wars they fight. While soldiers "are not ... entirely without volition," he says, "[t]heir will is independent and effective only within a limited sphere." This sphere contains only those tactics and maneuvers soldiers are engaged in, like training, loading their weapons, engaging in particular live-fire skirmishes, handling prisoners, and so on. It would thus constitute unfair "class legislation" for us to hold soldiers like these responsible for the justice of the wars they fight. We should focus on those most to blame: the elite, powerful leaders who set the war in motion.[12] But from the fact that political leaders are, I admit, *mostly* to blame for the crime of aggression, does it follow that they are *solely* to blame, as Walzer here insists? In my view, the more compelling alternative would be to suggest that, for the many reasons Walzer mentions, there should be a presumption against holding soldiers responsible for the crime of violating *jus ad bellum*. But this presumption does not preclude us from concluding, in particular cases based on public evidence, that: some soldiers of a particular aggressor state either *did* know, or *really should have* known, about the injustice of the war they were fighting; that they could have refused to participate in it; and thus that they may be held responsible, albeit with much lesser penalties than the elites. Such soldiers would be like minor accomplices to a major crime. This is one way in which I do not believe in the absolute separateness of *jus ad bellum* and *jus in bello*.[13]

Soldiers who fight for an aggressor do not have strict moral equality with those who fight for a victim or defender. The former are not mainly to blame for the aggression but they still are to blame, in a smaller but material sense. Soldiers are not automatons. Their merely professional function does not dislodge the ordinary human duty not to inflict severe, unjustifiable harm on others. Soldiers must inform their beliefs regarding the justice of the wars they are ordered to fight. Exceptional ones, upon seeing injustice, will refuse service, or else surrender to the other (just) side at the first non-life-threatening opportunity. Ordinary soldiers, when confronted with the fact that the war they fight is unjust, will probably still go along with the crowd of their buddies and fight—the pressures to do so are very strong. For them, we reserve the moral right to criticize and castigate them at war's end. Perhaps we will finally excuse them, on the basis of these pressures, but perhaps also, in some well-documented cases, we will have to prosecute them as minor accomplices to the one large "crime against peace" which is aggression.[14]

1.1.2. Engaging in Harm

Even if we agree with my proposal that some soldiers may be held responsible for *jus ad bellum* violations, can we still concur with Walzer's idea that all soldiers *generally* remain legitimate targets during wartime? After several false starts, Walzer offers us a compelling reason to do so: soldiers, whether just or unjust, are "engaged in harm." Soldiers bear arms effectively, are trained to kill for political reasons, and are "dangerous men": they pose serious threats to the lives and interests of those they are deployed against, whether for a just cause or no. Walzer suggests that an armed man trying to kill me "alienates himself from me ... and from our common humanity" and in so doing he forfeits his right to life. This establishes, I believe, a strong *prima facie* (i.e., "first glance") case that soldiers targeting other soldiers with lethal force is justified. Soldiers, whether for just or unjust reasons, remain among the most serious and standard external threats to life and vital interests. Only public, compelling, and accessible knowledge about the injustice of the cause of his own country can undermine a soldier's entitlement, in the face of such an opposing threat, to respond in kind.[15]

The converse of this general principle, of course, is that those who are not "engaged in harm" cannot be legitimate targets during wartime. This is the clearest sense of who is "innocent" in wartime: *all those not engaged in creating harm*. The first application, of this converse rule regarding harm, has to do with soldiers themselves: when soldiers no longer pose serious external threats—notably by laying down their weapons and surrendering—they may no longer be targeted with force and should, in fact, be extended what international law calls "benevolent quarantine" for the duration of the war.[16]

1.1.3. Benevolent Quarantine and Torturing Terrorists

"Benevolent quarantine" means that captured enemy soldiers can be stripped of their weapons, incarcerated with their fellows, and questioned verbally for information. But they cannot, e.g., be tortured during questioning. Nor can they be beaten, starved, or somehow medically experimented on. They cannot be used as shields between oneself and the opposing side, and in fact the understanding is that captured enemy soldiers are to be incarcerated far away from the front lines. Very basic medical and hygienic treatment is supposed to be offered—things like aspirin, soap, water, and toothbrushes—and, while making captives engage in work projects is permitted, the Geneva Conventions actually require that, in that event, captives be paid a modest salary. I have never heard of that actually happening—the incredible detail of the Geneva Conventions means they don't always get realized—but it is fairly common for combatants to disarm, house, and feed their captives, keeping them out of harm's way and ensuring their basic needs are met until the war ends. When it is all over, they are then usually freed, often in exchange for POWs on the other side.[17]

Controversies here focus around when, or if, aggressive questioning becomes a form of torture, and also around when non-state actors, like terrorists, are taken prisoner. The latter issue concerns whether non-state captives deserve the same quality of treatment as state captives. There's a sense that a soldier fighting for his community deserves better than a terrorist fighting for his pet cause. I think this distinction can be difficult to sustain and that, generally, non-state actors brought into capture by soldiers should be accorded the same rights as captured enemy soldiers. If soldiers fighting for an unjust cause deserve this treatment, then surely so do terrorists—whose method, if not the cause, is likewise unjust. In other words, if it's wrong to torture Nazi soldiers—whose cause was heinous and irredeemable—then it's wrong to torture radical Islamic terrorists (much less mere suspects). This topic has recently been highlighted regarding America's round-up and detainment of alleged terrorists, post 9/11, in Guantanamo Bay, Cuba. The facility still functions today, with over 150 detainees.[18]

The incidents in Abu-Ghraib prison, in Iraq, also come to mind. In the late spring of 2004, the world saw some shocking photos of American troop conduct in that jail. Iraqi prisoners—captured during the war and the subsequent insurgency—were subjected to rough treatment. Some of the practices—such as deliberate, prolonged sleep deprivation, and the use of dogs to attack or threaten already prone and naked people—clearly violated the Geneva Conventions. Others might have been visually disturbing but don't obviously count as human rights violations, such as forcing the prisoners to wear dog collars, or having American women ridicule their private parts, or putting female panties on their faces temporarily. (These might sound silly, but they are deeply humiliating in the prisoners' culture.) Clearly what went on was a violation of both the letter and the spirit of the principle of benevolent quarantine. Some of the US soldiers involved have since been charged, tried, and sentenced (which I would argue shows official American acceptance of the idea that non-state captives deserve the same treatment as state captives).[19]

There was an investigation as to whether any authorization of this treatment came from higher-up the US chain of command. It does seem unlikely, after all, that some "mere" reservists would repeatedly conduct such flagrant prisoner abuse on their own, and apparently there was a vaguely-defined policy of "softening up" prisoners for subsequent anti-terrorist questioning by the CIA. Perhaps the very vagueness of such a policy was itself a moral error, even if direct orders did not explicitly authorize prisoner abuse (as the investigation concluded).[20]

I suppose we might condone efforts at psychological pressure—mocking, aggressive cross-examination, ridiculing, criticizing, etc.—when the goal is getting information which might save innocent lives. Questioning is, after all, permitted under the Geneva Conventions. But the infliction of physical harm cannot be, even if it supposedly serves the questioning process. Why? Because it's impossible to square the infliction of physical harm with the concept of benevolent quarantine. Benevolent quarantine may not mean actually being nice to your prisoners but it certainly cannot, logically, include things the Geneva Conventions define as torture: prolonged sleep deprivation; starvation; slapping, punching, biting or strangling; the breaking or severing of limbs or digits; urging or allowing an animal to attack; any kind of drowning-based, or electrocution-based, session; sexual assault or rape; poisoning or medical experimentation; shooting; and so on. These things are simply prohibited. Not even war—not even a just war—can justify the deliberate infliction of such things upon other human beings, even if such people are suspected, or even guilty, of terrible things themselves. In domestic society, e.g., we do not permit prison guards to torture anyone—even those convicted of the very worst crimes. So why should we allow it in international society? The thing to do with terrorist suspects is to question them within the rules, and then prosecute them for war crimes and, upon conviction, send them to jail—not to strip them, beat them, and sic dogs after them. Dare I say, such activities are not only unjust but against the very self-perception of being "civilized" on the part of the forces and countries performing them. To speak more frankly, that's just not the American way. The forces of civilization must remain civilized even as they confront ruthless barbarism.[21]

As important as it is to prevent future terrorist attacks, and to protect innocent lives, torture is universally agreed to be one of the very worst things a person can do. Torture is everywhere banned in the laws of war and human rights law.[22] The methods cause revulsion and disgust—as we saw in worldwide reaction to the Abu-Ghraib photos. Torture also hardens the heart, and corrupts the character, of the torturer. It inflicts absolutely devastating pain upon the tortured—who must endure not only the raw pain of the act(s) but also the experience and knowledge of being utterly enslaved to the whims of another. Torture inflicts severe pain, combines slavery with violence, disregards human autonomy, and even renders the torturer worse off. It is, as a method, intrinsically corrupt and even evil. Moreover, torture is extremely questionable as an information-gathering device because evidence shows that people will say *anything*—even deny things they know are true, and assert things they know are false—just to get the torture to stop. After a threshold of pain, the over-riding objective of the victim becomes to please the torturer so that he'll stop—and, if this includes lying, then so be it. Plus, as should be expected, the experience of torture negatively impacts accurate recall, cognitive sharpness, and correct inference. Combine it all, and you have serious questions about anything worthwhile being extracted from such a process. Torture is not the answer to terrorism; it is a surrender to a world of brutality and barbarism—a world where the terrorist already resides. I'm not saying torture and terrorism are morally equivalent—presumably torture is more discriminating and localized than terrorism. What I am saying is that, as methods, they are both wrong—*always*—and ultimately indefensible regardless of the cause they supposedly serve.[23]

1.1.4. Civilian Immunity

The second application of the harm principle deals with civilians. Even though some civilians may inwardly approve, or even have voted in favor of, an unjust war effort, they nevertheless remain externally non-threatening. They do not bear arms effectively, nor have they been trained to kill, nor have they been deployed against the lives and vital interests of the opposing side. Civilians, whatever their internal attitude, are not in any external sense "dangerous men." So they may not be made the direct and intentional objects of military attack.[24] Although I endorse this conclusion, it remains controversial with others.

Some people—including Osama bin Laden[25]—argue that the fact that civilian taxes fund the military renders null and void any pretense of their being "innocent." Civilians are causally involved in financing the harm soldiers do. Others view nationality as shared destiny, or suggest that modern warfare is totalizing anyway and so wonder what the point of discrimination really is, in our age. If you're at all in the enemy country, you're fair game.[26] These are not trivial arguments but they fail to persuade. It is hard to see, e.g., how infants and young children could be anything other than innocent during wartime. Only the most dogmatic believer in collective responsibility could deny this, and then at the cost of his credibility. Just because a baby—through no fault of her own—happens to live in the enemy country, she's fair game? Even though she's not even old enough to be morally responsible for anything? It makes no sense.

And the relationship between paying one's taxes and the execution of military acts remains, on an individual level anyway: 1) *coerced*, since taxes are everywhere mandatory; and 2) *extremely indirect*, with manifold agents, transfers, and responsibilities intervening in-between. The degree to which the state is centrally involved in this coercion and transfer process—of taxes-to-warfare—renders *it* clearly the vastly larger, indeed the only, concrete permissible target. The state—its agents and appendages—is the main organizer and focal point of warfare. It always has been and always will be. It is thus *the* legitimate target and no attempt to "fuzzify" the difference between a government and its people can overcome this. Belligerents target civilians in warfare not because they think the people deserve it but, rather, because they think this will give them leverage against the state, which remains the armed, potent threat—the true adversary and target. It's sort of like kidnapping a rich man's family, so as to force *him* to pay you blackmail: give in, or your favorite innocents get it! Just war theory and international law command, by contrast, that you may only attack the true adversary in warfare: i.e., that entity directly engaged in physical harm.[27]

There is, moreover, little evidence that modern warfare is intrinsically totalizing: the 1991 Persian Gulf War, e.g., or the 2001–03 take-downs of the regimes in Afghanistan and Iraq, or the 2011 Libyan intervention, did not escalate into indiscriminate bloodbaths. Indeed, what seems obviously more the recipe for ever-increasing slaughter is the idea that civilians may be targeted as readily as soldiers. No doubt, there are some questions about the exact specification of "innocents" in wartime but I follow just war theory, and international law, in believing that it remains an important just war category, needed *not only to restrain violence* but also to express our strong—almost foundational—moral commitment to *punish only those who truly deserve it.* In the midst of "the fog of war," one of the most concrete and verifiable ways to cash out such deserving is to define it in terms of external engagement in serious harm. In the midst of war, we cannot peer into the hearts of every civilian; we can only look sweepingly at external behavior. When we do so, we notice a large and obvious difference between those engaged in harm—i.e., those inside "the war machine"—and those not. Since harm is a vital concept for justice and morality, it makes sense to say that it establishes a dividing line between those who may, and those others who may not, be targeted with force.[28]

Difficulties arise, of course, when we consider those people who seem, simultaneously, to be both civilians and engaged in harming, such as civilian suppliers of military hardware. What is the status of such people? Walzer suggests that "the relevant distinction is ... between those who make what the soldiers need to fight and those who make what they need to live like all the rest of us." So targeting farms, schools, and hospitals is illegitimate, whereas targeting weapons factories is legitimate. Walzer stresses, however, that civilians engaged in the military supply effort are legitimate targets only when they are engaged in that effort, so to target them while at home in residential areas would be illegitimate: "Rights to life are forfeit only when particular men and women are actually engaged in war-making or national defense." Walzer agrees with Thomas Nagel's explanation that "hostile treatment of any person must be justified in terms of something *about that person* [Nagel's italics] which makes the treatment appropriate." We distinguish combatants from non-combatants "on the basis of their immediate threat or harmfulness." And our response to such threats and harms must be governed by relations of directness and relevance. It is only military—and military-related—targets which pose a *direct* and *relevant* threat of serious harm; thus, it is only they which may be resisted with lethal force.[29]

Walzer's overall judgment on targeting—which is very helpful, and essentially condenses international law—is this: soldiers may target other soldiers, their equipment, their barracks and training areas, their supply and communications lines, and the industrial sites which produce their supply. Presumably, core political and bureaucratic institutions are also legitimate objects of attack, in particular things like the Defense Ministry. Illegitimate targets include residential areas, schools, hospitals, farms, churches, cultural institutions, and non-military industrial sites. *In general, anyone or anything not demonstrably engaged in military supply or military activity is immune from direct attack.* Walzer is especially critical of targeting basic infrastructure, particularly food, water, medical, and power supplies. He criticizes American conduct during the 1991 Persian Gulf War on this basis, since very heavy damage was inflicted on Iraq's water treatment and sewage system, and presumably he would also frown upon NATO's targeting the Serbian electric power grid during its 1999 armed intervention on behalf of the ethnic Albanian Kosovars. The aim there had very little to do with *bona fide* military tactics; it was a raw demonstration of sheer power designed to "shock and awe" the enemy into submission with an overwhelming display of "kinetic capability." And that it did: the Serbs couldn't turn on a toaster, watch TV, heat their homes, run their businesses, etc., unless NATO said so. You can see how this would give the Serbs rather strong incentive to please NATO. While it is true that soldiers cannot fight well without food, water, medicine, and electricity, those are things they—and everyone else in their society, including innocents—require *as human beings* and not more narrowly as externally threatening instruments of war. Thus, the moral need for a direct and relevant response only to the source of serious harm renders these things ethically immune from attack.[30]

1.1.5. The Doctrine of Double Effect

Another serious perplexity about targeting concerns the close real-world proximity of illegitimate civilian targets to legitimate military and political ones: weapons factories, after all, are often side-by-side with non-military factories, and at times just around the corner from schools and residential areas. This raises the complex issue of the Doctrine of Double Effect (DDE).[31] The core moral problem is this: even if soldiers intentionally aim only at legitimate targets, they can often *foresee* that taking out some of these targets will still involve collateral civilian casualties. And if civilians do nothing to lose their human rights, doesn't it follow that such acts will be unjust, since civilians will predictably suffer some harm or even death?

The DDE stipulates that an agent A may perform an action X, even though A foresees that X will result in *both* good (G) and bad (B) effects, *provided all* of the following criteria are met: 1) X is an otherwise morally permissible action; 2) A only intends G and not B; 3) B is not a means to G; and 4) the goodness of G is worth, or is proportionately greater than, the badness of B. The DDE, at first, can seem overly technical, and thus for some people "fishy." (And, admittedly, it does not have universal endorsement amongst ethical experts.)[32] But what the DDE is, is an idea rendered complex by the complexity of the situation it deals with. Since it is a common wartime situation, however, we can't avoid it. Let's break it down. It is a doctrine of "double effect" since it deals with actions which are going to have two effects: one good and one bad. It seeks to respond to the question: "Can one ever perform such an action?" It answers "yes," provided the criteria just listed are *all* satisfied; if even one criterion fails to be satisfied, the doctrine forbids the performance of the action. Assume now, using these criteria, that A is an army and X is an otherwise permissible act of war, like taking aim with a weapon at a military target. The good effect G would be destroying the target, the bad effect B any collateral civilian casualties. The DDE stipulates that A may still do X, provided that A only intends to destroy the military target and not to kill civilians; that A is not using the civilian casualties as means to the end of destroying the military target; and that the importance of hitting the target is worth the collateral dead.[33]

The first objection commonly raised against the DDE concerns its controversial distinction between *intending* Z's death (or harm) and *merely foreseeing* that one's actions will result in Z's death (or harm). Some have argued that the DDE is so elastic as to justify anything: all an agent has to do, to employ its protective moral cloak, is to assert: "Well, I didn't intend *that*; my aim, rather, was this...." It is clear, however, that agents are not free to claim whatever good intention they want in order to justify their actions, however heinous. Intentions must meet minimal criteria of *logical coherence* and, moreover, must be *connected to patterns of action* which are publicly accessible. The criminal justice system of most countries is based on these ideas: for such serious crimes as murder, the case must be made by the prosecution that the accused had *mens rea*, or the intent to kill. This is done by offering publicly-accessible evidence which is tied to the accused's actions, behavior, and assertions leading up to the time of the murder. Also needed is a consideration of whether the accused had both incentive and motive to commit the crime. Juries, as reasonable and experienced persons, are then invited to infer the accused's state of mind. The plausibility of this procedure undermines the popular academic claim that the DDE can be used to justify *any* heinous action, whether in war or peace. Walzer agrees, suggesting that we know the intentions of agents through their actions: "(T)he surest sign of good intentions in war is restraint in its conduct." In other words, when armies fight in strict adherence to *jus in bello*—taking aim only at legitimate targets, using only proportionate force, not employing intrinsically heinous means—they cannot meaningfully be said to intend the deaths of civilians killed collaterally. Their actions, focusing on military targets and taking due care that civilians not be killed, reveals their intentions.[34]

What exactly constitutes "due care" by armies that civilians not be killed during the prosecution of otherwise legitimate military campaigns? For Walzer, it involves soldiers accepting more risks to themselves to ensure that they hit only the proper targets: "We draw a circle of rights around civilians, and soldiers are supposed to accept (some) risks in order to save civilian lives." Walzer suggests we locate the limits of additional risk-taking—that soldiers can and should shoulder on behalf of those civilians they endanger—at that point where "any further risk-taking would almost certainly doom the military venture or make it so costly that it could not be repeated."[35] This principle might entail, for instance, that soldiers use only certain kinds of weapons, and avoid others. America has, e.g., recently pioneered the use of so-called "smart bombs" that use satellite technology to improve drastically the "hit rate" on desired targets. America also employs laser- and satellite-guided cruise missiles, which can be exceptionally precise (and are exceptionally expensive). Compare these advances with the older method of simply flying over a target, dumping one's bomb load, and beating a hasty retreat before getting shot down.

The due care principle might also mean moving in more closely on the military target to increase the likelihood of hitting it, and avoiding collateral civilian damage. America encountered criticism, in this regard, during the armed intervention in Serbia over Kosovo in 1999. Some, such as Michael Ignatieff, contended that the extensive bombing was not really that "smart," and that too much of it came from too high a distance. In other words, the participating American pilots were *willing to kill but not willing to risk dying*—and in opposition to the due care principle they actually went out of their way to increase the distance between themselves and their targets. This is permissible activity, in my view, only if one's bombing payload is not conventional explosives—with their disturbingly high rate of collateral damage—but, rather, reliable smart technology. If one's payload is otherwise, Ignatieff's criticism is both sound and scathing: it is a violation of the warrior ethos itself. (We shall revisit this theme below in connection with drones.)[36]

Although this might sound silly at first, the due care principle might also, under certain conditions, require some kind of advance warning to nearby civilians. Consider, e.g., that the Israeli military occasionally does this. Say it decides to destroy a building which it believes serves as a haven for pro-Palestinian terrorists. If this building is in a residential area, the Israeli military has sometimes been known to announce publicly its intent to destroy this target, declaring that civilians left in the area at the declared time will not be its responsibility. This warning might, admittedly, allow terrorists to escape with valuable equipment, but the Israelis still believe it valuable to destroy military-use targets while showing clear respect for civilians.[37]

What the due care principle implies, above all else, is this: *tactics and maneuvers must be carefully planned, in advance, with a keen eye towards minimizing civilian casualties.* This demands competent and well-trained officers and soldiers, as well as the need to gather and analyze quality intelligence on the precise nature of suspected targets. While Kant thought spying morally decrepit since it involves deception, I argue that: a) with advances in technology, intelligence gathering need not involve deception; and b) in any event, intelligence gathering can serve the vital ethical need of being more precise in targeting, knowing what to hit and what is out of bounds.[38]

So Walzer, in the end, maintains that civilians are not entitled to some implausible kind of fail-safe, or absolute, immunity from attack; rather, they are owed neither more nor less than this "due care" from belligerent armies. Providing due care is, in fact, equivalent to "recognizing their rights as best we can within the context of war." This is precisely the reality in the laws of armed conflict.[39]

We've seen explanations of the first two, of the four, criteria of the DDE. What about the third, regarding the prohibition on the use of the bad effects (like civilian casualties) to produce the good ones (like eliminating the military target)? An example of such a violation would be the deliberate bombing of the residential area around a weapons factory, with the rationale that most of the workers in that factory probably live in the neighborhood. And so, even if you miss the factory itself, you're still going to render it useless by taking out its workforce. It seems possible to discern whether a belligerent, such as country C, is employing civilian casualties as a means both to its immediate end of hitting the legitimate target and to its final end of victory over rival country D. If there are systemic patterns—as opposed to unavoidable, isolated cases—of civilian bombardment by C on the civilians of D, it is compelling to conclude that C is directly targeting the civilian population of D. Conversely, if the systemic pattern of C's war-fighting indicates its targeting of D's military capabilities, with only incidental and occasional civilian casualties resulting, then it is reasonable to infer that C is not trying to use civilian casualties as a pressure tactic to force D to retreat and admit defeat.

The truly difficult aspect of the DDE, in my view, is the final criterion: contending that the goodness of hitting the legitimate military target is "worth," or proportional to, the badness of the collateral civilian casualties. A pacifist, for example, will always deny this. Is the need to hit a source of military harm sufficient to justify killing people whom just war theory admits have done nothing to deserve death? Does the source of harm have to pass some threshold of threat before one can speak of the need for its destruction outweighing civilian claims? If so, how to locate that threshold? More sharply, can one refer to the ultimate "worth" of hitting the military target to justify collateral civilian casualties without referring to the substantive justice of one's involvement in the war to begin with? Personally, I fail to grasp how it can be morally justified to foreseeably kill innocent civilians in order to hit a target which only serves the final end of an aggressive war. The only justification sufficient, in my mind, to justify the collateral civilian casualties would be that the target is materially connected to victory in an otherwise just war. This suggests, importantly, that aggressors not only violate *jus ad bellum*, but in so doing face grave difficulties meeting the requirements of *jus in bello* as well. To be as clear as possible: to satisfy the *jus in bello* requirement of discrimination, a country when fighting must satisfy all elements of the DDE. But it seems that only a country fighting a just war can fulfill the proportionality requirement in the DDE. Thus, an aggressor nation fighting an unjust war—for that very reason—also violates the rules of right conduct. Here too we see that traditional insistences on the separateness of *jus ad bellum* and *jus in bello* are not sustainable. Kant was more correct when he remarked on the need for a consistent normative thread to be run through conduct during all three phases of war: beginning, middle, and end.[40]

1.1.6. Child Soldiers

One recent issue, of grave concern, connected to non-combatant immunity is that of child soldiers. These are not unknown in history—Hitler notoriously conscripted German boys during the final, losing days of World War II, desperate as he was for any kind of manpower—but the modern concern revolves around Africa. Experts concur that, in the early 1980s, rebels in Mozambique fought a civil war against government forces. Outnumbered, the rebels tried to even the odds by kidnapping boys—some as young as 8!—from their parents, conscripting them into the rebel cause. The rebels would brainwash the boys, train them, abuse them, arm them, and then unleash them on government forces. Often, the child soldiers would be threatened and coerced, given drugs or alcohol, and be told that the whole thing was a giant game. Since then, child soldiers have been used extensively throughout African conflicts (and also in Asia). It is estimated that over 250,000 child soldiers have been used in Africa alone since 1980. Child soldiers, *as soldiers*, remain legitimate targets in wartime—they are, after all, still firing at you—but, in 2012, the use of child soldiers in armed conflict was declared a war crime by the International Criminal Court (the "ICC"; more in Chapter 6), punishable against those adult leaders brutal enough to use them. There are also necessary, encouraging efforts by such organizations as "Save the Children" to help rehabilitate former child soldiers back into productive life after a war, or after they get liberated from the fighting.[41]

1.2. PROPORTIONALITY

The *jus in bello* version of proportionality mandates that soldiers deploy only proportionate force against legitimate targets. The rule is not about the war as a whole; it is about tactics within the war. Make sure, the rule commands, that the destruction needed to fulfill the goal is proportional to the good of achieving it. The crude version of this rule is: don't squash a squirrel with a tank, or swat a fly with a cannon. *Use force appropriate to the target.* Walzer is as uncertain about this requirement as he was about its *jus ad bellum* cousin, and there is reason to follow him in this regard. He notes that while the rule is rightly designed to prohibit "excessive harm" and "purposeless or wanton violence" during war, "there is [nevertheless] no ready way to establish an independent or stable view of the values" against which we can definitively measure the costs and benefits of a tactic. One case where he talks about, and endorses, a form of proportionality involves the Persian Gulf War. During the War's final days in early 1991, there was a headlong retreat of Iraqi troops from Kuwait along a road, subsequently dubbed "The Highway of Death." So congested did that highway become that, when American forces descended upon it, it was a bloodbath whose aftermath was much photographed and publicized. Although the Iraqi soldiers did not surrender, and thus remained legitimate targets, Walzer suggests that the killing was "too easy." The battle degenerated into a "turkey shoot," and thus the force deployed was disproportionate. Perhaps another example, from the other side of the same war, would be Saddam Hussein's very damaging use of oil spills, and oil fires, as putative means of defense against a feared amphibious invasion of Kuwait by the Allies.[42] As with the *jus ad bellum* case, we note that it is much easier to diagnose a *disproportionate* use of force than a merely proportionate one. The common sense of the abstract need for balance and moderation is clearly there, but it remains very difficult to define precisely, especially under battlefield conditions. Here, too, it may turn out that proportionality is more of a limiting factor, a negative condition, so to speak—setting outside constraints on force—than it is a positive condition which adds new content to the just war equation.

1.3. PROHIBITED WEAPONS

Walzer insists that the "chief concern" in wartime is the question of *who* may be targeted with lethal force. Thus separating out civilian, from military, targets is all-important. The question of *what means* may be employed in the targeting is, in his view, "circumstantial." He suggests that the elaborate legal rules—contained in the Hague and Geneva Conventions—defining what means may, and what others may not, be employed during war are beside the point. These rules—such as those prohibiting the use of chemical weapons on the battlefield—may be desirable, he says, but are not morally obligatory. After all, if soldiers may be killed, how much can it matter by what means they are killed? While that is a persuasive way of putting the matter, Walzer should not be flippant about setting these rules aside, or assigning them second-place status in *jus in bello*, behind discrimination and the DDE. For the robust and elaborate set of legal rules banning the use of certain weapons in wartime seems to indicate a high level of international consensus. There is a vast number of relevant conventions and legal treaties on this issue, aside from the canonical Hague and Geneva Conventions, such as those banning the use of chemical (1925 and second protocol 1996), biological (1972), and "excessively injurious weapons" (1980). Also relevant are the conventions against genocide (1948) and against methods of warfare which alter the natural environment (1977). Prohibiting weapons also puts an added restriction upon belligerents and, as such, is consistent with the deepest aim of *jus in bello*, namely, to limit war's destruction. It's simply not enough, in my view, to let weapons development proliferate, as if to say: "Develop and deploy whatever weapon you want, just don't aim it at the suburbs." So I think international law corrects a weakness in Walzer by adding this further rule regarding weapons prohibition.[43]

The legal conventions regarding *jus in bello* are much more detailed, specific, and thickly textured than those mentioning *jus ad bellum*. It is interesting to reflect on the disparity. I suggest it has to do with two factors. First, usually those with the war power—like the executive branch—also negotiate international treaties, and they want maximum latitude in connection with reasons for going to war. Second, *jus in bello* seems to have developed first,[44] coming out of ancient and medieval conventions regarding chivalrous ways of battling, rules for knights' fighting tournaments, and so on. Indeed, even the Old Testament talks about not laying waste to fruit trees when attacking enemy cities.[45] So *jus in bello* has had more development than *jus ad bellum*, and so we should expect more detail. Just to sample the flavor of *jus in bello* rule in international law, consider the following snippet on "booby traps" from the convention banning excessively injurious weapons:

1. Without prejudice to the rules of international law applicable in armed conflict relating to treachery and perfidy, it is prohibited in all circumstances to use:
   (a) Any booby-trap in the form of an apparently harmless portable object which is specifically designed and constructed to contain explosive material and to detonate when it is disturbed or approached, or
   (b) Booby-traps which are in any way attached to or associated with:
      (i) Internationally recognized protective emblems, signs or signals;
      (ii) Sick, wounded or dead persons;
      (iii) Burial or cremation sites or graves;
      (iv) Medical facilities, medical equipment, medical supplies or medical transportation;
      (v) Children's toys or other portable objects or products specially designed for the feeding, health, hygiene, clothing or education of children;
      (vi) Food or drink;
      (vii) Kitchen utensils or appliances except in military establishments, military locations or military supply depots;
      (viii) Objects clearly of a religious nature;
      (ix) Historic monuments, works of art or places of worship which constitute the cultural or spiritual heritage of peoples;
      (x) Animals or carcasses.

2. It is prohibited in all circumstances to use any booby-trap which is designed to cause superfluous injury or unnecessary suffering.[46]

In addition to these remarkably detailed legal conventions, one might suggest that there is a widely shared moral convention which stipulates that, even though soldiers may be targeted with lethal force, some kinds of lethal force—such as burning them to death with flame-throwers, or asphyxiating them with nerve gas—inflict so much suffering, and express such cruelty, that they are properly condemned. Moreover, the reasoning which distinguishes between legitimate and illegitimate weapons is very similar to the reasoning which generates the combatant/non-combatant distinction. For example, there is a legal ban on using bullets which contain glass shards. These shards are essentially impossible to detect. If the soldier survives the shot, and the bullet is removed by surgery, odds are that some glass shards will still remain in his body. These shards can produce massive internal injuries, long after the soldier has ceased being "a dangerous man" to the other side. Parallel reasoning was behind the 1999 passing into law of the International Treaty Banning Land Mines: land mines, too frequently, remain weapons of destruction long after the conflict is over. (And they disproportionately injure children, who play in long-forgotten mine-fields.)[47] Finally, restrictions on weapons can play a causal role in reducing destruction and suffering in wartime, something which *jus in bello* as a whole is designed to secure. Walzer doesn't even explicitly object to particular weapons on grounds that they are more likely than not to have serious spillover effects on civilians, and thus run afoul of discrimination. Biological weapons would fall under this category, as would many land mines. Such a stance would be consistent with other judgments one might expect, but does not hear, from him, such as criticizing America's extensive use of napalm and Agent Orange in Vietnam, which inflicted long-term damage to Vietnamese agriculture. The aim, at the time, was to defoliate all the jungle vegetation which was providing such effective cover for the Viet Cong. The consequences include abnormally low soil fertility even today, with serious effects on staple crops such as rice. Walzer is curiously unreflective about these considerations, and I cannot agree in this regard: in addition to the general *jus in bello* principles, all belligerents must adhere to the applicable international laws regarding weaponry.[48]

Walzer recovers his reflectiveness about weaponry only when he considers nuclear arms, which for a number of reasons have not clearly been declared illegal by ratified international treaty. (The main reason, of course, is that the major powers are all nuclear powers, and they would never agree to such a treaty, as it would eliminate a major military advantage they all share.) "Nuclear weapons explode the theory of just war," Walzer famously declares.[49] This is a graphic and gripping, but unfortunate, formulation since it seems to endorse the popular academic view that just war theory is out of date in the post-Hiroshima world. But Walzer cannot believe this, for he believes that the atomic bombing of Japan was unjust. Thus, what his dramatic declaration must really mean is that nuclear weapons can never be employed justly. Why not? First, and most crucially for Walzer, they are radically *indiscriminate* weapons. Perhaps only a handful of the most volatile biological weapons are more uncontrollable in their effects. Second, nuclear weapons are unimaginably destructive, not just in terms of short-term obliteration but also long-term radiation poisoning and climate change, so that their use will always run afoul of *proportionality*. Finally, there is the hint in Walzer that, owing to these two factors combined, the deliberate use of nuclear weapons—and emphatically an all-out nuclear war—would be an act *evil in itself*.[50]

Some people, perhaps first starting with Henry Kissinger, believe it might be possible to use nuclear weapons in a discriminate way. Their notion is to use very low-yield nuclear bombs directly on a battlefield against the enemy. I suppose in theory that might be possible but then: 1) there's still the question of proportionality; and 2) what would be the real difference between such bombs and conventional explosives? Perhaps it would just be the expense and strategy of 5 low-yield nukes versus 50 conventional, very high-yield conventional bombs (such as the "Daisy-Cutter," used recently to destroy mountain ranges in Afghanistan, aiming to bury the cave networks underneath believed to harbor terrorists). But I suspect the real strategy behind having nukes in the first place is the massive intimidation factor, in which case the low-yield nukes are useless. Low-yield nukes might be more discriminating—though it would be comforting to hear nuclear scientists say this rather than foreign policy strategists—but then their deterrent and intimidation factors would be undercut. The most useful aspect of nuclear weapons is precisely the deterrent and intimidation properties brought about by their highly destructive yield. But it is that exact yield which is morally objectionable, owing to the incredible destruction and lack of discrimination. In other words, perhaps nukes can be made discriminate but in such an event they won't be much different than conventional missiles—maybe save you a few bucks on transportation. The really useful nukes, so to speak and by contrast, are precisely the ones it's never morally permissible to use—wildly powerful and indiscriminately destructive.[51]

What about building, testing, and threatening to use such nukes but never actually using them (except twice on Japan)? Some moral thinkers believe that it's wrong to *threaten* to do something which it's *actually* wrong to do (e.g., threaten to murder someone), and so there are deep moral questions to be raised even about this. (Our legal systems reflect this: it's a separate crime merely to utter a death threat.) On the other hand, some politicians and historians credit America's nuclear deterrence with having stopped Soviet expansion, and with having won the Cold War. These latter are sweeping claims, and probably untrue—communism still expanded massively in the 1945–85 era, after all, so what exactly did American nuclear deterrence stop? I thus think that, from a just war point of view, nuclear weapons are going to be pretty dimly viewed no matter how they are interpreted. Nuclear deterrence does, though, raise issues of realism and emergency which we'll return to in later chapters. In particular, someone might admit that there are these serious moral problems with having, and certainly with using, such weapons but, given that "the genie is out of the bottle," isn't it alright to seek such weapons more for self-protection than anything else? The morality of having/using such weapons occurs in a context, not a vacuum, and given that the context is one in which others already have/use them, isn't it consistent with state duties to protect to try to avail themselves of these weapons—at least so they can't be bullied by those with the intimidating nuclear deterrent? This problem—a real one—is in my view best dealt with in our forthcoming discussions of emergencies and particularly realism, and the question of to what degree must just war theory make accommodations in its direction. The short answer now, for which we'll explain more then, is that it might—under very rare conditions—be *excusable* to build or even perhaps to use nuclear weapons but that it will never be *morally justified* to do so.

1.4. NO MEANS *"MALA IN SE"*

There is a traditional ban on "means *mala in se*," Latin for "methods evil in themselves." The imprecise yet interesting idea here is that some weapons and means of war are forbidden not so much because of the badness of the consequences they inflict but, more importantly, because they themselves are intrinsically awful. Using rape as a tool of warfare—e.g., to drive a population off a territory, or to "reward" one's troops after battle—is a clear example. Rape is ruled out not so much because of all the pain it produces, or because it is aimed at civilians, but because the act itself is rights-violating, a disgusting disregard for the humanity of the woman raped: a coercive violation of her bodily integrity and her entitlement to choose her own sex partner(s).[52] Methods like campaigns of genocide, ethnic cleansing, and torture probably also fall under this category. We don't have to do a cost-benefit analysis to determine whether such are impermissible in warfare: we already judge such acts to be heinous crimes because of their very nature. We have an almost visceral rejection of them. Indeed, the international community passed a convention in 1948 banning genocide, and recently resorted to armed force over Kosovo in Serbia to punish its practice (though it failed to do so earlier in Rwanda, and later in Darfur). Arguably—following upon our above discussion—the use of child soldiers ought also to be considered a means *mala in se*.[53]

1.5. REPRISALS

Reprisals are not permitted in the laws of armed conflict: there is a prohibition on them. At the same time, they have happened in history, are rather frequently threatened during wartime, and such just war luminaries as Walzer allow for reprisals in their theories. Let's examine the controversy. The reprisal doctrine permits a violation of *jus in bello* rules—but only in response to a prior violation by the opposing side. To his credit, Walzer refuses to condone any violation of the rule of discrimination as part of reprisal: "we must condemn all reprisals against innocent people." What of proportionality and no means "*mala in se*"? While he does not say so, one supposes Walzer cannot allow a violation of the latter rule for mere reprisal purposes. His single example of a justified reprisal focuses on proportionality and prohibited weapons. He claims that Winston Churchill was "entirely justified when he warned the German government early in World War II that the use of [poison] gas by its army would bring an immediate Allied reprisal." Such threats by heads of state have apparently become rather commonplace, since American President George Bush, Sr. warned Iraq in 1991 that, should it deploy chemical weapons on the battlefield, America would reserve the right to deploy other weapons of mass destruction, up to and including nuclear armaments. It is important to note here that, presumably, Walzer means that not only the threat but also the threatened action are grounded by his doctrine of reprisal.[54]

Walzer justifies his permission for retaliations on the need to enforce the rules of the war convention during battle: "It is the explicit purpose of reprisals ... to stop the wrongdoing *here* [his italics] with this final act" of *jus in bello* violation. Reprisals are designed to make the enemy stop its own *jus in bello* transgressions: state S violates proportionality, say, and state T responds in kind so as to punish S and hopefully prevent future violations.[55] Can we come up with relevant modern examples? Perhaps America's 1986 bombing of Libya, as retaliation for the latter's involvement in previous terrorist strikes, or America's 1998 bombing of suspected terrorist sites in Sudan and Afghanistan as reprisals for presumed involvement in American embassy bombings throughout Africa in the '90s.

Walzer's reprisal doctrine is worrisome. It ignores the serious likelihood that reprisals, far from chastening the organization which originally violated *jus in bello*, will actually spur further violations. Libya, after all, sponsored the Lockerbie jet bombing in 1988—*after* the American strike—and we know that the US cruise missile attacks on al-Qaeda training sites in 1998 didn't deter 9/11 in 2001. To put it in just war terms, reprisals have dubious probability of success. After all, what government is likely to simply sit there and suffer a violation of *jus in bello*? If it's the government that committed the first, unbidden, violation, why would it hesitate to commit a second one in response? It's not the kind of group that would be "scared straight." If it's the government that received the first violation, then it will, not implausibly, fear that a failure to respond in kind will only whet its opponent's appetite for more destruction. Reprisal, in short, is a recipe for escalation, at its extreme risking the onset of total war, a phenomenon just war theory utterly rejects.

Walzer might contend that a certain kind of reprisal may well succeed in stopping escalation. Of course it *may*, but what kind of reprisal is that likely to be? Realistically, it seems, only a very severe, disproportionate one. And while Walzer extends his reprisal permissions solely in terms of relaxing proportionality (and not, thankfully, in terms of relaxing discrimination/non-combatant immunity), we can still ask: how much is too much relaxation? Or is there too much relaxation at all when it comes to reprisals? Might Walzer, for example, condone the Gulf War "turkey shoot" incident on the Highway of Death if it were in reprisal, say for Iraq setting Kuwait's oil wells on fire? Or if state T were to lose one brigade of its soldiers to nerve gas unleashed unbidden by state S, does that mean for Walzer that, to ensure an effective enforcement of the rules, T should now gas two, three, four brigades of S's soldiers in response? Or perhaps deploy a tactical nuclear device against S's battlefield positions? For me, these are rhetorical questions.

Reprisal is a very tempting option in warfare, especially when one notes that, given its nature, the aggressor nation will most likely be the one which first violates *jus in bello*. And while relaxing proportionality against legitimate targets may feel like a fitting response to prior violations of a principle as important as discrimination/non-combatant immunity—for instance, gassing enemy soldiers who engaged in civilian massacre—it is unlikely to achieve its more reasoned goal of deterring future violations. As deterrence, reprisal is dubious. As retribution, reprisal may seem elemental, yet it is unlikely to achieve more than a modest, temporary satisfaction of popular outrage. It would thus seem far better to adhere to the policy adopted from a familiar phrase: *winning well is the best revenge*. This is to say the aim should be to win the war without violating *jus in bello* at all. But what if, Walzer would ask, one cannot put the two together: what if winning cannot be had, in the real world, by fighting well and by resisting the sinful pleasures of revenge? What if, ultimately, violating *jus in bello* seems the only way to stave off devastating loss?

Walzer notes that, when it comes to war, "we want to have it both ways: moral decency in battle and victory in war; constitutionalism in hell and ourselves outside."[56] We are therefore confronted with a grave dilemma when it looks as though we can win the war only by setting aside the rules of right conduct. Walzer, to his credit, refuses to indulge the fantasy that such situations cannot actually happen. His way out of this dark dilemma, however, is one of the most difficult and controversial aspects of his just war theory. It is his doctrine of *supreme emergency* and it permits not merely violation of proportionality against enemy soldiers but even violation of discrimination/non-combatant immunity against enemy civilians. It is something like the ultimate, no-holds-barred reprisal against the ultimate threat. How does Walzer pose, and then respond to, this grave problem? This is such a difficult question that it deserves a separate chapter, the next one.

1.6. RULES FOR THE RICH?

Before moving on to internal *jus in bello*, we must confront a criticism of external *jus in bello*. There are some people who argue that only rich and powerful nations can afford to satisfy these rules. These rules are thus unfairly stacked in their favor. Poorer countries, lacking things like smart bombs and drones, are thus doubly condemned: condemned to lose; and condemned as war criminals for using the "dirtier," older, and less discriminate weapons and tactics, which are within their means. I agree with these people that the rules must be fair but disagree with the rest of this complaint. It boils down to the analogous claim that poor people can't be ethical. This elitist claim, with a history going back to Plato and Aristotle, is not true. Perhaps poor people can't give as much money to charity as rich people but they are just as capable of being honest, kind, decent, hard-working, courageous, moderate, and just. And poor people, in domestic society, are perfectly capable of obeying laws against murder, rape, and assault. Similarly, poor nations can fight in accord with these *jus in bello* rules. It's not too much to ask them to refrain from bombing or terrorizing civilians, torturing prisoners, dropping down nukes, engaging in reprisals, and so on. They might resent the wealth and weaponry of rich nations, but these emotions don't give them a "poor man's right" to fight dirty. We know from history, after all, that wealth and advanced weaponry are no guarantee of decent behavior on the battlefield. Indeed, aggression is usually committed by powerful nations against the weak. Fundamentally, whether rich or poor, a nation makes a decision to fight decently or dirtily: you can fight within your means decently, or fight within your means dirtily. In other words, it's not a question of means but rather of moral choice. Fighting decently is no guarantee of victory, I concede. But there's never any guarantee that doing the right thing is always going to serve one's interests, or make one happy. Think of personal cases where you do your duty (e.g., avoid stealing) even though it prevents you from doing something which would make you more happy (e.g., getting a new car without having to pay for it). Poverty, or relative under-development, is no justification for committing war crimes. This complaint is a pathetic plea for excuses—of terrible actions—when none are justly warranted.

1.7. EMERGING MILITARY TECHNOLOGIES (EMTS)

There are four EMTs which get mentioned the most today:

- *Cyber-warfare*. This is the use of advanced computer-based, and Internet-based, technologies for: *espionage* (i.e., data-gathering); or for spreading *disinformation* (i.e., damaging, embarrassing lies); or for *sabotage* (i.e., destruction). Cyber-warfare deserves its own extended treatment, next chapter.

- *Non-lethal weapons.* These are otherwise known as "incapacitating agents." Today's militaries are anxious to keep the body count low in war, as publics—especially in voting democracies—don't like to see big and bloody casualty totals. Incapacitating agents range from such everyday law-enforcement tools as pepper spray and Taser electric-shock guns to sophisticated, military-scale weaponry. The US military, e.g., possesses a weapon (the "Dazzler") which, if deployed on the battlefield, would result in permanent blindness for anyone not wearing their specially-fitted eye-gear. It is an intensely bright, dazzling laser discharge which, essentially, fries the retinas of everyone within eye-sight unless they have specially-calibrated eye shields. The thinking is that such incapacitated enemies would then promptly surrender, and have their lives—but not their eye-sight—saved. (More below.)[57]

- *Soldier enhancements.* Militaries know that they are limited, significantly, by the limits of the human body. This is especially true for the land-based army. They are thus keenly interested in anything which will enhance soldier performance on patrol, and especially in battle. Thus, vision-, smell-, and hearing technologies are constantly being improved upon. Of special interest are drug-related enhancements designed to minimize the need for rest and sleep, and to maximize battle-ready alertness and energy levels. The US military, e.g., has designed (but does not use) a "souped-up" cocktail (of forms of cocaine, adrenaline, caffeine, testosterone, etc.) which allows some soldiers to maintain battle-ready energy, with no sleep, for 72 hours—three days!—straight.[58]

- *Unmanned systems.* These refer to robots and drones. Voting publics don't like losing their own soldiers, and so increasing use is being made of weapons systems which are un-manned, and operated either by robots, or from a distance by remote control using satellites and GPS technology. Probably the highest-profile of these are drones, which are unmanned small planes which can be flown remotely, often without enemy radar detection, and can be used for espionage and surveillance, or to drop bombs and shoot missiles. The US military has rapidly escalated its use of drone technology over the past 10 years, especially as part of the War on Terror for surveilling rogue regimes and attacking terrorist bases, particularly throughout the MENA region. (Analysis below.)[59]

International law often plays catch-up to new technology, as states are slow to come to both full understanding and full agreement. So, when we consider the EMTs, we cannot draw on existing international law treaties, as there are none. We are thus squarely within the field of ethics and just war theory. As an exercise, then, how might just war theory evaluate two of these EMTs: 1) "The Dazzler"; and 2) drones?

"The Dazzler," as mentioned, hasn't actually been used in battle yet, in spite of the fact that it's been around for a while. My own view is that the likely reason for this is that the US military has had a hard time squaring "The Dazzler" with the principles of just war theory. First, the light blast is *indiscriminate*, and anyone within the field of vision who's not wearing the special defensive goggles will be rendered blind. There is thus a serious risk of the weapon hitting civilians (unless it's deployed in a truly isolated battlefield, such as the desert or the high seas). The last thing the US military wants, from a public relations standpoint, is a collection of innocent civilians rendered permanently blind by one of its weapons. There is also the concern that, because the effects of the weapon are permanent, it may be *disproportionate*, with negative consequences lasting long after the targeted soldiers have ceased being "dangerous men." And there is the whole issue of what sight means to us, and how deeply we associate it with our experience of life. Thus, intentionally robbing someone of something so central to their identity and functioning might be seen as *especially cruel and vicious*, perhaps verging on a "means *mala in se*."

The reason why the weapon was developed in the first place was with the hunch that it might actually be humane, in the sense that those struck by "The Dazzler" would, presumably, surrender upon being rendered blind. They would then have their lives spared. Fair enough, but suppose we were to ask soldiers: which would you choose—certain blindness (but survival), or else take your chances on the battlefield, with possible risk of death? I don't pretend to know how most soldiers would vote in this regard, but I do think that the answer would be by no means clear-cut, and that some may well prefer the latter instead of the prospect of a life without sight. Finally, there's the risk with this weapon that, should one's own soldiers make errors with the fitting-on of the goggles, they too would be rendered blind, and obviously no military wants to be responsible for permanently damaging its own.[60]

Drones, by contrast, have been used, and used a-plenty. Since their invention, their use has sky-rocketed, especially as a tool in the War on Terror.[61] Does this mean that the US military believes that drones pass the principles of just war theory? Presumably so, but what's interesting is how much criticism this program has come in for, since its inception. What are the pros and cons of drones?

The pros include the following. First, drones clearly save lives on your own side, as they are un-manned systems. If they get shot down, not one of your own soldiers is going to die. B.J. Strawser has argued that, to the extent to which a government possesses such a weapon, yet refuses to use it, it is derelict in its duty to do what it can to protect its own people.[62] Second, drones make extensive use of both espionage data and precise satellite and GPS technology, rendering them perhaps the "smartest," most precise targeting systems yet invented. They are thus, arguably, a tribute to the principle of discrimination/non-combatant immunity. Third, drones are cost-effective. While they are very expensive on a per-unit basis—since they are such advanced pieces of technology—they are very cheap compared to what it would cost to land soldiers on the ground, deep in enemy soil, and task them with achieving the same objective. Fourth, drones excel at achieving surprise, as they can patrol at ultra-high altitudes, far-away from their intended target. It's axiomatic of military strategy that you want to achieve a surprise strike, if you can. Finally, drones are an expression of technological advantage and excellence, and thus telegraph strength to the international community and, as such, arguably serve not only as weapons of targeted destruction but also as tools of deterrence. If enemy countries, or terrorists, realize that now, in addition to the threat of soldier invasion, there is the silent-yet-deadly, removed-yet-immediate, threat of suffering a drone strike, then perhaps this may constitute one further tool by way of frustrating their agenda and aims. Shouldn't we encourage such people to feel that they are being surveilled continuously, and that they may suffer a severe price if they keep up their aggressive ways?[63]

On the other side of the ledger, there have been recorded cases of drones missing their intended targets—or having been fed inaccurate data—resulting in civilian casualties. Verified exact figures are not agreed-upon, but we can predict that this would be true at least to some extent, given that it's been true of every other weapons system. The real question is: are drones especially likely to be sloppy in this regard? Are they uniquely unreliable and indiscriminate? We need a fuller disclosure of information before we can pronounce definitively. However, recent studies have suggested: 1) that rates of civilian casualty by drones are getting smaller through time; and 2) they are actually smaller than rates produced by other weapons systems.[64] Another criticism of drone technology, harkening back to Ignatieff's concerns, connects to the so-called "warrior ethos." There seems to be something weird and distasteful about drones being piloted and guided by computer programmers half-a-world away, isolated from the action and removed from the battlefield. Is such not an act of cowardice? Won't that degree of removal from the situation make targeting errors much more likely, resulting in needless and perhaps innocent death? What becomes of the image of the warrior when drone warfare is at play? We now seem to have something more like the figure of the video-gamer, as opposed to the courageous commander-on-the-field, leading his troops into battle.[65] Finally, there is the notion that drone warfare makes killing all-too-easy, and thus is a serious temptation in favor of disproportionate violence, or maybe even secret warfare, in violation of the public authority rule. Some thinkers are convinced that, the easier we make killing, the more likely we are to resort to it, and thus these weapons are not weapons of peace but, rather, weapons for escalation. And this ties into the claim regarding deterrence: isn't the constant threat of drone strikes more likely to fuel more rage amongst terrorists? They are unlikely to be deterred by this technology—but they are likely to be angered by it, and to whip up public anger against it and against the perceived arrogance of those who can unleash such awesome destruction, unseen from the heavens above.[66]

Whenever there is new technology, there is a lot of unease about it, and many exaggerated claims both pro and con. It may well be that, in the birth-pangs of this technology, all the above claims—on both side—are true, and efforts are now being made to feed the drones better data, program them with more reliable targeting, and thus lessen concerns with discrimination. As for making killing easier, this is true of every weapon which has ever been invented, and thus drones don't seem to suffer unduly from it. As for the notion of the warrior ethos, we do in our culture have a clear commitment to the ideal of the brave soldier, present on the battlefield, risking his or her life for the sake of defending those who can't defend themselves. This is an admirable ideal. However, it seems unlikely that drones will ever replace the need for having soldiers on the ground, certainly when it comes to regime change and post-war reconstruction, when people have to be present and visible, involved and responsible.[67] But the use of drones as first-strike weapons within the broader War on Terror can be rendered consistent with that ideal: soldiers need an array of tools to best defend the community whose lives and rights they represent. And drones seem especially cost-effective, and effective at striking targets deep within the territory of a country unable, or unwilling, to do its part in co-operating in the War on Terror. There is also something to be said in favor of being removed from the immediate situation, wherein fear, rage, chaos and confusion can cloud one's judgment, and lead to battlefield mistakes—whereas remote targeting systems can allow one to be more cool and dispassionate. This leaves the real concern, for me, which is the issue of the feeding of intelligence and the need to do the due diligence required before ordering a drone strike, and ensuring that, ultimately, any drone program is controlled properly by public authorities and that there is a proper chain of command which features, at least amongst its own people, accountability and a public rationale for the use of this kind of long-range weapon wherein denial-of-use, and stealth use, are constantly possible. Thus, I don't think there's anything to the drone weapon-as-such which violates just war principles, but I do think certain ways in which drones are currently deployed could be improved upon: not having the CIA be completely in charge; being totally transparent about the role this weapon plays; and constantly being vigilant about improving collateral civilian casualty rates.[68]

2. Transition from External to Internal *Jus in Bello*

We've argued that, externally or vis-à-vis the enemy, a society in the midst of war must adhere to the following rules: 1) discrimination and non-combatant immunity; 2) benevolent quarantine for POWs; 3) due care for civilians; 4) the DDE; 5) proportionality; 6) no means *mala in se*; 7) no reprisals; 8) no use of banned weaponry; and now 9) something like, "proceed cautiously, under the guidance of just war theory, when it comes to new EMTs." Now, what of the internal issue? How should a government, in the midst of war, conduct itself vis-à-vis its own citizens? This is not a question commonly asked, much less answered, by conventional just war theorists. But we wish to go beyond convention and be as comprehensive and up-to-date as we can. Manifestly, these are issues of justice in wartime, and thus fall under the logical scope of just war theory. So consider the principles which follow.

3. The Internal Rules

3.1. ADHERE TO THE EXTERNAL RULES

This principle, simply put, is this: follow the external rules, both in terms of *jus ad bellum* and *jus in bello*. How is this an "internal" rule? It is internal owing to the force and grounding of its sense and meaning, as well as to draw tight conceptual and moral linkages between the internal and external rules. The branch of government constitutionally entitled to the war power should commit to following all the external rules not only because of its duties regarding its relations with the enemy country, or with the international community either politically or legally, but also because of its duties to its own people. This is to say that it is a fundamental obligation of every government not to engage in aggressive war or to commit war crimes. This was already established above, but what this section highlights is that this duty is owed to several entities: it stretches out to the international community, and especially to any enemy countries, but also pulls inward to one's own populace. One is, after all, declaring war in their name, launching war to protect them and to vindicate their fundamental rights, whether as individual persons or national communities. They are not entitled to engage in aggression or war crimes and, since their individual human rights ultimately ground all the war entitlements under investigation here, one is not entitled to engage in aggressive war or war crimes on their behalf. One needs to make a firm, sincere, public commitment—whether by public declaration, statute, or constitutional entrenchment in those provisions outlining the war power—to adhere to each and every one of the external rules. One owes it to one's own people to wage war only in conformity with *jus ad bellum*, and then to fight that war without resorting to war crimes.

3.2. RESPECTING DOMESTIC HUMAN RIGHTS

The second, and perhaps most vital, internal rule is to respect the human rights of one's citizens—be they soldier or civilian—as far as possible during wartime. This norm is codified in the "Protocol I Additional" to the Geneva Convention.[69] Let us discuss some of the most fundamental issues, as well as stress their vital importance. This is not an idle thought experiment: human rights protection comes at a price. It takes real resources and commitment to make rights real. During a serious war, there will be strong incentive for even legitimate governments to use as many resources as possible—including some previously devoted to domestic rights satisfaction—in order to fight the war with maximum effect. In fact, this consideration of rights protection on the domestic front is an especially important aspect of just war thinking, since some of the most gruesome human rights violations in wartime (e.g., the Holocaust and the Rwandan genocide) have occurred within, and not between, national borders. Belligerent governments are not entitled to use the cloak of war with foreign powers in order to commit massive human rights violations domestically, usually victimizing some disfavored racial, ethnic, linguistic, and/or religious minority. More recently, in connection with the aftermath of 9/11, legitimate governments around the world have drafted controversial sets of anti-terrorist, or emergency regime, legislation which legal scholars (among others) have questioned, especially regarding whether such extraordinary powers are genuinely needed to fight the war on terrorism and whether, in fact, they count as excessive abrogations or curtailments of civilian rights.[70]

3.2.1. Rights on the Civilian Side

Much of the literature on this complex issue focuses on what a regime, which finds itself embroiled in an emergency, may or may not do regarding the suspension or abrogation of human rights on the domestic front.[71] The so-called "Paris Minimum Standards," and the 1977 Second Amendment to the Geneva Convention, were both designed with this explicitly in mind, and they enshrine a list of human rights which are to be regarded as "non-derogable"—which is to say untouchable or absolute—even in such a public emergency as war.[72] These rights include: life; not to be tortured; not to be enslaved; not to be taken hostage; "minimal judicial guarantees"; non-discrimination; not to be subject to medical experiment; not to be subject to retroactive laws; recognition as a legal person; freedom of thought, conscience, and religion; a fair trial; a subsistence level of food and water; and special protections for children.

While that is a very laudable list, there seems to be movement, within the international human rights community, away from the very concept of derogability. Derogability, after all, suggests that, under usual circumstances, there is a set of human rights which governments are to respect as a condition of legitimacy.

However, when push comes to shove—e.g., during an emergency like wartime—the state can cut back on some human rights, but must still preserve a small core, the so-called "non-derogables," such as those listed above. The preference nowadays, and certainly my own, is that human rights must be thought of as forming an interlocking whole, for instance that entire set of entitlements demanded when we focus on the one concept of guaranteeing to every human being a minimally good life. Since human rights form an interlocking whole, there is no question of picking some over others for privileged protection, while the others may fall away when pressure is put on public resources. It is all or nothing, and I believe this is demanded by the quest for consistency in human rights theory: to what extent can we refer to the ones which may be "pruned away" as genuinely human rights at all? Better not to refer to them in that way, owing to the primary value and importance we wish to attach to human rights as, in John Rawls's words, constituting the very foundation of political and legal morality in our era.[73]

Failing to endorse derogability does not mean that one must, fancifully, commit a government shouldered with the real burdens of fighting a just and difficult war to an extravagant agenda regarding human rights fulfillment. It means, rather, that one has to be both strict and frugal when one is deciding what truly counts as a human right in the first place. There has been a noticeable trend of "human rights inflation" over time, according to which ever more, and ever more luxurious, items have been claimed as a matter of human right. But human rights are precious things, and they are cheapened when people try to elevate any old claim or preference they have into the status of a struggle over human rights. As I have written elsewhere,[74] as human beings we are only entitled as a matter of human right to claim those objects we genuinely need to live a minimally good life in the modern world. A minimally good life is one where we are both assured, as Jim Nickel says, of *having* a life (i.e., the minimal subsistence and physical security conditions we require to exist in society) and of *leading* that life as well (i.e., the freedom, social recognition, and non-discrimination we each require to pursue our own life plans). Moreover, all such claims must be such as to put only reasonable, bearable burdens upon the shoulders of others and social institutions. I have already argued that this means that we all have claims to only five foundational human rights objects: personal security; material subsistence; personal liberty; elemental equality; and social recognition.

All this by way of considering, in a deeper sense, what rights standards ought to be adhered to by governments hard-pressed in wartime. The general answer is that governments must be committed to respecting each and every *bona fide* human rights claim made by civilian or soldier. The human rights outlined above form a package. *They are a whole, not a hierarchy.* It is not true that as human beings we need security more than we need subsistence, or subsistence more than we need freedom. We need them all if we are to lead minimally good lives, as creatures who both have a life and can lead it as well. Thus, for example, to prune away the freedoms (or civil liberties) on the grounds that such pruning is needed to provide for greater security is in principle fallacious and misguided: it doesn't give up what is less important in exchange for what is more; it gives up something just as important as the other and actually attacks people's ability to lead minimally good lives in any event. To take it to the extreme, why should citizens care if they still have their lives if such lives are not minimally good anyway—if they feel their lives are not worth living?

We should reject the thinking that turns rights into mere social privileges, granted by generous governments. Human rights are not mere privileges, they are *entitlements* which government *owe* to their people. Nor are human rights mere social utilities; in fact human rights were explicitly designed to guarantee a minimally good life to everyone in the face of utility calculations and pressures to make social trade-offs which favor the majority. Human rights form a coherent, non-hierarchical whole where each of them is needed as a component of what it means to live a minimally good or decent life in the modern world. Without their satisfaction, no one has reason to sign on to the social contract constitutive of political order in the first place.

3.2.2. *Curtailing Human Rights?*

History contains a litany of massive overkill when it comes to government suspension of civil liberties in wartime. While the one end of the spectrum deals with such terrible events as the Holocaust, the more moderate end of the spectrum deals with events like the forced internment of Americans and Canadians of Japanese descent during World War II.[75] Legitimate governments, like other governments, enjoy power and have internal bureaucratic impulses towards the expansion of that power. It is very natural for them to take advantage of the wartime atmosphere to pursue that agenda, when resistance will be distracted or minimal. But governments have as their ultimate point and purpose the fulfillment of the human rights of all their citizens, and thus cannot consistently engage in an attack on, or derogation of, those same human rights, even if during wartime. In my view, most (but perhaps not all) emergency regime legislation is probably not morally justified, but rather constitutes an unjustified invasion of civil liberties and human rights by governments which are either panicked by a severe, yet temporary, external crisis and/or which have their own internal impulses towards government growth at the expense of those very entitlements whose realization actually constitutes their reason-for-being. Suspension of such things as freedom of peaceful assembly, free speech, and freedom of the press, we know, are things which cannot contribute in any meaningful way to augmenting the resources one has to fight a war. They merely make criticism of government, and protests against its war policy, more difficult. Suspension of *some* aspects of freedom of movement might, by contrast, be more defensible in wartime. While people might still otherwise be free to move around the country or to leave it altogether, it makes for clear sense to prevent them from wandering into battle zones. In this event, the heaviest burden rests with any government proposing any such restriction—it must have a clear and manifest connection to the legitimate operation of an otherwise justified war.

Suspension of the right to vote is an especially fearsome thing. While it might be argued that running an election in the midst of war has *bona fide* costs—running into many millions, which might be otherwise spent on the war effort—the risks in favor of tyranny, or at least an unjustified extension and growth of government power at the expense of civil liberties, are simply too extreme. Plus, there are relevant historical cases here. Take a big country like America, where running elections is indeed a huge and costly enterprise. Both Abraham Lincoln and Franklin Roosevelt won presidential elections which were held under deeply pressured wartime conditions. Surely, then, elections can run be run elsewhere, in smaller countries with fewer voters facing less severe challenges. Or there might be reasonable, middle-of-the-road solutions, such as the requirement laid out in Canada's Charter of Rights and Freedoms which allows, in time of warfare, for Parliament to continue sitting beyond the normal maximum of five years provided that no more than one third of the current elected members oppose such a move.

The story is similar when it comes to the suspension of due process rights, which are among the most frequently targeted by a government in the midst of war. It might be argued that running a proper police and court system is quite expensive, and such resources could be used instead to fight the war. In the current War on Terror, moreover, it is argued that, owing to the suddenness with which the enemy can exert incredibly deadly force, the slowness of police and court procedures actually puts public safety in jeopardy. To a point, these are true claims. Yet entitling a government to run roughshod over due process rights is extremely dangerous, in some cases looking much like the regular practice of a rights-violating (and thus illegitimate) regime. There might be room for plausible middle-of-the-road compromises here, which retain much of the substance of the right without sacrificing its principle. For instance, powers of seizure, arrest, and detention might be augmented, enabling for timely and efficient capture of suspects, but then the court system and due process remain fully intact so that those genuinely innocent will be fully empowered to be released and exonerated in due course as well. Suspects are quickly off the street and in custody, yet still fully entitled to due process. It fits in with this line of thinking, e.g., to note that the US Supreme Court decided, in June 2004, that terrorist suspects detained in Guantanamo Bay, Cuba, can avail themselves of US court procedures to determine whether their detention is appropriate under American law. Here you have the mix of rapid detention alongside material aspects of due process.[76]

3.2.3. *Conscription*

In terms of the just war literature, by far and away the most written-about aspect of domestic rights fulfillment during wartime is the issue of conscription. A just, rights-respecting society ought, on the basis of the human right to freedom of conscience, to abide by the good-faith claims of conscientious objectors, and/or pacifists, to be exempt from military service. A just state in the midst of a serious and justified war may, however, reasonably ask for some assistance from conscientious objectors, such as clerical or administrative work, in return for respecting their personal beliefs that they ought not to kill (much less be forced to kill) for political reasons. So, a state ought to meet its military needs through voluntary enlistment, where possible. There are many incentives which armed forces can, and do, employ to keep enlistments at the desired levels: subsidized post-secondary education, housing, and food, alongside guaranteed job slots, are some of the most popular. As most military experts agree, very rarely is there a credible military—as opposed to political—case for universal conscription: there are diminishing marginal returns, and huge inefficiencies, when it comes to dealing with such an enormous body of conscripts. The whole trend in the military arts is away from huge, labor-intensive fighting forces in favor of more nimble, less-manned and more technology-laden solutions, in any event.[77]

3.2.4. *The Judiciary*

The judiciary ought to be empowered when it comes to determining any proposed infringement or suspension of any civil liberty or human right during wartime. We just noted how the US Supreme Court asserted itself in this regard, in connection with the Guantanamo detainees. The judiciary is one of the bulwarks protecting human rights in most legitimate societies, and so it should here play a manifest and integral role. Its expertise in diagnosing, in detailed instances, when a civil liberty or constitutionally guaranteed right has been infringed *must* here be drawn upon. There is no reason why the standard slowness of the judicial process should be an objection to this proposal. During wartime, or leading up to wartime, government lawyers could for instance propose desired curtailments directly to higher levels of the judiciary in special sessions. Opponents of any such curtailments, such as bar societies, civil liberties lawyers, civil society or non-governmental organizations, could be welcomed into such hearings as "friends of the court," entitled to give counter-arguments and counter-proposals. But the judiciary's decision ought to be recognized as decisive, and in my view must give the heaviest priority to ensuring human rights satisfaction and ensuring that those very rights-respecting principles which make governments legitimate are not taken away in haste or else insidiously eroded under the auspices of security.

In sum, we can predict how, in crisis, even legitimate governments will naturally incline towards utility-based thinking: "national security"; "the public or greater good"; "what's good for the country"; etc. But the whole point of rights—or, at least, of human rights—is not merely to benefit people in general, or to protect the well-being of the majority, but also to be mindful of *every individual* human being's need for protection. There is no defensible hierarchy according to which one can sacrifice one human right for the sake of another—they all go together and form a package. There is also historical evidence showing standard overkill regarding civil liberties suspension, and so we should wonder not only about the morality but also about the strategic usefulness of any proposed wartime clipping of vital entitlements.

3.2.5. Rights on the Soldier Side

What human rights can soldiers claim vis-à-vis their own governments in the midst of war? It is often thought that any such claims must be minimal, if they exist at all. Soldiers are, after all, the very agents of war, and wars cannot effectively be fought if soldiers are busy clogging up the court system with human rights litigation against their own government. While this is true, as far as it goes, it is manifestly untrue that soldiers fail to have human rights. As human beings, they are entitled to the foundational five rights: to security, subsistence, liberty, equality, and recognition. The question, we've seen, has less to do with their forfeiture of any of these claims and more to do with the precise meaning of them in a wartime, soldierly context. Let's run through our list of "the foundational five" and consider the human rights issues more fully.

The right to personal security This phrase is older than, and without the misleading associations of, the phrase "right to life." It means something quite different in a soldierly context than it does in a peacetime civilian context. It does not mean that soldiers have a right not to be killed, or not to be put in circumstances where it is foreseeable that some of them might be killed. That is a promise which simply cannot be squared with the very practice of being a soldier. What it does mean is that—given that being a soldier is an inherently dangerous profession, undertaken in defense of someone else's life and liberty—soldiers have the right: to sound and serious military training; to be free from severe and dangerous inaugural or "hazing" rituals; to be free, as female soldiers, from sexual assault and harassment; and to have good, functional equipment and weapons which enable them to perform their job. A government which fails to provide these to its soldier class violates their human right to physical security: it fails to deliver the goods needed to realize the principle in the relevant context.

As part of this entitlement, soldiers also have the right to have had their commanding officers competently trained, so that they do not order strikes or actions which are so poorly planned as to constitute a negligent failure to provide that minimal level of personal security which even a soldier has the right to expect. Of course, military mistakes do get made, and sometimes they cost lives. War is a very dangerous business, and people are going to die. That is not at issue. What is at issue is a failure of officer training, and/or sloppy command-and-control design over military orders, so grievous that what results, predictably, is a senseless slaughter of one's own troops. Historical instances of deploying troops as mere "cannon-fodder," for instance, plausibly count as internal human rights violations in my view. World War I was rife, disastrously, with such cases.[78] By becoming soldiers, these men and women do not "contract out" of all their human rights. In the absence of human rights-violating or criminal behavior on their part, soldiers as human beings retain all their human rights, whether their enlistment was voluntary or through conscription. What changes upon enlistment is that the specification of what their human rights entitles them to, in their context, is different in many respects from analogous civilian claims. So soldiers have the right to good training, sound equipment, and to decently-planned strikes, not only in terms of military effectiveness but also in terms of their adherence to *jus in bello* norms. *Soldiers have the right not to be ordered to commit war crimes.* Finally, soldiers have, as part of their personal security entitlement, a subsidiary claim to a due process of military justice wherein any alleged violation of protocol on their part can be tried and considered fairly. Though war be hell, we try (often failingly) to make it a rule-bound hell; and though a soldier's life be hard, he too is owed a predictable form of rule-bound discipline as an extension of his right to personal security.

Subsistence is straightforward compared with security. A soldier has claims on his government to means of material subsistence (or at least an income sufficient to purchase such means). Most states—even ostensibly impoverished ones—have little difficulty in providing subsistence to their soldiers, often offering a mixture of salary with subsidized food, housing, and health care services. Though a soldier's life will never be the road to riches, it does seem that governments may have some work to do assisting soldiers, to a greater degree than presently, with subsistence after their enlistment ends. While this may not involve the generosity of the G.I. Bill—which provided extensive education and housing benefits to American veterans of World War II[79]—it should involve things like: career counseling and placement services; marketable job training; considerations of subsidized housing; health benefits for service-related disabilities; and participation in a decent pension scheme to provide for subsistence in retirement. These subsistence claims should flow to the immediate family (i.e., spouse/partner and dependents) of a soldier as well, especially when he is away on a tour of duty, or killed/missing in action. Why should soldiers be provided such things as a matter of human right? The short answer is because they lead such difficult lives in defense of our own. They do much more, and risk much more, than the average citizen in defense of our common security from aggression, and so they can plausibly make a slightly larger claim on public resources for their subsistence needs. Not at the expense of the subsistence needs of others, of course: a just government must do everything reasonable to meet everyone's subsistence needs. By and large, this is readily achievable and affordable in most societies, since the majority of people can provide subsistence for themselves, not needing direct assistance but, rather, only respect for their rights in their property. Taxation, authorized through representative means, thus allows for the small minority who genuinely cannot provide it for themselves to be provided with subsistence assistance from the state.[80]

Freedom for soldiers is more problematic. The limitations flow here more plausibly and readily than with any other human rights object. Command and control, and obedience to hierarchy, are of the very essence of military life, and are drilled into a soldier's head from day one of enlistment. Cohesion is, indeed, necessary to achieve an effective fighting force. Soldiers may not have much freedom of movement but, as citizens, they must for instance retain the right to freedom to vote. I also believe that the conjunction of personal security and freedom gives soldiers the right to refuse to be subjected to medical or biological treatments or agents (e.g., "immunizing" agents, or some of the new EMT "soldier enhancements") which have risks they are not willing to take. This was an issue in the 1991 Persian Gulf War, for both American and Canadian soldiers, who were essentially forced to receive an injection which would supposedly protect them in case Saddam Hussein used chemical weapons. This injection may, however, have itself caused long-term health problems for these soldiers. I think soldiers should have a right of refusal here, based on their bodily integrity. Of course, the armed services may, in return, justly refuse that soldier the opportunity to fight or circulate alongside his comrades. What about the larger issue, mentioned earlier, of whether soldiers should be allowed to pick and choose which wars they wish to fight in?

Vitoria argued, and Walzer agrees, that extending any such right would result in "grave peril" for a political community. If by this he meant that it would make it harder for a state to defend itself effectively from aggression, I disagree. Soldiers, generally, are spoiling for a fight. Usually ultra-patriotic, they are often eager to use their training in a real context. If it really were a justified war against aggression, I very much doubt that the state in question would find a problem regarding a slippery slope of defections leading to helplessness in the face of aggression. In fact, I would argue that enshrining this entitlement would only make it more difficult for a regime to mount an aggressive war, something it is not entitled to do in any event. If, by his warning, Vitoria was hinting that a military force might become harder to control by civilian authorities, then I admit that could be a concern. Societies must always be vigilant to keep the military under representative civilian control, and perhaps empowering soldiers to pick and choose which wars to fight might enable them to thumb their nose at civilian authorities, perhaps holding out for more pay, or even make a play for political power. Provided, however, that this is a mature and stable representative regime in view here, this seems empirically unlikely, since the deep political culture of that society will make soldiers personally committed to civilian control. I think that offering some choice is consistent with the availability of a sufficient number of fighters. Recent history shows some evidence of this. In my view, this case is less about potential military blackmail of civilian control and more about religious or conscientious pacifists objecting to conscription. The number of soldiers who will refuse to fight in any particular war will, predictably, be few and far between—all the pressures point the other way. Yet there might remain some who do. They should, like the civilian conscientious objector, be given administrative support or training roles in exchange for respecting their freedom of conscience that this was the wrong war to fight.

Equality might be hard to see, in the midst of so hierarchical a place as the armed services, but its substance is actually comparatively easy: all soldiers are equally entitled to all these claims. And it may be worth stressing that this is whether they are male of female, gay or straight, majority or minority.

In terms of *recognition,* the armed services can be impersonal. But what is meant by this value, in this context, is that soldiers still be acknowledged by the military command and state hierarchy as *persons* entitled to these rights while working towards the common moral purpose of defense and security, and not merely as useful cogs in a well-oiled killing machine. Here too arises the issue of entitlements which endure after enlistment ends. Soldiers often experience re-adjustment problems, whether with marital breakdown, post-traumatic stress disorder, or with controlling the violence they've been conditioned to deploy. Their human right to social recognition as soldiers demands something deeper than the civilian equivalent, which centers on recognition as a rights-bearing person before the law. Soldiers, in exchange for the deeper sacrifices they make on behalf of secure citizenship, are owed more efforts by governments on this front than they have recently been given. Medals and official days of honor and gratitude are forms of superior recognition, yet they strike superficially on the surface of what the substance of this right entails, which is the provision of resources needed to live a life of minimal value in the modern world.

4. Summary

In the midst of war, a state should adhere to two sets of rules: one external, the other internal. The external rules are the familiar *jus in bello* rules, and they regulate one's conduct with the enemy. They include: discrimination and non-combatant immunity; benevolent quarantine for POWs; due care for civilians; the DDE; proportionality; no means *mala in se*; no reprisals; compliance with all international laws on weapons prohibition; and proceed with caution regarding EMTs. The internal rules, just as important but not stressed nearly enough, concern one's conduct with one's own citizens, be they citizen or soldier. Ultimately, these rules boil down to the need to realize their human rights to the extent that can reasonably be expected during wartime.

Notes

1 Immanuel Kant, *The Metaphysics of Morals,* trans. and ed. Mary Gregor (Cambridge: Cambridge UP, 1995), 117.

2 W. Michael Reisman and Chris T. Antoniou, eds., *The Laws of War* (New York: Vintage, 1994). For more sources on the laws of war, see Appendix A.

3 Michael Walzer, *Just and Unjust Wars,* 3rd ed. (New York: Basic Books, 2000), 42–43, 135.

4 Walzer, *Wars,* 37, 40, 136; James M. Dubik, "Human Rights, Command Responsibility and Walzer's Just War Theory," *Philosophy and Public Affairs* (1982): 354–71.

5 Walzer, *Wars,* 135.

6 Walzer notes the British prosecutor's arguments in his *Wars,* 38. For the trials, see Chapter 6. See also Thomas W. Pogge, *Realizing Rawls* (Ithaca, NY: Cornell UP, 1989); David Rodin and Henry Shue, *Just and Unjust Warriors* (Oxford: Oxford UP, 2008).

7 Walzer, *Wars,* 127, 39.

8 Walzer, *Wars,* 39.

9 Kirsten Schulze, *The Arab-Israeli Conflict,* 2nd ed. (London: Longmans, 2008).

10 Walzer, *Wars,* 128; Reisman and Antoniou, eds., *Laws,* 41–57.

11 Jane Caplan, ed., *Nazi Germany* (Oxford: Oxford UP, 2008).

12 Walzer, *Wars,* 40, 138.

13 I'm joined in this regard by Jeff McMahan and David Rodin: Jeff McMahan, *Killing in War,* 2nd ed. (Oxford: Oxford UP, 2011); David Rodin, *War and Self-Defence* (Oxford: Oxford UP, 2005).

14 Jeff McMahan, "Preventive War and the Killing of the Innocent" in David Rodin and Richard Sorabji, eds., *The Ethics of War* (London: Ashgate, 2006), 169–90; David Rodin, ed., *War, Torture and Terrorism* (London: Wiley-Blackwell, 2009).

15 Walzer, *Wars,* 142.

16 Walzer, *Wars,* 142, 46.

17 Reisman and Antoniou, eds., *Laws,* 35–230; F. Borch, *Geneva Conventions* (New York: Kaplan, 2010).

18 Eric Saar and Viveca Novak, *Inside the Wire* (New York: Penguin, 2005); Michael Ratner and Ellen Ray, *Guantanamo: What the World Should Know* (New York: Chelsea Green, 2004); Derek P. Jinks, *The Rules of War* (Oxford: Oxford UP, 2013).

19 Mark Danner, *Torture and Truth: America, Abu Ghraib and the War on Terror* (New York: New York Review of Books, 2004).

20 Seymour M. Hersh, *Chain of Command: The Road from 9/11 to Abu Ghraib* (New York: Harper Collins, 2004).
21 Yuval Ginbar, *Why Not Torture Terrorists?* (Oxford: Oxford UP, 2010).
22 Reisman and Antoniou, eds., *Laws*, 153–393; Ian Brownlie, ed., *Basic Documents in International Law*, 4th ed. (Oxford: Oxford UP, 1995), 255–388.
23 Brian Innes, *The History of Torture* (New York: St. Martin's, 1998); Jonathan Glover, *Humanity* (New Haven, CT: Yale UP, 2001).
24 Walzer, *Wars*, 146–51.
25 Rohan Gunaratna, *Inside Al-Qaeda* (New York: Berkley Group, 2003).
26 Michael Gelven, *War and Existence* (Philadelphia: Penn State UP, 1994).
27 Igor Primoratz, ed., *Civilian Immunity in Wartime* (Oxford: Oxford UP, 2010).
28 Robert K. Fullinwider, "War and Innocence," *Philosophy and Public Affairs* (1976): 90–97.
29 Walzer, *Wars*, 146, 219; Thomas Nagel, "War and Massacre," *Philosophy and Public Affairs* (1971/72): 123–43.
30 Walzer, *Wars*, xx; R. Charli Carpenter, *Innocent Women and Children* (London: Ashgate, 2006); Eric L. Haney, *Beyond Shock and Awe: Warfare in the 21st Century* (New York: Berkley, 2008).
31 P.A. Woodward, ed., *The Doctrine of Double Effect* (Notre Dame IN: U of Notre Dame P, 2001).
32 Bob Martin, e.g., questions whether it's true that an intrinsically bad means ought never to be used to generate a good outcome. We might for instance imagine a case where an action which is otherwise impermissible and/or intrinsically bad—such as lying—might under certain circumstances generate good consequences (or, at the least, avoid terrible ones). So, while the DDE is clearly part-and-parcel of just war thinking, stretching back to Aquinas, other moral thinkers question it, not only in war but in other morally-loaded circumstances.
33 F.M. Kamm, *The Moral Target* (Oxford: Oxford UP, 2012).
34 Walzer, *Wars*, 106.
35 Walzer, *Wars*, 151, 157.
36 Michael Ignatieff, *Virtual War: Kosovo and Beyond* (New York: Viking, 2000).
37 Walter Laqueur and Barry Rubin, eds., *The Israel-Arab Reader*, 7th ed. (New York: Penguin, 2008).
38 Toni Erskine, "Moral Agents and Intelligence," *Intelligence and National Security* (Spring 2004): 38–54; Joel H. Rosenthal et al. *Ethics of Spying* (Lanham, MD: Rowman Littlefield, 2009).
39 Walzer, *Wars*, 152 and 156, in the note; Reisman and Antoniou, eds. *Laws*, 80–84.
40 Brian Orend, *War and International Justice: A Kantian Perspective* (Waterloo, ON: Wilfrid Laurier UP, 2000).
41 Peter W. Singer, *Children at War* (Berkeley, CA: U of California P, 2006); Roméo Dallaire, *They Fight Like Soldiers, They Die Like Children* (Toronto: Vintage; Amnesty International: <http://www.amnesty.org/en/news/landmark-icc-verdict-over-use-child-soldiers-2012-03-14>.
42 Walzer, *Wars*, 129 and xxi.
43 Walzer, *Wars*, 42 and 215; Reisman and Antoniou, eds., *Laws*, 35–132; William Boothby, *Weapons and the Laws of Armed Conflict* (Oxford: Oxford UP, 2009).
44 James Turner Johnson, *Ideology, Reason and the Limitation of War* (Princeton, NJ: Princeton UP, 1981).
45 Deuteronomy 20:19.

46 Convention II, Article 6, of the Convention on Prohibitions or Restrictions on the Use of Certain Conventional Weapons which may be Deemed to be Excessively Injurious or to have Indiscriminate Effects. This Convention was ratified in 1980. From Reisman and Antoniou, eds., *Laws*, 53.

47 Jody Williams et al., *Banning Landmines* (New York: Rowman and Littlefield, 2008).

48 Richard J. Regan, *Just War: Principles and Cases* (Washington, DC: Catholic U of America P, 1996), 87–99, 136–50.

49 Walzer, *Wars*, 282. While there have been two UN General Assembly resolutions, in 1961 and 1972, banning the use of nuclear weapons (see Reisman and Antoniou, eds., *Laws*, 66–67), and one in 2004 calling for the ultimate dismantling of them all, these do not carry the binding force of a ratified international treaty.

50 Walzer, *Wars*, 263–83.

51 Regan, *Just War*, 100–22; Henry Kissinger, *Diplomacy* (New York: Harper Collins, 1995); Joseph S. Nye, Jr., *Nuclear Ethics* (New York: Macmillan, 1986).

52 Walzer, *Wars*, 129–37; Catharine A. MacKinnon, "Crimes of War, Crimes of Peace" in Stephen Shute and Susan Hurley, eds., *On Human Rights* (New York: Basic Books, 1993), 83–110.

53 Reisman and Antoniou, eds., *Laws*, 84–94; Walzer, *Wars*, 257, 323.

54 Walzer, *Wars*, 207–22; Regan, *Cases*, 172–78.

55 Walzer, *Wars*, 207.

56 Walzer, *Wars*, 47.

57 Human Rights Watch, *Report on US Blinding Laser Weapons* (New York: Human Rights Watch, 1995).

58 Jonathan D. Moreno, *Mind Wars: Brain Science and the Military in the 21st Century* (New York: Bellevue, 2012); Kevin Dockery, *Future Weapons* (New York: Berkley, 2007).

59 Peter W. Singer, *Wired for War* (New York: Penguin, 2009); Matt J. Martin and Charles W. Sasser, *Predator: The Remote-Control Air-War over Iraq and Afghanistan* (New York: Zenith, 2010).

60 John M. House, *Why War? Why an Army?* (New York: Praeger Security, 2008).

61 It's estimated that, since 2000, the number of drone attacks has gone from zero to over 300 per year, and the amount of spending on drones has risen from $284 million USD to over $3.3 billion. Jeremiah Gertler, "US Unmanned Aerial Systems," study for the US Congressional Research Office (Jan. 2012): <www.state.gov/documents/organization/180677.pdf>.

62 Bradley Jay Strawser, "Moral Predators," *Journal of Military Ethics* (2010): 342–68.

63 Paul J. Springer, *Military Robots and Drones* (New York: ABC-CLIO, 2013).

64 Bill Roggio and Alexander Mayer, "Charting the Data for US Air Strikes in Pakistan, 2004–2012," *Long War Journal* (October, 2012): <www.longwarjournal.org/pakistan-strikes.php>.

65 Ignatieff, *Virtual*, passim.

66 Medea Benjamin, *Drone Warfare* (New York: Verso, 2013).

67 Bob Martin has noted how, here, appealing to the warrior ethos doctrine might actually support the absurd conclusion that we ought to go out of our way to make soldiers' lives *more* dangerous.

68 Christian Enemark, *Armed Drones and the Ethics of War* (London: Routledge, 2013). US President Barack Obama, in a vital national defence speech in May 2013, spoke of improvements to be made to drone policy in this regard. See <http://www.nytimes.com/2013/05/24/us/politics/transcript-of-obamas-speech-on-drone-policy.html?pagewanted=all&r=0>.

69 Reisman and Antoniou, eds., *Laws*, 84–87.

70 Ronald J. Daniels et al., eds., *The Security of Freedom* (Toronto: U of Toronto P, 2001); David Cole and James X. Dempsey, eds. *Terrorism and the Constitution*, 2nd ed. (New York: The Free Press, 2002); Richard C. Leone and Greg Anrig, eds., *The War on Our Freedoms* (New York: Public Affairs, 2003); M. Walker, *The Cold War: A History* (New York: Henry Holt, 1995).

71 On "emergency regimes" and rights-protection on the domestic front, see: James Nickel, *Making Sense of Human Rights* (Berkeley: U of California P, 1987), 131–46; Allan Rosas, "Emergency Regimes: A Comparison" in Donna Gomien, ed., *Broadening the Frontiers of Human Rights* (Oslo: Scandinavian UP, 1992), 162–200; The International Commission of Jurists, *States of Emergency: Their Impact on Human Rights* (New York: ICJ, 1983); Joan Fitzpatrick, "Protection against Abuse of the Concept of Emergency" in Louis Henkin and John Lawrence Hargrove, eds., *Human Rights: An Agenda for the Next Century* (Washington, DC: The American Society for International Law, 1994), 203–28; and Joan F. Hartman, "Derogation from Human Rights Treaties in Public Emergencies," *Harvard International Law Review* (1981): 1–52.

72 Lists of so-called "non-derogable" human rights also exist in both the International Covenant on Civil and Political Rights and the European Convention on Human Rights. But the Second Amendment and the Paris Standards are the most comprehensive, and hence discussed here. See: Jaime Oraa, *Human Rights in States of Emergency in International Law* (Oxford: Oxford UP, 1997); Subrata Roy Chowdhury, *Rule of Law in a State of Emergency* (London: Palgrave, 1997) and Joan Fitzpatrick, *Human Rights in Crisis* (Philadelphia: U of Pennsylvania P, 1994).

73 John Rawls, *The Law of Peoples* (Cambridge, MA: Harvard UP, 2000).

74 Brian Orend, *Human Rights: Concept and Context* (Peterborough, ON: Broadview, 2002).

75 Brian Masaru Hayashi, *Democratizing the Enemy* (Princeton, NJ: Princeton UP, 2004); Pamela Hickman and Masako Fukawa, *Righting Canada's Wrongs* (Toronto: Lorimer, 2012). Less widely known is the internment of people of German or Italian descent in both countries, of people of Ukrainian descent in Canada, and, bizarrely, in the US of native Alaskans, and in Canada, of Jewish refugees from the Nazis. This last group, considered "enemy aliens," were held in Canadian concentration camps which also held Canadian fascists and German prisoners-of-war (see <http://www.vhec.org/currentexhibits.html>).

76 Ronald Dworkin, "What the Court Really Said," *New York Review of Books* (12 August 2004): 26–9. (Not that there aren't other issues of due process we can raise in connection with the Guantanamo detainees, notably about freedom from torture, and access to lawyers. See section 1.1.4.)

77 Walzer, *Wars*, 34–40, 138–43; Wesley K. Clark, *Waging Modern War* (New York: Public Affairs Group, 2002).

78 John Keegan, *The First World War* (Toronto: Vintage, 2000).

79 Glenn C. Altschuler and Stuart M. Blumin, *The GI Bill* (Oxford: Oxford UP, 2009).

80 For more on the overall affordability of human rights, including those to subsistence, see Orend, *Human Rights*, 129–54.

5

Jus in Bello #2

SUPREME EMERGENCY AND CYBER-WARFARE

"(W)e have a right, indeed are bound in duty, to abrogate for a space some of the conventions of the very laws we seek to consolidate and reaffirm."

—WINSTON CHURCHILL[1]

This chapter examines two fascinating cases which test the very limits of *jus in bello*: 1) the proposal for a "supreme emergency" exemption from the rules; and 2) the recent emergence of cyber-war (sometimes a.k.a. "informational warfare"). Though these two subjects may seem rather different, they are actually similar in that:

- There is an absence of international law in their connection.
- They deal with dramatic, high-stakes circumstances for modern political communities.
- They thus pose unique challenges for constructing coherent and useful *jus in bello* rules.
- They help us explore more deeply the inter-connections between *jus ad bellum, jus in bello,* and *jus post bellum*.
- Thus making for a nice transition into examining (in the following two chapters) the subject of war termination and post-war reconstruction.

1. Supreme Emergency

The supreme emergency exemption is a doctrine which pushes to the very limits the relationship between *jus ad bellum* and *jus in bello*. Though it is nowhere written into international law, the supreme emergency exemption nevertheless has high profile support, including such luminaries as Churchill (quoted above), John Rawls, and Michael Walzer. But it is Walzer who is fundamentally responsible for this proposed exemption within just war theory—Churchill merely inspires it, and Rawls merely apes it.

As Walzer defines it, the supreme emergency exemption allows a country victimized by aggression to set aside the rules of *jus in bello* and fight however it wants, provided: 1) there is public proof the aggressor is just about to defeat the victim militarily; and 2) there is similar proof that, once it does so, the aggressor will not simply crush the political sovereignty of the victim community but, moreover, institute a brutal policy of widespread massacre and enslavement against its individual members. Walzer's favorite, and only, example of such an aggressor is Nazi Germany.[2] More on this example shortly: let's now push our definitions, and sense of the stakes, toward greater clarity.

We saw last chapter that (external) *jus in bello* contains a number of general moral rules within which the stunning number of legal conventions and prohibitions can be located. These abstract rules include: 1) noncombatant immunity from direct and intentional attack; 2) benevolent quarantine for captured soldiers; 3) due care to civilians; 4) the DDE; 5) use of proportionate means only against legitimate military targets; 6) no reprisals; 7) no prohibited weapons; 8) no use of means "*mala in se*"; and 9) be guided by just war theory when considering new EMTs. Walzer is saying here that, under supreme emergency conditions, the country with *jus ad bellum* on its side (i.e., the victim of aggression) may set aside all *jus in bello* rules and fight *however it wants to*—without restraint—to stave off the threat posed by the aggressor. In particular, the victim country may willfully violate non-combatant immunity, and do such things as deliberately attack enemy civilians with lethal force. Traditionally, we've seen that such transgression has counted as the clearest violation of *jus in bello* rules, and has been viewed as one of the very worst war crimes. Indeed Hugo Grotius once said that noncombatant immunity is a rule so powerful that it "cannot be changed, even by God."[3] So, what we have in the supreme emergency exemption is probably the most controversial, and consequential, amendment to just war theory ever proposed. The stakes regarding its acceptance into just war theory are enormous, and disturbingly relevant to an era well-acquainted with genocide and weapons of mass destruction (WMD).

1.1. WHICH CASES COUNT?

Churchill, Walzer, and Rawls concur that Britain experienced a supreme emergency in the early 1940s. By 1940, Nazi Germany stood triumphant in Western and Central Europe as well as Scandinavia, following its shattering success during the Blitzkrieg. Neither the USA nor the USSR were, at this point, in the war to drain the pressure off Britain. Hitler indeed had plans to invade the UK, and was "softening up the target" with *Luftwaffe* bombing raids, especially on Coventry and London. These Nazi bombing raids were indiscriminate and terrorist. Churchill, who coined the phrase "supreme emergency" in this regard, argued that as Prime Minister he had to authorize exceptional measures under such ultra-menacing conditions. He suggested that the British were "fighting to re-establish the reign of law and to protect the liberties of small countries. Our defeat would mean an age of barbaric violence and would be fatal, not only to ourselves, but to the independent life of every small country in Europe." "It would not be right," Churchill declared, "that the aggressive power should gain one set of advantages by tearing up all laws, and another set by sheltering behind the innate respect for law of its opponent. Humanity, rather than legality, must be our guide." And so Churchill authorized the Royal Air Force (RAF) to begin bombing raids on German cities, knowing full well—even intending—that German civilians would be killed. (More below, in Section 1.2, regarding how the DDE applies to this choice.) This was partly in retaliation, or reprisal, for Hitler's own original bombings of London and Coventry, but was also designed to deter any conquest of Britain. It was thought that the German people, delirious with the Blitzkrieg's success, had to be made to feel the sting of war—needed some wind taken out of their sails—lest their approval drive Hitler's armed ambitions even further. Air power was the only tool at Churchill's disposal in this regard, and he employed it to the full during this period, which culminated in the Battle of Britain—when so few did so much for the safety of so many. The fact that Hitler then gave up his UK invasion plans and turned his murderous attention towards the Russian border was cited by Churchill as evidence his supreme emergency strategy worked.[4]

Walzer and Rawls agree with all of this, yet are even more permissive than Churchill himself regarding the time during which Britain experienced a supreme emergency. After all, Britain "stood alone" against the Nazis in the West until America entered the theater in substance, in 1942. Even then, the Allies didn't experience much success until the campaigns in North Africa and Italy in 1943. In the East, the Soviets didn't get involved until 1942, and initially suffered terrible set-backs. Both American thinkers are inclined to believe Britain's supreme emergency lasted from 1940 until well into 1943, and thus all RAF bombing of German residential centers during this time was permissible. Walzer puts the core moral issue in the stark terms we need to reflect on: "(C)an one do *anything* [his italics], violating the rights of the innocent, in order to defeat Nazism?" He answers yes, and justifies himself in a phrase already quoted (in Chapter 2) but worth repeating here: "Nazism was an ultimate threat to everything decent in our lives, an ideology and a practice of domination so murderous, so degrading even to those who might survive, that the consequences of its final victory were literally beyond calculation, immeasurably awful. We see it—and I don't use the phrase lightly—as evil objectified in the world."[5]

When supreme emergency conditions evaporate, however, the justification for deliberate civilian targeting dissolves. So Walzer and Rawls argue that continued Allied bombing of German cities—and emphatically the fire-bombing and razing of Dresden in 1945—was unjust. Indeed, Churchill himself grew to regret the later bombings, admitting they were motivated more by bloodlust, the passions of war-fighting, and—above all—by a desire for revenge for the London and Coventry bombings, than by any plausible moral or even strategic concern.[6]

Rawls, in his writings on supreme emergency,[7] is mostly concerned with using the doctrine as a tool for criticizing America's use of the atomic bomb on Japan in 1945. He suggests that perhaps the only thing which could justify the use of nuclear weapons—which, of course, are wildly destructive and unusually indiscriminate—is the experience of a supreme emergency. But America in August 1945 was not in a supreme emergency at all; on the contrary, it had just triumphed in Europe and had Japan by the throat. In fact, America was one of the most powerful and privileged societies on earth at that time. So the moral case for its using WMD was nil. In Rawls's view, US President Harry Truman's decision to do so anyway was a cynical piece of *realpolitik,* designed to show Japan and the world just how powerful America had become. The bombing was not done to stave off devastating loss; it was done to secure whatever terms of Japan's surrender America wanted—at minimal cost to the US—as well as to impress potential future rivals like the Soviets and Chinese with American capability. How stunning, then, was Truman's notorious comment that he never hesitated at all to order the bombing, that he never lost a moment's sleep over it. Walzer reflects insightfully on Truman's problematic cost-benefit approach: "Commonly, what we are calculating is *our* benefit (which we exaggerate) and *their* cost (which we minimize or disregard entirely) [his italics]."[8]

Truman's reply would be that the atomic bombings, in spite of their destructiveness, actually saved lives. How so? The Japanese, in July and August 1945, were irrationally refusing to surrender when they were clearly beaten and after their other former allies, Italy and Germany, had already given up. Moreover, in the previous battle of Okinawa—the first piece of Japanese territory on which US and Japanese forces clashed—the Japanese showed themselves capable of some of the most ferocious and bloody resistance in military history. So US decision-makers were in a dilemma: the Japanese were beaten yet refused to admit it, and apparently the only way to force surrender was an invasion of Japan itself. But Okinawa foretold that such an invasion would be an absolute slaughter for both US forces and Japanese soldiers and civilians: one million dead was the minimum predicted casualty total. By contrast, the Hiroshima and Nagasaki bombings killed about one-quarter that number—and they forced the Japanese to surrender without a blood-soaked invasion. So the bombings, while dramatic and using unprecedented technology, actually served both sound military and even moral objectives of forcing the surrender of an unjust aggressor while minimizing casualties.[9]

Walzer and Rawls refuse to be swayed by this reasoning. The figure of one million dead, and so many more injured, seems completely speculative and thus probably inflated. It's always convenient when we construct counter-factual numbers and arguments—and they end up "revealing" that our choices were right, leaving our opponents no way of either confirming or refuting the "evidence." Moreover, even if the numbers were true, Walzer and Rawls insist that they miss the point. The point is not to minimize the casualties while pursuing policies designed to advance majority interests regardless of whether there is rights violation or not. The point is to minimize casualties while pursuing policies, and using means of war, which do not violate human rights. And they believe the atomic bombings violated human rights because the explosions violated the core principles of discrimination and non-combatant immunity. It was foreseen, and intended, that innocent civilians would die *en masse* in both cities as a result of the bombings: that was supposed to happen to provide the leverage on the Japanese government to surrender and not risk suffering even more threatened bombings in the future. That was indeed what happened—but even if that was a happy consequence (i.e., the final surrender of an unjust, aggressive Japanese regime) it doesn't provide after-the-fact justification for the rights violation used to generate it.

What's also interesting in Rawls's reflections is that they are not merely backward-looking, designed to render correct judgment regarding historical cases. They are also forward-looking, in that they provide criteria for future use of controversial war-time measures. It's a clear inference from Rawls's reflections that a country suffering from a supreme emergency might be justified in using nuclear weapons, and perhaps other WMD, to prevail against an aggressor.

Which leads me to speculate whether we might imagine possible future instances. Consider the case of Israel. Israel, of course, occupies a quite precarious position in the Middle East: very small geographically, surrounded by hostile (or, at best, cool) neighbors, each of which it has encountered in war in the past 65 years. The concentration of population in its few major cities also makes Israel quite an easy target for utterly devastating widespread destruction. The continuing controversy over the Palestinians, moreover, fuels an almost constant security crisis in Israel, and remains a *cause célébre* among Arabs, fueling rage and terrorism. What if a dystopian future unfolded, according to which Israel found itself in a condition of supreme emergency at the hands of its neighbors and/or domestically-located terrorists? If so, what may Israel permissibly do at that moment, especially in connection with its nuclear arsenal? Could it contemplate nuking Tehran, Riyadh, or Damascus? More bitingly, what about its own West Bank, or Gaza Strip, holdings? This horrible hypothetical underlines the continuing relevance of the proposed supreme emergency exemption—it's not just an outdated device for contemplating "Churchill versus the Nazis." In fact, in the era of terrorism and WMD, it's every bit as relevant as when Hitler darkened the world.[10]

Some academics and politicians, in the immediate aftermath of 9/11, argued that America was then in a condition of supreme emergency (or something very close to it). Former US Secretary of Defense Donald Rumsfeld repeatedly made this assertion, as did former NYC mayor Rudy Guiliani; even former President George Bush, Jr. appeared to claim this, with his references to the "axis of evil" and his frequent claim that nothing less than civilization itself was at stake in the War on Terror. All three men drew direct analogies between the on-going war against "radical, violent Islamo-fascism" and the World War II struggle against Nazi Germany and Imperial Japan. Guiliani most directly—and I suppose not surprisingly, given his experience that day of 9/11—has drawn an absolute analogy between the War on Terror and the situation of Churchill's Britain during the Nazi Blitz. These men have all argued that we need completely new rules to regulate wartime since it is a completely new era, owing to the potential blending between terrorists and WMD. Just war theory—quaint, decent, state-centric—must go the way of the dodo bird in the harsh, post 9/11 world.[11] But I doubt it.

Historically, we've heard the death of just war theory—and even international law—pronounced many a time before, and never has it turned out to be the case. The moral truth has a reassuring stability and resilience to it, and can survive trendy proclamations of its imminent demise and the dawn of a new era of brutality, wherein we can and should fight however we want, as bare-knuckled and bloody as we want.

We should be very hesitant to agree that America, in the War on Terror, remains—or ever was—in a supreme emergency, and we should consider skeptically the motives and incentives of those who do so. Why might they want to hype the notion that America suffers from supreme emergency? Well, perhaps that makes it easier for them to start and justify controversial wars, as in Iraq in 2003. A mega-crisis atmosphere would also make the detention and even torture of terrorist suspects much easier, and could create an environment wherein the people would rally around the government in patriotic panic. The government might then enact forceful legislation at odds with many classical civil liberties, as discussed last chapter.

Declaring a supreme emergency in America, post 9/11, is an invitation to: 1) irrationality (since it's not true, and stimulates panic); 2) moral violation or even atrocity (on far-away battlefields and prisons); 3) internal political repression in the name of patriotism; 4) external strategic mistakes (Abu-Ghraib, and probably Iraq in general); and 5) experiencing deep regret later, when the country comes to realize that, in knee-jerk reaction to the shock of 9/11, it accidentally authorized a whole slew of controversies which it should have resisted.

When we look at the three criteria for a supreme emergency, we see that America meets only one: it was genuinely victimized by aggression on 9/11. But there's little to show that America's military defeat, then or now, was close or imminent, much less that America will soon suffer widespread massacre or enslavement. Indeed, America has gone on the military offensive since 9/11, quite decisively taking down two regimes in countries on the other side of the world. America faces security threats of varying severity, but not plausibly a supreme emergency. It's difficult to imagine any state actor, or combination of such, putting America in such a position, much less a non-state actor.[12] The only way would be in connection with WMD: if a group could somehow detonate enough WMD to truly devastate America—a very big, massively populated, resourceful, and diverse country—then that would fulfill the three supreme emergency requirements of: 1) victimization by aggression; 2) military collapse; and 3) imminent threat of widespread massacre and/or enslavement. This indeed gives America, and other legitimate countries, strong reason to be very vigilant regarding the spread and control of WMD.[13]

(After all, it is often said that terrorists don't want such weapons for deterrent purposes, since they aren't states with territorial interests to protect. Terrorists want WMD for either blackmail or actual use; and, in that sense, can—in some circumstances—be even more dangerous than enemy states, even though they generally have much fewer resources. This is true, and it underlines the seriousness of contemporary terrorist threats and ambitions, as well as being resolute and determined in confronting them.)

But this possible use of WMD certainly does not, as yet, give Western nations reason to deliberately attack civilians in the on-going War on Terror. The 9/11 attacks were outrageous and shocking acts of aggression, and they justified the return strike on the Taliban in Afghanistan, since that regime was sponsoring al-Qaeda in the way defined in Chapter 3. But the attacks manifestly did not put America into a condition of supreme emergency, with all the permissiveness and laxity in targeting which Walzer has it imply. When it comes to genuine victims of supreme emergency, we are much more likely to find them at the other end of the power spectrum—the small, weak, and vulnerable communities which are decidedly unlike the one and only "hyper-power" (even "global colossus") which the United States has become.[14]

Consider, for instance, communities targeted with, or victimized by, genocide, such as Turkish Armenians in the 1910s, European Jews in the early 1940s, Rwandan Tutsis in the mid-1990s, and perhaps both Albanian Kosovars in the late 1990s and black Christian Sudanese, in the Darfur region, in the 2000s. If any community experiences a genuine supreme emergency, it is those confronted with genocide, which means trying to kill or enslave an entire people. Examples more distantly rooted in history might include Native Americans at the hands of the Spanish conquistadors or Black Africans on the eve of the armed slave trade.[15] Reference to all these instances of genocide is done to underline the reality and urgency of the supreme emergency debate—to illustrate that it's not just about the Nazis, or science fiction scenarios sketching out nuclear wars between Russia and America. Supreme emergencies—thank goodness—are not regular occurrences, even in war. But they seem actually to have happened several times in history and, if the record of warfare teaches us anything, it's that we should not be surprised at the depth and breadth of violent atrocity of which humanity is capable. As responsible thinkers, we must confront this proposed exemption and consider its nature.

1.2. OPTIONS REGARDING SUPREME EMERGENCY

There seem to be five major—insightful, influential, and logical—options for considering how to conceive of the supreme emergency doctrine. Let's examine each of them in turn.

Before we do, we should note how the Doctrine of Double Effect (DDE)—very often called upon by just war theory to solve difficult wartime dilemmas—is not a viable option when dealing with supreme emergencies. Why? Because, as we saw last chapter, the DDE (among other things) only lets one perform actions which are otherwise permissible, and in which the unintended bad effects are not the means to producing the intended good ones. But in supreme emergencies, the actions contemplated are not otherwise permissible (e.g., deliberately killing civilians), and the bad effects *are* the means to producing the good (e.g., hoping, as Churchill did, that the civilian casualties will, somehow, quell the aggressor's appetite and force it to back off).[16]

1.2.1. Option #1: No Such Thing

This first perspective, or option, asserts that there really is no such thing as a supreme emergency, and that Walzer's proposal is thus a bastardization or corruption of just war theory. The objection here is rooted both conceptually and historically. In the conceptual sense, the supreme emergency conditions might seem too abstract, and subject to interpretive disagreement, to be useful and immune from gratuitous, self-serving abuse. Consider the vagueness of Walzer's conditions. First, they require that there be a clear victim, and perpetrator, of "aggression." We are all now quite familiar with disputes regarding what exactly counts as "aggression" and "defense" from it—witness the whole debate on anticipatory attack. Second, Walzer says there must be "public proof" of imminent military defeat and subsequent massacre or enslavement. Such "proof," though, can be hard indeed to come by. The famous saying, after all, is that "truth is the first casualty of war." Discerning the future tides of war-fighting, and the intent of one's opponent, can be very difficult, especially amidst the heat of battle. We know generally that, in war, people overestimate the risks they face. Everything seems like a super-heated crisis. We have also recently witnessed, in connection with America's 2003 Iraq attack, the apparent failure of even the best-funded intelligence agencies to come up with plausible and well-grounded conclusions, in this case regarding a connection between Iraq and al-Qaeda, as well as Iraq's possession of WMD before the attack. Third, there is the issue of what counts as an imminent "military defeat." Is it simply a big, crushing loss in a high-profile battle? Is it loss of one's political capital to the enemy?

Or is it, as I would suggest, something more like: the total collapse of an effective armed forces capability, rendering you literally defenseless? Next, there is vagueness regarding what "close and imminent" means. Are we talking weeks, days, or hours? Are we agreeing, with Oliver Wendell Holmes, that the threat of supreme emergency must (merely) be "a clear and present danger?" Or are we saying something more stringent, as I'd be inclined to believe, such as: you have imminency only when you'll lose and then be massacred unless you switch to exceptional measures of war-fighting? Finally, the criteria require that, after the military defeat, you know you will be subjected to "widespread massacre and/or enslavement." Massacre and enslavement seem fairly straightforward in meaning, but "widespread" is not. How much is widespread: 5%, 10%, 50% or more of your population? Or a distinctive sub-set of your population—such as a visible or especially powerful minority group—even if, overall, it doesn't add up to many numbers, or a large percentage?

This first, skeptical perspective might also wonder whether the one example that these theorists all seem to agree on—namely, Britain in 1940—actually was a supreme emergency. After all, while Nazi invasion seemed imminent, Britain's military collapse was not, or at least it's not a clear causal connection to go from suffering invasion to suffering total military collapse. We also can't forget Churchill's political self-interest in exaggerating the threat that Britain faced: doing so would drive the British people to greater efforts, and it would also serve as a strong rhetorical and moral tug on the United States finally to get involved in the war (on the Allied side). Moreover, Walzer and Rawls surely err when they talk of Britain "standing alone" against the Nazis at this time. For Britain had all of its colonies and ex-colonies fighting alongside it from the very first days in 1939. They included Australia, Canada, India, New Zealand, and the Caribbean island nations. This is to say that Britain had far greater resources to draw on than any of the Continental countries that fell to the Nazis during the Blitzkrieg, including France. In fact, Britain probably had more resources to draw on than all those countries put together, and to boot had the advantage of geography: an island has a natural ring of defensive water all around. To what extent, then, did it actually face a supreme emergency, as Walzer defines it? Drawing on these considerations of conceptual vagueness and questionable historical application, the skeptical perspective might well conclude that the supreme emergency exemption is a big, bad, dangerous moral loop-hole in just war theory, and we're better off without it. Perhaps this is why it appears nowhere in the international laws of armed conflict. The rules are the rules; and we shouldn't allow for exceptions to them, or ways for belligerents to get around them.[17]

While I do think that this perspective adds some very healthy precautionary skepticism regarding the supreme emergency exemption, in the end I believe it fails to persuade. While far too many just war theorists accept the exemption uncritically, and apparently on little more than Walzer's authority, it really does seem as though supreme emergencies can be real. Witness the examples of genocide offered last section. Also, from the fact that supreme emergencies can be hard to define conceptually, it does not follow that we should get rid of, or dismiss, the very idea itself. There is, after all, a whole roster of hard-to-define but vitally important ideas in moral and political philosophy—e.g., freedom, equality, human rights, justice, democracy—that we'd have to throw out as well, if that were the case. The conceptual difficulty just means that our jobs aren't easy. The same holds for the objection regarding the abuse of the concept of supreme emergency for self-serving ends. We know full well that, subjectively, all belligerents in every war will try to claim for their side any concept which justifies their actions. There's an old saying: "Even the Devil can quote Scripture." Just because people or countries claim that their actions are justified does not make it so. The task for them, as we've strongly asserted, is to show that their subjective beliefs correspond to objectively defensible standards and to inter-subjectively plausible evidence. This is an absolutely vital point, not just for supreme emergency but for all of just war theory and international law, and it seems it cannot be made forcefully enough, or repeated often enough.

1.2.2. Option #2: Churchill's Consequentialism

This second perspective states that, when in supreme emergency, only *jus ad bellum* matters, therefore the rules of *jus in bello* may be set aside. Churchill clearly believed this, and Walzer partially believes it. (More on Walzer's nuanced view below.) Other exemplars of this view may be Generals Grant and Sherman during the US Civil War. Both believed that the South was the aggressor, and that its social system of slavery was so unjust that it could not, under any condition, be allowed to win. Thus, they both took a very permissive view regarding what the North was entitled to do to bring about victory. Note, for instance, Sherman's notorious "scorched earth" policy against the state of Georgia wherein, after his divisions conquered territory, they set it ablaze so as to ruin it for any Southerners who might re-group to plan future military action.[18]

The strength of this view, that supreme emergency makes any action acceptable, is that it offers a morally coherent response to a terrible dilemma. And, depending on your ethical views, it may offer you complete satisfaction on this issue. Upon reflection, though, I think this perspective has four fatal flaws to it.

The first flaw is precisely that it violates the human rights of enemy civilians, understood by international law and just war theory to be noncombatants. As such, this view violates our core commitment not to punish the innocent. As Thomas Nagel eloquently puts it: "hostile treatment of any person must be justified in terms of something *about that person* [his italics] which makes the treatment appropriate." We distinguish combatants from noncombatants "on the basis of their immediate threat or harmfulness." And our response to such threats and harms must be governed by relations of directness and relevance.[19] But it's not the enemy civilians who are threatening us, it's their military machine, and so it is impermissible to strike out deliberately at the civilians, because even in a supreme emergency it is not they who are the direct and active agents of the brutal force.

Churchill's consequentialism is also problematic because it seems to endorse the proposition that "the ends justify the means." We all know the flaws in this proposition, notably the one that it violates the principle never to treat persons as mere things to be sacrificed against their will, for the sake of some glorified social project. Individuals all have autonomy unless they themselves forfeit it, and this nicely ties in with the previous claim about the human rights of enemy civilians, and how they do nothing to forfeit them. Believing and acting on this proposition—that the ends justify the means—can also be morally corrupting in the following sense: isn't civilian murder the very thing feared at the hands of the aggressor? If so, what entitles you to commit the very same action?[20]

Thirdly, why have *jus in bello* at all if *jus ad bellum* is what ultimately matters? Now some people, apparently Grant and Sherman, seem to believe this: "war is hell," whether just or unjust, so at least let's make sure that the just side wins. Let's give the just side wide, or even complete, sway regarding its selection of tactics and targets. This attitude, however, ignores the compelling reason we have in favor of maintaining *jus in bello* rules: they prevent escalation into indiscriminate slaughter and total, no-holds-barred warfare. And if just war theory stands for anything, it's that total warfare must be avoided. The very essence of just war theory, we now know, is to insist on restraints in the reasons for fighting, and in the means used in fighting.

Finally, Churchill's consequentialism is at odds with our moral convictions in an analogous inter-personal case of supreme emergency. Suppose that aggressor person A brutally attacks victim B with murderous intent, and B drags in innocent bystander C, to serve as a shield between him and A. How should we evaluate B's actions during his own "personal supreme emergency"? I suggest that none of us, upon reflection, would argue that B's actions are morally justified. Indeed, the immediate reaction, normally, is that B is behaving like a selfish and despicable coward, endangering an innocent person's life instead of confronting his own danger like a man. Upon consideration, though, it seems that this immediate response may be too judgmental, since it is offered by those of us who reflect in comfort upon a fellow person's desperate choices amidst terrifying danger. (We like to comfort ourselves by supposing we would make better choices under such conditions. But until we experience similar extraordinary pressure and fear, we might want to climb down from our tower of condemnation.) It seems equally erroneous, however, to pretend there's nothing wrong with B doing whatever he wants—including sacrificing C—to save his own life. Yet that is precisely what Churchill's consequentialism would here imply. Clearly, B has no right to violate C's rights in this case: C has done nothing wrong, nothing that would render her rights forfeit. She is an innocent bystander that B decides to use as a mere tool in service of his own end of survival. B utterly disregards C's humanity in this instance; he treats her as a prop, not a person.[21] In my view, he is almost as culpable for her death as A, should she succumb from her injuries sustained while serving as a shield between the two.

The most complete and accurate judgment of this inter-personal analogy seems to be this: B has no right to drag C into the situation, and if he does so he commits a severe moral wrong-doing. However, we might be willing to excuse B's actions, on grounds that the terrible duress and mortal fear operative on him, in the situation, drove him to make the terrible choice he did. Like any animal filled with mortal terror, he desperately reached out for any means necessary to stave off death. This doesn't make his choice *right* or morally justifiable; it merely makes it *understandable* and, depending on the exact circumstances, *excusable* from criticism or punishment. It will be excusable if we determine that the pressure, in the case, was so extreme that B acted more out of animal instinct than out of a morally-culpable decision-making capacity. We would say, under such conditions, that he was forced to do something terribly wrong. This case, and this distinction between having moral justification for doing X, and being excused for doing X, are vital in my mind to a proper understanding of a supreme emergency.

1.2.3. Option #3: Strict Respect for Jus in Bello

This third perspective says that, even in supreme emergency conditions, one must still scrupulously respect the rules of *jus in bello*. Colloquially, this is the view that "let justice be done, though the heavens fall." Kant and Socrates are probably exemplars of this view, as is a different part of Walzer, and the international laws of armed conflict themselves. Nowhere, in any piece of international law, does it say that military necessity is a valid reason for setting aside the rules of armed conflict. In fact, in several places it is stated quite clearly that, since the rules have been framed in the first place with military necessity already in mind, no appeal to necessity can override the need to respect the rules.[22]

This view has seductive strengths from the moral point of view. Notably, it avoids each of the four problems detailed with Churchill's consequentialism. Unlike that perspective, this one respects the human rights of enemy civilians, does not endorse the proposition that "the ends justify the means," maintains *jus in bello* as a meaningful category, and can be brought into accord with our considered judgment in the inter-personal analogy. It is also a consistent and coherent response to the supreme emergency dilemma and, if one has certain moral leanings, it may offer total satisfaction in this regard. Think of Socrates's powerful pronouncement that it is always better to suffer injustice than to inflict it oneself.[23] Yet this view, in spite of its moral force, also has flaws.

The first flaw with this view is that it seems quite unrealistic. Strict respect for *jus in bello,* in this case, might result not just in victory for the aggressor, but also the kind of horrible slaughter or slavery previously detailed. Realistically, who is going to follow the advice of this option? Respecting *jus in bello* is, to an extent, agreeing to fight with one arm tied behind one's back. Now, this might be fine so long as one can still win, or at least if one loses, it is simply a "run-of-the-mill" military defeat involving things like territorial concessions. But that is not what we're talking about with supreme emergency: we are talking about not just defeat but slaughter, slavery, and total catastrophe. In the face of such a threat, who in their right mind is still going to fight with one arm tied behind their back?

John Fialia says that Kant will still agree to fight with one arm tied, but only because he has a philosophy of history—i.e., a system of beliefs about how history will unfold—which guarantees the eventual, complete victory of liberal democracy. In other words, one day the planet will be covered with nothing but legitimate, rights-respecting regimes. So Kant can relax about the occasional supreme emergency, and insist on respect for *jus in bello,* since in the end rights-respecting democracies are destined to triumph, and brutal, rights-violating aggressors will disappear from the face of the Earth.[24] While that is an accurate description of Kant's philosophy of history—about which, more in the next two chapters—I don't believe that that is why Kant still insists on respecting *jus in bello*. Kant, elsewhere, says there's no guarantee that doing the right thing will improve the world, or even serve your self-interest. Doing one's duty might not make one happy—but it remains one's duty. Perhaps this is just an instance of this conviction. Here in supreme emergency we perhaps discern the full strength and import of Kant's commitment to morality: you are to adhere to moral demands, even if it costs you your life. Morality is thus revealed to be the single most important thing in life for Kant: the act which shows humanity at its very best.[25] Something of the same can be said of Socrates, with his own personal example of sticking to his principles even though it led to him being forced by the Athenian court to drink poison and die.[26] Critics of Kant and Socrates (and we can hear them baying at this point) alternatively suggest that first you have to survive, and then you can be moral. Existence precedes ethics, so to speak.

The second weakness with this option is that, as Walzer notes, it is fundamentally irresponsible on the part of the victim country's government, which has an obligation to protect its country's citizens from massacre and enslavement. There's a vital moral duty which the government owes its own people to do what it can to stave off the horrifying suffering and death which are part-and-parcel of the supreme emergency condition. Walzer says that if the state has any moral value at all, it is precisely to defend those whom it represents. Failure to provide such defense is an abdication of office, and it dissolves the social contract which formerly united rulers and ruled, the people and their state. (Deliberate standing-down in the face of a holocaust even more so.) In other words, it is one thing to sacrifice oneself for one's own principles, like Socrates; it is quite another to sacrifice others. The state's duty to protect implies that it cannot deliberately sacrifice its own citizens when effective resistance might still be available.[27]

1.2.4. Option #4: Walzer's Paradoxical Dirty Hands

As previously mentioned, Walzer endorses Churchill's consequentialism, but also supports Kant's strict respect for the rules. Walzer thinks that being politically realistic in supreme emergencies drives one towards the former, while being morally sensitive inclines one towards the latter. We have, on the one hand, his remark, quoted above, that one can do anything to defeat Nazis. Similar to it is his recommendation that one should, during a supreme emergency, "wager this determinate crime (the killing of innocent people) against that immeasurable evil (a Nazi triumph)." On the other, Walzer also tells us that civilians are not in any material sense "dangerous men." Thus, "they have done nothing, and are doing nothing, that entails the loss of their rights." So they may not be made the direct and intentional objects of military attack. He declares, moreover, that "the destruction of the innocent, whatever its purposes, is a kind of blasphemy against our deepest moral commitments."[28] He then asks: "How can we, with our principles and prohibitions, stand by and watch the destruction of the moral world in which those principles and prohibitions have their hold? How can we, the opponents of murder, fail to resist the practice of mass murder—even if resistance requires us, as the phrase goes, to get our hands dirty (that is, to become murderers ourselves)?"[29]

Walzer accordingly describes his position on supreme emergency as paradoxical. The victim community may set aside *jus in bello* rules, so as to protect its people and defend itself from slaughter, yet doing so is still morally wrong, in that it will involve the murder of enemy civilians. Walzer says that when "the very existence of a community may be at stake," "the restraint on utilitarian [or consequentialist] calculation must be lifted. Even if we are inclined to lift it, however, we cannot forget that the rights violated for the sake of victory are genuine rights, deeply founded and in principle inviolable."[30] The deliberate killing of innocents, though murder, can nevertheless be justified in a supreme emergency: it is simultaneously right and wrong. At the same time, and with respect to the same action, we say: "yes and no." Bomb the residential areas deliberately—murder those civilians—but do so only because you are "a nation fighting a just war [which] is desperate and survival itself is at risk." "(I)n supreme emergencies," Walzer concludes, "our judgments are doubled, reflecting the dualist character of the theory of war and the deeper complexities of our moral realism; we say yes *and* no, right *and* wrong [his italics]. That dualism makes us uneasy; the world is not a fully comprehensible, let alone a morally satisfactory place."[31]

Walzer's position underlines the sheer difficulty of the supreme emergency dilemma, whereas the other positions might seem simplistic and one-sided by contrast. His reconstruction of contemporary just war theory possesses great authority, and is aimed in this specific regard at balancing the insights of the two extreme positions of respecting the rules scrupulously, on the one hand, and discarding them completely, on the other. Yet we might wonder about the coherence of his doctrine, as well as its action-guiding properties. The upshot of just war theory, after all, is precisely to devise coherent rules that statesmen and soldiers can refer to as they make choices under pressured wartime conditions. This has been a major objective throughout this book. With Churchill's consequentialism, the nature of the advice is—in spite of its substantive problems—quite clear: disregard *jus in bello,* and do whatever you can to stave off supreme emergency. Kant's doctrine, despite its limitations, likewise provides coherent guidance: you must still adhere to *jus in bello* even in the teeth of a supreme emergency. Where, we might ask, is the coherent advice in Walzer's position of paradox? He seems, after all, to stress that the various options in a supreme emergency are *both* right and wrong. Consider the most relevant quote here: "A morally strong leader is someone who understands why it is wrong to kill the innocent and refuses to do so, refuses again and again, until the heavens are about to fall. And then he becomes a *moral criminal* [my italics] ... who knows that he can't do what he has to do—and finally does."[32] It is in reflection on this curious pronouncement that we see Walzer's position is, ultimately, not so evenly balanced between the two options as his self-reference to paradox would have us believe.

In the final analysis, Walzer leans a little bit towards Churchill's consequentialism, and this allows him at least to offer coherent advice, but it comes at the cost of some of the moral controversy attaching to that attitude. Walzer's advice to statesmen and soldiers in a supreme emergency is this: you must set aside *jus in bello* and do what you can to stop the supreme emergency, even though this will involve horrible wrongdoing. You actually have a duty to do this—to get your hands dirty, to shoulder personally the burden of this crime—because the function of your office is to defend your people. This is coherent advice, but still somewhat paradoxical: you have an important moral duty to violate another important moral duty; you have the right to do something that's not right. Even though Walzer urges this "dirty hands policy" upon statesmen and soldiers, he says they should not face war crimes trials after the war ends. They should, at most, be criticized and shamed after the war. Walzer here cites approvingly the British policy to withhold highest honors to RAF Commander Arthur Harris, who was humiliated by being the only senior UK military official denied such honors after the Second World War.[33] (Known as "Bomber Harris," or even "Butcher Harris," he advocated, devised, and implemented area bombing techniques designed to maximize civilian destruction, suffering, and death.)

1.2.5. Option #5: Moral Tragedy, Prudential Strategy

The point of this section—the fifth perspective—is to present an alternative way of thinking about supreme emergency which, on balance, is superior to all the previously-discussed rivals.[34] I stress that what follows applies only to the *external* issue of how to treat one's enemies. In my view, the *internal* issue of domestic human rights satisfaction remains as discussed last chapter. The entry point of this option reminds us that we can look at a person, or action, from at least two different perspectives. Consider, for example, Kant's thoughts on the nature of a human being. Famously, Kant argued that humanity is a composite of "animal instinctuality" and "free rationality." Considering the human being as *phenomenon* (i.e., as a physical being revealed by our senses), we see a quite limited, corporeal animal entity, subject to all the physical laws of nature, hard-wired to seek its own survival and satisfaction. Considering the human being as *noumenon* (as an object in-itself, not filtered through our perception), we see not so much finite body as expansive mind, we discern moral freedom instead of physical necessity, and we witness commitment to reason and justice even at the cost of our own happiness, and perhaps sometimes even of life itself. It's the exact same object—the human person—yet seen as possessing radically different properties depending on the perspective chosen. While Kant clearly sided with the noumenal self, he knew the phenomenal self to be in some sense inescapable, and in fact viewed much of life as a struggle between the two for primacy.[35] I propose that much can be gained from viewing the supreme emergency condition analogously under two different perspectives: the moral and the prudential. Morally, a supreme emergency is a terrible tragedy. Prudentially, it is a struggle for survival.

From the moral point of view, a supreme emergency is a moral tragedy. A moral tragedy occurs when, all things considered, each viable option you face involves a severe moral violation. It's a moral blind alley: there is no way to turn and still be morally justified. Colloquially, in a supreme emergency, "you're damned if you do, and damned if you don't." You're damned if you do, so to speak, because if you "do," you violate *jus in bello* and commit widespread civilian murder. You're damned if you don't, on the other hand, because if you "don't," you fail to protect your own civilians from widespread murder. On this understanding, there is no supreme emergency "exemption"—no moral permission or loophole. *The whole thing is a wretched moral tragedy and, no matter what you do, you're wrong.* This option differs from Walzer's in two important respects. First, it captures and highlights not merely the *difficulty* of the dilemma but its full-blown *tragedy*. I think reflection upon war's tragedy is something which just war theory can benefit from, and which has hitherto been ignored.[36] Not everything in war can be morally justified—in supreme emergency we hit a wall where we see that, morally, we run out of permissible options. Yet still we *must* choose and act—the world forces this upon us. Second, this option retains no aspect of paradox, as Walzer's still does. Walzer suggests that, in a supreme emergency, you have the right to do wrong, and/or a duty to violate duty, whereas no such confounding claims are here made, resulting I believe in a more coherent understanding. You don't have the right to do wrong, nor a duty to violate duty: *if you do wrong, you do wrong,* even under the pressure of supreme emergency conditions.

From the prudential point of view, a supreme emergency is a desperate, Hobbesian struggle for survival, and as a matter of fact any country subjected to it will do whatever it can to prevail. The animal instincts are going to kick in, just as in our inter-personal analogy involving A, B, and C. Yet these instincts can still be channeled by rules of rational choice—you want your self-saving actions to work, after all. Which rules would here help? First, make sure that resort to supreme emergency measures are, in fact, *a last resort.* Wartime can create an overheated crisis atmosphere, in which people discern "emergencies" which aren't, in fact, there. There are a great many options, permissible according to standard just war theory, to be tried prior to actions which violate the rules. As the war goes badly, perhaps things like conscription or assassination should be tried. Perhaps, as the Russians have sometimes done historically, the thing to do is pull back from one's borders, moving one's people and maybe strategically despoiling some territory, so as to put distance between oneself and the aggressor. We have to make sure supreme emergency measures aren't taken hastily, out of a failure of imagination surrounding standard military tactics.

A second rule of prudence is *to declare publicly* what one intends to do. This ties into last resort: it gives the aggressor pause, articulating the extreme measures to be taken if he, in fact, persists to push one into a condition of supreme emergency.

The public declaration should also serve as an appeal to the international community. The international community clearly has a moral duty of humanitarian intervention to aid a country in supreme emergency, and to do everything reasonable to stop the aggressor. The victim has every self-interest in appealing for such intervention, just as individuals in "personal supreme emergencies" should yell "help!" "police!" or "fire!" to bring in outside support. At the same time, the reaction of the international community has, sadly, been known to be inefficacious, half-hearted, or absent altogether—we think here of Rwanda[37]—and so, pending the imminence of the supreme emergency, the victim must always act of its own accord and not pin inflated hopes on the historically fickle replies of the international community.

Fourth, one must, to the extent possible, keep one's mind clear of other temptations, such as the passions of revenge and bloodlust, or just an inclination to destroy: to take others down with you, so to speak. This is to say that, even here, there should be *a right intention*—not one of moral purity, but rather one of prudential effectiveness, namely, that the purpose of one's actions is one's survival.

Any supreme emergency measures, above all, must have a *reasonable probability of success*. This fifth rule is absolutely vital: are the extreme measures contemplated actually going to make a difference? This is particularly important in connection with civilian targeting: if it's the aggressor's military machine which is pushing one into supreme emergency, how is killing his civilians actually going to help? To be blunt—if it came down to this—why not employ a tactical WMD against the aggressor's front line, instead of unleashing civilian slaughter?[38] Churchill argued that his policy of civilian bombing worked, because Hitler gave up his UK invasion plans. True, but the bombing didn't actually beat Hitler—what did was standard tactics, aimed at his military machine and industrial supply, for several sustained years after that. In my view, the probability of success regarding deliberate civilian targeting is probably very limited, and more utility can likely be had by violating other *jus in bello* rules while still aiming at legitimate military targets, notably the ban on prohibited weapons. And we should note that probability of success is relevant on several levels: not just, will our first strike stave off supreme emergency? But how is the aggressor likely to respond to that first strike? Can we withstand his response, and then formulate a forceful second strike? And so on.[39] This is, of course, very difficult to do under the crush of these conditions, yet some consideration simply must be given to it, since the ultimate goal remains one's survival.

Having this two-fold perspective on supreme emergency is very advantageous. It raises the important issue of moral tragedy, and it contains more detailed, practical rules of thumb for soldiers and statesmen than any of the other four approaches. It thus provides concrete, considered advice. I suppose the final question is this: which perspective is more important, the moral or the prudential?[40] I view this as a loaded and misleading question. Both perspectives are vital to a complete analysis: victims of supreme emergency are going to fight to survive, and they need rules of thumb to help them achieve that goal. At the same time, supreme emergency measures—while (hopefully) prudentially useful—remain morally wrong (insofar as they involve *jus in bello* violations). I view the scenario as directly analogous to the inter-personal case: the victim was forced to do wrong. The measures remain wrong, even though aimed against a terrible aggressor. Owing to the severe duress of the supreme emergency condition, the victim resorted to immoral measures to stave off disaster and death. Owing to this duress, we can *excuse* the victim's actions, but *never justify* them. And I think the excuse from punishment should be extended to everyone involved in the extreme measures. Picking out one official, like Bomber Harris, for public shaming seems both *pro forma* and unfair. *Pro forma*, because it's purely symbolic, and unfair because in Harris's case many others—including Churchill himself—were involved in the bombing, but only he was singled out.

I do believe that the victim country, supposing its supreme emergency measures to succeed, owes its citizens and the international community a full public accounting, after the war, for what it did and why. But that's all—no war crimes trials, no shaming, no symbolic hand-wringing. It was forced to do terrible things in order to survive. Indeed, depending on the circumstances, the international community might also have some explaining of its own to do, regarding why it failed to intervene effectively and to stop the situation from becoming so desperate and bleak in the first place. (I refer the reader back to our discussion of armed humanitarian intervention (AHI) in Chapter 3.)

1.3. SUMMARY OF SUPREME EMERGENCY

This section considered the case of supreme emergencies, which are nowhere defined, or permitted to be cited, in international law. Discussion of them has continued, however, owing to historical and recent events, speculation on dark scenarios, and the authority of figures like Rawls and Walzer. We considered five options for thinking about ethics with such emergencies. We rejected four of the most common—namely, skepticism about whether such emergencies exist at all, Churchill's consequentialism, Kant's strict respect for the rules, and Walzer's paradoxical dirty hands—and settled on the fifth option, which suggested that violating *jus in bello* in crisis remains morally wrong but might nevertheless be excused on grounds of duress and tragedy. There are still prudential (and familiar) rules of thumb which should be followed, and of course a genuine supreme emergency is perhaps the clearest instance demanding AHI from the international community. So here, too, we see that deep, sustained reflection on one concept of just war theory—i.e., supreme emergency within *jus in bello*—necessarily raises material connections to the other categories, especially *jus ad bellum*. Ultimately, it all relates—and the tone of the relation is first established by issues of just cause and political legitimacy. We'll witness something similar, as we turn our attention to cyber-warfare.

2. Cyber-warfare

Cyber-warfare is a cutting-edge topic in armed conflict. It can be defined, at least initially, as attempting to use the Internet, and related advanced computer technologies, to substantially harm the fundamental interests of a political community. And cyber-space has been referred to as "the fifth dimension of warfare," after land, water, air, and space.[41] Yet, much confusion surrounds cyber-warfare, both regarding its present realities and its future potential. How much damage can cyber-attacks actually do? Is it even appropriate to liken computer-based cyber-attacks to physical ("kinetic") violence? Is "informational warfare," as cyber-war is otherwise known, changing the very nature of political conflict in our time (indeed, for all time)? This section aspires to clear up some—but certainly not all—of this fog which surrounds the fifth dimension. It will do so by means of critically examining two important distinctions in this regard, and also by meditating on how just war theory should approach this subject.[42] But first, some workable definitions are required.

2.1. QUICK DEFINITIONS

As offered above, "cyber-warfare" is an umbrella term, referring to the aggressive use of advanced computer technologies in a way deliberately designed to substantially harm a political community.[43] Cyber-warfare, generally, can take one of three forms:

1) *espionage* (i.e., using the Internet, etc., to gather information which a country has taken steps to protect as a matter of national security, such as secret, confidential, or classified information);
2) *the spread of disinformation*, via the same means, in a manner which harms the security interests of the target country; and/or
3) *sabotage* (i.e., using these means to bring about the non-functioning, or destruction, of various systems which are integral to the basic interests of a political community. The systems most often mentioned include: electricity and power; water and fuel distribution; computerized parts of manufacturing facilities; transportation systems, such as air or rail; banking and the stock market; and even the Internet itself, or at least the most used websites (like Google or Facebook), Internet service providers, and/or the most basic operating systems).[44]

Cyber-attacks would then refer to any specific use of any of 1–3 above, as tools within the overall cyber-warfare strategy. The countries most frequently mentioned today as developers, victims, or perpetrators of cyber-war technology include America, Britain, China, France, India, Israel, Pakistan, and Russia.[45]

2.2. THE FIRST DISTINCTION: "CYBER-WAR-SKEPTIC" VS. "CYBER-WAR-SALESMAN"

An example of a *cyber-war-skeptic* is Howard Schmidt, who declares that "there is no such thing as cyber-warfare."[46] A cyber-war-skeptic believes that the threat from such measures (as 1–3 above) is minimal or, at least, not at all on a level where talking about a military response is appropriate. A cyber-war-skeptic might also believe that the whole extended analogy—between information attacks and computer viruses, on the one hand, and kinetic warfare and physical casualties, on the other—is: 1) crude and factually incorrect, perhaps even a "category mistake" confusing two completely different kinds of things; 2) fear-mongering, capitalizing on the common person's (relative) intimidation by, and lack of knowledge regarding, advanced computer technology; and 3) deliberate exaggeration, or even fraud, communicated by those with a vested interest in the business of cyber-security, ranging from cash-strapped military departments looking for fresh resources to greedy software programmers drooling at the prospects for profit. (And the financial stakes are very considerable: The Pentagon has publicly disclosed that, in the first half of 2009 alone, it spent over $100 million USD "responding to, and repairing damage from, cyber-attacks.")[47]

A *cyber-war-salesman*, on the other hand, would be someone who wildly exaggerates the threat of cyber-war, and the disruption to be suffered from such. It needs to be stressed that such a figure doesn't have to be a cyber-war profiteer, as just mentioned at the end of last paragraph. Consider that the US Director of National Intelligence testified before a Congressional committee in 2010 that the "information infrastructure" on which the US is so dependent is "severely threatened" by cyberattack.[48] The US mainstream broadcasting company CBS reported, in an evening national TV broadcast, that, in 2007, the US federal government suffered "an espionage Pearl Harbor" when some unknown sources downloaded "terabytes of classified government and even military information." (Note the similarity between the spoken sound of "terabytes" and "terror bites.")[49] Indeed, in 2010, the US Joint Forces Command issued a statement expressing its conviction that "adversaries have already taken advantage of computer networks and the power of information technology... to plan and execute savage acts of terrorism."[50] Even the normally staid *New York Times* reported that a malware program (i.e., a malicious software virus) which had infected some US factory computers should be "considered the first attack on critical industrial infrastructure that sits at the foundation of modern economies."[51] Finally, consider the closing lines in one of distinguished journalist Michael Gross's important articles about information warfare in general, and a virus called "Stuxnet" (more below) in particular:

> Cyber-conflict makes military action more like a never-ending game of uncle, where the fingers of weaker nations are perpetually bent back. The wars would be secret, waged by members of anonymous, elite brain trusts, none of whom would ever have to look an enemy in the eye. For people whose lives are connected to the targets, the results could be as catastrophic as a bombing raid, but would be even more disorienting. People would suffer, but would never be certain whom to blame.
>
> Stuxnet is the Hiroshima of cyber-war. That is its true significance, and all the speculation about its target and its source should not blind us to that larger reality. We have crossed a threshold, and there is no turning back.[52]

Within all these various dramatic comments, one takes special note of the multiple references to terrorism and to the Second World War. And the question naturally arises: who's right? Who, between the cyber-war skeptic and the cyber-war salesman, is more correct?

2.2.1. *Middle Ground Judgment*

On the one hand, there is no denying that cyber-attacks are real, and they have had some surprisingly serious consequences, at times very much akin to actual, kinetic warfare. So, in this sense, the cyber-war skeptic is wrong and the cyber-war salesman, right. Several quick, illustrative examples:

- In 1982, during the height of The Cold War, a Canadian oil and gas company thought they had a Soviet (Russian) spy in their midst. They contacted America's military. The Canadians and Americans launched a joint scheme: they would let the spy steal what he was after: a computer-control system for regulating the flow of oil and gas. (The Russians wanted this to modernize their pipeline system in Siberia.) But the Americans programmed the computer system with "a logic bomb" designed to make the pipelines malfunction and eventually explode after it was implemented. And that is exactly what happened, with some loss of life and a substantial set-back for a key sector of the Soviet economy.[53]

- In 2007, Russia launched a cyber-attack on Estonia, a neighboring country. There was a dispute between them regarding the movement of a war statue of great meaning to the Russians. When the Estonians moved it, Russia responded with a crippling cyber-attack on the websites of the Estonian government, media, and its richest banks. For nearly a week, these institutions could not conduct any business online, nor could their citizens/customers contact them, or access anything through them. The attack came to an end only when Russia decided to release its grip.[54]

- From May to December, 2010, India and Pakistan traded over 1,000 separate cyber-attacks against each other, directed not only against official government and military websites but also selected high-profile companies, universities, and research institutes. While most of these attacks were mere "defacements" of the various websites (and thus more a form of disinformation, or graffiti, than sabotage), they nevertheless revealed both the involvement of these countries in cyber-war activities as well as the degree to which they were capable of gaining access and demonstrating control.[55]

- More seriously, in 2010, Iran was attacked by a computer virus or "worm" commonly believed to have been the joint-creation of both America and Israel (nick-named "Stuxnet"). A piece of malware, this very sophisticated computer virus was planted in a German-made component of one of Iran's nuclear reactors. When it was activated, the virus eventually disabled the reactor, forcing it to shut down—lest it melt-down and cause enormous damage—for an unspecified time (thought to be at least for months, and perhaps even over a year). The goal, reputedly, was to set-back Iran's progress towards developing nuclear weapons.[56]

- Perhaps relatedly, in 2012 the "Flame" virus entered public knowledge. Reputedly, Flame went undetected for over 5 years. Its main purpose seems to have been espionage or information-gathering. Experts have pronounced it "more than 20 times more powerful" in its sophistication than Stuxnet and, by time of discovery, it was confirmed to be present in over 5,000 computers, almost all in the Middle East (with a special concentration in Egypt, Iran, and Israel).[57]

- The country most associated with cyber-attacking today is China. Unlike American and Russian attacks, though, which have tended to feature sabotage, the Chinese seem to prefer espionage, both of the commercial and political variety. Many of the top US high-tech firms, such as Google, Microsoft, Apple, and various weapons companies, have complained of sustained cyber-attacks from China which have accessed tons of their highest-security information, including especially product design and patent information (as well as, intriguingly, human resources data, such as personal information about top executives). The companies have pressed the US government to respond, but thus far all that have been issued are verbal warnings.[58]

Thus, informational warfare is real; and it can have—and has had—very serious consequences, including loss of life. (Though, admittedly, these most serious consequences seem more rare and exceptional rather than regular and expected, as with direct kinetic warfare.) On the other hand, the cyber-war skeptic seems correct to insist that it's important not to exaggerate people's fears about the likelihood of their being victimized by such strikes, or to make colorful but unhelpful analogies to weapons (such as Hiroshima's bomb) which can kill hundreds of thousands of people. And it certainly seems compelling to note that all this talk, and all this activity, surrounding cyber-warfare does serve some vested interests, out to gain narrow advantage, and we should regard their claims with some sober second thought, and ask for proof.

After all, if the Pentagon is spending at least $100 million USD every six months on cyber-defense, one must admit that a pot of money that large is likely to attract not only legitimate and defensible, but also questionable and grasping, attention.

2.3. WHAT TO DO? JUST WAR THEORY'S PERSPECTIVE

Cyber-warfare is here, and it's real; and so the question arises: what, if anything, should we do about it? An obvious response would be to try to regulate it with the law. At present, there is no international law whatsoever regarding informational warfare. In 2011, America, China, and Russia got together for a high-level meeting of officials—very preliminary "talks about talks"—regarding a possible negotiated treaty between them on the acceptable methods and means of cyber-war (analogous to the many such treaties on kinetic warfare, notably the Hague and Geneva Conventions). But the talks fell apart, amidst bitter mutual accusations.[59]

It's vital to note that, in the absence of an international treaty on this, all the major countries have simply (and resoundingly) declared that—as a matter of their foreign policy—they will consider any "severe" cyber-attack against them as a *casus belli*, i.e., a justification for war, a reason to resort to war (presumably, either of the new informational, or the traditional physical, kind).[60]

In the absence of law, one turns to ethics for guidance. We've seen this already in connection with the EMTs last chapter, and with supreme emergencies above. This book, obviously, has been urging the merits of just war theory as the best approach to ethics in wartime. What might just war theory have to say about cyber-warfare?

2.3.1. *Application of* Jus ad Bellum *Rules to Cyber-war*

JUST CAUSE

As shown in Chapter 2, the gold standard of *casus belli* is a kinetic physical attack, usually involving some kind of armed invasion across a border. As such, a cyber-strike does not seem to constitute aggression in the traditional meaning of the term. But two thoughts suggest themselves:

1) sometimes, as we've seen, cyber-attacks can actually lead to traditional, physical damage, including loss of life. Such would have to be construed as straightforward instances of aggression, ethically and legally enabling a forceful response.

2) an argument could be made that the concept of aggression itself needs to be amplified and expanded (but responsibly so) precisely to allow for cyber-attacks as a kind of aggression. This thinking would need to stress the new and pervasive role which advanced computer technologies have

> come to play in our lives (especially in the developed world), and the degree to which damage aimed at them could rise to the level of a very serious, society-wide attack. Indeed, some might even argue that, e.g., a cyber-strike on the stock market—causing it to crash, and costing millions of people billions of dollars—might actually be more damaging in long-term consequence than, e.g., an army unit lobbing a missile across a border, resulting in the physical injury (or death) of only, say, three soldiers on border patrol. This is to say that: a) a powerful cyber-strike might actually be more damaging than a physical strike; and b) if the latter counts as aggression, then the former ought to, as well. The key notion here would be that our thinking of what constitutes aggression needs to keep pace with the times and the new technological realities of our lives.[61]

I think the second argument requires more thorough explanation, moving forward, but I do support the general notion that these just war concepts, to remain relevant, must be considered in light of the latest technologies and deep, ongoing developments in the contours of our lives. My own considered view is that a cyber-strike probably will not justify anything more than an in-kind cyber-response, and that the burden of proof rests on anyone arguing that it may justify something further, such as an armed kinetic attack in reply. While there is much defensive, deterrent-based wisdom in the status quo—i.e., of warning others that any "severe" cyber-strike will be considered a *casus belli* (especially one involving sabotage against core, society-wide, basic infrastructure)—more sustained efforts at deeply developing these concepts need be made.[62]

PROPORTIONALITY (AND PROBABILITY OF SUCCESS)

Proportionality would clearly support the notion that a cyber-strike probably justifies only an in-kind cyber-response, and not an armed kinetic war in reply. And probability of success demands that we ask, for any such cyber-strike: is it likely to achieve its aims? How so? What kind of confidence can one have in that regard, especially as regards the minimization of any over-spill onto civilians, and the likelihood that one can have favorable control over the consequences?

LAST RESORT

There is a real danger, and some evidence from the actual uses thus far, that a major temptation with cyber-strikes is that they be used not as a last resort, but rather as a first-strike, either on their own or else to disorient and "soften up" the target for an actual kinetic attack, such as with drones, missiles, or even an armed invasion of soldiers.

It might be argued that cyber-war could be rendered consistent with this principle, and find its own proper slot in the moral hierarchy of foreign policy tools, with diplomacy at the ground floor, as the most accessible (and encouraged) level, and with kinetic force at the top: the rarest, riskiest, and most controversial. Cyber-strikes could be located either just beneath kinetic warfare, or else perhaps on par with sweeping economic sanctions, which often are similarly targeted at foundational aspects of the target country's economy.[63]

PUBLIC DECLARATION BY A PROPER AUTHORITY (AND RIGHT INTENTION)

Here there is no question that the vast majority of actual cyber-attacks thus far have violated this rule of just war. Indeed, has *any* government publicly declared, and accepted responsibility, for *any* cyber-attack? One of the seductions of this technology is its supposed anonymity (though, almost always, the doer's identity does come to be known: see more below). We know that, historically, those with the war power prefer to use it in secret and with few, or no, checks-and-balances on them. Cyber-war may thus provide terrible temptations in favor of "easy war" and "secret war" which ought, obviously, to be resisted. This raises the related issue of right intention, as those who wish to conduct war in secret—almost invariably—do so because they have something objectionable to hide.

Experts in the field talk repeatedly of "the attribution problem," noting how cyber-attackers—especially those suspected to be linked, in some way, with China—go out of their way to hide their tracks and conceal the ultimate source of the strike. This is of great concern, as it would no doubt color our judgment of whom it is permissible to strike back at.[64] Yet, while being ignorant of the sophisticated details of how these things get determined, I would want to point out, as mentioned above, that eventually—and rather quickly, actually—the cyber-community seems to have been able to come up with pretty reliable attributions thus far. Is cyber-strike attribution really so different from, and so much more difficult than, say, the investigations which went into determining who was responsible for the 9/11 attacks (i.e., al-Qaeda), and how the then-government of Afghanistan was complicit in them as well?[65]

2.3.2. *Application of* Jus in Bello *Rules to Cyber-war*

We saw last chapter that there are many rules of *jus in bello*, but most of them concern only physical, kinetic warfare, and they are not directly applicable to cyber-war. The one principle which most clearly is, though, is *jus in bello*'s most important: discrimination and non-combatant immunity.

DISCRIMINATION AND NONCOMBATANT IMMUNITY

If one engages in a cyber-strike, one ought to take every effort to ensure that civilians are left out of it, and that only legitimate targets bear the brunt of the cyber-attack. The best, contrasting examples from the above list of cases would be the Russian cyber-strike on Estonia, on the one hand, and Stuxnet, on the other. The Russian strike clearly impacted every citizen in Estonia, as (for the week or so in which it was on-going) such citizens could not have contact with their democratically-elected government online, nor could they access personal funds from their own bank accounts, and so on. This, clearly, was a substantial and intended interference with the basic rhythms of their daily lives. Ironically, Estonia (and the other Baltic states) had been, up until that point, at the fore-front of so-called "e-government": i.e., making as many government services deliverable over the Internet as possible. The cyber-strike from Russia, unfortunately, showed the potential disadvantages of such a progressive and technologically advanced approach. In any event, it clearly violated non-combatant immunity.

Stuxnet, by contrast, was elaborately constructed to harm only the nuclear power capability of the Iranian government. And it seems to have succeeded in that regard, and not one civilian was even harmed in the process. (The virus, after it struck, was programmed to "evaporate": i.e., to write itself out of existence, so it could do no further harm.) Now, I suppose one could talk about the potential harm to the public, had the Iranians not known how to handle the situation: things may, indeed, have taken quite a frightening turn. Obviously, the perpetrators (rumored to be the US and Israel) had confidence that the Iranians would recognize what was happening, and would have the wherewithal to shut the reactor down and not risk broader public damage from a Chernobyl-style meltdown. In any event, these two broad examples show what just war theory would view as a permissible cyber-strike: a discriminate one aimed only at a legitimate target, and with clear measures taken to minimize or eliminate any negative consequences on civilian populations. Especially to be ruled out—as the equivalent, really, of WMD—are potent, society-wide, cyber-strikes involving sabotage of basic core infrastructure (such as electricity or water treatment) seeing as how such would predictably involve large-scale damage, harm, and loss of life.[66]

2.3.3. *Application of* Jus post Bellum *Rules to Cyber-war*

It's unclear exactly how "post-war" norms apply to cyber-war, or broad-based computer attacks. (I myself think there's much room for both maneuver, and hard, ground-breaking work, on this subject.) All I wish to point out is that there is a post-cyber-war phase, just as there is a post-conflict phase for every other kind of armed conflict, and so some principles of post-cyber-attack justice must come into play. One I would recommend, above all, would be to "*Clean-up, and Aid with*

Restoration" following a cyber-strike. Now, obviously, it depends crucially on the details of the strike: Stuxnet, e.g., evaporated and didn't cause spill-over damage to civilians, and so it's hard to see what duties of clean-up might meaningfully have been called for. But in the Russia/Estonia case, where people may have suffered real (mainly financial) hardship during their week of being blocked out from their banks, and not having access to government services, etc., some kind of actual monetary restitution might be in order.

Relatedly, it seems that there would be a *jus post bellum* norm calling for "*Public Accountability*," in terms of a public declaration, and explanation, of why a country resorted to a cyber-strike, and/or why it responded either kinetically or in a cyber way, to a cyber-attack. Both *jus ad bellum* and *jus post bellum* unite together to call, very strongly, for public accountability and transparency both before, and in the aftermath of, war.

As war crimes trials are called for *après la guerre*, so it would seem that cyber criminals need to be held accountable, and investigated for charges, following a cyber-strike. Such "*Trials for Cyber-Criminals*" would serve to underline and enforce the seriousness of their actions, and the attitude of the international community towards things like theft of intellectual property, espionage, and especially harm-causing acts of sabotage. Legal innovations are called for here, in order to bring such into reality.[67]

Finally, it would seem as though some "*De-cyber-ization*" might be called for, if we follow the standard logic of demilitarization post-war (more next chapter). If cyber tools were used in an aggressive attack, then the international community, and especially any victims, are entitled to some reasonable security that they will not be made victim once more, in the near future, to the cyber-schemes of the aggressive power. How, exactly, to go about such stripping or curbing of cyber-power is, of course, beyond the ambit of this section (and the cyber-skills of its author).

2.4. OPTIMISM VS. PESSIMISM

Which brings us to the second and final distinction here: will we be able to achieve such control, such progressive agreement about when it is proper, and when illegal, to use cyber-warfare? The optimist says: why not? If we did it with something as ferocious as atomic and nuclear weaponry, surely we can do it with cyber-war technology. The pessimist would be inclined to cite how different cyber-technology is—how widespread and diffuse and more easily hidden it is—and comment darkly as to how, in many ways already, the world has devolved into a situation where, in cyber-terms, it is somewhat like a Hobbesian war of "all against all," or at least every country against every country.[68] The middle ground judgment here, in my view, would thus be that, while the pessimist probably provides an accurate description of the state-of-play as it presently stands, there are some historical grounds for believing that, if we've been able to bring other forms of very destructive technology under control through international laws and arms control agreements, then we ought to be able to do the same things with the tools of cyber-war. There should be new international laws on informational warfare, and they can and should draw upon the values and resources located within the rules of *jus ad, in,* and *post bellum*.[69]

2.5. SUMMARY OF CYBER-WARFARE

This section—striving to dispel some of the fog surrounding the fifth domain of warfare—first sought to define its terms, and then to consider in a substantial way two "big picture" distinctions surrounding informational warfare: 1) that between cyber-war-skeptic and cyber-war-salesman; and 2) that between optimist and pessimist. With regard to each distinction, it was argued that a middle ground judgment between the two seems the best and most promising way to understand the issue, and to wrestle with the many, and profound, challenges which cyber-war technology now poses to the community of nations. Just war theory was offered as a (stubbornly and perhaps surprisingly) useful tool to draw upon, as we move boldly forward into the new age of cyber-conflict.

3. Conclusion

This chapter examined two fascinating and controversial cases, which take to the very limits the nature of the *jus in bello*: what it means on its own, and how it hooks into the other just war categories of *jus ad bellum* and *jus post bellum*. After discovering the nature (and cases) of supreme emergencies and cyber-warfare, argument was made that a just war analysis of both situations can offer action-guiding rules which are both plausible and principled. And so now we ask: can such also be done during the termination phase of war?

Notes

1 W. Churchill quoted in Michael Walzer, *Just and Unjust Wars*, 3rd ed. (New York: Basic Books, 2000), 245. For primary sources: Winston Churchill, *The Gathering Storm* (London: Macmillan, 1961), 488–90; Winston Churchill, *The Hinge of Fate* (New York: Bantam, 1962), 770 f.

2 Walzer, *Wars*, 251–68.

3 Grotius quoted in Paul Christopher, *The Ethics of War and Peace* (Englewood Cliffs, NJ: Prentice Hall, 1994), 109.

4 Churchill, *Storm*, 488; Churchill, *Hinge*, 770; John Keegan, *The Second World War* (New York: Penguin, 2005).

5 Walzer, *Wars*, 253.
6 Churchill, *Storm*, 490–92; Churchill, *Hinge*, 770; Frederick Taylor, *Dresden* (New York: Harper Collins, 2004).
7 John Rawls, *The Law of Peoples* (Cambridge, MA: Harvard UP, 1999), 98–105; John Rawls in *Dissent*'s Summer 1995 symposium on the bombing of Hiroshima.
8 Michael Walzer, *Arguing About War* (New Haven: Yale UP, 2004), 39.
9 John Costello, *The Pacific War* (New York: Harper, 1982).
10 James L. Gelvin, *The Modern Middle East*, 3rd ed. (Oxford: Oxford UP, 2011).
11 Davida E. Kellogg, "Reaping the Whirlwind: Terrorism, Supreme Emergency and the Abandonment of *Jus in Bello* Restrictions on Attacking Enemy Civilians," Unpublished paper, 2002, University of Maine; Rowan Scarborough, *Rumsfeld's War* (New York: Regnery, 2004); Rudolph Guiliani, *Leadership* (New York: Miramax, 2002), 3–28, 341–80; Bill Adler, ed., *The Quotable Guiliani* (New York: Pocket, 2003), 23–54; the post-9/11 speeches of President George W. Bush, all available in complete text at <www.americanrhetoric.com>.
12 In terms of state actors, we could I suppose imagine a grisly scenario involving war between the USA and, say, Russia and/or China. The latter two probably do have enough WMD to put America into supreme emergency.
13 Olivia Bosch and Peter van Ham, *Global Non-Proliferation and Counter-Terrorism* (London: Brookings Institute, 2006).
14 Niall Ferguson, *Colossus* (New York: Penguin, 2005).
15 Thanks to Neta Crawford for these examples. On the history of genocide, see Frank Chalk and Kurt Jonassohn, eds. *The History and Sociology of Genocide* (New Haven, CT: Yale UP, 1990); and Samuel Totten et al., eds., *Century of Genocide* (New York: Garland, 1997).
16 For more on the DDE, see Walzer, *Wars*, 151–60 and our discussion last chapter. Thanks to Alex Moseley for discussions on this.
17 Thomas W. Pogge, "Loopholes in Moralities," *Journal of Philosophy* (1992): 79–98.
18 Walzer, *Wars*, 29–34. This is the option Walzer describes as "the sliding scale."
19 Thomas Nagel, "War and Massacre," *Philosophy and Public Affairs* (1973): 133–41.
20 Defenders of consequentialism may well note more everyday circumstances in which it might seem quite plausible to assert, and act on, the notion that the ends might justify the means. But *in this case* of supreme emergency, the means contemplated are so extreme and controversial—widespread, deliberate civilian murder—that it shows an instance where the principle breaks down. Thanks to Bob Martin for discussion on this.
21 Onora O'Neill, *Constructions of Reason* (Cambridge: Cambridge UP, 1989).
22 W. Michael Reisman and Chris T. Antoniou, eds., *The Laws of War: A Comprehensive Collection of Primary Documents Governing Armed Conflict* (New York: Vintage, 1994); Adam Roberts and Richard Guelff, eds., *Documents on the Laws of War* (Oxford: Oxford UP, 1999).
23 Plato, "Gorgias" in *Plato: The Collected Dialogues*, ed. Edith Hamilton and Huntingdon Cairns (Princeton: Princeton UP, 1961), 229–307.
24 Andrew Fiala, "Terrorism and the Philosophy of History: Liberalism, Realism and the Supreme Emergency Exemption," *Essays in Philosophy* (Vol. 3, 2002): 1–15; Michael W. Doyle, *Ways of War and Peace* (New York: W.W. Norton, 1997); Michael W. Doyle, "Kant, Liberal Legacies and Foreign Affairs," *Philosophy and Public Affairs* (Vol. 12, 1983): 205–54 and 323–53; Michael Edward Brown et al., eds., *Debating the Democratic Peace* (Cambridge, MA: MIT, 1996).

25 Brian Orend, *War and International Justice: A Kantian Perspective* (Waterloo, ON: Wilfrid Laurier UP, 2000).

26 Plato, *Collected*, 3–100.

27 Walzer, *Wars*, 251–68.

28 The quotes, in order, from: Walzer, *Wars*, 231, 259, 146–51, 262–68.

29 Walzer, *Arguing*, 37.

30 Walzer, *Wars*, 195, 228.

31 Walzer, *Wars*, 325–28 and 251–68.

32 Walzer, *Arguing*, 45.

33 Walzer, *Wars*, 251–68; Michael Walzer, "Political Action: The Problem of Dirty Hands," *Philosophy and Public Affairs* (1972/3): 160–80.

34 I wish especially to thank Patrick Hayden, Danny Statman, and Toni Erskine for stimulating and sharpening my thoughts regarding what follows.

35 Orend, *Kantian Perspective*, 10–36.

36 Another concept which just war theory might gain by adding would be mercy.

37 Gérard Prunier, *The Rwanda Crisis: History of a Genocide* (New York: Columbia UP, 1995); Roméo Dallaire, *Shake Hands with the Devil: Humanity's Failure in Rwanda* (New York: Random House, 2003).

38 In other words, and as an accommodation to realism, I do admit there might be extreme, very rare conditions when WMD use—perhaps including nukes—might at least be excusable (but probably never justifiable). More on realism in Chapter 8.

39 Thanks to Neta Crawford for emphasizing this.

40 Toni Erskine has urged this question, and choice, upon me. But I don't think I have to choose, for reasons explained.

41 The Economist, "Special Report on Cyberwar: War in the Fifth Domain." *The Economist* (1 July 2010): 18–26.

42 See also Martin Cook, "'Cyberation' and Just War Doctrine" *Journal of Military Ethics* (2010): 417–22.

43 Jeffrey Carr, *Inside Cyber Warfare* (London: O'Reilly, 2010).

44 Richard A. Clarke, *Cyber-War: The Next Threat to National Security and What to Do About It* (New York: Ecco, 2012).

45 Ibid.

46 Howard A. Schmidt, *Patrolling Cyberspace* (Washington, DC: Larstan, 2006).

47 Richard A. Clarke, *Cyber War* (New York: Harper Collins, 2010).

48 Admiral Dennis C. Blair, testifying before the Select Committee on Intelligence of the Senate, 2 February 2010. Quoted in the US Senate bill S. 2105 (112th): The Cybersecurity Act of 2012.

49 CBS news, *60 Minutes*, broadcast 6 November 2009.

50 USJFC, *Cyberwar_Report*, released 18 February 2010: <www.jfcom.mil>

51 New York Times, "Malware Hits Computerized Industrial Equipment," *New York Times*, 24 September 2010.

52 Michael Joseph Gross, "The Fog of Cyber-War," *Vanity Fair* (April 2011): 155–98, with quote at 198.

53 The Economist, "Special Report on Cyberwar: War in the Fifth Domain," *The Economist* (1 July 2010): 18–26.

54 Athina Karatzogianni, ed., *Cyber-Conflict and Global Politics* (London: Routledge, 2008).
55 Berg P. Hyacinthe, *Cyber-Warriors at War* (New York: XLibris, 2011).
56 Michael Joseph Gross, "The Stuxnet Cyber-Weapon," *Vanity Fair* (April 2011): 152–98.
57 Oliver Stallwood, "Flame Virus: How Malware Became the New Weapon of War," *Metro News* (London, UK: 26 June 2012).
58 Michael Joseph Gross, "Enter the Cyber-Dragon," *Vanity Fair* (September 2011): 220–234
59 Heather Harrison Dinniss, *Cyber-Warfare and the Laws of War* (Cambridge: Cambridge UP, 2012).
60 Jeffrey Carr, *Inside Cyber-Warfare,* 2nd ed. (London: O'Reilly, 2011); William J. Lynn III, "Defending a New Domain: The Pentagon's Cyberstrategy," *Foreign Affairs* (Sept./Oct. 2010): 97–108.
61 Luciano Floridi, *Information* (Oxford: Oxford UP, 2010); Luciano Floridi, ed., *The Cambridge Handbook of Information and Computer Ethics* (Cambridge: Cambridge UP, 2010).
62 Susan Brenner, *Cyber Threats: The Emerging Fault Lines of the Nation-State* (Oxford: Oxford UP, 2009).
63 Brian Orend, *Introduction to International Studies* (Oxford: Oxford UP, 2012), Chap. 4.
64 Clark, *Cyber-War,* 20–42.
65 Randall R. Dipert, "The Ethics of Cyberwarfare," *Journal of Military Ethics* (2010): 384–410.
66 George R. Lucas, "Just War Theory and Cyber-War," paper delivered at The First International Workshop on "The Ethics of Informational Warfare," University of Hertfordshire (UK), 1 July 2011.
67 See both Dinniss, *Laws,* and Hyacinthe, *Cyber-warriors,* for more on the technicalities.
68 Randall R. Dipert, "The Probable Impact of Future Cyberwarfare," paper delivered at The First International Workshop on "The Ethics of Informational Warfare," University of Hertfordshire (UK), 1 July 2011.
69 Daniel Ventre, *Cyberguerre* (Paris: Hermès-Lavoisier, 2010); Daniel Ventre, *Cyberespace et actueurs du cyberconflict* (Paris: Hermès-Lavoisier, 2011). In April 2013, an independant body of experts released a suggested draft treaty to govern cyber-warfare, called "The Tallinn Principles" (in honor of Tallinn, capital of Estonia). The full draft of these 95—!—principles can be found at: <http://www.nowandfutures.com/large/Tallinn-Manual-on-the-International-Law-Applicable-to-Cyber-Warfare-Draft-.pdf>.

6

Jus post Bellum #1

OVERLAPPING CONSENSUS, AND RETRIBUTION

"The object in war is a better state of peace."

—B.H. LIDDELL HART[1]

How should wars end? It might seem surprising, but only very recently has the issue of justice after war—or "*jus post bellum*"—come into the prominence it deserves. All too often, still today, just war theorists stick with the first two categories—of *jus ad bellum* and *jus in bello*—and pretend like that is all they have to talk about. International law, sadly, has joined just war theory regarding its relative silence on proper war termination.[2] This is a decrepit state of affairs that must be remedied, both for conceptual and concrete historical reasons:

1) War has three phases: beginning, middle, and end. So if we want a complete just war theory—or a comprehensive international law—we simply *must* discuss justice during the termination phase of war. After all, there's no guarantee that if you fought justly, for the sake of a just cause, that you will automatically impose a just set of peace terms upon your vanquished enemy. Mistakes are possible, and made frequently, during each of the three phases. It is, indeed, difficult to fight a truly just war.

2) Failure to include *jus post bellum* in your just war theory leaves you open to a sharp, potentially devastating objection from both realists and pacifists, namely, that just war theory fails to consider war in a deep enough, systematic enough kind of way. It simply considers war on a case-by-case basis, dusting off its precious old rules for yet another ethical application. Pacifists, e.g., have long objected that just war theory, with its hitherto narrow focus, is fundamentally passive and complaisant about war—that it doesn't ultimately care why war breaks out and doesn't seek to improve

things after war's end (so as to make the international system more peaceful over the longer term). I believe this objection succeeds against just war theorists who have no account of *jus post bellum*; if we are not to meet their sorry fate, we must include such an account to surmount this challenge.

3) More concretely, recent armed conflicts—in Bosnia and Kosovo, in central Africa, in Libya and Afghanistan, and twice in Iraq—demonstrate the difficulty and illustrate the importance and controversy surrounding a just peace settlement. The major issues of contemporary international affairs simply demand we look at *jus post bellum*. We know, for instance, that when wars are wrapped up badly, they sow the seeds for future bloodshed. For example, some people think that America's failure to remove Saddam Hussein from power after they first beat him in 1991 prolonged a serious struggle and eventually necessitated the second war, of regime change, in 2003. Would the second war have happened at all had the first been ended differently—i.e., more properly and thoroughly, with a longer-range vision in mind? Many historians ask the exact same question of the two World Wars and the recent, related Serb wars: first in Bosnia and then over Kosovo.

4) Failure to construct principles of *jus post bellum* is to allow unconstrained war termination. And to allow unconstrained war termination is to allow the winner to enjoy the spoils of war. This is dangerously permissive, since winners have been known to exact peace terms which are draconian and vengeful. The Treaty of Versailles, terminating World War I in 1918–19, is often mentioned in this connection. It is commonly suggested that the sizable territorial concessions, and steep compensations payments, forced upon Germany created hatred and economic distress, opening a space for Hitler to capitalize on, saying in effect: "Let's vent our rage by recapturing our lost lands; and let's rebuild our economy by refusing to pay compensation and by ramping up war-related manufacturing."[3]

5) Failure to regulate war termination probably prolongs fighting on the ground. Since they have few assurances or expectations regarding the nature of the settlement, belligerents will be sorely tempted to keep using force to jockey for position. Since international law imposes very few clear constraints upon the winners of war, losers can conclude it is reasonable for them to refuse to surrender, to continue to fight. Perhaps, they think, "we might get lucky and the military tide will turn. Better that

than just throw ourselves at the mercy of our enemy." Many observers felt this reality plagued the Bosnian civil war, which we saw (Chapter 3) had many failed negotiations and a three-year "slow burn" of continuous violence as the very negotiations took place.[4]

Peace treaties should still, of course, remain tightly tailored to the historical realities of the particular conflict in question. But admitting this is not to concede that the search for general guidelines, or universal standards, is futile or naïve. There is no inconsistency, or mystery, in holding particular actors, in complex local conflicts, up to more general—even universal—standards of conduct. Judges and juries do that on a daily basis, evaluating the factual complexities of a given case in light of general moral and legal principles. We should do the same regarding war termination. The goal of this chapter, accordingly, is to consider a general set of plausible principles to guide communities seeking to resolve their armed conflicts fairly and decently.[5]

1. Starting Assumptions

The first step is to answer the question: what may a participant rightly aim at, with regard to a just war? What are the goals to be achieved by the settlement of the conflict? We need some starting assumptions to focus our thoughts on these issues. First, the two *jus post bellum* chapters will mainly consider classical cases of interstate armed conflict to provide a quicker, cleaner route to the general set of post-war principles sought after. But I do believe that these principles, owing to their generality and moral strength, clearly apply as well to non-classical cases, such as those discussed in Chapter 3. The point here is to fashion an overall blueprint which can be amended, as details demand, in particular and especially unconventional cases.

The next assumption is that the forthcoming set of post-war principles is offered as guidance to those participants who want to end their wars in a fair, justified way. Not all participants do, of course—and to that extent they act unjustly during the termination phase. Violations of *jus post bellum* are just as serious as those of *jus ad bellum* and *jus in bello*. Like *jus ad bellum*, responsibility for fulfilling *jus post bellum* is primarily political (as opposed to military), although some cases may blur that line: e.g., if there is a need to impose short-term, direct military occupation over a shattered society. A related assumption is that there is no such thing as "victor's justice." The raw fact of military victory in war does not, of itself, confer moral rights upon the victor, or ethical duties upon the vanquished. It is only when the victorious regime has fought a just and lawful war, as defined by international law and just war theory, that we can speak meaningfully of rights and duties, of both victor and vanquished, at the conclusion of armed conflict.[6]

This is to say, importantly, that when or *if an aggressor wins a war, the peace terms will necessarily be unjust*. The injustice of the aggression which caused the war infects the conclusion of the war, as readily as it infected the conduct, which I argued for in Chapter 4 (in connection with proportionality and the DDE). The three just war categories are not separate but, rather, connected. And *jus ad bellum* sets the tone and context for the other two categories, and to that extent is probably the most important. This is not to say that meeting *jus ad bellum* will automatically result in your meeting *jus in bello* and *jus post bellum*. But it *is* to say, conversely, that failure to meet *jus ad bellum* results in automatic failure to meet *jus in bello* and *jus post bellum*. Truly: *once you're an aggressor in war, everything is lost to you, morally*.

Now, we might still say that some terms which a victorious aggressor imposes are better or worse than others which it could have. A winning aggressor might—though it's unlikely—have milder peace terms than we expected. But we cannot call these terms just, since they remain the product of a war which, overall, was unjust. So, for the rest of this chapter, I shall assume that the winning side fought the war with *jus ad bellum* on its side. It is in this sense that I develop an "ideal" conception of post-war justice, to arrive at some rules and values against which we can measure and evaluate the non-ideal cases with which the world confronts us.

With these assumptions declared, let's return to our opening question: what are the ends or goals of a just war? Some say that the just goal of a just war is the proverbial *status quo ante bellum*: the victorious regime ought simply to reestablish the state of affairs which obtained before the war broke out. Restore the equilibrium disrupted by the aggressor, traditionalists advise. As Michael Walzer points out, however, this assertion makes little sense: we should not aim for the literal restoration of the *status quo ante bellum*—because that situation was precisely what led to war in the first place![7] How is going back there going to improve things, or show the war was worth it? Also, given the sheer destructiveness of war, any such literal restoration is empirically impossible. War simply changes too much. For better and for worse, war remains a major generator of historical change. So the just goal of a just war, once won, must be a more secure and more just state of affairs than existed prior to the war. What might such a condition be?

The general answer is a *more secure possession of our rights*, both individual and collective. The aim of a just and lawful war, we know, is the resistance of aggression and the vindication of the fundamental rights of societies, ultimately on behalf of the human rights of their individual citizens. I have already argued (Chapter 2) that these deepest values revolve around the concept of a minimally just and hence legitimate community. Such a community is one which does all it reasonably can to: 1) gain recognition as being legitimate in the eyes of its own people and the international community; 2) adhere to basic rules of international justice and good international citizenship, notably non-aggression; and 3) satisfy the human rights of its individual members (to security, subsistence, liberty, equality, and recognition).

From this general principle—that the proper aim of a just war is the vindication of those rights whose violation grounded the resort to war in the first place—more detailed commentary needs to be offered. For what does such "vindication" of rights amount to: what does it include; what does it permit; and what does it forbid? The last aspect of the question seems the easiest to answer, at least in abstract terms: the principle of rights vindication forbids the continuation of the war after the relevant rights have, in fact, been vindicated. To go beyond that limit would itself become aggression: men and women would die for no just cause.[8] This bedrock limit to the justified continuance of a just war seems required in order to prevent the war from spilling over into something like a crusade, which demands the utter destruction of the demonized enemy. The very essence of justice of, in, and after war is about there being firm limits and constraints upon its aims and conduct. Unconstrained fighting—with its fearful prospect of degenerating into barbaric slaughter—is the worst case scenario, regardless of the values for which the war is being fought.

This emphasis on the maintenance of some limits in wartime has the important consequence that there can be no such thing as a morally-mandated unconditional surrender. The principles vindicated successfully by the just state themselves impose outside constraints on what can be done to an aggressor following its defeat. This line of reasoning might spark resistance from those who view favorably the Allied insistence on "unconditional surrender" during the closing days of World War II. But we need to distinguish here between rhetoric and reality. The policy of unconditional surrender followed by the Allies at the end of that war was not genuinely unconditional; there was never any insistence that the Allies be able to do whatever they wanted with the defeated nations, as it was for instance standard to do in ancient Greek and Roman times. Churchill himself said that "we are bound by our own consciences to civilization ... [we are not] entitled to behave in a barbarous manner."[9] At the very most, the policy which the Allies pursued was genuinely unconditional only vis-à-vis the governing regimes of the Axis powers, but not vis-à-vis the civilian populations in those nations. Such a more discriminating policy on surrender may be defensible in extreme cases, involving truly abhorrent regimes, but is generally impermissible. For insistence on unconditional surrender is usually disproportionate and will prolong fighting as the defeated aggressor refuses to cave in, fearing the consequences of doing so. Walzer believes this was the case during The Pacific War, owing to America's insistence on Japan's unconditional surrender. Japan kept fighting because of this insistence, and eventually America resorted to atomic weapons to end the struggle. Walzer believes that the atom bombs wouldn't have been necessary at all had America had a more reasonable policy regarding surrender in the first place.[10]

It is thus the responsibility of the victor to communicate clearly to the losing aggressor its sincere intentions for post-war settlement, intentions which must be consistent with the other principles of post-war justice here developed. This means that some serious planning must go into the post-war phase right from the start. Winners—like America over Iraq in 2003—should never find themselves in a position where they've won the war but now they don't know what to do, and so they start making up post-war policy "on the fly." That's irresponsible, and the potential for bad decisions skyrockets.[11]

2. Overlapping Consensus: The Thin Theory of Post-War Justice

What does the just aim of a just war—namely, *rights vindication, constrained by a proportionate policy on surrender*—precisely include or mandate? It seems as though we can diagnose two basic answers to this question, two fundamental theories about post-war justice: *Retribution* and *Rehabilitation*. These two main theories of post-war justice share some principles. This overlapping consensus constitutes a "thin theory"—a minimum we'll want to go beyond. These shared principles include the need to have: publicly declared peace terms; an official apology for aggression; an exchange of prisoners-of-war (POWs); the need for the aggressor to give up any and all war gains; some demilitarization of the defeated aggressor; and war crimes trials.[12] Let's consider each in turn below.

2.1. PUBLICITY

Do the terms of the peace settlement, whatever they are, need to be public? On the one hand, war settlements often exert deep impact on people's lives. They are thus entitled to know the substance of peace settlements, and especially how these are predicted to affect them. Kant, for one, was vehement about this publicity requirement in his famous writings on war.[13] But someone might challenge this publicity principle, for instance by citing a counter-example. Consider the Cuban Missile Crisis of 1962. At the height of the Cold War, America discovered that the Soviet Union was installing nuclear-tipped missiles on Cuba at Fidel Castro's invitation. These missiles were thought to pose unacceptable first-strike capabilities against the United States—since Cuba is so close—and US President John F. Kennedy demanded their removal. He even put Cuba under quarantine to ensure that more missiles weren't on their way. We know that part of the reason why the Soviet Union backed down during this crisis was because of JFK's secret assurances that America would remove missiles from Turkey shortly after the Soviets removed theirs from Cuba.[14] But this "counter-example" does not deal with a full-blown war, much less a post-war period, and so it is not directly analogous. People who have suffered through a war do, indeed, deserve to know what the substance of the settlement is.

This does not mean that the people must explicitly and immediately endorse the proposed settlement: e.g., through a plebiscite or referendum. Nor does it mean that the settlement must be drafted up in a formal treaty. Both things are clearly permissible, and perhaps desirable as well: a show of popular support for a settlement might bolster its endurance; and writing out the peace terms can enhance the clarity of everyone's understandings and expectations. But it seems needlessly strict to insist that both features must be there for the settlement to be legitimate. We can imagine numerous and serious practical difficulties with running a referendum in the immediate post-war period. We can also imagine communities coming to an understanding on the settlement—even going so far as to adhere to it—without nailing down every possible contingency in a detailed legal document. After all, the 1919 Treaty of Versailles was a detailed legal document, and it didn't work out all that well; whereas the 1945 post-World War II settlement was just as sweeping but left at an abstract level intentionally, lest too much fussing over each exact detail spoil the deal. In a sense, settlements are processes, and while on the one hand they represent the end of a war, in another sense they inaugurate transition and change. There needs to be a certain flexibility and sensitivity as one tries to fix and solidify the terms for moving on.[15]

2.2. APOLOGIES

We should also expect a formal apology by Aggressor to Victim, and any Vindicator, for its aggression. While it is right to agree with Walzer that "official apologies somehow seem an inadequate, perhaps even a perfunctory, way" of atoning for aggression,[16] this is no reason to rule such an apology out of the terms of the peace. For even though formal apologies cannot of themselves restore territory, revive casualties, or rebuild infrastructure, it is obvious that they do mean something real and important. If not, why do such formal apologies, and victim's campaigns to secure such apologies, generate considerable political and media attention? If not, why do informed people know that Germany has apologized profusely for its role in World War II, whereas Japan has hardly apologized at all? Walzer must concede that we expect wrongdoers eventually to admit their wrongdoing, and to express their regret for it. We feel that victims of wrongdoing are owed that kind of respect, and that aggressors must at least show recognition of the moral principles they violated as part of their own rehabilitation. Apologies are an integral aspect of a complete peace settlement.[17]

2.3. EXCHANGE OF POWS

Obviously, a just peace settlement further requires that any and all prisoners-of-war (POWs), described in Chapter 4, be returned safely to their home countries.[18]

2.4. GIVING UP UNJUST GAINS

Another elemental aspect of any decent post-war settlement is to require that the unjust gains from aggression must be eliminated. If, to take a simple example, the aggression has involved invasion and taking over a country, then justice requires that the invader be driven out of the country and secure borders re-established, much as what happened regarding Iraq and Kuwait in 1990–91. The equally crucial corollary to this principle is that the victim of the aggression is to be re-established as an independent political community, enjoying political sovereignty and territorial integrity. Other examples: during its initial campaign in 1992–94, the Serb side of the Bosnian Civil War (Chapter 3) initially conquered 70% of Bosnia, way beyond the area traditionally occupied by ethnic Serbs. More dramatically, during the Blitzkrieg of 1939–40, Hitler's Germany conquered Belgium, France, The Netherlands, Poland, and the Scandinavian countries. This principle requires that, at war's end, the aggressor give back all such unjust gains.[19]

2.5. DEMILITARIZATION

The aggressor state might also require some demilitarization, depending on the nature and severity of the aggression it committed and the threat it would continue to pose in the absence of such measures. "One can," Walzer advises, "legitimately aim not merely at a successful resistance but also at some reasonable security against future attack."[20] Aggressor may be required to demilitarize, at least to the extent that it will not pose another serious threat to Victim—and other members of the international community—for the foreseeable future. The appropriate elements of such demilitarization will clearly vary with the nature and severity of the act of aggression, along with the extent of Aggressor's residual military capabilities following its defeat. But they may, and often do, involve: the creation of a demilitarized "buffer zone" between Aggressor and Victim (and any Vindicator), whether it be on land, sea, or air; the reducing and capping of certain aspects of Aggressor's military capability (troops, weapons, or weapons-deployment systems); and especially the destruction of Aggressor's weapons of mass destruction (WMD). Why may an aggressor's WMD be destroyed, while those of other nations remain intact? As mentioned in Chapter 3, the key thing with WMD is not their mere possession so much as a responsible record of having such weapons and a stable recent history of non-aggression. By committing aggression, Aggressor has broken any trust—or, at least, tolerance—offered by the international community in this regard. Aggressor has shown itself to be capable of aggressive destruction and international criminality. It is simply too great a risk to allow it to keep WMD. Besides, from a more global point of view, the fewer WMD, the better. Non-proliferation seems the route to greater global security.[21]

Proportionality must be brought to bear upon this general principle of demilitarization: the regime in Aggressor may not be so demilitarized as to jeopardize its ability to fulfill its function of maintaining law and order within its own borders, and of protecting its people from other countries who might be tempted to invade—for whatever reason—if they perceive serious weakness in Aggressor. The world, after all, has some rough neighborhoods. Another way this requirement could be met would be for the victors to provide reliable security guarantees to the people of Aggressor, for instance by keeping military garrisons in the country.[22]

2.6. WAR CRIMES TRIALS

The final element of the thin theory of post-war justice concerns putting on trial those who've committed war crimes during the course of the war. As this is, generally, the most written-about aspect of post-war justice, it merits sustained attention. The normative need for such trials follows from Walzer's dictum that "there can be no justice in war if there are not, ultimately, responsible men and women."[23] Individuals who play a prominent role during wartime must be held accountable for their actions and what they bring about. There are, of course, two broad categories of war crimes: those which violate *jus ad bellum* and those which violate *jus in bello*.

Jus ad bellum war crimes have to do with "planning, preparing, initiating and waging" aggressive war, as we have defined it. Responsibility for the commission of any such crime falls on the shoulders of the political leader(s) of the aggressor regime. Such crimes, in the language of the Nuremberg prosecutors, are "crimes against peace."[24]

2.6.1. Nuremberg

The Nuremberg trials were the very first set of modern war crimes trials, held right after World War II in the German city of that name. (There were Japanese war crimes trials, too, in Tokyo.)[25] In Nuremberg, much of what was left of the Nazi hierarchy was put on trial for both war crimes (i.e., starting an aggressive war) and crimes against humanity (i.e., The Holocaust). While every war crime is also a crime against humanity, the converse is not true, since crimes against humanity can be committed in peacetime and cover a broader range of terrible actions, such as torturing political dissidents.[26]

Even if the Nuremberg trials perpetrated "victor's justice"—that is, injustice forced on the losers—as some have claimed, it's clear that this is not an adequate view of all of the trials' features. The process, after all, was rigorous, open, and fair. All those charged had lawyers, could cross-examine witnesses and experts, and present their own evidence. The trials operated on rules known to all. Consider also the raw numbers: 22 Nazi elites were tried over the course of a year, 3 were found innocent, 19 guilty. Of the guilty, 11 were sentenced to death and 8 to prison sentences of varying lengths. This conviction rate, of just over 86%, is in line with the average rate of conviction for non-war-crimes in most developed societies.[27] (If that seems high, consider: 1) that prosecutors often drop charges against those they feel they can't convict; and 2) there are many social and psychological factors—apart from the case's evidence—which incline judges and juries to convict, such as desires to re-establish order and to offer the victim some solace.) Combine this percentage at Nuremberg with the variety of outcomes in sentencing there, and it looks like you have a fairly well-developed, reasonable judicial process looking at the evidence in each individual's case—as opposed to one which sweepingly condemns and convicts them all because they happened to be on the losing side.[28] Plus, the first international war crimes trials had to happen sometime. The notion that the Nuremberg trials operated on principles just then being invented is silly: there had been talk since the 1800s of having post-war criminal tribunals, and the codes of proper military conduct, such as the Hague Conventions (1899–1907)—to say nothing of basic moral decency—were known to all who were charged. But actual trials were a new phenomenon, and whenever there is innovation there is bound to be controversy, especially when something like war is involved. It wasn't perfect, but the Nuremberg trial process was decent and defensible. Decent, because it followed standard due process regulations. (Ironic and notable, indeed, that these Nazis, when in power, denounced the rule of law and due process—and yet benefited from them during these trials.) And defensible, because the Nazis were culpable for horrendous crimes, and at the time the only people capable of running a trial for them were the winners of the war. It was a bold institutional move, for proper moral motives, which has resonated down to today.[29]

2.6.2. Contemporary Tribunals

Resonated how, exactly? In a three-fold sense. First, the Nuremberg trials directly inspired some future war crimes trials. After the brutal Bosnian civil war of 1992–95, and the near-genocidal Rwandan massacres of 1994 (both discussed in Chapter 3), the international community decided to convene proceedings regarding war crimes and crimes against humanity. Both are on-going: Bosnian proceedings in The Hague in Holland (long a place associated with international diplomacy and institutions), and the Rwandan proceedings in neighboring Tanzania. Both tribunals actually confront huge backlogs in trials and workloads. These *ad hoc*—"one-time"—criminal procedures feature the same commitment to rigorous due process as Nuremberg did. (This is a partial reason for the back-log.) They have also, unlike Nuremberg, tried some of the biggest fish: the ex-prime minister of Rwanda; and the ex-president of Serbia/Yugoslavia, both seen as heavily complicit in the respective conflicts. The results: ex-Serb president, Slobodan Milošević, died during his trial before sentencing could be determined; but Jean Kambanda, ex-prime minister of Rwanda, pleaded guilty to genocide charges, and is now serving a life term in prison.[30]

Partly to overcome the limitations of *ad hoc* trials, and to institute something more lasting, there arose in the late 1990s a movement to create a permanent international criminal court (or ICC). In 1998, the Treaty of Rome was signed, paving the way for the ICC to be formed, also at The Hague. Since it will be permanent, and fully international, the ICC repels accusations regarding "revenge motives" and "victor's justice." Its permanence and global resources will also allow it to become a more experienced and efficient court process than, say, either the Bosnian or Rwandan efforts, which continue to be starved of resources. Although Americans continue to object to the ICC, and have not ratified membership—fearing that it could be "politically hijacked" to feature "show trials" of US servicemen—the ICC has gone ahead anyway, and there are principled reasons to support the court.[31]

First, there's the *deterrence benefit*. If all war crimes, in all wars, are prosecuted and punished by an impartial world court, then it stands to reason that future, would-be war criminals might well be deterred from committing their ghastly actions if they know that they will, themselves, pay a personal price for their crimes. Second, there's the *war termination benefit*. The having of a permanent and non-partisan world court can assist nations in wrapping up their armed conflicts, punishing acts which need punishment in an impartial manner. Third, there's what we might call the *world system benefit*. The global community has already witnessed the huge benefits of having an international system based on rules of law which are reasonable, impartial, and applicable to all. The trade sector is the clearest and most recent example of this. The construction of a permanent world criminal court helps complete the international landscape, thereby adding to the existence of a global system which can run smoothly on a consistent and comprehensive set of shared values, notably human rights. History shows that specialist agencies of the United Nations (UN)—i.e., those manned by trained professionals and focusing on a specific task—enjoy a much higher success rate than the generalist and politicized agencies, such as the General Assembly and Security Council.[32] Finally, there's the *commitment benefit*. The construction of a permanent war crimes court encourages the world community to keep its commitments to the core values of peace, security, and human rights. A world court enhances peace by punishing deeds which, if left unpunished, could sow the seeds of future wars. This augments global security more broadly.

The third effect of Nuremberg—apart from the recent *ad hoc* trials and the ICC—concerns the much more active willingness of national armed forces, at least in developed nations, to investigate and prosecute members of their own services for alleged war crimes. The activity here is real and quite remarkable. Consider the American military prosecuting and punishing those of its own soldiers who engaged in the infamous My Lai Massacre during the Vietnam War (Chapter 3). Frustrated by civilian support for, and hiding of, Viet Cong soldiers, one American unit—under Lt. William Calley—morally snapped and deliberately massacred the inhabitants of the village of My Lai. More recently, the Canadian Armed Forces prosecuted and punished some members of its Airborne Unit which served in the 1993 intervention in Somalia (Chapter 3). Thuggish members of that Unit caught a Somali civilian stealing from their supplies, and beat him to death. Then there's the case of the US reservists facing charges in the 2004 Abu-Ghraib prisoner abuse in Iraq (Chapter 3). Convictions came down in Spring, 2005. The list here can go on and on: the developed world's armed services drill their soldiers in the rules of engagement, and the ethics of war and peace, and they quite vigilantly oversee them. In some engagements, I've actually heard servicemen say—only half-jokingly—that they are more afraid of their own service's military lawyers than they are of enemy soldiers. It should be noted, for those still anxious about the ICC, that it's empowered to act only when a given national armed service fails to act on and investigate an alleged war crime. It does not replace or supersede the national military justice systems.[33]

2.6.3. Jus ad Bellum *War Crimes*

Enough about Nuremberg, and its sizable rippling consequences over time. Back to the ethical principles behind *jus ad bellum* war crimes. Subject to proportionality, the leaders of Aggressor are to be brought to trial before a public and fair international tribunal and accorded full due process rights in their defense. Why subject this principle of punishment to proportionality constraints? Why agree with one commentator who says that "it isn't always true that their leaders ought to be punished for their crimes"?[34] The answer is that sometimes such leaders, in spite of their moral decrepitude, retain considerable popular legitimacy and thus bringing them to trial could seriously destabilize the polity within Aggressor. The international community recently faced this situation twice. The first was in Somalia, in 1992–93, when attempt was made to arrest faction leader Mohamed Farrah Aidid for war crimes, resulting in serious escalation in the conflict, which ultimately backfired and resulted in the international force withdrawing from the country. The second time was in Bosnia, in 1994–95, when charges against Bosnian Serb leaders Ratko Mladić and Radovan Karadžić seriously increased tensions and delayed the onset of a not unreasonable peace agreement. Care needs to be taken, as always, that appeal to proportionality does not amount to rewarding aggressors, or to letting them run free and unscathed despite their grievous crimes. Yet this care does not vitiate the need to consider the destruction and suffering which might result from adhering totally to what the requirements of justice as retribution demand. (And, patience can be a virtue: eventually both Mladić and Karadžić were turned over, freely, by their own domestic governments, to the *ad hoc* tribunal—after the post-war passions had calmed down, their symbolic nationalist/ethnic status had ended, and people acknowledged the plain truth that, if someone commits a war crime, they need eventually to face justice for such a severe assault on human rights and global peace.)[35]

Should political leaders on trial for *jus ad bellum* violations be found guilty, through a public and fair proceeding, then the court is at liberty to determine a reasonable punishment, which will obviously depend upon the details of the relevant case. Perhaps the punishment will consist only of penalizing the leaders financially. Or perhaps, should the need for political rehabilitation be invoked, such leaders will need to be stripped of power and barred from political participation, or perhaps even jailed. Some figures in the Bosnian Serb community, e.g., have been prohibited from running in subsequent elections. It's clear that it's not possible, *a priori*, to stipulate what exactly is required with regard to such personal punishments. The point here is simply that the principle itself—of calling those most responsible for the aggression to task for their crimes—must be respected as an essential aspect of justice-after-war. The actual enforcement of this principle might constitute a non-trivial deterrent to future acts of aggression on the part of ambitious heads of state. If such figures have good reason to believe that they will themselves, personally, pay a price for the aggression they instigate and order, then perhaps they will be less likely to undertake such misadventures in the first place.

2.6.3.1. HEADS OF STATE

Walzer stresses that a head of state cannot escape judgment, at any such trial, by appealing to the function of his office. The fact that he "represents" his people on the world stage, and rationalizes his actions in terms of "reasons of state," can provide no exoneration for the crime of launching an unjust war. Why not? "Representative functions [far from exonerating representatives] are instead peculiarly risky ... because statesmen ... act for other people, and with wide-ranging effects." Heads of state covet power, actively seek it, enjoy its exercise, and exert enormous influence. If they "hope to be praised for the good they do, they cannot escape blame for the evil." Heads of state are as subject to blame—both moral and legal—as the rest of us, probably even more so since their actions have larger consequences. Walzer suggests that, when fishing for *jus ad bellum* war crimes, we cast our net wider than the head of state. No doubt, we must first look to the head of state but then should move down the chain of authority to see if other individuals are also decisively implicated. There will probably be others, such as the heads of the various armed forces, the head of national security, the head of intelligence gathering, the defense minister, certain top-level civil servants, and so on. It was also argued in Chapter 4, against Walzer, that some soldiers might meaningfully be included in this chain of authority.

The general principle we are to apply in this regard is the following: *the greater a person's influence on his country's actions in wartime, the greater his responsibility for them.*[36]

2.6.3.2. COLLECTIVE DEMOCRATIC RESPONSIBILITY

Some of Walzer's most interesting reflections, in this regard, concern the collective responsibility that citizens of a democracy face when their country launches an unjust war, as Walzer believes America did during Vietnam. Walzer suggests that we discern their responsibility by first considering what the responsibility of citizens in a perfect democracy would be. By such a "perfect democracy," Walzer means something like Jean-Jacques Rousseau's ideal society: a small participatory (or direct) democracy, peopled by enthusiastic citizens animated by the general will: i.e., a sincere regard for the common good of the community in which they are all equal members. Walzer asserts that, in this idealized case, even though "it cannot be said that every citizen is the author of every state policy," it remains true that "every one of them can rightly by called into account." So who would be responsible for an aggressive war in this idealized instance? "(A)ll those men and women who voted for it and who cooperated in planning, initiating and waging it ... All of them are guilty of the crime of aggressive war, and of no lesser charge." Those who voted against the war are not to blame, whereas those who didn't even bother to vote "are blameworthy, though they are not guilty of aggressive war." Why is this the case? Walzer suggests we recall the parable of the Good Samaritan, which illustrates our agreement that if it is possible for one to do good without great cost to oneself, then one ought to do it. Walzer says that when it comes to resisting aggressive war, "the obligation is stronger" than in the Good Samaritan story, because "it is not a question of doing good but of preventing serious harm, and harm that will be done in the name of my own political community—hence ... in my own name." An engaged citizen, in a perfect democracy which is waging an aggressive war, "must do all he can, short of accepting frightening risks, to prevent or stop the war." Presumably, political action, canvassing, arguing, organizing, protesting, advertising, running for office oneself, giving money to the cause, are all things on his mind here. In general, "the more one can do, the more one has to do."[37]

Very few of us, however, live in a perfect democracy. How then does this idealized model of democratic responsibility translate under conditions of an actual, imperfect, contemporary democracy? Walzer believes it crucial to get the right description down. Such a democracy has a fairly large, diverse, and scattered population, and is "governed at a great distance from its ordinary citizens by powerful and often arrogant officials." While these officials are periodically endorsed through elections, "at the time of the choice very little is known about their programs and commitments" or, at least, their actual willingness to follow through on them. Active political participation is the rare exception rather than the regular rule, and knowledge about the justice of wars fought is "occasional, intermittent ... [and] partially controlled by these distant officials ... which ... allows for considerable distortions." One is powerfully reminded here, e.g., of the controversy—discussed in Chapter 3—surrounding official US and UK intelligence estimates of Iraqi WMD, in 2003, as grounds for war.[38]

Under these normal conditions in an advanced Western democracy, the bulk of the burden for waging aggressive war will still fall most heavily on the governing elites and intelligentsia who support the war. We know this excuses those citizens who vote against the war and emphatically those who also protest against it, rally opposition to it, and so on. But does it completely excuse those citizens who support the unjust war effort? It does so, Walzer says, only if the information required to make a plausible judgment is seriously distorted by the elites, and correct information is exceedingly difficult for the citizenry to get its hands on. It does not excuse the citizenry if, with some effort, they could come across this information and make principled judgments. If citizens choose not to seek out such information, preferring either to "zone out" in front of the TV, or to endorse the war out of unreflective patriotism, then they are blameworthy, though not of the full charge of aggressive war. What they are guilty of, Walzer suggests, is "bad faith as citizens." The information about the war's injustice is available, say through credible media sources; it is critically important to do what one can to prevent serious harm (especially that being done in one's name); so failure to do so constitutes, at least, a failure to meet the moral requirements of decent democratic citizenship. Widespread bad faith, in Walzer's eyes, constitutes a searing indictment of the democracy in which it occurs. It reflects poorly on its system of education, on its media outlets, on its political system and representatives, and, above all, on the very character of its people and their moral maturity.[39]

2.6.4. Jus in Bello *War Crimes*

Jus ad bellum war crimes trials, we know, are not the only ones mandated by just war theory and international law. Attention must also, in the aftermath of conflict, be paid to trying those accused of *jus in bello* war crimes. Such crimes include: deliberately using indiscriminate and/or disproportionate force; failing to take due care to protect civilian populations from lethal violence; employing weapons which are themselves intrinsically indiscriminate and/or disproportionate (such as those of mass destruction); employing intrinsically heinous means, like rape campaigns; and treating surrendered prisoners of war in an inhumane fashion, e.g., torturing them. Primary responsibility for these war crimes must fall on the shoulders of those soldiers, officers, and military commanders who were most actively involved in their commission. Officers and commanders carry considerable moral burdens of their own during wartime. They are duty-bound not to issue orders which violate any aspect of the laws of war. Furthermore, they must plan military campaigns so that foreseeable civilian casualties are minimized, and they must teach and train their soldiers not only about combat but also about the rules of just war theory and the laws of armed conflict.[40]

A critical aspect to note here is that, unlike *jus ad bellum* war crimes, *jus in bello* war crimes can be—and usually are—committed by all sides in the conflict. It's fair to say that at least a few *jus in bello* violations are usually committed by every side in every armed conflict. So, care needs to be taken that Victim/Vindicator avoid the very tempting position of punishing only *jus ad bellum* war crimes. In order to avoid charges of having a "double-standard," or engaging in revenge punishment, the Victim/Vindicator—despite the justice of its cause in fighting—must also be willing either to try its suspected soldiers within its own military justice system or else to submit them to an impartially constructed international tribunal, such as the ICC. The exact kind of punishment for *jus in bello* war crimes (as for *jus ad bellum* violations) cannot be specified philosophically in advance of considering the concrete details of the case in question. It may involve such things as: disciplinary action within the service; demotion within, or expulsion from, the armed forces; jail time; perhaps the paying of personal restitution; and so on.

Let's consider the two defenses soldiers most often employ in *jus in bello* war crimes cases: that of battle frenzy; and that of superior orders. The idea behind the first defense is that a particular battle, or even a whole war, is so intense, chaotic, and brutalizing that, although it starts out measured and discriminating, it ends up escalating to the point where atrocities get committed. This was a line of defense taken by Calley and his comrades regarding the My Lai Massacre. We are right to be skeptical of this argument. Even in alleged cases of battle frenzy, other soldiers present at the scene seem to retain their control and combat savvy under the same conditions as those who fly off the handle and commit atrocities, such as slaughtering civilians. Indeed, it was because some of these more sober soldiers were present, but non-participating, at the My Lai Massacre that Calley and his comrades were arrested, tried, and convicted. The only plausible case for this implausible defense, as Walzer suggests, is when a senior officer actually encourages battle frenzy as a way of cementing the fighting spirit or unity of his troops. But this is, at best, a mitigating factor in punishment, not an excuse or justification for a finding of innocence. Walzer notes that such an officer is not only stupid—since soldiers fight best when they are disciplined and controlled, not wild and frenzied—he is issuing a blatantly immoral order; and the soldiers under him should not, and are usually taught not to, follow such an order.[41]

This ties into the second defense most frequently offered by soldiers in defense of *jus in bello* war crimes charges: superior orders. Such a defense strategy invokes savage scorn, almost automatically, owing to its extensive use by the Nazis at Nuremberg. But we should not indulge in such easy, black-and-white criticism. From the first day of induction into the armed forces, a soldier is literally drilled into obeying the orders of his commanding officers. This is the case in both just and unjust societies. Failure to obey always comes with punitive measures, some truly painful and serious. The very point of military training is to habituate soldiers to follow orders under the most hellish conditions of war, so that they can retain fighting coherence and achieve their objectives. Even so, ordinary soldiers, by common sense if not by training, know when they are confronted with a blatantly immoral order (such as massacring civilians), and they remain duty bound not to follow it. If they do follow it, they should be charged with war crimes. The only excuse here would be if the blatantly immoral order was coupled with a credible threat of execution for disobedience. Nazi officers, e.g., would routinely shoot their own disobedient soldiers in front of their entire unit to enforce compliance. A soldier with a gun at his head, clearly, is a man acting under extreme duress and so cannot be held readily responsible for his actions. The person to be held responsible here would be the person who issued the immoral order, and coupled it with the grievous threat as a matter of policy—i.e., the commanding officer. The excuse of superior orders will hold only if the penalty for disobedience is extremely severe, such as execution. There is always some penalty for disobedience, but not any old penalty will suffice as an excuse here. The threat of demotion in the ranks, for instance, is obviously not enough to excuse murder. It has to be something very grave, such as execution, to count. And, again, it counts only as an excuse or mitigation in punishment, and never as a justification for a verdict of innocence.[42]

So officers and commanders are duty-bound not to issue orders which violate any aspect of the laws of war, nor are they to threaten excessively severe penalties for failing to comply with an order. The orders they give, in other words, must all fit within the general structure of permissible action established by the laws of war and just war theory.

3. Retribution

The traditional model of post-war justice combines the thin theory, as explained above, with clear aspects of retribution (sometimes called "revenge"—though "retribution" is the more neutral, and thus preferred, term). The core intuition behind retribution theory is that *the defeated aggressor must be rendered worse-off than prior to the start of the war*. This is thought to be required for proper punishment, and the elemental demands of justice. Why must there be punishment at all? Why can't we just cancel Aggressor's unjust war gains, and then "live and let live"? Three reasons are articulated by retribution theorists, such as Robert Nozick. First, the obvious—yet powerful—one of *deterrence*. Punishing past aggression deters future aggression, or at least does so more than if we had no punishment at all. No punishment seems a lax policy which actually invites future aggression. Secondly, proper punishment can be an effective spur to atonement and change on the part of Aggressor (since presumably it doesn't want to suffer through such punitive measures again). Finally, and most powerfully, failing to punish the aggressor degrades and disrespects the worth, status, and suffering of the victim. Thus, it's not enough merely to take away the unjust gains of Aggressor, and force it to apologize publicly. It must suffer some retribution as a matter of balance and fairness. This is the same reasoning which explains and articulates criminal punishment in domestic society: if someone, e.g., has stolen something, we don't just make him give it back, and apologize to his victim: we make him suffer further—make him worse-off than prior to his deed—for instance by making him pay a fine, or spending some time in jail.[43]

So, how should we make the defeated Aggressor worse-off than prior to the war? Demilitarization, as discussed above: yes. War crimes trials for those individuals complicit in aggression: absolutely. But two further things get advocated by retribution theorists: 1) a backward-looking system of compensation payments, from Aggressor to Victim(s); and 2) a forward-looking system of sanctions, placed by Victim and the international community on Aggressor. The goal of the first is to offer some reparation to Victim, to help it pay for its costs incurred during the fight for its rights. The second is to hamper, deliberately, the economic growth of Aggressor moving forward, as a kind of fine for, and lesson about, the commission of aggression. Let's consider these proposals in turn.

3.1. COMPENSATION AND DISCRIMINATION

Since aggression is a crime which violates important rights and causes much damage, it does seem (at first glance) reasonable to contend that, in a classic context of inter-state war, Aggressor owes some duty of compensation to Victim. This is the case because, in the absence of aggression, Victim would not have to reconstruct itself following the war, nor would it have had to fight for its rights in the first place, with all the death and destruction that implies. It has been said that the deepest nature of the wrong which an aggressor commits is to make people fight for their rights: i.e., to make them resort to violence to secure those things they have an elemental entitlement to in the first place, and which they should enjoy as a matter of course.[44] To put the compensation issue bluntly, Aggressor has cost Victim a considerable amount, and so at least some restitution seems due. The critical questions are: how much and from whom in Aggressor is the compensation to be paid out?

The "how much" question, clearly, will be relative to the nature and severity of the act of aggression itself, alongside considerations of what Aggressor can reasonably be expected to pay at war's end. Care needs to be taken not to bankrupt Aggressor's resources, if only for the reason that the civilians of Aggressor still, as always, retain their claims to human rights fulfillment and the objects of such rights require that resources be devoted to them. In short, there needs to be an application of the principle of proportionality here. The compensation required may not be draconian in nature. We have some indication, from the financial terms imposed on Germany at the Treaty of Versailles, that to beggar thy neighbor is to pick future fights.

This reference to the needs of the civilians in Aggressor gives rise to important considerations of discrimination in answering the "from whom" question: when it comes to establishing terms of compensation, care needs to be taken by the victorious Victim, and/or any third-party "Vindicators" who fought on behalf of Victim, not to penalize unduly the civilian population of Aggressor for the aggression carried out by their regime. This entails, for example, that any monetary compensation due to Victim ought to come, first and foremost, from the personal wealth of those political and military elites in Aggressor who were most responsible for the crime of aggression. Walzer seems to disagree, as he suggests that such a discriminating policy on reparations "can hardly" raise the needed amount. But he ignores the fact that, historically, those who launch aggressive war externally have very often abused their power internally to accumulate massive—sometimes obscene—personal fortunes. Saddam Hussein, for example, skimmed billions from Iraqi oil sales and used them to live lavishly, to secure the loyalty of his Republican Guard, and to build up enormous foreign bank accounts in case things turned bad.[45]

In light of this supposed shortfall—between the fortunes of dictators and what their victims are owed—Walzer argues that, since "(r)eparations are surely due the victims of aggressive war," they should be paid from the taxation system of the defeated Aggressor. There ought to be a kind of post-war poll tax on the population of Aggressor, with the proceeds forwarded to Victim. In this sense, he says, "citizenship is a common destiny." I believe, however, that such a proposal probably fails to respect the discrimination principle during war termination. Though Walzer insists that "(t)he distribution of costs is not the distribution of guilt,"[46] it is difficult to see what that is supposed to mean here: why not respond by asking why civilians should be forced, through their tax system, to pay for the damage if they are not in some sense responsible for it? Respect for discrimination entails taking a reasonable amount of compensation only from those sources: 1) which can afford it; and 2) which were materially linked to the aggression in a morally culpable way. If such reparations "can hardly pay" for the destruction Aggressor meted out on Victim, then that fiscal deficiency does not somehow translate into Victim's moral entitlement to tax everyone left over in Aggressor. The resources for reconstruction simply have to be found elsewhere.

The one exception to this would be if Aggressor's destruction was of such magnitude that Victim can no longer afford to be a minimally just state, whereas

Aggressor's post-war resources are clearly in a surplus over that threshold level. Provided that is the case, and provided the fortunes of the guilty in Aggressor were first exhausted, then we could justifiably talk about some kind of broader, Walzer-style transfer from Aggressor to Victim. Victim at least has the right to that level of post-war resources sufficient to provide minimally just governance to its people. If the reason it fell below that level was enormous wartime expenditures fighting off Aggressor, then it makes sense to say Aggressor owes it at least that. But if both Victim and Aggressor, after war, retain resources clearly above the minimal level, then the financial restitution coming from Aggressor to Victim must be limited to the assets of the guilty. That is what discrimination requires, and I believe such a more moderate policy would render the issue of compensation a lot less complicated and conflictual than what it has been in the past.

One application of these thoughts to recent events can be seen by considering the following question: should America have levied a post-war poll tax on the citizens of Afghanistan, to increase the funds needed to compensate and care for those who lost loved ones during the 9/11 strikes, or else to re-build New York's shattered financial district? The principles just developed argue against such a tax, since there is a serious question of its affordability to Afghanistan, and an even sharper one regarding responsibility, since the available evidence points to a collusion between the now-routed Taliban regime and the al-Qaeda terrorist network as the source of the 9/11 attacks. Commendably, there has been little to no talk of any such punitive measure on Afghanistan, and Americans have instead turned towards each other to raise the needed reconstruction resources. For example, right after 9/11, American celebrities and singers hosted a televised fund-raiser for the widows and injured of the bombings.

3.2: SANCTIONS

A further implication of respect for discrimination in settlements is a ban on sweeping socio-economic sanctions. The reasoning is clear: sanctions which cut widely and deeply into the well-being of the civilian population are not only punitive, they surely end up punishing some—perhaps a great many—who do not deserve such treatment. When such treatment strikes at their vital welfare, such sanctions are properly condemned as inappropriately targeted and morally wrong-headed. People have argued over whether US-imposed sanctions on Iraq—following the Persian Gulf War in 1991 and lasting until 2003—count as such morally-questionable sanctions or not. On the one hand, statistics show a sharp drop-off in Iraqi GDP during those years, as well as a sharp rise in indicators of poverty and preventable disease. On the other, supporters of the sanctions argue that Saddam Hussein's regime could have prevented any humanitarian damage by improving access to resources, and giving his military and ethnic clique less (so that the majority could have had more and been alright). Saddam failed to do this for his own selfish reasons, and so he's the one to blame. We'll return to this debate when we focus on the Persian Gulf War settlement more broadly at the end of this chapter. In any event, for now, there is a vocal and growing community of thought which commends instead sanctions which target only the guilty elites: e.g., by freezing their personal assets, banning their foreign travel, and blocking any weapons trade. For example, the American assets of some organizations alleged to be involved in terrorism have been frozen since 9/11.[47]

3.3. LEAVING THE DEFEATED REGIME IN POWER

The major ways in which the retribution model of post-war justice differs from the rehabilitation model (to be described in full next chapter) are three. Retribution: 1) requires compensation payments from Aggressor to Victim; 2) recommends economic sanctions on Aggressor, moving forward; and 3) is very skeptical about trying to change the defeated regime in Aggressor by force, preferring instead to leave it in power, and hampering its ability to commit future aggression by imposing demilitarization and economic sanctions. I have shown above some weaknesses, and amendments, which ought to be considered in connection with the first two suggestions. But what about the third? On the one hand, leaving the regime in Aggressor in place is simpler, less costly, and allows the victorious Victim/Vindicator to leave the defeated society promptly after the war has been won. Further responsibility for reconstruction is disavowed—or, rather, "left to the locals"—and that's that. On the other, history gives us some reason to believe that leaving the regime in power might only be an apparent and short-term savings, as too often such regimes have found ways to re-build and—since they were willing to commit aggression once—come to commit aggression yet again, thereby necessitating a costly second war to finally be rid of them. Hussein's Iraq is a very recent and instructive case study in this regard (see below), as is Milošević's Serbia.

3.4. SUMMARIZING RETRIBUTION'S PROS AND CONS

To summarize the pros of the retribution model: it's simple and straightforward; it's the historical norm (and I guess there's some value in long-standing habitual practice); there's no messing around with complex, costly, and controversial regime change and post-war reconstruction; and, if one believes that justice requires retribution as a matter of principle, then one is going to be deeply moved by retribution's claims.

At the same time: if one doesn't believe that justice requires retribution, then the retribution theory is going to strike one as being animated by angry revenge and not by balanced justice; the reparations and sanctions called for by retribution theory very often wind up hurting innocent civilians, and thus violate discrimination;

and finally, in historical cases where retribution has been employed, there often has been imperfect or even quite shoddy results (the revenge creates bad feelings and new generations of enemies, and the aggressive regime is left in place, combining together over time to produce—rather regularly—a second war), thus negating any supposed "savings" of not trying to rehabilitate the decrepit regime.

My own considered view, reflecting on these pros and cons, is that, though some measured and targeted compensation/sanctions might be justified—as outlined above—in general the retribution model is overall not as compelling as the rehabilitation model. I shall describe this in detail, and defend this claim in full, next chapter, following the retribution case study below of the terms of peace of the Persian Gulf War.

4. Case Study: The 1991 Persian Gulf War Settlement

Let us consider, as helpful illustration, the justice of the post-war settlement with Iraq in 1991 following the Persian Gulf War. (We'll look at the justice of the post-war arrangements in the second, 2003 war next chapter.)

We argued, in Chapter 2, that the American-led Allies had a just cause in resorting to war against Iraq in 1991, following Iraq's invasion of Kuwait in 1990 and the subsequent plundering and brutality. Let us, to facilitate analysis, assume that the war on the part of the Allies also met the other criteria of *jus ad bellum*. And let us bracket for the meantime the question of how well *jus in bello* was fulfilled on both sides. Given these assumptions, how just and lawful was the termination phase of this otherwise justified war?

Consider first the aim of a just war: vindicating rights. When did the Allies terminate the war? The *de facto* (actual) end to the war came on February 27, 1991, when American President George Bush, Sr. ordered the Allied forces to adhere to a cease-fire, following the rout and flee of Iraqi forces from Kuwait. The *de jure* (legal) end to the war came more than a month later, on April 3, 1991, when UN Security Council Resolution 687 proclaimed its end. Did the Allies have just cause to terminate the war when they did? It seems that the answer to this question is probably yes. It appears that the rights of the Kuwaiti people were reasonably vindicated, first and foremost by having the Allies cease the Iraqi aggression and, indeed, drive the Iraqi aggressors out of Kuwait entirely. Kuwait was then re-established as an independent community acknowledged by international society.

Between March and April 1991, terms of the cease-fire were hammered out under the auspices of the UN Security Council. These terms, which were publicly announced, included the following requirements of Iraq: 1) it had to cease hostilities and declare a formal end to them; 2) it had to rescind its claim to Kuwait, and return looted property; 3) it had to release immediately all prisoners of war (POWs); 4) it had to accept liability for loss, injury, and damage in Kuwait which resulted from its invasion; and 5) it had to provide to the UN total disclosure of its program for making WMD and commit itself to that program's destruction, subject to verification by on-site UN inspectors.

Items 1–3 of these terms of the Persian Gulf War peace agreement are essential elements of agreeing to end a war: to stop fighting; to accept responsibility for aggression; to renounce unjust claims; and to release POWs. Article 4 provides for the targeted kind of compensation for aggression that was defended in limited fashion above. The compensation was paid out in the following way. Following the war, the UN established a "compensation fund" that was financed by a gradual lifting of the oil embargo that was leveled on Iraq after its initial invasion of Kuwait. Under the terms of the lifting, 30% of the oil export sales of Iraq were allowed to be kept by its government, with the (purely verbal) stipulation that such monies be employed to provide for the humanitarian needs (foodstuffs and medicine) of its people. The remaining 70% was split among: 1) the compensation fund for Kuwait; 2) a special fund designed to pay for the expenses of the on-site UN weapons inspectors; and 3) an escrow "incentive account," which was to be handed over to Iraq once full compliance with the terms of settlement was achieved. Such an account seems to have been an enlightened and sophisticated actualization of a targeted compensation principle.

Article 5 of the cease-fire provided for that partial disarmament and demilitarization of the aggressor, defended above as part of the goal of achieving a more secure and peaceful international order than was the case prior to the war. In addition to the verifiable dismantling of Iraq's WMD program, the Security Council also established demilitarized zones within Iraq, north of the 36th parallel (to greater protect Israel, Turkey, and the Kurdish minority within Iraq) and south of the 32nd parallel (to greater protect Kuwait, Saudi Arabia, and the Shiite community within Iraq). Iraq pledged neither to fly nor to occupy those areas for an indeterminate amount of time. It also acquiesced to Allied air patrols of the no-fly zones (NFZ), for enforcement purposes. It seems that such terms were also entirely in line with the criteria of *jus post bellum* defended above: Iraq was to be demilitarized not to the point of collapse but at least to the point where it could not pose a short-term threat to international peace and security within the region.

One criticism which might be leveled at this arrangement was that, because it was indefinite and open-ended, flare-ups were bound to occur. The first time was in January 1993, when Iraq tested the Allies by flying into both NFZs, and quickly crossing the border into Kuwait to retrieve some weaponry it had abandoned during the retreat back into Iraq during February 1991. The US retaliated with three air attacks and missile strikes on military targets, albeit with at least one errant missile striking a residential section within Baghdad. Military fire was exchanged several times in 1996. Then, starting in late 1997 and moving into the summer of 1998, Iraq refused to comply with the UN weapons inspectors anymore. By December 1998 American President Bill Clinton ordered Operation Desert Fox.[48] British and American forces combined to bombard military targets in Iraq for four days. The "operation"—a serious military offensive—attempted to enforce compliance with the inspections regime and, in any event, to set back that part of Iraq's WMD program which had eluded inspection. The latter aim may have succeeded but not the former: Iraq as of 1999 absolutely refused to let any UN weapons inspectors back into its territory. This was, of course, cited as one major cause of war for the 2003 regime take-down.

One aspect of *jus post bellum* which clearly was not met was the failure to commit to holding any war crimes trials at all, on either side. There was nothing credible in the cease-fire agreement to this effect, nor was there any public commitment on the part of the Allies, particularly the USA.

Another aspect of controversy here concerns discrimination. When Iraq invaded Kuwait in August, 1990, much of the developed world responded with sweeping economic sanctions. These were substantially maintained by the peace treaty and, in fact, lasted until the very fall of the Hussein regime after the 2003 regime take-down, or 13 years in total. As noted before, soon after the war, the Allies partially eased the economic embargo on Iraqi oil exports, stipulating that the 30% Iraqi take from such new sales be devoted to meeting the humanitarian needs of its people (foodstuffs, medicine, and infrastructure repairs). However, perhaps it could be argued that this was too strict and indiscriminate a policy on the part of the Allies. After all, everything that everyone knew about the Hussein regime indicated that the funds would be used for its own buttressing and benefit, and there were no effective enforcement mechanisms built into the terms of Iraq's receiving this money. (They tried to change this somewhat in 1996, with the so-called "Oil-for-Food" program, but that policy was deeply troubled—and, it turns out, deeply riddled with corruption.) So perhaps it was disingenuous for the Allies simply to leave the matter at that—particularly with regard to the damage that their bombing had inflicted on part of the water treatment supply system in Iraq. Perhaps effective enforcement mechanisms could have been built into the receipt of that cash, and/or perhaps more could have been made available, from the oil fund, to non-governmental aid and relief agencies. In the absence of such measures, the Allies might have been guilty of some callousness with regard to the post-war sufferings of the Iraqi people in the 1990s.

Of course, this is not at all to exonerate the Hussein regime, whose truculence and indifference to the well-being of its own people must loom large in any fair-minded account of why the Iraqi populace seemed to suffer such deprivations during and after the war. It is to apportion only some of the blame for this suffering: more should have been done for the Iraqi people than to say "Look, we give Saddam 30% of the oil revenue for you, but he uses it for himself and his army." Funding international relief agencies to go in with actual food and medicine seems an obvious way around this, which should have at least been tried. To the extent to which this settlement violated discrimination, it also raises issues of proportionality. In other words, the strictness of the sanctions, and the widespread effects they had on civilians, revealed that the treaty involved disproportionate punishment.[49]

Perhaps it might be said that the fact that the Allies created so-called "safe havens"—protected by military force and liberally supplied with humanitarian aid—within both demilitarized zones for the Kurdish and Shiite communities does, in fact, indicate substantial adherence to the rule of discriminating between the *people* of a given aggressor and the aggressive *regime* itself. And so it does. However, the account cannot be left to end at this point. After all, during the war Bush himself explicitly, and publicly, called on the Iraqi people to overthrow Hussein. And the Kurds and Shiites heeded that call, but were crushed in the immediate post-war period by the remnant of Hussein's armed forces. It is arguably true that such a call, and such a response, created an obligation independent of the principle of discrimination on the part of the Allies, especially the United States, to create safe havens for those persecuted people in the wake of war.

Despite these substantial difficulties, it needs to be admitted that the majority of the post-war measures were directly targeted at the aggressor regime: forcing it to abandon its claims; reducing its military capacity; limiting its resources and regional sway; and so on. So, the judgment with regard to discrimination seems quite difficult and conflictual. It seems that, on the whole, the Allies did indeed focus on punishing the regime—they clearly intended to target the regime—but the extent and depth of Iraqi civilian deprivation in the aftermath leaves one wondering whether the Allies could have done more to ease their suffering, without providing any comfort to their aggressor regime.

The big failing with the Persian Gulf War settlement concerns rehabilitation, in two senses. First, there was little attempt to reform Kuwait's political structure after its independence was re-established. Second, there was no attempt to reform the Hussein regime in Iraq. There are probably two reasons why this was the case. The first is the idea that the just cause for going to war was the invasion and brutality against Kuwait. Once the Allies reversed the invasion and restored the Kuwaitis to some security, the reasons justifying the war ended. It seems Bush Sr. sincerely believed in this, because many of his generals asked for permission to go into Baghdad to take out the Hussein regime, and he denied them. He had a quite conservative, cautious understanding of just war principles. The second reason for refraining from rehabilitating Iraq at that time was a belief that the various peace treaty terms would sufficiently contain the Hussein regime from further misadventures.

This choice not to rehabilitate was a mistake, and it is partly because of this Iraq experience that we have compelling evidence that forcible post-war rehabilitation can be, in some cases, a good long-term idea. This may be one reason why the mood in favor of rehabilitation is so much stronger today. Failing to rehabilitate Kuwait diminished the overall value of the war: while the war made Kuwaitis much better off than during the Iraqi occupation, did it make them better off than before the whole business? Not obviously so, and wars which fail to do this cannot be viewed very brightly. Failing to rehabilitate Iraq cost much more. First, the Kurdish and Shiite resistance to Hussein was sold down the river. Second, the costs of the ongoing military containment programs were considerable. Third, the whole weapons inspection process could have happened much more quickly, and effectively, under a different regime instead of lasting for over a decade and escalating into a cause for another war. Fourth, all the fretting about Saddam supporting terrorism could have been avoided. Indeed, perhaps the whole second war could have been prevented. Above all, the Iraqi people would've been saved from: 1) the ravages of the sweeping sanctions; and 2) the rights-violating tyranny of the Hussein regime. What's morally the most striking, and repeatedly observed, about the Persian Gulf War settlement terms is the insensitivity to, and hence culpability for, the continued misery and rights-violation suffered by ordinary Iraqis. This experience, and others throughout the 1990s, have rightly lessened concerns about undue interference and intervention, and instead strengthened the moral and even strategic case for progressive post-war rehabilitation measures.[50]

Now, it's very easy indeed to point out flaws and mistakes a long time after a serious decision has been made, and we've been able to see the flow of history in-between. "Monday morning quarterbacks" always seem to know the right play after the results are in. We must resist this temptation. Wartime decision-making is incredibly pressured, the evidence often not as decisive as one wishes, and the long-term consequences are, at times, very difficult to see. We shouldn't envy those whose job and responsibility it is to make such choices. Bush Sr. stuck to a cautious interpretation of just war theory and international law, and thus believed that the Allies had to stop after they drove Iraq out of Kuwait. He must have been eager to stop the war, too—America's first major war since Vietnam. And the international scene was quite delicate at that time: the USSR and its Eastern European client states were all imploding; and so Bush Sr. wanted to be prudent and cautious so as not to unwittingly spark something else far more severe. All very understandable and reasonable positions at the time. And that must really be our standard: *what was it reasonable to believe and do at the time*? At the time, perhaps regime change did seem incredibly risky, especially with the Vietnam quagmire looming large in memory and with not wanting to convey to collapsing communist states that America favored bold, Western-led social re-engineering around the world. But we've learned much since the '90s, about regime change in general and about that regime in particular, and so perhaps the 1991 decision was a failure by history's harsh, long lights. This is not so much to criticize Bush Sr. so much as to learn from his example for the benefit of future decision-makers. It's not a personal criticism; it is a statement that the policy failed as a result of its effects. But, in my view, Bush Sr. can be more readily criticized for the maintenance of the sanctions. In spite of the safe havens, it was predictable at the time that Saddam's clique would always take care of itself, and thus nation-wide sanctions would bite into civilian well-being. There were mitigating factors, we've seen; even so, not quite enough effort was made in thinking that one through. And so the situation dragged on and on, the sanctions bit and bit, and serious problems were created for the Iraqi people and both the Clinton and Bush Jr. administrations. It was also reasonable to see, in 1991, that if you let the weapons inspections process run indefinitely, that eventually Iraq would chafe and challenge it. Firm deadlines should have been given, to prevent all the subsequent skirmishes and serious misunderstandings, which of course were partly responsible for sparking another war.

Notes

1 Basil Henry Liddell Hart, *Strategy* (New York: Random House, 1974), 338.

2 In *War and International Justice: A Kantian Perspective* (Waterloo, ON: Wilfrid Laurier UP, 2000), 218–23, I refer to some pieces of international law in the Hague Convention which *do* mention war termination, but such laws are: 1) very dated, almost 100 years old now; and 2) radically thin and lacking in substance. I suppose there are pieces of international human rights law which international lawyers would say also apply to post-war situations. Fair enough—and good—but it remains true that these pieces aren't specifically designed to guide states during that post-war phase, which is what I'm talking about here. There is the related issue of foreign occupation, and there is some international law on that, but we'll discuss it next chapter on regime change.

3 Manfred Franz Boemeke, ed., *The Treaty of Versailles* (Cambridge: Cambridge UP, 1998). Though, we shouldn't make the mistake of believing that the Treaty exonerates the German people from allowing Hitler to come to power. The Treaty may have been *one* factor in laying the groundwork for World War II but it can hardly be considered the only one. The failure of rival German elites to challenge Hitler, the ruthless thuggery of the Nazis, and the electoral appeal of simple solutions in a time of complex crisis, were all important domestic factors in Germany. For an excellent study, see Margaret Macmillian, *Paris 1919* (New York: Macmillan, 2003).

4 David Reiff, *Slaughterhouse: Bosnia and the Failure of the West* (New York: Simon and Schuster, 1995).

5 This is not to deny the existence, or the importance, of the robust conflict resolution literature. Much of that literature is relevant to the present concern, but not much of it is located within the explicitly *ethical* values and commitments of just war theory, whereas this chapter is. For more on conflict resolution in general, see: Stephen J. Cimbala, *Strategic War Termination* (New York: Praeger, 1986); Paul R. Pillar, *Negotiating Peace: War Termination as a Bargaining Process* (Princeton: Princeton UP, 1983); Stuart Albert and Edward C. Luck, eds., *On the Endings of Wars* (London: Kennikat, 1980); and Fen Osler Hampson, *Nurturing Peace: Why Peace Settlements Succeed or Fail* (Washington, DC: US Institute of Peace, 1996).

6 Immanuel Kant, *Perpetual Peace and Other Essays*, trans. Ted Humphrey (Indianapolis: Hackett, 1983); see also the forthcoming Brian Orend, ed., *Kant's "On Perpetual Peace,"* trans. Ian Johnston (Broadview, 2014).

7 Michael Walzer, *Just and Unjust Wars* 3rd ed. (New York: Basic Books, 2000), 119, xx.

8 Walzer, *Wars*, 109–24.

9 Churchill quoted in Walzer, *Wars*, 112.

10 Walzer, *Wars*, 109–24, 263–68; M. Walzer, [Untitled], *Dissent* (Summer 1995), 330.

11 Rowan Scarborough, *Rumsfeld's War* (New York: Regnery, 2004); James Carroll, *Crusade: Chronicles of an Unjust War* (New York: Metropolitan, 2004).

12 Compare and contrast to: Larry May and Andrew Forcehimes, eds., *Morality, Jus Post Bellum and International Law* (Cambridge: Cambridge UP, 2012).

13 Immanuel Kant, *The Metaphysics of Morals*, trans. Mary Gregor (Cambridge: Cambridge UP, 1995), 114–24; Orend, *Kantian Perspective*, passim.

14 Martin Walker, *The Cold War: A History* (New York: Henry Holt, 1995), 160–83.

15 Andrew Arato, *Civil Society, Constitution and Legitimacy* (Lanham, MD: Rowman and Littlefield, 2000).

16 Walzer, [Untitled] 330.

17 Alice C. MacLachlan, "Government Apologies to Indigenous Peoples" in Alice C. MacLachlan and C. Allen Speight, eds., *Justice, Responsibility and Reconciliation in the Wake of Conflict* (Dordrecht: Springer, 2013), 183–204; Linda Radzik, *Making Amends* (Oxford: Oxford UP, 2009).

18 Sibylle Scheipers, ed., *Prisoners in War* (Oxford: Oxford UP, 2010).

19 Reiff, *Slaughterhouse*, passim.

20 Walzer, *Wars*, 118.

21 Olivia Bosch and Peter van Ham, *Global Non-Proliferation and Counter-Terrorism* (London: Brookings Institute, 2006).

22 David A. Cummings, *Demilitarization* (London: Biblioscholar, 2012).

23 Walzer, *Wars*, 288.

24 Walzer, *Wars*, 292–301.

25 Walzer, *Wars*, 319–22; W. Michael Reisman and Chris T. Antoniou, eds., *The Laws of War* (New York: Vintage), 337–50; Yuki Tanaka, *Hidden Horrors: Japanese War Crimes in World War II* (Boulder, CO: Westview, 1997); Tim P. Maya, *Judgment at Tokyo: The Japanese War Crimes Trial* (Lexington, KY: U of Kentucky P, 2001).

26 Geoffrey Robertson, *Crimes Against Humanity* (London: Penguin, 2012).

27 Reisman and Antoniou, eds., *Laws*, 332–33.

28 Admittedly, however, there was a 100% conviction rate in the Tokyo trials, which rightly raises eyebrows. There's no denying, looking at the events of 1945–46, that the Americans truly had it in for the Japanese.

29 Walzer, *Wars*, 292–96; Reisman and Antoniou, eds., *Laws*, 318–37; Joseph E. Persico, *Nuremberg: Infamy on Trial* (New York: Penguin, 1995); Michael R. Marrus, *The Nuremberg War Crimes Trials 1945–46* (New York: St. Martin's Press, 1997).

30 Victor Peskin, *International Justice in Rwanda and The Balkans* (Cambridge: Cambridge UP, 2008); Richard H. Steinberg, *Assessing the Legacy of the ICTY* (London: Brill Academic, 2011); Gerald Gahima, *Transitional Justice in Rwanda* (London: Routledge, 2012).

31 William Schabas, *The International Criminal Court* (Oxford: Oxford UP, 2010).

32 Brian Orend, *Introduction to International Studies* (Oxford: Oxford UP, 2012), Chap. 5, "International Law and Organization."

33 Walzer, *Wars*, 309–16; Reisman and Antoniou, eds., *Laws*, 357–70; William Schabas, *An Introduction to the International Criminal Court* (Cambridge: Cambridge UP, 2001); Saymour M. Hersh, *My Lai 4* (New York: Doubleday, 1970); Peter A. French, ed., *Individual and Collective Responsibility: The Massacre at My Lai* (Cambridge: Harvard UP, 1972); Seymour M. Hersh, *Chain of Command: The Road from 9/11 to Abu Ghraib* (New York: Harper Collins, 2004).

34 Walzer, *Wars*, 123.

35 Richard J. Regan, *Just War: Theory and Cases* (Washington, DC: Georgetown UP, 1996), 172–212.

36 Walzer, *Wars*, 290–91, 298.

37 Walzer, *Wars*, 299–301.

38 Walzer, *Wars*, 301; US Congress, *The 9/11 Commission Report* (Washington, DC: US Congress, 2004).

39 Walzer, *Wars*, 301–03.

40 Walzer, Wars, 304–28; Martin L. Cook and George R. Lucas, Jr., *The Moral Warrior* (Albany: SUNY, 2004).

41 Walzer, Wars, 309–16; Hiromi Sato, *The Execution of Illegal Orders and International Criminal Responsibility* (Dordrecht: Springer, 2011).

42 Walzer, *Wars*, 305–16.

43 Robert Nozick, *Anarchy, State and Utopia* (Cambridge, MA: Harvard UP, 1974).

44 Walzer, *Wars*, 113.

45 Walzer, *Wars*, 113, 119; Efram Karsh and Inari Rautsi-Karsh, *Saddam Hussein: A Political Biography* (New York: Grove, 2003); C. Coughlin, *Saddam: King of Terror* (London: Ecco, 2002).

46 Walzer, *Wars*, 297.

47 Ramsey Clark, *The Impact of Sanctions on Iraq* (London: World View Forum, 1996); Anthony Arnove and Ali Abunimah, eds., *Iraq Under Siege* (London: South End Press, 2000); Geoff Simons, *The Scourging of Iraq*, 2nd ed. (New York: Macmillian, 1996); Albert C. Peirce, "Just War Principles and Economic Sanctions," *Ethics and International Affairs* (1996) 99–113; and the multi-essay exchange on the issue between Joy Gordon and George A. Lopez, from pp. 123–50, in *Ethics and International Affairs* (1999).

48 Some were scandalized that Clinton ordered the operation on the night before the first scheduled vote on his impeachment in the US House of Representatives. Others noted the unhappy

title of the operation, since "Desert Fox" was Nazi General Erwin Rommel's nickname during World War II.

49 See the sources in Note 47.

50 Information for this section on the Persian Gulf War has been drawn from the following sources: Regan, *Cases*, 172–79; Lawrence Freedman and Efraim Karsh, *The Gulf Conflict: Diplomacy and War in the New World Order* (London: Faber and Faber, 1991); Wolfgang F. Danspeckgruber and Charles Tripp, eds., *The Iraqi Aggression Against Kuwait* (Boulder, CO: Westview, 1996); US News and World Report, *Triumph without Victory* (New York: Random House, 1992); James Turner Johnson and George Weigel, eds., *Just War and Gulf War* (Washington, DC: UP of America, 1991); and Alan Geyer and Barbara G. Green, eds., *Lines in the Sand: Justice and the Gulf War* (Louisville, KY: John Knox, 1992).

7

Jus post Bellum #2

REHABILITATION, AND WARS-WITHOUT-END

"They can only be made to accept a new constitution of a nature ... unlikely to encourage their warlike inclinations." —IMMANUEL KANT [1]

In the previous chapter, we introduced the concept of post-war justice, and noted three broad theories about its nature: 1) the overlapping, consensual "thin" theory; 2) the retribution model; and 3) the rehabilitation model. We saw that the thin theory of post-war justice advocates: publicity in post-war settlements; exchange of prisoners-of-war (POWs); official apologies for aggression; war crimes trials; and for the aggressor not only to give up its unjust war gains but to suffer some demilitarization after the fighting has ended. The retribution model builds on these claims, and advocates further that: 1) there be mandatory compensation payments slapped onto the defeated Aggressor, and forwarded to Victim; 2) that Aggressor's future economic growth be restricted with sweeping sanctions; and 3) that the war winners have no responsibility for forcible social or political reconstruction of Aggressor after these measures have been put into place. (Implement these proper measures of post-war punishment, and then leave ASAP, leaving any political transformations up to the local population.) We closed off last chapter explaining the strengths and weaknesses of this retribution model, promising to show, in this chapter, the superiority of the rival account of post-war justice: the rehabilitation model. That is precisely the main aim of this chapter, the last on just war theory and international law.

Yet, before leaving just war theory completely—to consider its major rivals (realism and pacifism)—attention will also be given, towards the end of this chapter, to the complex and contested case of protracted warfare. A protracted war is one which lasts decades, or even longer, and is one which—when it has gone on so long, and has become almost an entrenched way of life—can seem like a conflict without hope of resolution. The main instance nowadays, of course, is the Arab-Israeli conflict. Such struggles can seem like wars-without-end: so how would just war theory evaluate such, and seek to guide belligerent behavior in this regard? After all, if just war theory talks about justice "of," "in," and "after" war, how can it help advise us in cases where there seems to be no real "after," no true "end," no reasonable prospect of closure?

1. The Rehabilitation Model of Post-War Justice

As mentioned last chapter, there is no sharp split between the retribution and rehabilitation models. They share commitment to the following aspects of a decent post-war settlement: the need for publicity in settlements; official apologies; exchange of POWs; trials for criminals; some demilitarization; and the aggressor's return of any unjust gains. Where the models differ is over three major issues. First, the rehabilitation model *generally rejects sanctions*, especially on grounds that they have been shown, historically, to harm civilians and thus to violate discrimination. (We saw last chapter that the rehabilitative model might accept some carefully targeted sanctions—aimed only at elites—but is generally hostile to sanctions, and emphatically hostile towards sweeping sanctions applied to an entire country.) Second, the rehabilitation model *rejects compensation payments*, for the same reason. In fact, the model favors investing in a defeated Aggressor, to help it re-build and to help smooth over the wounds of war. Finally, the rehabilitation model *favors forcing regime change* in the defeated Aggressor whereas the retribution model views that as too risky and costly. Those who favor the rehabilitative model may agree on the risk and cost, but they would suggest that it can be worth it over the long-term, leading to the creation of a new, better, non-aggressive—even progressive—member of the international community. To those who scoff that such deep-rooted transformation simply can't be done, supporters of the rehabilitative model reply that, not only *can* it be done, it *has* been done. The two leading examples are West Germany and Japan after World War II.

1.2. REBUILDING GERMANY AND JAPAN AFTER WORLD WAR II

World War II's settlement was not contained in a detailed, legalistic peace treaty. This was partly because Germany and Japan were so thoroughly crushed and had so little leverage. But World War II's settlement was sweeping and profound, with immense effects on world history. It was worked out, essentially, between America and the Soviet Union at meetings in Tehran and Yalta, but with participation from the UK, France, China, and other of the "lesser" Allies. Both Britain and France kept control over their colonies, but everyone knew that powerful forces of anti-colonialism—abetted by the exhaustion of England and France—would soon cause those old empires to crumble. As for the new empires, it was understood that the USSR would hold sway in Eastern Europe, ostensibly to serve as a barrier between itself and

Germany, preventing another Nazi-style invasion from the west. (It also, though, provided for the export and spread of communism from the east.) The USA, by contrast, would get Hawaii, a number of Pacific Islands, and total sway over the reconstruction of Japan. As for Germany, it was agreed that America, Britain, France, and Russia would split it, into Western and Eastern halves. Ditto for the German capital Berlin, which was otherwise entirely within the Eastern, Soviet territory. Within this Soviet sphere, police-state communism came to dominate as readily as it did in Russia.[2] But within the West, there was a concerted effort to establish genuine free-market, rights-respecting democracies. In Japan, the same experiment was undertaken, but there the US military, under the firm leadership of Douglas MacArthur, held more direct control than it did in West Germany, and for longer.

The Allies, genuinely working with nationals in both countries—more so in Germany than Japan, perhaps—first undertook a purging process, which in Germany came to be known as "denazification." All signs, symbols, buildings, literature, and things directly associated with the Nazis were destroyed. The Nazi party itself was abolished and declared illegal. Surviving ex-Nazi higher-ups—but not all of them[3]—were put on trial, put in jail, or otherwise punished and prohibited from political participation. The militaries of both Germany and Japan were disbanded, and for years the Allied military became the military, and the direct ruler, of both Germany and Japan.

After the negative purging process, the Allies in both countries established written constitutions or "Basic Law." These constitutions, after the period of direct military rule ended, provided for bills and charters of human rights, eventual democratic elections, and—above all—the checks and balances so prominently featured in the American system. Since government had grown so huge and tyrannical in both Germany and Japan in the 1930s, it had to be shrunk down, and then broken into pieces, with each piece only authorized to handle its own business. Independent judiciaries and completely reconstituted police forces were an important part of this—and they went a long way to re-establishing the impersonal rule of law over the personal whims of former fascists. The executive branches, much more so than in the American system, were made more accountable to the legislative branch, and more closely tied to it. The goal, of course, was to ensure that the executive couldn't grow into another dictator. By design, there were to be no strong presidents. So Germany and Japan became true parliamentary democracies, more in the European than American style.

Western-style liberal democracy was not the only change forcibly implemented. The education systems of both Germany and Japan were overhauled, since they played huge propaganda roles for both regimes and the content of their curricula had been filled with racism, ultra-nationalism, and distorted ignorance of the outside world. Western experts re-designed these systems to impart concrete skills needed to participate in reconstruction, as well as to stress a more objective content favoring the basic cognitive functions ("the three Rs") as well as critical thinking and especially science and technology. The curricula were radically stripped of political content (though, of course, some lessons on the new social institutions and their principles were required).

The Americans quickly saw that their sweeping legal, constitutional, social, and educational reforms would lack stability unless they could stimulate the German and Japanese economies. The people needed their vital needs met, as well as a sense of hope that, concretely, the future would get better. Otherwise, they might revolt, and the reforms fail. Instead of making the (World War I) mistake of sucking money out of these ruined countries through mandatory reparations payments, the Americans were the ones who poured money into Germany and Japan. America shunned the retribution paradigm and embraced the rehabilitative one. A staggering sum of money was channeled in, through the Marshall Plan. Money was needed to buy essentials, as well as to clear away all the rubble and ruined infrastructure. It was also just needed to circulate, to get the Germans and Japanese used to free market trading. Jobs were plentiful, as entire systems of infrastructure—transportation, water, sewage, electricity, agriculture, finance—had to be rebuilt. Since jobs paid wages, thanks to the Marshall Plan, the people's lives improved and the free market system deepened. But it wasn't just the money. American management experts poured into Germany and Japan, showing them the very latest, and most efficient, means of production. Within 30 years, Germany and Japan had not only rebounded economically, they had the two strongest economies in the world after America itself, based especially on quality high-tech manufacturing, for instance of automobiles.

The post-war reconstructions of Germany and Japan easily count as the most impressive post-war rehabilitations in modern history; rivaled perhaps only by America's re-building of its own South after The Civil War (1861–65). Germany and Japan, today, have massive free market economies, and politically remain peaceful, stable, and decent democracies. They are both very good citizens on the global stage. In addition, these countries are by no means "clones" (much less colonies) of America: they each have gone their own way, adding local color, and pursuing political paths quite distinct from those that most interest the United States—consider especially Germany's formative role in the European Union. So we have clear evidence that even massive and forcible post-war changes need not threaten a nation's character, or what makes it unique and special to its people. But such success did come at a huge cost in terms of time and treasure: it cost trillions of dollars; took trillions of "man-hours" in work and expertise; it took decades of real time; it took the co-operation of most of the German and Japanese people; and, above all, it took the will of the United States to see it through. It was American money, American security, American know-how, American patience, and American generosity which brought it all into being. Such is the magnitude of commitment needed by any party bent on successfully implementing substantial post-war rehabilitation.[4]

1.2. CONNECTING START AND FINISH: E.G., IN IRAQ & AFGHANISTAN

I've stated repeatedly throughout this work that the three phases of war (beginning, middle, and end) are interconnected, and so should be the three categories of just war theory (*jus ad bellum, jus in bello,* and *jus post bellum*). In particular, when it comes to *jus post bellum* it is axiomatic that if there was no justice at the start of the war, there will be no justice at the end. In other words: *the less just your start of war, the fewer your rights in the post-war phase.* Coherence entails that injustice in the beginning infects both the middle and end of war. It's hard to imagine—logically, causally, and historically—a war which X began unjustly yet, when X won and imposed its will, that justice was somehow ultimately served. In those three senses, it seems more accurate to quip that it's "garbage in, garbage out": rotten inputs don't generate sublime outputs. So if we concern ourselves with justice after war, we must ensure we involve ourselves in a just war to begin with.

Some might ask: can't we imagine a war unjustly begun, yet justly concluded? Some might say that America's 2003 Iraq attack was unjustly begun, yet it was fought quickly and with reasonable adherence to *jus in bello*. (The prison tortures came later, during the occupation). And if America succeeds in reconstructing Iraq, that's just, no? Compared to Saddam's dictatorship? Well, justice isn't just about results, though of course these are important. Justice is also about not violating rights, and about following a certain procedure. *Jus ad bellum* violations are violations of rights, and it has always been my contention[5] that we should understand each of the three just war categories coming together to form one long procedure which demands getting each step right before moving on to the next one. So, *jus ad bellum* failure corrupts the whole resulting project. We might therefore speak of Iraq being better off, if—*IF*—American-led reconstruction eventually "works," but not of it having been fully just if we seriously doubt, as I do, the justice of America's inauguration of that conflict. In other words, even if it all somehow turns out well, that still won't make the original decision just; it will simply mean that the post-war situation wasn't as bad as it might have been.

The connection between the categories means that the only party with post-war entitlements regarding regime change will be the one which fought on the side of justice to begin with. As Kant said, the raw fact of military victory only changes the power situation; it does not, and should not, change our *moral* assessment of the war, which is at the level of enduring principle and not merely of contingent power.[6] There is no guarantee the just side will actually win, of course, but it's quite another thing—surely, a mistaken thing—to interpret victory in war as itself imbuing the war, or post-war measures, with moral value. Nazi Germany won the Blitzkrieg phase of World

War II, yet this hardly justifies what it subsequently did to Poland, Scandinavia, the Netherlands, and France. The Communists, in the early- to mid-1900s, won their civil wars in Russia and China, but that doesn't justify how they later governed those territories. And so on.

As I argued in Chapter 3, the American-led war of regime change against the Taliban in Afghanistan satisfied *jus ad bellum*, whereas that against Saddam Hussein's regime probably violated it. Why? In the first war, in late 2001, strong evidence showed the Taliban provided state sponsorship—of resources, weapons, and safe havens—to the terrorist group al-Qaeda, which had just committed aggression against America on 9/11. The Taliban did so because it shared al-Qaeda's radical Islamist ideology, which mandates the violent take-over of all governments in traditional Arab lands and their conversion into strict Islamic theocracies wherein there is a unification of "church" and state modeled after the Taliban's Afghanistan or, to a lesser extent, Iran. These groups despise the West because it is not Islamic and particularly target America because of its support for Middle Eastern regimes they would love to overthrow, in particular Saudi Arabia (the holy land of Islam) and Israel (which they claim is on traditional Arab land). Most just war theorists, and 28 other countries, agreed with America that it was just to respond with force when the Taliban refused to hand over al-Qaeda suspects in November 2001. Owing to that large consensus on the justice of the start of that war, we can speak meaningfully of large post-war entitlements of the Allied force in Afghanistan.

Regarding Iraq, only seven countries agreed with America, and I think a majority of just war theorists disagreed with the war. International lawyers were perhaps the most incensed of all, since no clear Security Council permission vote was held. In Chapter 3, I argued that the main cause of the war—pre-emptive self-defence against an imminent WMD strike by Iraq, or Iraq-supplied terrorists—was not proven to the degree it had to be. While I did admit that armed humanitarian intervention (AHI) provided the best case for that war—Saddam's regime not being minimally just—it clearly wasn't "the shot being called" and, besides that, the attack ran afoul of issues of proper authority, last resort, probability of success, and proportionality. So I must conclude that post-war entitlements in the Iraq case are much smaller than in the Afghanistan case. But even though I believe America has few, if any, rights in post-war Iraq, this doesn't mean I think America should just up and leave. That is because I endorse the much-publicized "Pottery Barn Rule": *if you break it, you buy it.* In March-May, 2003, America broke Iraq—there can be no doubt about that—and that act brought with it separate responsibilities to help put Iraq back together. In other words, America has few rights, but many duties, regarding post-war Iraq. This means that it still makes sense to hold America to standards, such as aiding the creation of a minimally just community in Iraq. Even if I think the Iraq war unjust, and thus cannot ever pronounce America's post-war policies fully just, I can—we have established—still pronounce them better or worse, according to the extent to which they would satisfy the ideal, had the inauguration of the conflict been different.

1.3. THE GOAL OF JUST REGIME CHANGE

Before considering in detail the latest efforts regarding post-war reconstruction in Afghanistan and Iraq, let's speak of the ideal goal of justified regime change in general. The goal of justified post-war regime change—whether permitted by rights or demanded by duties—is the timely construction of a minimally just political community. As we saw in Chapter 2, such a community makes every reasonable effort to: 1) avoid violating the rights of other minimally just communities; 2) gain recognition as being legitimate in the eyes of the international community and its own people; and 3) realize the human rights of all its individual members. We provided there a justification for having this standard, and we recall attention to it here since the imposition of any standard in the post-war environment is such serious and controversial business. The ideal of a human rights-respecting, minimally just political community is a justified one because:

- It is in every individual's self-interest;
- It respects everyone's potential for autonomy and self-direction;
- It thus has universal appeal;
- It already enjoys very strong international consensus;
- It is based on thin, reasonable, and accessible values, such as living a minimally good life;
- It generates good consequences, especially in terms of average quality of life; and
- It promotes long-term international peace and stability.

It is these values—their strength and moral resonance—which ground regime-changing measures in a post-war environment. These are not extreme, narrow, "crusading," or "imperialistic" values; they are modest, secular, widely accepted, and based on appeal to the first principle of respecting individual rights as well as to after-the-fact considerations of generating concrete beneficial consequences for everyone. Let's now examine in some detail how well the on-going—and nearly "done"—reconstruction processes in Afghanistan and Iraq are faring, relative to these standards and goals.

1.4. AFGHANISTAN AND IRAQ: HOW FARES THE GOAL?

Afghanistan has been in a period of post-war reconstruction since early 2002; Iraq since mid-2003. (These dates refer to when the regime fell in each society, as a result of American invasion, leading then to US military occupation (i.e., when country X's military controls the affairs of another country Y).)[7] It seems true that the international community, as led by America, has—more or less—been trying to construct a minimally just society in each instance. It has been a very difficult process, in both countries, and has seen a mixture of both successes and failures.

1.4.1. Successes

The major post-war successes, in both nations, have been the replacement of aggressive, rogue regimes with new governments. The old regimes have been purged; and these new governments enjoy democratic legitimacy—through multiple elections, in both countries (most recently in 2010)—and are based on written constitutions crafted by locals. The gains in terms of personal freedom, in both societies, have also been huge. Finally, in Afghanistan anyway, the gains in terms of gender equality have been very substantial with, e.g., the international community (including Canada) building and staffing many new schools for girls and women.[8]

The problem, though, is that the evidence suggests that it's not things such as individual liberty and gender equality which matter most when it comes to the success and durability of post-war reconstruction. The historical data suggest, rather, that the most important things are physical security (i.e., personal safety) and economic growth. Jim Dobbins, probably the leading scholar on this issue, has distilled all this data into one crystal-clear rule-of-thumb regarding post-war success: *the war-winning occupier, and the new local regime, have about 10 years to form an effective partnership and to devote themselves in particular to making the average person in that society feel better off—more secure and more prosperous, especially—than they were prior to the outbreak of the war.* If they can do this, post-war reconstruction will probably succeed. If not, there will be failure, and a serious risk of back-sliding into armed conflict.[9]

Using this rule of thumb, we note that the approximate deadline for achieving this in Afghanistan would have been 2012, and in Iraq, 2013. Now, the US occupation of Iraq has been declared "officially over" (as of December, 2011), but the reality is that a substantial number of US troops remain indefinitely to help train the new Iraqi army, and to protect Iraqi oil infrastructure.[10] And, in Afghanistan, NATO troops have committed to being there until 2014. So, will physical security and economic improvement be achieved in the very short time remaining?

1.4.2. Challenges

SECURITY

While the capital of Afghanistan, Kabul, is quite secure, the same cannot be said for the rest of the nation: there is a deep urban-rural split in this regard. Afghanistan is a highly weaponized society, with nearly all men owning guns and with local tribal leaders protecting their families' farms (and crops) with their own armed militias. The Taliban is making a come-back in rural areas by clamping down on these local tribal "war lords," and promising a return to the very strict (religious) law-and-order state they feel they achieved when in power. So, would the average Afghani feel more secure now than back when the Taliban were in power? Maybe not, and this is one reason why US President Barack Obama ordered a fresh surge of US troops into Afghanistan over the next few years (largely, cycling them out of Iraq and into Afghanistan). He has done this to: bring security; turn the tide against a resurgent Taliban; and deal more effectively with the border area between Afghanistan and Pakistan, keenly focused on ensuring radical Islamic extremists don't use it to re-build and potentially strike America once more.[11]

Things were so bad, security-wise, in Iraq during 2005–06, that experts spoke openly of there being a civil war between the three main groups: Kurd, Sunni, and Shi'ite. At the time, President George W. Bush ordered a big surge of more US troops into Iraq and, as led by General David Petraeus, they have succeeded beyond anyone's expectations in cutting down group-on-group violence and in keeping the peace. (This success is what inspired Obama to order the same for Afghanistan.) But is it enough? Dobbins would remind us that more security now than in 2006 is not the same thing as more security than back when Saddam was in power in 2003. Saddam was a brutal tyrant, but he did keep law-and-order. So would the average Iraqi say they feel safer and more secure than before the war? It's hard to say, and might depend on which group one is asking: the Kurds and Shi'ites might well say yes, whereas Saddam's own Sunni ethnicity might well say no. While there have been clear security gains since 2006, all the groups are quite concerned as to what might happen once the US pulls out entirely.[12]

ECONOMY

Would average Afghanis, and Iraqis, say they are more prosperous now than prior to the war? Thankfully, the Americans did not implement the retribution model in either case, and instead have sent investment flowing into both countries. Iraq probably has a better shot here, since (at least) it has lots of oil and gas, as well as a large and reasonably educated workforce. Yet huge challenges remain. The near-constant war since 1979, plus the effects of the sanctions from 1991–2003, devastated Iraq's basic infrastructure and well-being. So much re-building needs to be done. Unemployment remains a terrible problem. One solution would seem to be to pay the unemployed to perform all the re-building, but the costs would be enormous—in the dozens of billions, or more—and the Americans have been reluctant to pay the bill all on their own. But other countries, for their part, reply that it was America's war, and so America needs to pay the price.[13]

Afghanistan is one of the world's poorest countries, where two-thirds of the population lives on $2 USD/day. The same proportion of the population is thought to be functionally illiterate, and unemployment is thought to afflict half the workforce. Afghanistan faces the same issues of ruined infrastructure, and the brutal consequences which constant warfare has inflicted on the economy. (These consequences can be condensed as follows: *would you open a business in a war zone?*) Afghanistan's economy is a toxic mixture of war and drugs. Poppies grow well there, and farmers can earn much more growing them than legal crops like wheat or corn. It is estimated that one-third of Afghanistan's economy comes from poppy production, and the heroin and opium trade which comes out of it. Transforming Afghanistan's economy from one of war and drugs to a peaceful and legal economy rooted in broad-based, healthy economic growth is proving terribly hard. It's deeply unclear whether clear success will happen on this front, but at least here the Americans can count on international support, as all of NATO is involved. The UK, e.g., is thinking of buying Afghanistan's poppies and using them for medical-grade opiates in Western hospitals (e.g., for pain-killers). Canada and Germany are heavily involved in building and running schools for Afghan children. Even Russia, in 2010, signed an agreement to help co-operate in stopping the narcotics trade, as much of Afghanistan's drugs wind up on the streets of Moscow (as the closest big city).[14]

The upshot is this: by the three criteria of minimally just communities, the nearly-done processes of reconstruction in Iraq and Afghanistan have produced mixtures of success and failure. There has been much success in the prevention of more international aggression, the re-building of genuinely legitimate governments, the augmentation of personal freedoms, and the bringing into the political and social fold groups which were formerly excluded and discriminated against (notably, the Kurds and Shi'ites in Iraq; and the women in Afghanistan). But real challenges, or perhaps even failures, are more evident when one considers physical security and material subsistence in these countries, and leading post-war scholars like Dobbins have argued that these things are, in fact, more important to the endurance of a new post-war order. Thus, even if post-war reconstruction is somehow determined to be an "overall success" in Iraq and Afghanistan, it seems clear that it will not be of the same order of magnitude as what was achieved in Japan and (West) Germany in 1945–55. But, maybe that is all that can reasonably be expected in these situations, as Japan and Germany represent the historical best cases, and we can't expect every new case to turn out as well as the historically best ones. Maybe we thus have to settle for what Aristotle once wisely described as "the second-best solution": all serious efforts are made towards the best possible ideal—over a period of 10–15 years—but realizing that, by the end of that time, we may instead be left with an imperfect mixture of success and failure.[15]

1.5. BACK TO THE IDEAL

It's important to consider these real-world—and very relevant and timely—cases of post-war reconstruction, and measure them up to our ideals and standards. But it must be stressed that the serious problems in Afghanistan and Iraq do not show that forcible, progressive post-war regime change cannot actually be done, and so we must abandon the effort. Successful coercive post-war regime change was actually done in Germany and Japan, and so it is neither conceptually nor empirically impossible. In fact, a review of the literature shows something of an ideal 10-point recipe for transforming a defeated aggressor into a minimally just regime.

Before sketching out this recipe, consider Kant's interesting and provocative opening quote. He clearly believed forcible regime change permissible. His moral test involved considering whether one's policies or actions would, if everyone else did the same thing, lead to contradiction or inhumanity. A brutal, rights-violating state obviously acts inhumanely, and if all states behaved like aggressors it would "make peace among nations impossible." Thus, states failing minimal justice forfeit rights of existence. Kant hastens to add, however, that other states shouldn't simply carve up and "ingest" the offending state and its territory, since that would ignore completely the wishes and rights of the local population. The local population does have the right to exist as a people, but it doesn't have the right to establish an aggressive or rights-violating state. Kant concludes that the most reasonable, middle-ground solution is that the people stay together as a people but they must accept a new, "less war-like constitution." Forcible regime change is actually a sound compromise between the two extremes of conquest (on the one hand) and (on the other) of letting terrible regimes exist and thrive.[16]

This puts the vital issue of entitlement nicely: regimes which aren't minimally just have no right to govern, and so are in no position to complain should they be overthrown. But what about the right of the people there to be self-governing? National self-determination is not an end-in-itself; it is good only insofar as it results in a minimally just society. A people never has the right to establish an aggressive or human rights-violating regime, any more than a crook has the right to beat up people as a form of his "freedom of expression." We can imagine cases—indeed, know of cases—where a people lacks the means for constructing a minimally just society. Perhaps they lack the resources and expertise, are deeply divided, have been exhausted by war, or flat out refuse out of blinkered nationalism or ideology. In all these cases, they can justly be forced to accept a new, minimally just regime in the post-war period provided the war was just. If the war was not just, they can't be so forced but they should certainly be helped if they freely request it. Owing to the power of the idea of a minimally just political community, we shouldn't be surprised to see locals clamoring for this option and for help. The new regime must then eventually get endorsement and show its local legitimacy—ideally through direct election—and then that effectively cements its right to govern. If the locals still don't like it, they can turf the government out and start again—but always within the confines of minimal justice.

So, and this is the heart of this chapter, forcible post-war regime change is permissible provided: 1) the war itself was just and conducted properly; 2) the target regime was illegitimate, thus forfeiting its state rights; 3) the goal of the reconstruction is a minimally just regime; and 4) respect for *jus in bello* and human rights is integral to the transformation process itself. The permission is then granted because the transformation: 1) violates neither state nor human rights; 2) its expected consequences are very desirable, namely, satisfied human rights for the local population and increased international peace and security for everyone; and 3) the post-war moment is especially promising regarding the possibilities for reform. And the transformation will be successful when there is: 1) a stable new regime; 2) run entirely by locals; which is 3) minimally just.

1.6. THE "REHABILITATION RECIPE"

According to sound empirical research analyzing the cases,[17] the core blueprint for transforming defeated, rights-violating aggressor regimes into minimally just societies is:

- *Adhere diligently to the laws of war during the regime take-down and occupation.* This is morally vital for its own sake, as well as to help win the hearts and minds of the locals. America, of course, has notoriously run afoul of this principle in Iraq, owing to the prisoner abuse scandal at the Abu-Ghraib prison.

  (Speaking of the laws of war, there is a body of rules referred to as "occupation law" but it is much in dispute, even regarding whether it is still in force. As Simon Chesterman explains, occupation law demands that any occupation be temporary. It does allow occupation forces to defend themselves. And it requires that the occupier provide for civilian well-being, especially in connection with vital needs and basic infrastructure. But it stridently stipulates that the occupier *not* change any of the existing laws or structures within the occupied society. So, Chesterman observes, occupation law "provides little support for regime change." Thus, this 10-point recipe is in the domain of just war theory and political philosophy, not international law. Yet, not entirely so, since the UN Security Council has authorized recent regime-changing actions in Afghanistan, Cambodia, East Timor, Kosovo, and Libya, so the principle isn't completely foreign to international law. Additionally, what if the war causes the existing state structure to collapse? It seems irrational to suggest that the occupying power may not change such a condition of destroyed rubble; such change could only be for the better, would it not? And what about those cases of truly abhorrent regimes, like the Nazis or Khmer Rouge? The old ban on changing regimes seems predicated on a belief that the existing state structures don't have anything seriously, irredeemably wrong with them. But we know that's not always true. And so the clarity and utility of occupation law is much to be wondered at, and that's why here we focus on theory.)[18]

- *Purge much of the old regime, and prosecute its war criminals.* Much, but not necessarily all. Clearly, anyone materially connected to aggression, tyranny, or atrocity cannot be permitted a substantial role in the new order. They've lost the right to govern. But others—say, middle-ranking civil servants—might be kept on for their local knowledge and bureaucratic expertise. There always needs to be some continuity, even in the face of a sea-change in institutions.

- *Disarm and demilitarize the society.* The target military does need to be disarmed and demobilized—but then something needs to be done with them. Many critics of the American occupation of Iraq argue that a key decision which helped spark the insurgency was the US choice to promptly disband the 400,000-strong Iraqi army—then leave them to their own devices. Plans for employing these potentially dangerous men, providing them opportunity, should have been developed.[19]

- *Provide effective military and police security for the whole country.* Most experts suggest a two-stage approach here: the successful "attack and overthrow" war divisions be replaced by other divisions specifically trained in post-combat peace-keeping and nation-building. Whether this latter force should be multinational, or UN-led, is taken up below. But the transition should be as seamless as possible, and the ratios are crucial. The nation-building research shows you need about 20 soldiers per 1,000 residents to stabilize and secure post-war populations. (Incidentally, both the Afghanistan and Iraq occupation forces are—and have always been—well short of this ratio.) The moral is to go in big, with plenty of "boots on the ground," boots tutored in what The Pentagon labels "stability operations." Show the locals strong—not hesitant—intentions to protect them and to provide a secure backdrop for the development of law and legitimacy.[20]

- *Work with a cross-section of locals on a new, rights-respecting constitution which features checks and balances.* Limited government is required to prevent re-growth of tyranny; legitimate government is needed both for moral fitness and for stability. The picture here is of a genuine political partnership between the war-winner and the local civilian population. The facts show that the meaningful participation and support of both is absolutely necessary, and usually more extensive international participation is desirable as well. Constitution-making is a process, and so we can't rationally expect perfection or closure the first time out. Even the most developed societies occasionally change their constitutions and/or take several tries before creating a workable one in the first place. So while the post-war atmosphere is pressured, and there's a desire to rapidly end foreign occupation, some patience is required on the part of everyone. Good things often take time. In terms of inclusion in the constitution-building process, Andrew Arato reminds us that every group must be included: 1) whose non-participation could ruin any subsequent arrangement; and 2) who is committed to the creation of a minimally just state. If these two conditions are met, all relevant groups—as guided by the war-winner—are to develop an inclusive framework for limited, accountable, and rights-respecting government.[21]

- *Allow other non-state associations, "civil society," to flourish.* Civil society associations refer to all groupings which don't involve the state. They range from chambers of commerce to little league sports associations, from religious organizations to rock music bands, and from volunteer charities to online social media groups. Research stresses how important such associations are, not only to enjoyment of life but also to people's commitment to their society. These groupings connect people to each other, provide satisfaction, and promote non-political aspects of life. They serve to take pressure off the state (by providing diverse outlets for energy), they help to legitimize the society (by increasing participation and happiness) and they also indirectly limit state power (by showing there's more to life than politics). It's always the mark of a tyrannical government when there is little activity within civil society. Robust civil societies are thus an important ingredient in creating mature, legitimate social conditions.[22]

- *Forego compensation and sanctions in favor of investing in and re-building the economy.* In the last chapter we saw that many modern peace arrangements—notably the Treaty of Versailles and the terms ending the Persian Gulf War—unraveled, or created perverse consequences, when they included hefty compensation terms and sweeping sanctions.[23] Targeted compensation might still be justified but, beyond that and war crimes trials, punitive settlements don't seem to work. The goal of proper regime change is the creation of a stable, minimally just social condition. This is difficult enough as it is; trying to achieve it while sucking resources out of the target country becomes nigh impossible. Thankfully, in Iraq in 2003, the old punitive sanctions were dropped, and investment started to flow in. This need for funds is a strong argument for including international partners in reconstruction. Realistically speaking, though, such partners will probably volunteer their resources only if they believe the war was justified to begin with.

- *If necessary, revamp educational curricula to purge past propaganda and cement new values.* The fascists in the 1930s used school systems to warp future citizens so that they would subscribe to highly destructive doctrines of racial and national supremacy, with the flip-side being hatred and aggression against "Others." In Afghanistan under the Taliban, and elsewhere still in the Middle East, great controversy attaches to the teaching of Islamic extremism and its attitudes towards violence, Israel, the West, and women in particular. Much development research powerfully shows the beneficial effects of massive commitment to the education of girls and women. Indeed, some have even pronounced this one of the few "silver bullets" in development, which correlates very strongly with such other desirable social outcomes as economic growth, higher life expectancy, lower crime rates, and internal political stability.[24]

- *Ensure that the benefits of the new order will be: 1) concrete; and 2) widely, not narrowly, distributed.* As Michael Walzer says, you've got to increase everyone's stake in the new, developing order. In particular, you must avoid a situation where it seems that the foreign occupier is favoring one group above the rest, giving that group most of the power. That group will soon be marked as traitors and foreign agents, and will lose legitimacy and popular support. This was frequently the case during the European colonial era—particularly with France and Belgium—when the colonizer would select an elite group to rule, creating bitter ethnic and communal rivalries which persist today. The reconstructions of Germany and Japan showed, by contrast, that there must be widespread concrete benefits distributed throughout the population to make reconstruction work. Political things like getting to vote and run for office where you couldn't before; civic things like having your daughter go to school where before she couldn't; social things like starting up reading clubs where they used to be banned; and, above all, economic things like an average rise in living standards within a reasonable time.[25]

- *Follow an orderly, not-too-hasty exit strategy when the new regime can stand on its own two feet.* This requires walking a fine line. On the one hand, the foreign occupier can't stay forever—for that's conquest, not reconstruction. The locals must see that occupation will come to an end and they will return to full sovereignty. This knowledge should diffuse some tension. On the other hand, if you're going to do something as important as post-war rehabilitation, you should try to do it well. Plus there's a moral responsibility not to "cut and run." A botched reconstruction benefits no one, including impatient locals.

This ten-point recipe for reconstruction is only a general blueprint; clearly, in particular cases, some things will need to be emphasized over others. The best recipes always allow for individual variance and input, depending on time and the ingredients at hand. We should also note the heavy interconnectedness of many of these elements. US Major-General William Nash is probably only exaggerating a bit when he declares: "The first rule of nation-building is that everything is related to everything, and it's all political."[26] Further, in spite of the variances among aggressive, rights-violating societies—different geography, history, language, economy, diet, ethnic composition—there has been striking similarity in the kind of regime here in view. Think of the major twentieth century aggressors and dictatorships: the USSR; Fascist Spain and Italy; Nazi Germany; Imperial Japan; North Korea; Communist China; Pol Pot's Cambodia; Muammar Gaddafi's Libya; Saddam Hussein's Iraq; the Taliban's Afghanistan. In spite of all the differences among them, the regimes shared large affinities: a small group of ruthless fanatics uses force to come to power; it keeps power through the widespread use of violence, both internally and externally; it engages in massively invasive control over every major sphere of life, with no other associations allowed to rival the state's prestige; the rule of law is jettisoned; the military, or "in-party," becomes all-important; human rights are trampled upon, and so on.[27] To a remarkable extent, in spite of all the other differences, it's been the same kind of regime. And this shouldn't, in the end, come as so much of a surprise: they all learned from each other and sought to emulate what worked elsewhere. The modern police state only has so many precedents to draw upon, and might in fact be located ultimately in such early examples as Napoleonic France, or most probably Robespierre's Reign of Terror during the French Revolution.[28] So, then, we shouldn't be all that shocked, surprised, and skeptical if it turns out that one general recipe can, in fact, be found for transforming such regimes and societies away from rampant rights-violation into ones which are at least minimally just.

1.7. KNOWING VERSUS DOING

Al Pierce has wisely noted that there's a difference between *knowing* what to do, and actually *being able* to do it. In other words, even if we do know the general recipe for pro-rights reconstruction, there's still the issue of whether we are able to implement that knowledge in particular instances. In Iraq, e.g., there was quite fierce armed resistance to both American and Iraqi attempts to implement the general recipe there. This does highlight the distance between the ideal and the real, which can never be ignored in international affairs. I agree with the moral logic of Pierce's position but it's hard to state what it finally means for the thesis advocated here. We can't be overconfident of success; we must expect resistance and impatience; and we must meaningfully involve the local population in the reconstruction of its own regime. But there have been actual cases of successful pro-rights, post-war reconstruction. We think of Germany and Japan post-World War II especially. These cases have even occurred in social contexts—like Japan in 1945—with no appreciable background commitment to any of the needed attitudes, habits, and values. So it *can* be done; there is no abstract, sweeping "can't." Perhaps it can't be done in particular cases—but how are we to know without trying? Pierce's point is important, and rightly cautionary. But it doesn't show that post-war rehabilitation shouldn't be tried at all, or that it is misguided in principle. We can still have it as our ideal plan, even if it turns out we can only partially realize it in particular cases (as conceded above).

Some also say that the process imagined here is only going to work in very rare cases, like Japan and Germany, wherein the target country was completely crushed during the war. In this sense, pro-rights reconstruction still "can't be done" in the majority of cases, where there is less-than-total victory. The locals simply won't agree to it.[29] Fortunately, this view is skeptical speculation, with shaky empirical backing. Consider that right now there are on-going pro-rights, post-war reconstruction processes underway in Afghanistan, Bosnia, East Timor, Kosovo, and Iraq. None of these regimes—Bosnia least of all—was crushed to the extent that Nazi Germany and Imperial Japan were. Yet they all find themselves on the same road to reconstruction. Now, there *are* real difficulties, as noted above. But there have also been real successes, especially in Bosnia-Kosovo and East Timor. New institutions, based on human rights, are developing; there is relative stability and peace; there have been free elections and, in the case of Bosnia and East Timor, there is almost fully restored sovereignty. Bosnia and East Timor have been utterly transformed from societies bloodily battered by foreign invasion and civil war to peaceful, near-sovereign nations. Admittedly, there's a shorter time-span with these cases, so we can't pronounce them successes on the order of a Germany or Japan. But they clearly offer support for the thesis that post-war rehabilitation is possible even without achieving crushing military victory, unconditional surrender, and total sway over the local population. The locals in Bosnia and East Timor did agree to the values of post-war reconstruction here in view, and so again we see the incorrectness—the easy, fashionable pessimism—of the notion that "the locals won't go for it," that "it simply can't be done." No one enjoys foreign occupation, to be sure. But most people can see that it's the quality of governance which matters most, not the source of its genesis. If a foreign source can help create a minimally just society where none existed before, it can't rationally be rejected merely on grounds of foreign participation. Indeed, if you look back far enough, it's hard to think of any country which hasn't had some "foreign" contribution to its political structure. (Consider the USA itself, and the role that American Indians, British, and French had on its founding structures—and waves of foreign immigrants have had on its society.) The point is that the process be just, not that it be "purely local" in its origins.[30]

1.8. WHO'S IN CHARGE?

This leaves the large issue of who should be the main players in post-war reconstruction. The war winner? The international community? The locals? The Dobbins Report, interestingly, finds in repeated cases that the commitment, presence, and investment of the war winner is most necessary to the success of post-war reform. That's apparently a fact of which we need to be mindful. There's also the value of the goal of minimal justice and our desire to see it actualized, which calls our attention to these power realities. Another fact is this: reconstruction needs to take place within a secure context, and the war-winner is clearly best positioned to provide this—at least initially. There's the relative responsibility argument, too: the war winner, after all, was the one who overthrew the regime. Having "broken it," the war winner "bought it": i.e., shouldered the main responsibility for aiding the reconstruction of a replacement regime.

This is not a clarion call for triumphant unilateralism, much less "neo-imperialism." It's a judgment informed by: 1) the facts of who can secure the society; 2) who most bears responsibility; and 3) who can effectively leverage successful post-war regime change. Clearly, local involvement and endorsement is, eventually, a make-or-break deal. Given the good values of just reconstruction (compared with what went before), we shouldn't worry about finding such support. Indeed, the cases show there are many locals to be found, in every society, who see the sense of minimal justice and who wish to take up leadership roles in the reconstruction process. It's more an issue of *when* and *how* to transfer reconstruction authority to a reconstituted and legitimate state structure, and that's clearly to be determined on a case-by-case basis. Local input—meaningful cross-sectional consultation—has to be there right from the start, and gradually grow to fully restored sovereignty, probably about 10–15 years later. The war winner must always understand—as Chapter XI of the UN Charter (which deals with "Non-self-governing territories") says—that it occupies a position of "sacred trust" in this regard. The war winner can't ever forget, as the International Commission on Intervention and State Sovereignty (ICISS) says, that its reconstructive activities must be aimed at "putting itself out of a job." The war winner's authority lasts only as long as the trust remains earned and the rehabilitative task—as defined here by the recipe—keeps progressing in the direction of minimal justice.[31]

What role should the international community play? Both watchdog and junior partner. Watchdog, to ensure that the power enjoyed by the war winner doesn't corrupt. And junior partner, in that sensible war winners will want to reach out and receive additional resources as well as world-wide expertise in the various fields of social reconstruction. The war winner shouldn't have problems attracting such outside aid if the war itself was just. There is, e.g., a large international presence in the reconstruction of Afghanistan. Nor should the international community hesitate to provide such aid, since it's not just a matter of charity but also of improving the peace and security of themselves and their own people. America, obviously, is having some problems in this connection with Iraq. Non-aid from erstwhile international allies is understandable—not wanting to reward and legitimize what they see as an unjust war. However such allies can't forget that the Iraqi people pay the price for such non-provision as well. I don't think non-aid violates a duty here but these consequences should still be kept in mind when making a decision whether to help a war winner engage in social reconstruction.

When it comes to United Nations involvement post-conflict, the UN does have much relevant, and recent, experience—e.g., in East Timor—which it would be wise to draw upon. Is such needed to confer legitimacy upon post-conflict reconstruction? I don't think so: the UN, while seasoned, has had some sour experiences as well, especially in African conflicts ranging from Congo to Somalia to Rwanda. The UN has also been involved in serious corruption scandals, so there's no guarantee that multilateralism ensures integrity in the process.[32] The exclusivity of such UN bodies as the Security Council also raises questions regarding its political—as opposed to legal—legitimacy. There's also the probability of success issue. On the one hand, you do want lots of resources, support, and diverse expertise; on the other, "too many cooks can spoil the broth." Is the Afghani reconstruction—featuring the UN and many countries—going much better than the Iraqi? To those in the know, not obviously so. The Taliban are not in power but still exist, especially in rural Afghanistan; most of the reconstruction is centered only around the capital, Kabul; rival clan lords retain armed militias, posing security threats; and there has been a failure to develop the legitimate economy, driving local farmers to poppy production, which feeds heroin addiction and provides illegal drug lords with resources and power.[33] Part of this checkered record, of course, is the sheer difficulty of the enterprise—which we should never underestimate—but another part might be that responsibility so widely divided can leave actors with insufficient incentive for ensuring overall success. In my view, fewer people worry about Afghanistan, despite its severe difficulties, because there's larger consensus on the justice of that war and accompanying regime change. Contrast this with the Iraq case, where the whole enterprise substantially rests on the shoulders of the Iraqis and the Americans. American prestige and possibly security are on the line, and the Iraqis have their very futures at stake. This illustrates, for me, that the key relationship in reconstruction always boils down to that between the war winner and the local population: they each bear big burdens, and the involvement of both is essential for enduring, successful reform.

1.9. RESISTANCE

We should predict a rough ride, especially at the beginning. Regime hold-outs, fanatics of various stripes, criminal elements, and foreign de-stabilizers might all actively resist forcible regime change, even if the initial war was clearly just. Assuming it was so, the war winner is entitled to combat the resistance, and embark on a "hearts and minds" campaign to win hold-outs over. But if for some reason the resistance genuinely takes on the character of widespread public resistance to occupation, and uprising against it, then careful consideration must be made of what to do next. Fact-finding is here vital: if the resistance is illegitimate—composed of those elements listed above—then it is legitimate to stamp it out, or at least control it through military and police measures. Social reconstruction is hugely difficult—but hugely worthwhile if successful. One can't just turn tail and run in the face of some car bombings and kidnappings. That would, irresponsibly, create an incentive in favor of violent resistance and be a breach of faith with the interests of the majority of the local population. One also can't allow the re-birth of a regime failing minimal justice—or else what was the point of the war? But if the resistance becomes deep, patterned, and genuinely widespread—involving things like general strikes, commercial and political boycotts, and regular mass protests—then clearly a change of strategy is demanded, almost certainly including a stepped-up transfer of sovereignty. The devil here is truly in the details of the case, and none of us should envy policymakers who must decide when the resistance is rough but illegitimate, and when it becomes so serious that justice demands a radical policy shift. Much of how the resistance question plays out, in my view, will be affected by perceptions of the justice of the war to begin with. There's simply no escaping the interconnections, here as elsewhere.

1.10. AIMING AT REGIME CHANGE FROM THE START

This perspective on rehabilitation—calling for disarmament, institutional reform, political transformation, and infrastructure investment—brings into focus important questions. Does it follow from all the above that the imposition of rehabilitation on an aggressor is itself a legitimate war aim? In other words, may a state set out, from the start of the war, not only to vindicate violated rights but, moreover, to impose institutional therapy upon the aggressor? If so, Walzer asks, what does that imply in terms of the use of force during war, since being in a position to impose institutional therapy after the war is at least linked to, and may even depend on, the achievement of a certain degree of military superiority at war's end? The therapy requires the strength to see it through. My sense is that the imposition of institutional therapy on an aggressor is consistent with, even implied by, the overall goal of a justified war argued for last chapter, namely, rights vindication constrained by a proportionate policy on surrender. The therapy is justly invoked when required to prevent future aggression and to enable the defeated community to meet the requirements of minimal justice. In terms of war-fighting, having regime change and rehabilitation as a war goal does not somehow diminish the responsibility to fight in accord with the *jus in bello* rules of right conduct. The importance of the end does not lessen the constraints just communities face when they vindicate their rights by force. Will insistence on rehabilitation as part of war settlement itself prolong the fighting? While it might do so as a matter of fact—relative to a less stringent or unjust settlement offer—seeing it through is not wrong provided the fighting continues to respect *jus in bello*. The duty falls on Aggressor to agree to reasonable terms of rehabilitation, not on Victim/Vindicator to avoid seeking those means necessary to secure adherence to them. Besides, as previously noted with reference to cases, the bringing of rehabilitation does not demand the infliction of a crushing military defeat upon the Aggressor.

1.11. CONTAINMENT INSTEAD OF CHANGE?

What of those who suggest that, instead of all these dramatic post-war regime transformations, we should settle for "merely" defeating and containing aggressors? Let's not muck around with the very structures of their society; let's simply defeat the aggressor regime and de-fang it, so to speak, so that it cannot cause more problems in the foreseeable future. Note, as Walzer does, that this recommendation is inconsistent with humanitarian intervention. For in such a case, it is precisely the depravity of the regime which invites the military maneuvers. It makes no sense to leave such a regime in place following its defeat: regime transformation is needed to stop the very crisis in question. So, the containment option only comes up in instances of cross-border aggression. How, in this regard, to compare and evaluate the merits of containment versus reconstruction and rehabilitation?

The core, defining difference between containment and reconstruction is this: with containment, one leaves the defeated regime in power whereas with rehabilitation, one ejects the regime and guides the process for creating a new one. A logically lesser distinction, but still a substantial one, is that containment is mainly concerned with preventing future cross-border aggression on the part of the defeated regime whereas rehabilitation is concerned not just with that but also with transforming the regime in a way which benefits the domestic citizenry. These further differences get us close to the Oxford English Dictionary definitions: containment means "to hold within itself, or to prevent from moving or extending" whereas rehabilitation means "to restore to effectiveness, or normal life, or proper condition by training, especially after prison or illness." Clearly, rehabilitation is a more ambitious policy. But is it more costly? Is it recklessly risky? Is it better? (Note the relationship between containment and retribution: they can go together, but they don't have to, logically: one could decide to merely contain but to forego further retributive measures. But, quite commonly, the two do get adapted together, historically: note the case study on the Persian Gulf War at last chapter's end.)

Let us first note one large area of agreement between containment and rehabilitation. This is the need to disarm the defeated regime. This suits both aims of preventing future aggression by the regime as well as, quite often, breaking its main source of domestic power. There is thus truly widespread consensus on the need for such common post-war disarmament measures as chopping the defeated regime's armed forces; capping future military capability; creating buffer zones between the regime and other countries; and cataloguing and destroying its weapons, especially those of mass destruction. We noted this in the preceding chapter.

It is after military disarmament that the two notions split. Consider that when a decision to contain is made, the question of war crimes trials goes out the window. This was, for instance, never brought up in the 1991 Persian Gulf War settlement. After all, you're leaving the regime in power, so you can't insist that its top people surrender to a war crimes tribunal. Conversely, when you decide to rehabilitate, you keep this option open. We think of historical links between rehabilitation and war crimes (or crimes against humanity) tribunals, whether at Nuremberg, Tokyo, or The Hague. This morally marks one up for rehabilitation over containment: containment sacrifices some justice for what it thinks is expediency. While war crimes trials can cause pain within a political community, so too can a failure to have them. Trials also de-legitimize unjust regimes in a way that inaction, obviously, never can.

There is a huge difference between the two notions regarding the treatment of the defeated country's economy. The logical goal of containment is to cut, or at least to limit, the target regime's resources so as to clip its capabilities for future aggression. Thus, some form of economic punishment, or at least non-engagement, is called for (and so we note again the dovetailing between containment and retribution). The 1991 settlement terms of the Persian Gulf War left intact the sweeping socio-economic sanctions leveled after Iraq's original invasion of Kuwait in 1990, and they also required Iraq to pay compensation to Kuwait, out of future Iraqi oil sales. The result of the sanctions was a humanitarian disaster for the Iraqi people throughout the 1990s. This disaster was the result not just of poor treaty drafting, but of the logic of containment itself. The treaty drafters, of course, should've known that civilian welfare was not a priority for Saddam, and so leaving it up to him was either naïve or callous, as argued for at the end of last chapter. The deeper point is that, because containment's focus is on preventing cross-border aggression, it is much more insensitive to local civilian suffering than many people want to admit. Since containment wishes to cut the regime's resources, this will necessarily leave less for civilians. And if nothing is done to change a regime which does not much care for its civilians, then material deprivation amongst the civilian population is a predictable consequence of containment. It's not just Iraq: there's no doubt, for instance, that American containment during the Cold War contributed to real economic hardships in such communist countries as Cuba. Whereas with containment resources are essentially sucked out of the regime, with rehabilitation the resources flow the other way: into the defeated country to aid in reconstruction and to ensure that the new regime can enjoy popular support without threat of backsliding into injustice and illegitimacy. This, we noted, is what is currently happening in Iraq and Afghanistan—though whether the amount of resources is sufficient might be wondered at—and of course it also happened, to great success, with Germany and Japan in the post-1945 period.

Another myth about containment is that it is non-violent, or at least relative to rehabilitation. The Iraq experience casts a cloud of doubt over this. First, the sanctions arguably were violent—inflicting physical harm—and in an indiscriminate way. Say what you will about forcible regime change, but taking out a regime with force is much more discriminating than slowly starving a country of resources. Now, there obviously is more military force involved in rehabilitation over containment, but it can be more discriminating. And even the military equation is not entirely obvious. There were, e.g., over two dozen military clashes, and one major combat operation, between America and Iraq during what we might call "the retribution and containment phase," from 1991 to 2003. These episodes generated scores of casualties, including some civilians. The violence and casualties can be predicted because the terms of containment, to be effective, need to be enforced. In Iraq's case, the no-fly-zones and the weapons inspection process both required repeated military enforcement.

Military clashes during containment can also be predicted out of frustration with what are often open-ended, long-lasting containment procedures. The recent containment of Iraq lasted 12 years, and only ended because America decided to attack instead. The reconstruction of Germany and Japan, by contrast—enormous undertakings—lasted about 10 years each. Containment is open-ended because its end is "negative"—merely preventive—as opposed to the "positive" goal of reconstruction in rehabilitation's case. How do you know when to stop the containment (or retribution)? The only sure answer seems to be: when the regime has changed. But that is precisely what rehabilitation seeks to do directly right from the start. As Walzer puts it perceptively, and concisely, "(l)egitimacy and closure are the two criteria against which we can test war's endings."[34]

Some people suggest that containment is more respectful of state rights to political sovereignty and territorial integrity than is rehabilitation. But consider that permissible reconstruction gets rid of an illegitimate, rights-violating regime, thereby enabling greater political participation and thus expression of national sovereignty. Illegitimate regimes, we've established, have no right to govern, and their removal enables all kinds—even democratic kinds—of expressions of national sovereignty. There are also the human rights of individuals to account for, too, and in that regard the containment theory must answer for its insensitivity to continued civilian suffering under the illegitimate regime which it allows to continue. Trading human rights violations for respecting state rights is not exactly a bargain to be bragging about.

Other people worry that rehabilitation is more costly and risky: *cost* in the form of overthrowing the regime and rebuilding the economy; and *risk* in the form of possibly botching reconstruction, leading to backsliding into illegitimacy or perhaps even civil war. These admittedly real risks of rehabilitation are somewhat mitigated by the fact that we do know the basic recipe for sound rehabilitation, discussed above. And we can't forget that containment has its own costs and risks: the cost of enforcing containment, both financially and militarily; the risk that civilians will continue to suffer material deprivations and rights violations (perhaps even more so under the straightened circumstances of containment); the risk that containment will be needed indefinitely; or the risk that containment will be ineffective and that armed conflict and forcible regime change will be needed anyway, as clearly seems to have been the case recently with the Taliban in Afghanistan and with Milošević in Serbia. Was the containment of Saddam a success? It may have stripped him of WMD, and Iraq did not seem to commit international aggression during those years—real achievements. But it did nothing to help the Iraqi people, and may have actually hurt them. If Iraq's containment was a success, clearly it was of a checkered kind.

My point here is this: the rewards for good rehabilitation are greater than those of good containment (and retribution), and so the greater risk can be reconceived as a more promising investment. We all know greater returns can only be had by assuming greater risks. And the return on good containment is, so to speak, merely negative: there's no more cross-border aggression. But with good rehabilitation you get not only that but also a better life for the civilians, greater rights realization, and a more secure international order.

In the end, our attitudes about containment versus rehabilitation boil down to two issues: war and governance. These are intimately connected, both historically and because war is ultimately about governance, i.e., about who gets to decide what goes on in a given territory. Defenders of containment are willing to tolerate an illegitimate and rights-violating regime in exchange for the avoidance of war. But there are moral reasons, sometimes, to doubt this tolerance. First, it's quite easy, perhaps smug, to tolerate somebody else's terrible regime. Second, there are good reasons to believe that terrible regimes eventually produce war anyway, and so containment merely postpones the inevitable. Which good reasons are these? First, historical ones: there's heavy empirical evidence that rights-violating regimes go on to attack others. Think of Mussolini, Hitler, Hirohito, Stalin, Kim Il Sung, Pol Pot, Idi Amin, Gaddafi, Hussein, and Milošević. Second, conceptual reasons. As Kant noted, if regimes are willing to violate the rights of their own citizens, why would they hesitate to do the same with foreigners, as soon as they are capable and willing? It's the regime which needs changing; and rehabilitation recognizes this, whereas containment doesn't (nor does retribution). At best, containment recognizes this but somehow views the tools of containment as better at achieving this than the tools of rehabilitation. This might, admittedly, be the case when the regime in question has nuclear weapons, as in the Cold War. I don't deny that containment sometimes makes great sense, for instance when the probability of success for regime overthrow and reconstruction are minimal or when the quantum of force needed to break the regime is simply too great, as in any nuclear case. But when these obstacles do not hold, I have suggested here that containment's tools are dull and slow, whereas those of rehabilitation are sharper and quicker. Containment's tools are not cheap, nor are they risk-free. They aren't even non-violent. They probably also avoid justice for mere expediency. Above all, containment's measures are more indiscriminate and insensitive to civilian suffering.

This all suggests that, in some cases of defeating an illegitimate regime in war, reconstruction is preferable to mere containment. I'm not going so far as to say that it's a duty to choose the former over the latter—I believe it's an option, and contingent upon the opportunities circumstances make available. There are the other just war rules to consider, too, notably probability of success and proportionality: is the regime really that bad? And will rehabilitating it likely achieve minimal justice? All I'm saying here is that there are strong general reasons for preferring reconstruction over containment, reasons which might be defeasible in particular instances.

1.12. COMPLETING THE REHABILITATION VS. RETRIBUTION COMPARISON

This leads naturally into a summary of the pros and cons of the rehabilitation model, especially as contrasted with its main rival, retribution. The two main cons of rehabilitation are these: 1) it takes a ton of time, effort, and resources; and 2) there's controversy attaching to the imposition of values. But the main pros are these:

1) in historical cases where it has worked well, the rehabilitation model has been an amazing success, well beyond what the retribution model could

ever have dreamed of achieving. (Indeed, in some historical cases, such as Germany, the rehabilitation model has been employed to clean up the messes left behind by the retribution model.)

2) the rehabilitation model does not leave behind rights-violating regimes which often serve as the causal agents of a second, and worse, war. The rehabilitation model does not leave the aggressive regime in place, nor does it trust that measures of punishment and/or containment will suffice to handle the issue of the bad regime. It views the bad regime as itself the main problem, and thus as needing tackling, through such rehabilitative measures as political therapy, defined above.

3) rehabilitation cannot be accused of creating a new generation of enemies, nor can it plausibly be seen as sowing the seeds of a second war. Clearly, this model is trying to help the people in the defeated Aggressor and, though complex emotions might be created by such actions, the desire for revenge is not typically one of them.

4) against the accusation that rehabilitation involves the infliction of narrow or parochial values, contention has already been made that rehabilitation ought to be limited to the construction only of a minimally just state, one characterized by values which are neither parochial nor narrow nor harmful: the values underlying the structure of a minimally just society.

Altogether, it adds up to a compelling case suggesting strongly that rehabilitation is a superior model of post-war justice, as compared with retribution (or retribution combined with containment).

2. War-Without-End

Now, it's one thing to commend the rehabilitation model during cases of post-war settlement. But what of those cases—or, are there cases?—wherein there is a sustained armed conflict, but it keeps going on, and on, and on, with no end in sight? What about hopelessly protracted wars or armed struggles, wherein no termination seems forthcoming, or even predictable? Can just war theory shed any light on cases of "wars-without-end"? I believe it can, and that the rehabilitation model is quite relevant here, too. But first we need to examine a relevant case, to better understand what we're considering. And it's hard to think of one more appropriate to our times than the Arab-Israeli conflict.

2.1 THE ARAB-ISRAELI CONFLICT

It is a mistake to think of the Arab-Israeli conflict as primarily a religious conflict. This conflict is complex and multifaceted, and has as much to do with territory and the desire of nations for security, as it does with spirituality. I should also stress that this is a very controversial subject, about which even the most basic concepts and terms are contested. Still, the subject cannot be ignored. Consider a quick synopsis.[35]

The Jews originated, in ancient times, in the Middle East, probably around Palestine. They grew to have prosperous Jewish kingdoms in the area, for instance as governed by Solomon the Wise and King David. But territorial control became an issue, with the Egyptians and the Romans contesting it, and eventually the Jews lost control over their homeland and, while a number stayed in the Middle East, many more left for Europe and North America. This is called "the Jewish diaspora."

It remained, for centuries, an object of Jewish yearning to re-establish a self-governing Jewish community in Palestine. This yearning came to be called Zionism (after Mount Zion, a hill in Palestine, on which once stood a fortress conquered by King David). At the end of World War I, in 1918, Palestine was governed by the Turkish, or Ottoman, Empire. This Empire—centered on Constantinople (today Istanbul)—was Muslim. And Palestine was inhabited by Arabs (an ethnic term referring to those whose ancestors came from the Arabian Peninsula, and who share certain physical commonalities, and especially a distinct language). The Ottoman Empire was on the losing side of World War I, and had only weak control over Palestine to begin with. Jewish leaders lobbied the heads of the winning Western governments to seize the initiative, and support Zionism. This would punish the Ottomans, and reward the Jews. The Western powers were willing to do the first but not quite (yet) the second. Britain took over Palestine as a result of its war winnings, but did not cede control over it to the Jewish people. It did, however, vaguely commit in principle to eventual Jewish self-governance via the Balfour Declaration.

At the end of World War II (1945), seizing upon the horrors of The Holocaust, Jewish leaders now demanded their own self-governed Jewish homeland, and a follow-through on the promise of the Balfour Declaration. In any event, they said: "Look, The Holocaust proves that we Jews can't count on the protection of any nation-state; and thus, we need our own, and there's no better place than our ancient Biblical homeland in Palestine." The Allies, especially the UK and USA, agreed, and they took measures to pave the way for the foundation of the new Jewish state, Israel. The substantial problem, though, was that there were many hundreds of thousands of Palestinian Arabs living on that land. Moreover, these Palestinians, quite plausibly, replied: "Look, we're not the Nazis; we had nothing to do with The Holocaust. And yet, because of it, we are going to lose our land?" The Palestinians had, after all, been living there for centuries.

The formation of Israel went ahead in May, 1948, to the great joy of many Jews and to the great despair of many Palestinian Arabs, who were coerced by the Allies into vacating their former homes, to make way for the Jews (some 700,000 Palestinians were deemed "refugees" by the United Nations, in a 1950 census). Thus began the Arab-Israeli conflict, which endures to this day. The Jews view the creation of Israel as both a necessity of survival—after The Holocaust—and, perhaps, as one step closer to the Jewish Promised Land. But Arabs world-wide view it as the displacement and disenfranchisement of the Palestinian Arabs, at the hands of both the Israelis and their Western supporters, especially America. Few things unite "the Arab Street"—i.e., public opinion amongst the majority in the Muslim world—more than sympathy for the Palestinians, and anger towards Israel.

When Israel's existence was first formally announced, a declaration of war was sent out by Israel's Arab neighbors: they attacked, trying to strangle the new nation in its infancy. But Israel—with Allied help—fought back and won. Since then, Israel has—at one time or another—been at war with every one of its Arab neighbors. It has won every time, and has even expanded its original 1948 territory through some of these wars, especially the important Six-Day War of 1967. Moreover, it has carved out for itself a decent democracy amidst what was—until very recently—a sea of poor and unstable authoritarian regimes (i.e., undemocratic governments, ruling by virtue of military force and police control and not by virtue of the consent of the people, as determined by free and fair public elections).

That much is to Israel's credit. On the down-side, however, Israel must maintain enormous vigilance, and massive military expenditures. (It is helped very substantially, in this regard, by America in particular, year-in and year-out. But, even so...) Every adult Israeli—man or woman—must serve a conscripted term in the Israeli Defense Forces (IDF), and everyone knows that Israel has nuclear weapons, even though it has never publicly acknowledged this. Israel's foreign policy with its neighbors is very difficult, ranging from livable peace agreements with Egypt and Jordan to outright hostility with Lebanon, Syria, and especially Iran, whose government is still officially committed to Israel's destruction. Israel's location, hostile neighbors, and small size (population: 7 million), make growing its economy difficult. And then there's the huge remaining issue of the Palestinians.

Displaced in their own land, the Palestinian Arabs have endured a long and varied journey with Israel, starting out as powerless, displaced victims and then transforming angrily—via the Palestinian Liberation Organization (PLO)—into a violent uprising against both Israeli citizens and the IDF. In the 1970s and '80s, this was very bleak, leading to thousands of deaths, resulting in no net gains for anyone, and leading the US government to declare the PLO a terrorist organization. But, after the end of the Cold War in 1990–91, and perhaps inspired by analogous examples in Northern Ireland and South Africa, the PLO agreed to renounce violence, give up terrorism, acknowledge Israel's right to exist, and enter a democratic and political process for pursuing its objectives. Israel responded positively, acknowledging the PLO as the official representative of the Palestinian people. The result was the 1993 Oslo Accords, a kind of cease-fire agreement and, more importantly, a deal to politicize the on-going territorial dispute, turning away from violence. The PLO-led Fatah party, together with the more radical Hamas faction, now jointly govern the Palestinian people—both those within Israel and those within the various Occupied Territories.

Though things have gotten better in this sweeping kind of way over time—moving from a very large-scale, regional conflict towards a more focused, smaller-scale struggle centered around the Occupied Territories and Israel's immediate neighbors, substantial violence still happens, and sometimes with unfortunate scale and force. For example, in 2006, a major armed conflict broke out between Israel and Lebanon, which resulted in the deaths of thousands, and the displacement of hundreds of thousands, on both sides. (The 2006 "Lebanon War" was actually the biggest armed conflict in the on-going Arab-Israeli struggle since the Six Day War in 1967.) In the Fall of 2012, another flare-up of violence occurred, as Israel attempted to destroy bases which Arab militants use for launching rockets into Israel (in 2011 alone, there were over 1,000 separate rockets shot into Israel from both its neighbors and the Occupied Territories).

The costs of the on-going war have been very substantial. Estimates place the death toll, from 1948-present, at around 95,000 dead. We know, for sure, that between 2000 and 2012 alone (and excluding the 2006 Lebanon War), over 7,000 people died as a direct result of the violence (the majority during that time period being Arab Palestinians). Many studies have cited the enormous economic drain which this struggle has brought to bear on both sides, and how the failure to come up with a definite peace agreement has only served to draw in other major powers, determined to tinker behind the scenes and affect the outcome of the conflict. The major external interveners include, on the Israeli side, the UK and USA, and, on the Palestinian side, almost every major Arab country, each for its own reasons but including especially Syria and Iran.

The Arab-Israeli conflict has never been a simple, two-sided conflict. All along, there have been those, in both camps, who have sought peace and accommodation with the other side, just as there have been those of extreme, radical belief, unwilling to compromise at all. For example, in 1995, Israeli Prime Minister Yitzhak Rabin was assassinated; and not by a Palestinian but by an Israeli extremist who thought Rabin was giving too much away to the Palestinians during peace talks. In general, there is a division within Judaism between reform and orthodox Jews, with the former being more moderate, and the latter more strict, regarding both the interpretation and the application of God's laws. In Israel, some so-called "ultra-orthodox Jews" have been firmly opposed to the Palestinian peace process, and they have taken to becoming "settlers" on some of the disputed territories, forming residential religious communities on them and standing their ground (which they are convinced has been gifted to them by God Himself). On the Palestinian side, there are moderates—indeed, statistics show that the majority, in almost any given religious or political population, are moderates—and extremists, too. For a long time, the extremists in the PLO had the upper hand, and they confronted Israel with indiscriminate armed resistance. Eventually, the moderates prevailed; violence was renounced; the peace process entered; and clear progress was made on making life better. Whenever we discuss these conflicts, and these groups, we must always be mindful of the spectrum of beliefs, and especially the omnipresent difference between compromising moderates (who reach out to "others," and hold their own beliefs more lightly) and uncompromising extremists (who turn away from "others," hold their own beliefs more tightly, and who are, generally, willing to act much more radically).

2.2. REHABILITATION AND PROTRACTED CONFLICT

Protracted wars, and especially the Arab-Israeli conflict, have much to learn from the rehabilitation model of post-war justice. One reason why this is: the enduring solution to this conflict—if there is any—seems so difficult that the most promising thing to do, in the meantime, would appear to be to focus on building up the affected communities so that they all have something real, concrete, and improving to look forward to, and thus might become better motivated to overcome the deep bitterness of the past.

The nub of the problem is this: you have two totally different peoples who want the same territory. This makes the Arab-Israeli conflict different from such other recent protracted wars as The Cold War (1945–1991), which featured hostile animosity aplenty—but, in the end, was a more standard struggle between rival states on different territories, featuring clashing ideologies and social systems. With the Israelis and the Palestinians, you have two peoples who are both clearly staying; and thus no kind of crushing, one-sided victory seems realistic. Increasingly, some kind of *modus vivendi* (or deal, or "workable way of living") has to be arrived at—and is actually, bit-by-bit, being constructed. But because of the violent past, raw feelings, lack of trust, and the magnitude of difference between these two peoples, such an arrangement is proving very complex. (Plus, there are a host of more practical issues whose enduring solution is deeply daunting, such as: access to water; labor mobility; and the exact drawing of final borders.)

Still, it's clear that any such eventual peace deal is going to—and should—have more in common with rehabilitation than retribution. Specifically, elements of rehabilitation which are instructive for helping to hasten the end of a severe protracted war (such as this) would include:

- The provision of physical security to all affected parties.
- The foregoing of any compensation and sanctions in favor of investing in, and rebuilding, the economies of all affected communities.
- Careful, voluntary, and mutual regime transformation, so that all sides can come to be represented by peaceful, legitimate, democratic governments.
- The development of minimally just, and efficient, systems of law, education and health care, so that everyone's basic human needs can be met, their human rights can be satisfied, curricula can be purged of hatred, and education can serve as a tool for both economic growth and tolerant inter-communal co-operation over time.
- Socially, those previously excluded (or discriminated against) need to be brought "into the tent" of social recognition, and heavy support ought to be given (ideally, from international sources) to building up civil society organizations—especially to those which straddle inter-communal divides.

We can see, over the long term, that this does seem to be the actual, general direction of the Arab-Israeli conflict, especially since the big leap in the early 1990s, when the PLO gave up violence, recognized Israel, and was recognized by Israel in return. This long-term trend seems encouraging, and is consonant with the kind of mutual confidence-building and socio-political transformation suggested by the rehabilitation model. Yet here, too, the most worrisome realities in this conflict are the same as those in Iraq and Afghanistan, and they just happen to be the two things most stridently stressed as required by reconstruction experts: 1) physical security for all; and 2) economic growth. These two forceful challenges plague the Arab-Israeli conflict, as fighting still routinely erupts (and, in fact, the past two to three years have not been encouraging) and as broad-based, reliable, self-generated economic growth for both communities proves elusive.

3. Summary

There have been successful pro-rights, post-war regime changes, and these make us mindful of an important option when wars end. Forcible regime change is permissible when the war itself was just, when it violates no rights, and when it promises the good consequences of instituting a minimally just regime. To that extent, aiming to impose rehabilitation right from the start of a just war is permissible, too. Without excluding the international community, the key reconstruction relationship is that between the war winner and the local population. The war winner occupies a position of enormous power and therefore trust, and is duty-bound to follow "the rehabilitation recipe" and to work with and nurture local leadership. The locals, for their part, must commit themselves to peace, to good faith interaction with each other, and, above all, to the development of a minimally just regime. Some resistance should be expected and the huge difficulties acknowledged—perhaps only partial realization of the ideal is possible. That is still better than nothing—or worse, not even trying—and in fact might be a reasonable definition of progress in such difficult circumstances. Furthermore, the advice and insights of the rehabilitation model can provide useful guidance for those communities trapped in wars apparently without end and, with its future-focus and positive orientation, rehabilitation provides a much more constructive model for such cases than does retribution.

Notes

1 Immanuel Kant, *The Metaphysics of Morals*, trans. Hugh Barr Nisbet in Hans Reiss, ed., *Kant: Political Writings* (Cambridge: Cambridge UP, 1991), 170.

2 Indeed, as Bob Martin has noted, the case of Germany post-World War II provides for a clear, compact, and gripping contrast between the retribution and rehabilitation models. In West Germany, as we'll see below, the Americans decided to implement rehabilitation—to great success. Whereas in East Germany, not only did the Soviets take over, they subjected the territory to retribution, and thus rendered it extremely poor, and very sub-optimal in terms of human rights respect, for decades. See Norman Naimark, *The Russians in Germany* (Cambridge, MA: Harvard UP, 1997).

3 Some especially useful ex-Nazis were provided safe havens in the West, particularly those who were working on Hitler's rocket program.

4 Leon V. Sigal, *Fighting to the Finish: The Politics of War Termination in America and Japan* (Ithaca, NY: Cornell UP, 1989); Howard B. Schonberger, *Aftermath of War: Americans and the Remaking of Japan* (Kent, OH: Kent State UP, 1989); Michael Schaller, *The American Occupation of Japan* (Oxford: Oxford UP, 1987); and Eugene Davidson, *The Death and Life of Germany: An Account of the American Occupation* (St. Louis, MO: U of Missouri P, 1999).

5 Brian Orend, *War and International Justice: A Kantian Perspective* (Waterloo, ON: Wilfrid Laurier UP, 2000).

6 Kant, *Metaphysics*, 169–71.

7 Eric Carlton, *Occupation* (London: Routledge, 1995).

8 Matteo Tondini, *Statebuilding and Justice Reform: Post-Conflict Reconstruction in Afghanistan* (New York: Routledge, 2010); US Government, *Afghanistan Reconstruction: Despite Some Progress...* (Washington, DC: Books LLC, 2011); Mokhtar Lamani and Bessma Momani, *From Desolation to Reconstruction: Iraq's Troubled Journey* (Waterloo, ON: CIGI, 2010).

9 James Dobbins et al., *America's Role in Nation-Building: From Germany to Iraq* (Santa Monica, CA; RAND, 2003); James Dobbins et al., *The UN's Role in Nation-Building: From Congo to Iraq* (Santa Monica, CA: RAND, 2005); James Dobbins et al., *Europe's Role in Nation-Building: From the Balkans to Congo* (Santa Monica, CA: RAND, 2008); James Dobbins et al., *The Beginner's Guide to Nation-Building* (Santa Monica, CA; RAND, 2009).

10 This was widely reported by Associated Press in December 2011, along with the following figures: the Iraq War lasted 9 years (2003–2011), costing over $800 billion USD, and involving 4,500 US military dead and 32,000 US military wounded.

11 US Government, *Afghanistan Reconstruction* (Washington, DC: Bibliogov, 2011); Dov Zakheim, *A Vulcan's Tale: How the Bush Administration Mismanaged the Reconstruction of Afghanistan* (Washington, DC: Brookings Institute, 2011).

12 US Special Inspector General, *Hard Lessons: The Iraq Reconstruction Experience* (Washington, DC: US Independent Agencies and Commissions, 2009).

13 Lamani and Momani, eds., *Troubled,* passim.

14 Zakheim, *Vulcan,* passim.

15 Aristotle, *The Politics,* trans. Carnes Lord (Chicago: U of Chicago P, 1985); Jeff Bridoux, *American Foreign Policy and Post-War Reconstruction: Comparing Japan and Iraq* (New York: Routledge, 2012).

16 Kant, *Metaphysics,* with both quotes at 170.

17 Ray Salvatore Jennings, *The Road Ahead* (Washington, DC: United States Institute of Peace, 2003); Antonio Donini, ed., *Nation-Building Unravelled?* (New York: International Peace Academy, 2004); and all sources in Note 9 above.

18 Simon Chesterman, "Occupation as Liberation: International Humanitarian Law and Regime Change," *Ethics and International Affairs* (2004): 51–64 with quote at 54.

19 International Commission on Intervention and State Sovereignty, *The Responsibility to Protect* (Ottawa: International Development Research Institute, 2001), 40–41; Kofi Annan, *The Causes of Conflict and the Promotion of Durable Peace in Africa* (New York: United Nations, 1998); Rowan Scarborough, *Rumsfeld's War* (New York: Regnery, 2004).

20 James Traub, "Making Sense of the Mission," *New York Times Magazine* (11 April 2004): 36.

21 Andrew Arato, "Constitution-Making in Iraq," *Dissent* (Spring, 2004): 32–36; Andrew Arato, *Civil Society, Constitution and Legitimacy* (Lanham, MD: Rowman Littlefield, 2000).

22 Michael Edwards, *Civil Society,* 2nd ed. (London: Polity, 2009); Robert D. Putnam, *Bowling Alone* (New York: Simon and Schuster, 2000).

23 Manfred Franz Boemeke et al., eds. *The Treaty of Versailles* (Cambridge: Cambridge UP, 1998); Anthony Arnove and Ali Abunimeh, eds., *Iraq Under Siege* (London: South End, 2000).

24 Brian Orend, *Introduction to International Studies* (Oxford: Oxford UP, 2012), Chap. 11: "International Aid and Development."

25 Michael Walzer, *Arguing About War* (New Haven, CT: Yale UP, 2004), 164–5.

26 William Nash, qtd. in Traub, "Making Sense," 35.

27 Jonathan Glover, *Humanity: A Moral History of the 20th Century* (New Haven, CT: Yale UP, 2001).

28 Lynn Hunt, ed., *The French Revolution and Human Rights* (London: Bedford, 1996).

29 Toby Dodge, *Inventing Iraq* (New York: Columbia UP, 2003).

30 Dobbins, *Nation-Building;* Dobbins, UN; Traub, "Making Sense," 32–62.

31 ICISS, *Protect,* 44–45; UN Charter, Articles 73 and 74.

32 Roméo Dallaire, *Shake Hands with the Devil* (Toronto: Random House, 2003); Kenneth Cain et al., *Emergency Sex and Other Desperate Measures* (New York: Miramax, 2003).

33 Traub, "Making Sense," 32–62.

34 Walzer, *Arguing,* 20.

35 Sources for this case study are: James L. Gelvin, *The Modern Middle East,* 3rd ed. (Oxford: Oxford UP, 2011); Kirsten Schulze, *The Arab-Israeli Conflict,* 2nd ed. (London: Longman, 2008); James L. Gelvin, *The Israel-Palestinian Conflict* (Cambridge: Cambridge UP, 2007); and Walter Laqueur and Barry Rubin, eds., *The Israel-Arab Reader,* 7th ed. (New York: Penguin, 2008).

PART TWO *The Alternatives*

8 EVALUATING THE REALIST ALTERNATIVE

"The general inclination of mankind is a perpetual and restless desire of power after power that ceaseth only in death." —THOMAS HOBBES[1]

The book so far has been devoted to explaining and mainly defending contemporary just war theory and, to a lesser extent, the current international laws of armed conflict. But there are two large and influential rivals to just war theory which must be explored in a comprehensive text on these issues. They are realism and pacifism: the first is taken up in this chapter, the second in the next.

1. Realism in General

The core propositions of realism express a strong suspicion about applying moral concepts, like justice, to the conduct of international affairs. Realists believe that moral concepts should be employed neither as descriptions of, nor as prescriptions for, state behavior on the international plane. Realists emphasize power and national security issues as well as the need for a state to forward its own self-interest. Realism is a form of national egoism, or selfishness in foreign policy. Above all, realists view the international arena quite darkly. They see it as a kind of anarchy—an un-governed condition—in which the will to power enjoys primacy among the players. The drive for augmenting one's own security, power, and resources is the prime mover in the realist's reality (hence the above quotation from Hobbes). Referring specifically to war, realists believe that it is a completely predictable part of an anarchical world system; that it ought to be resorted to only if it makes sense in terms of national self-interest; and that, once war has begun, a state ought to do whatever it can to win. So, if adhering to the rules of just war theory and international law hinders a state in this regard, it should disregard them and stick steadfastly to its fundamental interests in power, national interest, and security.[2] Classical realists include the ancient Greek historian Thucydides and the medieval Italian diplomat and writer Machiavelli. Modern realists include professors Hans Morgenthau and Hedley Bull, civil servant George Kennan, theologian Reinhold Niebuhr and former US National Security Advisor Henry Kissinger. Most so-called "foreign policy practitioners"—diplomats and ambassadors, and not a small number of military personnel—tend to see themselves as some kind of realist.[3]

Realists, Michael Walzer notes, view war as "a world apart," where "self-interest and necessity prevail. Here men and women do what they must to save themselves and their communities, and morality and law have no place." "(R)ealism," he observes, "imposes no moral requirements," either in war or more broadly in international affairs. Just war theory, designed to limit war's destructiveness and to protect rights during armed conflict, is viewed by realists as mere "idle chatter, a mask of noise with which we conceal ... the awful truth." This truth is that we are essentially "fearful, self-concerned, driven, [even] murderous" and war brings all these ugly traits to the surface and gives them free rein. Much of morality is rank self-deception (and self-glorification), and probably no more so than during wartime, when states and people are pushed to their very limits. Just war theory is, then, quite unrealistic in the literal sense of not applying meaningfully to the facts of our world. If realists endorse any rule at all with regard to wartime behavior, it's something like the old saying, "all's fair in love and war." In war's desperate circumstances, *anything goes*.[4]

Thucydides' *Melian Dialogue* offers a frank expression of realism. This memorable, well-known piece describes a historical meeting between ancient Athenian generals and the leaders of Melos, a Greek island. The expansionist Athenians want to annex Melos and supplement their power, whereas the Melians wish to preserve their independence and protect their own way of life. The generals propose that "all fine talk of justice" be put aside, and that everyone stare reality square in the face. This reality is that "they that have odds of power exact as much as they can, and the weak yield to such conditions as they can get." It's rule or be ruled in our rough-and-tumble world. The Melians refuse to play ball, citing their right as an independent and peaceful community not to be attacked; and subsequently they get invaded and crushed by the Athenians. Just war theory would view this as classic aggression, whereas realists simply view it as the way of the world.[5]

2. Descriptive Realism

2.1. CHARACTERIZATION

We should at this point distinguish, importantly, between *descriptive* or factual realism and *prescriptive* or normative realism. Descriptive realism is the doctrine according to which states, the primary actors in the international arena, are in fact motivated by self-regarding considerations of power, security, and national interest, and not at all by those of morality or justice. *States simply don't care about morality and justice; they only care about their own interests.* They might—and often do—pay lip-service to ethics but, in the end, they act to benefit themselves. These benefits reside not in ethical ideals but, rather, in basic material things like survival, security, economic growth, natural resources, power, and prestige.

The starting point for descriptive realism is an understanding of the nature of the international arena as one of anarchy. There is no reliable international government. The United Nations (UN) does exist, but it is neither reliable nor does it have much power or resources. Indeed, as its name shows, the UN is merely an association of nations, not a government over nations. Indeed, the UN is largely at the mercy of powerful countries, or blocs thereof. We think here, in particular, of the five veto-holding permanent members of the Security Council and, especially, the USA. The UN doesn't come close to having the same power over its "subjects" that national governments have over theirs.

Since there is no reliable international authority, all states are fundamentally insecure: they are always vulnerable to the attacks and encroachments of others. At the very least, they have no reliable assurances from the others that they will not attack or interfere in a damaging way in their affairs. This so-called "assurance problem" makes states fearful and insecure. Fundamentally, they can't trust, or count on, other countries. The lack of central authority means that, in the final analysis, states can rely on no one other than themselves to secure their interests. So self-help is the order of the day. It follows that each state will be, and is, concerned—first and foremost—with its own power and security vis-à-vis other states. Each state will, and does, act so as to maximize what it takes to be its own enlightened self-interest, and this involves relying on armed force, trying to assert and forward its own power and security, and in general doing the best it can vis-à-vis other states in terms of cultural, commercial, political, and military competition.

In light of this, Morgenthau for one argued that we cannot speak meaningfully of state behavior in terms of moral concepts and judgments. The only meaningful kind of discourse surrounding international relations is that centered on power, interests, and security. Moral concepts are *literally inapplicable* to the realm of foreign affairs. To appeal to moral judgment in international relations—like saying a certain war is unjust—would be to commit what is sometimes called a "category mistake." It would be like trying to apply the rules of baseball to football. Such simply does not fit. The rules which make sense in one context (i.e., interpersonally) fail to make sense in a completely different one (i.e., internationally). Werner Jaeger concurs, and opines that "the principle of force forms a realm of its own with laws of its own" which are unique and separate from the rules of ethics applicable among individual people living ordinary lives in developed, settled societies.[6]

Indeed some realists, like Edmund Wilson, even argue that the international arena is not actually a place wherein free choice—including morally responsible choice—plays a meaningful role at all. These realists frequently speak of the "necessity" of state action in the global context: states have no meaningful choice but to act on the basis of power and interest if they are to survive at all, much less thrive. The one thing that looms large, in all such accounts, is the bleak and dangerous picture of the international arena. On this view, war is seen as an entirely predictable, even inescapable, reality of the interstate system; it is a simple fact that the clash of national self-interest will sometimes spill over into armed conflict. It is another simple fact that states will do whatever they can, in the midst of war, to win. To hope otherwise—as just war theory does—is to engage in wishful thinking about the brutal facts on the ground in the international arena. So attempting to limit or constrain warfare—e.g., with a set of just war rules and laws—is, as Carl von Clausewitz contended, at odds with its very nature and the very animating force behind state action. Wars are rather like storms that just naturally break out every now and then. No one can influence them and they just have to be left alone to exhaust themselves, as it were, and blow over. US Civil War General W.T. Sherman once said, e.g., that "(w)ar is cruelty, and you cannot refine it ... You might as well appeal against the thunderstorm as against these terrible hardships of war."[7]

2.2. CRITICISM

The first criticism which can be made of descriptive realism—on behalf of just war theory—concerns the deep ambiguity of its appeal to the "inapplicability" of moral concepts to international affairs. This claim seems false. States, at least sometimes, really do seem to act on the basis of moral commitments, even when such actions seem manifestly at odds with their national interests. Although such examples are always complex and open to controversy, some have contended that Britain's efforts in the 1800s to outlaw the international slave trade constitute one such example, since its actions greatly increased the price of its own imports of such basics as sugar, tea, and cotton; and seriously aggravated its relations with America. But the British people, especially as inspired by Protestant preachers, simply wouldn't stand for it anymore. They rejected the practice morally, and forced their government to act accordingly. Jack Donnelly cites American participation in World War I as another case of moral motivation at odds with national interest. America intervened to pacify Europe—"to make the world safe for democracy"—not because its own territory or sovereignty was threatened.[8] Someone might argue the same thing with regard to the American interventions in Somalia and Bosnia in the early 1990s, discussed in part one of this book.

Even if it's controversial to say that states sometimes adhere to their moral beliefs before, or above, their national interests, at the very least it seems true to say that among a state's interests are its moral and political ideals. States want to see their moral and political beliefs realized in the world as much as individuals do— states *must* want this because they are, after all, composed of individual persons. If this is true, and it seems obviously so to me, then mixing moral talk with international affairs cannot be an "inapplicable" category mistake. Indeed, the category mistake would be to leave moral matters out of international issues like war and peace, and simply let states and peoples do whatever they want without fear of criticism or punishment.

A second criticism is that these realist accusations—regarding the "inapplicability" of morality—fly in the face of common, long-standing practice. We have had a very long history of utterly coherent ethical thought about international relations in general and warfare in particular. Just war theory is only one example in this regard, and it is centuries old. We all understand what someone is trying to say when they assert that a war is unjust, or that trade should be free, or that more aid should go to Africa—and we frequently make similar judgments ourselves. So if we all understand and participate in such talk—talk which evaluates international affairs ethically—how can it be systematically mistaken? How likely is it that, all this time, the realists have been right (as they condescendingly assert) and the rest of us have not known what we were doing? Not very likely, I'd say, especially since ethical evaluations of international affairs and war simply seem so meaningful, and they attract so much passion and engagement in response.[9]

Further evidence, of the weakness of realism's claim that moral talk in wartime is meaningless, concerns the similarities between morality and military strategy. Both discourses are devoted to evaluating the same course of action—the deployment of armed force in foreign affairs—and to enabling both justification and criticism of it. Both discourses offer firm, action-guiding rules, such as (in morality) "Do not directly attack civilians" and (in strategy) "Do not launch a frontal attack on a protected position." Both discourses presuppose a shared vocabulary, they appeal to public evidence for support, and they recognize the risks attending alternative courses of action. Both discourses presuppose that the alternatives in question are real and not merely apparent: the actors are genuinely confronted with free choices. Both offer norms for action. And though these norms can be ignored on the ground during the heat of battle, this does not detract from the intelligibility of the norms, nor even (perhaps) the overall commitment to adhere to them. In light of these profound similarities between morality and strategy, how can the realist completely ignore and even mock the one while emphasizing the importance of the other? How can the realist consistently exalt the importance of smart strategy during wartime while shouting down those who dare to forward moral arguments about military conduct?[10]

And what of all this realist talk about the "necessity" of state self-regard? It appears, upon reflection, to be quite misleading and ill-founded. As Walzer says, rarely is a state credibly threatened with extinction; and so the day-to-day reality of international affairs is much more a matter of probability and risk than it is of strict necessity and of adhering to the fierce requirements of survival. States, it seems, are much freer to choose between alternative courses of action than realists contend. This means that states are free, in a very clear sense, to choose to act on the basis of moral commitments and conceptions of justice, as well as upon considerations of their own national interest.[11]

It seems straightforwardly true that states do, indeed, act upon the basis of both national interests and moral commitments. This is perhaps clearest in democratic, representative regimes where the people simply insist that their governments take seriously the moral beliefs of the nation. Perhaps these states don't always listen, but they do so at their own peril, since the discipline of the ballot box remains. It follows from these thoughts that the ancient Athenian generals, e.g., were not actually forced to "rule or be ruled"; rather, they carried out a deliberate policy of aggressive expansion that was authorized by the Athenian assembly. The crushing of the Melians was not a "necessity of nature"—an "ingurgitation" of a small state by a big one—but rather the brutal outcome of a free collective decision by a group of Athenians giddy with power and lusting for more. Walzer notes that Thucydides omits these prior debates and decisions in his storied *Dialogue*. Walzer then rightly concludes that war is the inevitable product neither of the structure of nature nor of the international system; rather, war is "a human action, purposive and premeditated, for whose effects someone is responsible."[12]

The upshot is that descriptive realism seriously misunderstands the nature of moral discourse, particularly with regard to war. War is an *intentional* human activity: states *choose* whether or not to take the dramatic step of embarking down the road of war. They *deliberately decide* whether it is in their best interests to do so, and whether they think it is right to do so. It's an important fact about moral discourse that any intentional, deliberate human activity is one which can be subjected to moral scrutiny. Of any prospective choice in the realm of human action, we can always meaningfully ask: "What ought the agent to do?" Furthermore, war is not just any intentional human activity: it is one of the most extreme and destructive activities there is. The very activity inherent in warfare—namely, mass killing and destruction for political purposes—is so serious and far-reaching in its impact on our lives that it clearly demands moral judgment. Wars are not like storms spontaneously breaking out on the horizon, to be weathered with strength and luck. Wars, rather, are acts of mass violence deliberately set in motion by those empowered with the war authority. It follows that we can, we ought, and we actually do make meaningful moral judgments with regard to international relations in general and war in particular.

Walzer has a fascinating further point to consider here. He claims that states as understood by descriptive realism—those with only self-preservation and self-assertion as policy–would not last long. They would fail to inspire their people enough to keep the partnership alive. A collective association can endure, he says, only if there is a shared "commitment to the kind of belief or value that might inspire and sustain a common life and lift it out of mere existence." In other words, humans are much more complex and demanding than realists picture them: we want more out of our community than mere animal survival and economic growth. We are not simple creatures, even though we do have straightforward material needs. You can't reduce the complexity of human action and motivation into simplistic slogans, like Friedrich Nietzsche's "will to power." "It isn't really prudent," Walzer suggests, "to assume the malign intent of one's neighbors; it is merely cynical, an example of the worldly wisdom which no one lives by or could live by." We must, of course, tend to our elemental claims to physical security. We have human rights to such security, and in a very rare supreme emergency this must, as I admitted in Chapter 5, be our overriding objective. But this is not all we want, nor all we can expect under normal conditions. Our fuller desires and hopes reside in inhabiting a community in which our values are reflected, in which we enjoy equal membership, recognition, and even some fellow-feeling. We don't merely desire personal security, or political and economic expansion; we also want a place we can call our own and feel comfortable in, a political home. And we want our political home to make serious efforts at being just as opposed to unjust, ethical as opposed to evil. In other words, no one wants to live in a realist paradise; no one—not even an ancient Athenian—ultimately wants to live in a world dominated by the cynical, imperialistic generals of Athens.[13]

3. Prescriptive Realism

Prescriptive realism is the view that states *should* only care about maximizing what they take to be their own enlightened national interest. (Note that prescriptive realism need not be based on descriptive realism; it is its own doctrine and that is why we must examine it separately. Indeed, there's a point of logic here: if a state literally cannot act on moral principles, then it's idle (at best) to insist that this is what it ought to do.)[14] This leads to one more important distinction, namely, that between a prudential and a moral prescriptive realism.

3.1. THE PRUDENTIAL FORM

3.1.1. Characterization

Prudential prescriptive realism stipulates that nation-states ought, prudentially, to be motivated in their international relations only in terms of national interest. The bottom line here is that basing a foreign policy solely on an informed and sober understanding of selfish national interest is simply the smartest and most advantageous thing to do. Why? There's a self-interested reason, and a more universal one. The self-interested reason runs like this. Even if moral considerations can in principle be relevant to international affairs, most of the time what we actually see, for lack of a better phrase, is states behaving badly. Even if it's not a strict necessity, it's nevertheless a regularity to witness most states behaving in a realist kind of way—trying to maximize resources, "Looking Out For Number One." In light of this reality, you don't want to get suckered by behaving too nicely. If you're too moral, you'll be treated like a door-mat, taken advantage of, exploited. But that's not smart; what is, is to behave like a realist. Behave like a realist, and you'll do better for your own people than if you behave like a moralist.

The more universal grounding offered for prudential prescriptive realism is the notion that all states should be motivated solely in terms of prudence in their international relations because everyone would thereby be better off. If only every state minded its own business, from a purely hard-nosed prudential perspective, the world would be a much better place. Why? Because people get hot and bothered about their moral beliefs. They care deeply about their vision of justice, and are very reluctant to change their views about it. Think of how many past wars were (arguably) created by fanatical moralism: the Crusades; the Wars of Religion between Catholic and Protestant; the French Revolutionary Wars; and perhaps even World War II, owing to Hitler's conviction that it was just for the Germans to rule Europe because of their supposed racial superiority. The prudential realist will thus suggest that we would all be better off leaving our different moralities at home, and deal with each other internationally only in terms of interests all states share, such as sovereignty, secure territory, developing the economy, and tending to their people's well-being.

There is a version of this argument which realists make special use of against just war theorists. They accuse them of having a crusading mentality, and of actually increasing the destruction of war by linking it to passionately contested beliefs about justice. Just war theorists fill people's heads with talk of aggression, and dreams about securing justice through violence. And the result? Much more death and destruction than there would be if we de-linked warfare and morality. We should only link warfare to strategy, and leave all hot-blooded appeals to justice to the side (or simply confine them within our nation's justice system, or our interpersonal relations).[15]

So the view of war, on this realist understanding, is this: war is to be undertaken only if it is clearly in the nation's best interests to do so. Generally speaking, since war is such a momentous, costly, and risky undertaking, war should be considered only in the most serious cases where the nation's fundamental interests are demonstrably at stake. Furthermore, once a war has begun, the only principle which is to guide a nation's actions is again one of prudence: one should do whatever will maximize one's interests in terms of the war. Whether that involves adhering to just war rules constraining wartime action or not depends entirely on whether the nation in question sees such behavior contributing to its end of victory. But there is here no question of adhering to a set of restrictions or rules as a matter of principle or right; the guiding light emanates solely from the notion of protecting and enhancing national security and power. Indeed, the understanding here is that we should be cynical about warfare. War is not a moral business; it is a brutally violent thing which should be resorted to only when vital interests are genuinely, and severely, threatened. When we're cynical like this, fewer mistakes will be made, passions will be held in check, fewer people will die, and the war will be over more quickly.

3.1.2. Criticism

This is a challenging and provocative doctrine, and just war theory must respond. Consider first the argument about being suckered. I do agree that it *can* be relevant to one's behavior what most others around one are doing. If most other states are behaving badly, this does give grounds for being extra cautious, and for not forgetting to tend to one's fundamental interests. I demonstrated, in the supreme emergency chapter, an affinity with some aspects of realism: if the risk to oneself is truly terrible and mortal, then prudentially one must tend to one's survival. That being said, in the absence of such extreme conditions—which are very rare—I do not agree that the *mere risk* of being suckered and exploited justifies jettisoning moral beliefs and behaving in a completely egoistic way. First, one's moral beliefs are a part of one's fundamental interests, and one selfishly wants to see them realized as readily as one's interest in becoming more secure and wealthy. So it's not so easy to simply carve out, and dump, one's moral interests in favor of one's prudential interests. Often, moral beliefs are a crucial part of one's identity, be one a person or a nation. Second, under normal, non-emergency conditions, the moral defection and badness of others is not a sufficient reason for one to behave amorally or immorally oneself. If, e.g., "everyone else" is looting during a city-wide blackout, this does not justify—or make it smart—to engage in looting oneself. We could even understand such moments as testing one's moral character and integrity, rather than as providing one license to set them aside. One might find it more valuable to preserve one's integrity than to betray one's moral convictions, even under conditions of real risk.

At the least, then, it is not at all so obvious that the risk of being exploited renders it clearly better to behave like a realist than not.

Additionally, there is no reason why prescriptive realism should be thought to be more peaceful, or stabilizing, or advantageous, than alternative understandings of the imperatives of foreign policy. For every state, according to this view, is to be a self-regarding egoist. It does not take much imagination to see how having each state behave in a completely self-regarding way would, eventually and inevitably, lead to conflict. Indeed, one can easily imagine realism recommending more aggressive foreign policies—perhaps even more wars—than, say, a justice-based account of foreign policy. This is especially the case for a powerful state, which has less to lose and more to gain by exercising its influence, perhaps even by resorting to armed force.

This is not just an idle thought experiment. Even the most cursory glance at the historical record shows the bad consequences of states basing their mutual dealings solely on the basis of national egoism and the strategic struggle for power. The fundamental reason is that it makes trust between states very difficult to come by, and then the realist view of global anarchy and conflict becomes a self-fulfilling prophecy. We should all behave ruthlessly and selfishly—thus disintegrating any trust between us—and then the collapse of that trust causes all of us to behave that much more ruthlessly and selfishly. There's a downward spiral of mistrust, paranoia and eventually conflict. If we all adhered to realist advice, I don't think the result would be peace and prosperity. The result is more likely to be bitterness and suspicion, eventually paranoia and then conflict over natural resources, territory, and perhaps even over the mere fear that one's neighbors are getting too big for their own britches. Indeed, that used to be the famed "balance of power" thinking which dominated European foreign policy, permitted preventive war (Chapter 3), and culminated in the two World Wars.

To be sure, if we look more closely at the history of war (as the realist invites us to do) it's clear that, as often as morality has sparked wars, the clash of national interests has done so as well. Think of all the wars, from the 1400s to the 1900s, between the European powers regarding their various empires and struggles over colonial territory and resources.[16] Consider also that, in addition to his insane "racial" beliefs, Hitler invaded Poland in 1939 to get more territory so that populous Germany could have more *lebensraum*—"room to live." In 1914, a previous generation of Germans invaded tiny Belgium to get more land, show their power, and because they thought they could get away with it. And in 1870, an even previous generation of Germans—led by a master practitioner of *realpolitik*, Otto von Bismarck[17]—provoked the French into war so that he might win land and cement newly-formed German unity. Elsewhere in the world, Saddam Hussein invaded Kuwait in 1990 to capture its waterfront territory and oil supply, partly to help pay off his massive war debt from the Iran-Iraq war. Indeed, it is a common realist tactic to go to war externally not to resist any outside aggression but, rather, because it "solves"—or, at least, distracts attention from—some domestic problem one is having, like a sluggish economy. It's not at all clear, to say the least, that widespread adherence to realism would be better for the peace and prosperity of the world, compared to a justice-based account that has firm rules against this kind of aggressive behavior.

This point is quite separate from whether morality can plausibly be seen as the source of conflict which realism contends it is. There are real differences, of course, but also real similarities, between the world's many moral codes. Moreover, the similarities seem to focus around a growing international consensus in favor of respecting human rights. In other words, not all moral beliefs give rise to the kinds of tensions, threats, and insecurities that are endemic to the purely prudential approach. Indeed, as Thomas Pogge has argued, shared moral commitments serve as more promising bases of a secure international system, in that they are by no means as prone to change and renunciation as are those resulting from the latest cost-benefit calculation of interests. Generally speaking, people keep their moral commitments, even when doing so leads to a sub-optimal result in terms of their personal interests. Just think of how many times you have made some sacrifices in order to keep your commitments, especially to friends and family. This might even be part of what it truly means to have a moral commitment: that one sticks with it even in the face of temptation. So moral motivation in foreign policy, provided that it is universally accessible and minimally conceived—limited, say, to respecting human rights—need provide no grounds for worry about stoking the fires of inter-state conflict. Indeed, consensus around such moral beliefs can make international trust and rewarding cooperation possible, even strong and predictable, over time.[18]

What about the particular shot at just war theory? It is important, I admit, to consider whether "the justice motive" causes wars, and/or causes them to be especially destructive. The first thing to note, as I've stressed several times, is that the clash of subjective moral opinion over a war isn't enough to shatter just war theory. Just because belligerents say they have justice on their side doesn't make it so. Just war theory is designed to reduce such subjective clashes and passions by explaining and enumerating more objective grounds for morally judging warfare. Besides, it seems a very severe "solution" to suggest that, because moral opinions can differ and are often strongly held, we should ditch all of morality itself when it comes to judging warfare! Secondly, the notion that realism would allow wars to be better fought, with less killing and shorter duration, is pure speculation. Heads of state can make severe prudential mistakes about their national interests, too. Consider Saddam's 1990 invasion of Kuwait: was that a smart move? Did his realist motivation prevent a destructive conflict? Did the realist motivations of the European empires render the colonial era war-free?! Just war theory is not pro-violence and pro-destruction any more than realism is. Moreover, being cynical about warfare can lead decision-makers to be casual about it, with horrible death and destruction following. World War I is probably an example of this, both in its beginning and often in its conduct. Historians have well-depicted the comedy of errors, ruthless scheming, and mindless nationalism that set the war into motion. People actually thought it would be "a lovely little war." And generals on both sides have been roasted by historians for the ease and callousness with which they ordered their own men to their deaths.[19] People who believe that war can be sometimes morally justified aren't fans of warfare and violence; if sane, they believe wars are just as dangerous and destructive as any realist or pacifist. Third, just war theorists need not have a crusading mentality.[20] Some unfortunately may, but there's nothing essential to the theory which calls for this. Just war theory does not commit us to fighting unlimited crusades in pursuit of Pure Justice. Just wars, Walzer stresses, "are limited wars; there are moral reasons for the statesmen and soldiers who fight them to be prudent and realistic."[21] Such moral reasons include, perhaps above all, the need to minimize human suffering.

Another deep flaw with prescriptive realism—indeed, realism in general—is that it is incapable of ruling out from consideration state actions which are blatantly immoral. To that extent, realism seems at odds with some of our deepest commitments, which do indeed levy definitive prohibitions. As Donnelly says, there is nothing in realism which would be at odds with, say, colonialism or imperialism—or even slavery, torture, rape campaigns, killing the innocent, and genocide—provided the right conditions and calculations were met. The familiar point here is that the recommendations of realism are always contingent and subject to change; there are no rules which states are to adhere to on unchanging moral principle, as in just war theory or international law. This feeds back into the instability which realism—contrary to its self-image—fuels and furthers. If a state's foreign policy is always malleable (because it is based on the latest conditions and calculations of self-interest), then this can only add to the insecurity which all other states feel in wondering about its motives and future maneuvers, and what they ought to do next to forward their own power and security against it. In the most literal and biting sense, realism is an unprincipled perspective. This is clearest in its "anything goes" advice regarding warfare.[22]

Realism also favors and legitimizes the actions of the most powerful states in the interstate system. Realism benefits and buttresses—is biased towards—the actions and interests of the most powerful, which is perhaps one unfortunate reason why so much realist literature and thought comes out of major powers, such as America, China, and Russia.[23] If states ought to do what's in their best interests, and if the most powerful states have the greatest capability of doing what they want to do, then the result is a legitimation of the fact that powerful states are able to exert such incredible power over the interstate system in general and smaller states in particular. But this bias in favor of the powerful is at odds with our other values, e.g., democracy, sovereignty, and the self-determination of political communities. Also, if the only standard for praise and blame in the realm of foreign policy is a prudential one, this all-too-conveniently deprives smaller, less influential states of what is often their most powerful claim for global reform: moral criticism. In other words, realism is a doctrine powerful states—from ancient Athens to contemporary America—advance to render themselves immune from criticism. But we all know that, often, it's precisely the most powerful who deserve the most scrutiny.

3.2. THE MORAL FORM

3.2.1. Characterization

There is one last form of realism to consider: morally prescriptive realism. This might sound paradoxical, and perhaps it is, but the idea runs as follows: morally, nation-states ought to be motivated, in their international relations, only in terms of national self-interest. Morality itself demands realistic prudence on the international stage. There are two prominent grounds for morally prescriptive realism, just as there were for prudentially prescriptive realism. The first ground is impersonal or universal. The notion here is that all states ought to be animated internationally only in terms of self-regarding prudence because moral animation makes states intolerant, inflexible, arrogant, and disrespectful of the autonomy of other peoples, particularly those committed to a different set of moral values.[24]

The second grounding is more particularist or nationalist in nature. This nationalist form is based on the notion that there are no global moral duties. Moral demands alter radically along national borders; indeed, they alter so radically that only norms of prudence ought to be adhered to internationally. Why? First, a legitimate national government is a trustee, or advocate, or "agent-representative" of its people and, as such, its overwhelming and overriding duty is to look out for the well-being of its people, and only its own people. Secondly, individual identity is very closely tied to national membership. Shared values, languages, historical experiences, and customs tie together a moral community based on mutual recognition and regard—a kind of mutuality which is simply not present (at least not yet) at the international level. In other words, morality itself is rooted in community, and communities only exist nationally. People talk loosely about "the international community" but it's not a genuine shared culture, which is what you need to ground authentic moral duties. Whether universal or particular in terms of its grounding, morally prescriptive realism, in terms specifically referring to war, counsels that it is not only prudent but fully moral to base decisions to go to war on a calculation of national interests. And in the conduct of war, the best that a national government can do, morally, is to do the best it can by its own citizens, namely, by winning the war as quickly as it can, with as little cost to itself and its people as possible.[25]

Prescriptive moral realism, regardless of the way it is grounded, is a clever, sophisticated, and influential doctrine. Kennan, one of the chief architects of Cold War foreign policy in America, repeatedly contended that "the primary obligation" of a national government "is to the interests of the national society it represents ... its military security, the integrity of its political life, and the well-being of its people." And Kissinger has repeatedly claimed that it is morally offensive for states to be "morally-charged" in terms of their foreign policy, contending that the world is thereby made worse off. Strong moralism invites strong moralism in return, and this passionate process can easily create an insecure, threatening situation, as both sides dig in their heels over their clash of ideals.[26] Yet a contemporary just war theorist will reject such a view. On what grounds?

3.2.2. *Criticism*

The first thing to note is that, as a form of prescriptive realism, moral realism shares a number of fatal flaws with prudential realism—flaws we have already diagnosed. These include: 1) refusing to rule out atrocious actions, especially in war; 2) recommending a doctrine which, if widely adhered to, would result—and has actually resulted—in serious international instability and conflict; and 3) being biased in favor of the most powerful nation-states. In fact, moral realism is perhaps more offensive than prudential realism, with regard to this last remark, since it grounds pure national self-regard morally, as opposed to merely prudentially. It therefore offers moral cover and justification for the dominance of the most powerful and privileged states.[27]

Consider now the impersonal, universalist grounding for moral realism. The core claim is that moral motivation in international affairs is a source of arrogance and intolerance. Since there is radical moral diversity in our world, states ought not to base their dealings with the rest of the world in terms of their own (presumably provincial) morality. A contemporary just war theorist will object to this argument on grounds that it offers an excessively balkanized, fragmented conception of morality, hardly allowing for the existence of any shared moral values between admittedly diverse ethical traditions. Yet clearly there is considerable overlap amongst the world's most influential moral codes, at least in terms of their most basic propositions. Very rare, indeed, is the moral system which approves of murder, torture, cruelty, aggression, deception, and betrayal. Equally rare is an ethics code which doesn't, in some way, recommend honesty, courage, wisdom, friendliness, and respect for human dignity.[28] And consider human rights. Nearly every state on earth has ratified the United Nations' Charter, which mandates commitment to human rights. Human rights have thus been endorsed, in a substantial sense, by representatives of every major ethical tradition on the globe. Furthermore, the grounds typically offered for respecting human rights are utterly non-provincial, invoking the vital needs of the human person as such and the very widespread norm not to do serious harm to persons without just cause. There are thus grounds for believing that an international morality limited to respect for such human rights—such as that advocated in this book—will successfully avoid this realist accusation. In sum, it seems false to argue that a human rights-based foreign policy, and accompanying set of war actions, will produce or express arrogant intolerance.[29]

So much for the impersonal grounds of moral realism. What of the particularist or nationalist ones? The first particularist claim, recall, is that a legitimate national government is one which is a trustee or agent of its people and, as such, has an overriding moral duty to look after the interests and well-being of those it represents. There is obviously an important political truth in this claim, especially if one subscribes to values like democracy and the self-determination of communities freely and legitimately organized into minimally just states. The real question here is not whether such a claim is morally compelling; it is, rather: what does its truth actually justify? In particular, does its truth justify the supposed non-existence of cosmopolitan duties? To what extent does its truth allow national governments to put the interests and well-being of their own citizens over those of foreigners, especially in wartime?

By way of response, consider that a trustee or agent of any X is not morally entitled to do something which X may not himself do. A defense lawyer, for example, is neither morally nor legally entitled to do anything and everything on behalf of his client. He is not permitted, for instance, to bribe the judge or to murder a damaging witness. The lawyer has to maintain a set of rules; but within the parameters established by those rules, he is entitled to argue vigorously on behalf of his client. Analogously, we might say that, within a minimal set of fair and just standards applicable to all, the agent or trustee is entitled to be partial to the interests of his client. Are there any such minimal standards operative at the international level?

Following ideas developed throughout this book, it seems defensible to say that human rights establish the minimal set of rules and principles of justice which states are duty-bound to uphold on the international level. Such rights are, as John Rawls has said, the baseline requirements of political reasonableness and just conduct in our era. And human rights are crystal clear commitments mandated by international law. With respect to war, I suggest that just war theory—itself connected to human rights protection—serves as a set of minimal and universal rules, applicable to all, within which states are to operate on behalf of their citizens. These notions put paid to any ignorance, or degradation, of cosmopolitan duties. All governments are duty-bound not to violate human rights, regardless of the nationality of the rights-holder. They are not to violate any human rights because to do so is to do severe harm to human beings without just cause, something which no one is morally entitled to do. National governments may not do something which their own citizens may not themselves do. In Chapter 2, we established that state rights are legitimized, and delimited, by human rights. There are thus real, powerful, and principled limits on the degree of national partiality which moral realism can plausibly justify.[30]

It is important to note that this just war, or international law, claim is compatible with one aspect of the realist claim that national governments owe some degree of partiality to their own citizens. Just like the case of the defense lawyer, it seems cogent to contend that, above and beyond the minimal, universal threshold of human rights fulfillment required by international justice, national governments may feel free to do the best they can for those they represent. Above and beyond respect for human rights, and the rights of minimally just states, national governments need not treat all claims of foreigners on par with those of their own citizens, for instance with regard to tax treatment, access to government subsidies, social programs and welfare benefits, participatory rights, and so on. National governments may offer their own citizens much more than they offer foreigners but they cannot treat foreigners in a way less than the minimum respect established by human rights principles.

But what of the second nationalist claim often advanced by moral realists, namely, that moral duties are created out of a sense of moral community and belongingness which only obtains at the national level? It needs to be admitted, in response, that the global community obviously does not constitute a community in any way nearly as strong as that of a nation-state. It also seems as though a considerable part of an individual's self-understanding is shaped by her cultural and historical membership and thus that our communities enjoy a privileged position in our political thinking, especially when it comes to the international plane. But, that being granted, there are serious limits and ambiguities to this grounding of moral realism.

The first thing to note is that individuals can also feel quite alienated from, and disillusioned with, their own communities—and to place greater personal value on leaving them behind rather than on preserving their traditions and customs. Furthermore, it is very difficult to speak consistently about a shared, coherent national culture or identity which is worthy of the exalted status often claimed by nationalists (or "communitarians"),[31] given that no national culture is homogeneous. The reality on the ground is that almost every so-called "nation-state" is actually a multi-national state, with majority-minority dynamics and tensions, differences of language, gender, region, race, custom, interest, historical perception, political ideology, and so forth. In fact, we know from the historical record that most "shared cultures" have come to be that way through very questionable practices, such as wars of genocide, persecution of minorities and dissidents, propaganda campaigns, and so on. So, even if there were a truly "shared national culture," and even if it did play an enormous role in individual self-understanding, it would seem to be (at least somewhat) morally tainted by the way it came into being historically. At the very least, such knowledge cautions us from claiming too much on behalf of the nation-state. It certainly seems to prevent us from agreeing with the realist claim that such is the exalted moral status of the nation-state that, internationally, it ought only to act to forward its own power and interests vis-à-vis neighboring communities. That is one reason why I prefer, in my work, to speak only of minimally just societies, and the need to secure minimal justice. Too many people think far too highly of their own society and believe that it serves as a blueprint for mankind. Far better, I suggest, to leave such delusions behind and to focus instead on the more universally acceptable standard of minimal justice, and then let communities differ as they wish.

Pogge has come up with a telling point in this regard. Consider the human association which seems, obviously, to be most constitutive of self-identity, namely, the family. Even though we acknowledge many special measures on behalf of families in our social structures, we do not think that family ties justify any act on behalf of the family. We do not think that moral duties radically alter, perhaps to the point of dissolution, as soon as one walks out the front door of the house or apartment. We do not encourage families to think in terms of a desperate, paranoid struggle of "us versus them," of doing the best they can among themselves without any regard to how their acts impact upon their neighbors. And if we are not inclined to extend such permissive privileges to the family, why should we believe we ought to do so when it comes to the less influential nation-state?[32]

Another dubious aspect of moral realism is that, as Charles Beitz has contended, it seems to constitute another kind of groundless discrimination. Membership, on a moral realist account, is all-important: a state is only duty-bound to look after the interests and well-being of its own members, let the interests of others fall where they may. But what is political membership based on? In the vast majority of states, and for the vast majority of the world's people, membership is based on the place of one's birth. And yet no one had a choice where or when they were born, just as no one had a choice what sex or race into which they were born. And we do not argue on principled grounds in favor of racism or sexism. So how can we argue on principled grounds that political membership is to be absolutely determinative of how one gets treated in the contemporary world, especially during times as dangerous as those of war? Membership, by and large, is an arbitrary, unchosen characteristic for which no one can be held responsible; so how can so much turn on it, morally, in terms of what governments may and may not do to human beings?[33]

We see these issues in bold relief when it comes to what realism recommends in times of war: namely, an efficient victory, with minimal costs to one's own citizens.

In the illustrative words of Michael Gelven: "The value we place on the concerns of peace ... are challenged by those of war, which make up our communal meaning and allow us to posit the worth of what is ours against the challenge of what is alien." He makes an even stronger claim, that "war [is] grounded in the existential concern for the priority of the We over the They."[34] This red-blooded communalism—literally "us versus them"—implies the existence of only voluntary restraints upon the conduct of war with regard to foreigners. As with prudential realism, there are here no firm principles, such as rules of just war, restraining a nation's conduct during war. There is nothing which might be called the employment of intrinsically heinous means: everything is thought to be entirely contingent upon the situation and wishes of the nation in question. But surely this is morally dubious, and violates our other values. The employment of mass rape campaigns, e.g., or weapons of mass destruction, are usually actions we want to level non-contingent—i.e., firm, fierce, unchanging—prohibitions against. These are not idle thoughts: realism, with its emphasis on ending the war as quickly and as favorably as possible, would seem to recommend and endorse the employment of dirty means against the enemy state. For what quicker and more thorough way to crush an enemy, and minimize the total costs to one's own people, than by rapidly deploying overwhelming, disproportionate and indiscriminate force? Quick, dirty, ugly, and despicable wars are the predictable result of state adherence to moral realism.

4. Summary

Communities are to adhere, as a minimal condition of justice, to human rights. Even during times of war, human rights form the bedrock of cosmopolitan moral duties. Indeed, just war norms are designed to secure human rights insofar as they can be secured amid the grim circumstances of war. But above and beyond the threshold level of minimal justice established by human rights, states may justifiably pay much more attention, and give greater weight, to the interests of their own citizens. It does not, in other words, seem defensible to support national partiality all the way down, as realism does. There remains a residual, yet stubborn and real, threshold level of moral universality and cosmopolitanism. Compatriots may well owe each other more than they do foreigners, but they are not utterly free of all obligations with regard to even the most distant of strangers. Community, fellow-feeling, and even the maintenance of a part of one's sense of self, do not justify doing severe harm and grievous injury to other human beings.

While this amounts to an on-the-whole rejection of realism, it needs to be admitted that some aspects of realist thought have already been accommodated and integrated. Recall, from our Introduction, that we stressed that each of "The

Big Three" traditions has something important and enduring to share. We've just mentioned the maintenance of some national partiality on the part of a country's government and even its people's affections and affiliations. We also note that, while the international arena is not quite a bloody, Hobbesian anarchy, it clearly does lack sufficient ordering; in the final analysis, it's true that states must rely on self-help and be vigilant about protecting their rights and interests. Indeed, acknowledgment of this "realistic" fact is built into the just war argument in favor of permitting armed self-defense in the face of aggression (see Chapter 2).

Realism also makes us mindful of the current limits of international institutions, like the UN, and prevents us from putting too much faith in their capacity to resolve severe disputes pacifically. On the other hand, it might also drive us to improve such institutions, in the expectation that more developed and effective global governance can lessen the self-help strain too often left upon the shoulders of imperfect national decision-makers.

Realism highlights the fact that statesmen, and their states, very often succumb to temptation and behave badly, or at least greedily, insecurely, and shortsightedly. We need to know this as we reflect upon our own foreign policy choices and, again, to check any tendency towards naïve optimism. We want not only to be just but also smart. Realism, however, does not show that morality should not be a part of a nation's foreign policy, much less that it is an illusion. It might be rare, but states can act with moral motivation, and be fair and reasonable in their actions. They are at least capable of such; we should hold them to some standards and not merely let them do whatever they want. Governments unbound by principles are among history's most frightening creatures.

Realism, I believe, is best thought of as a healthy and needed antidote to those who—whether out of a privileged upbringing, little contact with distant strangers, or blinkered ideology—simply expect too much of flawed people behaving in an insecure environment. Against such utopians, realism offers a bracing tonic, a needed "negative" purging of their surreal optimism and lack of worldliness. Such utopians can sometimes actually be damaging do-gooders. But as a "positive" doctrine of foreign affairs, realism has far too many flaws—as shown throughout this chapter. With the exception—again, very rare—of a genuine supreme emergency, realism should not be the ruling doctrine of foreign affairs in general, much less wartime in particular. Indeed, when it comes to wartime, just war theory already incorporates much realist wisdom in the *jus ad bellum* rules of: last resort; probability of success; and proportionality. Each of these rules urges a sober caution regarding war, a clear calculation that it's probably going to be worthwhile, and a realistic appraisal that the problem is really so severe that war seems a fitting solution. Each of these rules is designed to make us mindful of the expected consequences of going to war and, as such, is consistent with realism's insistence that we look reality square in the face and make smart decisions about war within an accurate, not fanciful, context.

The same holds true for *jus in bello*. *Jus in bello* also features a proportionality rule, and its most important rule—discrimination and non-combatant immunity—can be interpreted as having clear strategic, as well as moral, value. For, generally, it's not going to be smart strategy to target an enemy's civilians. Such will often inflame anger and resolve within the enemy and, since the enemy's military is the main source of threat to oneself, attacking civilians will be at odds with economy-of-force and with directing one's strength at one's main adversary. The result will be an unwise wasting of finite resources on a target lacking in military value.

In terms of *jus post bellum*, the rehabilitation model shows prudential concern for avoiding a second war, and for not creating future generations of enemies. It seeks to clarify expectations, and provide mutually beneficial guidelines for both winners and losers, at war's end. It advocates a philosophy of enlightened self-interest in helping to re-build and better-develop former foes, so that rewarding future co-operation might be joined.

One concludes that, whatever strengths realism has, such are already incorporated within just war theory and international law. Thus, in light of its remaining—and very substantial—weaknesses, realism must on the whole be renounced, and put to the side.

Notes

1 Thomas Hobbes, *Leviathan*, ed. Aloysius P. Martinich (Peterborough, ON: Broadview, 2004), Chapter 11, 79–80.

2 Jeff McMahan, "Realism, Morality and War" (78–92) and David R. Mapel, "Realism and the Ethics of War and Peace" (180–200), both in Terry Nardin, ed., *The Ethics of War and Peace: Religious and Secular Perspectives* (Princeton, NJ: Princeton UP, 1996); Steven Forde, "Classical Realism" (62–84) and Jack Donnelly, "Twentieth Century Realism" (85–111), both in Terry Nardin and David R. Mapel, eds., *Traditions in International Ethics* (Cambridge: Cambridge UP, 1992). See also Robert O. Keohane, ed., *Neorealism and Its Critics* (New York: Columbia UP, 1986).

3 Hans Morgenthau, *Politics Among Nations*, 5th ed. (New York: Knopf, 1973); George F. Kennan, *Realities of American Foreign Policy* (Princeton, NJ: Princeton UP, 1954); Reinhold Niebuhr, *Christianity and Power Politics* (New York: Charles Scribner's Sons, 1940); Hedley Bull, *The Anarchical Society: A Study of Order in World Politics* (New York: Columbia UP, 1977); Kenneth N. Waltz, *Man, the State and War* (Princeton, NJ: Princeton UP, 1978); Henry Kissinger, *Diplomacy* (New York: Harper Collins, 1995).

4 Michael Walzer, *Just and Unjust Wars*, 3rd ed. (New York: Basic Books, 2000), 3–4, 117.

5 Walzer, *Wars*, 5.

6 Morgenthau, *Politics*, 16–22; Werner Jaeger, *Paideia*, trans. Gilbert Highet (New York: Random House, 1949), 402. Thanks to Christian Barry here.
7 Wilson cited in Walzer, *Wars*, 3–21; Carl von Clausewitz, *On War*, trans. Anatol Rapoport (New York: Penguin, 1994). Quote from William T. Sherman, *From Atlanta to the Sea* (London: Folio Society, 1961), 121–22.
8 Donnelly, "Realism," 85–111.
9 Walzer, *Wars*, 3–20.
10 Walzer, *Wars*, 13–16.
11 Walzer, *Wars*, 3–21.
12 Walzer, *Wars*, 5–10, 15.
13 Michael Walzer, "Nation and Universe," in Grethe B. Peterson, ed. *The Tanner Lecture on Human Values* (Salt Lake City, UT: Utah UP, 1990), 537–40.
14 I'm grateful to Bob Martin for suggesting this and other helpful points.
15 Thomas M. Franck, *The Power of Legitimacy Among Nations* (Princeton, NJ: Princeton UP, 1990), Appendix; David A. Welch, *Justice and the Genesis of War* (Cambridge: Cambridge UP, 1988).
16 David B. Abernethy, *The Dynamics of Global Dominance: European Overseas Empires 1415–1980* (New Haven, CT: Yale UP, 2001).
17 Theodore S. Hamerow, *Otto von Bismarck*, 2nd ed. (London: Heath, 1972).
18 Thomas W. Pogge, *Realizing Rawls* (Ithaca, NY: Cornell UP, 1989), 211–81.
19 John Keegan, *The First World War* (New York: Vintage, 2000).
20 Is a crusading mentality present in my own defence, last chapter, of forcible regime change? I don't think so: a crusading mentality denotes a narrow-minded, absolutist, simplistic, and probably religious world-view which perceives itself as entirely righteous and the other side as completely unjust and to be demonized and vanquished. The last chapter does not display such traits: what is defended there is an idea of *minimal* justice—not pure or maximal justice—which is rooted in modest, reasonable, secular values like individual human rights and the good consequences of greater international peace and the ability of everyone to lead a minimally good life. Please note again the difference between a *just* war and a *holy* war discussed in Chapter 1. Moreover, the conception of coercive post-war regime change endorsed last chapter was assuming that the target regime was the aggressor: the permission to start the war comes from the target regime's act of aggression, not from its rooting in different values. Further, my defence of forcible regime change was quite guarded, with many careful distinctions, exceptions, and noted needs for checks-and-balances: especially the constraints imposed by the ten-point rehabilitation recipe for regime reconstruction. Believing that clear improvements can and should be made in a defeated aggressor post-war is not the same thing, surely, as calling for a crusade against infidels.
21 Walzer, *Wars*, 122.
22 Donnelly, "Realism," 85–111.
23 There are other reasons why Americans show a predilection for realist thought. Their being "top dog" in the international arena has led them to be inordinately concerned with their own status and influence in the international system. Being top dog also makes one a target of those who wish to dethrone and replace the dog, or just to rough it up a bit. Either way, you can see how the top dog is going to be sorely tempted to view the world in a quite paranoid, conflict-ridden way, always watching his back. But there's nothing essential or universal

about that experience. If one neither is the top dog nor intends to harass or replace the top dog, then one is not very likely to be impressed in any way with the realist view of international relations. This is probably why so few "middle power" countries—like Canada, Australia, the Scandinavian countries—talk or behave like realists.

24 Kissinger, *Diplomacy*, passim.

25 Morgenthau, *Politics*, passim; Niebuhr, *Power*, passim.

26 Kennan, *Realities*, 48; Kissinger, *Diplomacy*, passim.

27 Donnelly, "Realism," 85–111.

28 Michael Walzer, *Thick and Thin* (Notre Dame, IN: U of Notre Dame P, 1994).

29 This is not to say that a foreign policy animated by more provincial values than human rights satisfaction would not run afoul of this criticism. It may well—but it is not a claim advanced here.

30 John Rawls, *The Law of Peoples* (Cambridge, MA: Harvard UP, 1999), passim; Thomas W. Pogge, "The Bounds of Nationalism," in Jocelyne Couture et al., eds., *Rethinking Nationalism* (Calgary, AB: U of Calgary P, 1998), 463–504.

31 Will Kymlicka, *Liberalism, Community and Culture* (Oxford: Clarendon, 1988); Michael J. Sandel, *Liberalism and the Limits of Justice* (Cambridge, MA: Harvard UP, 1982); Amitai Etzioni, *The Spirit of Community* (New York: Touchstone, 1994).

32 Pogge, "Bounds," 463–504.

33 Charles R. Beitz, "Cosmopolitan Ideals and National Sentiment," *Journal of Philosophy* (1983): 591–600.

34 C. Michael Gelven, *War and Existence* (Notre Dame, IN: U of Notre Dame P, 1994), 12.

9 EVALUATING THE PACIFIST ALTERNATIVE

"But I tell you not to resist an evil person. Whoever slaps you on your right cheek, turn the other to him also." —JESUS, *MATTHEW* 5:39

"He shall judge between many nations, and rebuke strong nations afar off; they shall beat their swords into ploughshares, and their spears into pruning hooks; nations shall not lift up sword against nation, neither shall they learn war anymore." —*MICAH* 4:3

There are many kinds of pacifism. It is not my task here to diagnose and describe all of them. Different pacifists define pacifism differently, and offer various kinds of justification for their beliefs. But it seems that what unites all forms of pacifism—the basic proposition, or lowest common denominator—is opposition to warfare. The logical core of pacifism, as Jenny Teichman says, is "anti-war-ism."[1] No matter what kind of pacifist you are, you believe that *war is always wrong;* there is always some better approach to the problem than warfare. So, unlike realists, pacifists believe that it *is* possible and meaningful to apply moral judgment to international affairs. In this, they agree with just war theorists. But they disagree with just war theorists regarding the application of moral judgment to warfare. Just war theorists say war is *sometimes* morally permissible, whereas pacifists say war is *never* morally permissible.

Jim Sterba has attempted to mesh just war theory and pacifism into what he calls "just war pacifism,"[2] and he has collected some support in this regard. But I don't buy it. It's a strange kind of pacifist, after all, who can endorse warfare. If they do endorse warfare under just war conditions, then I suggest that they are just war theorists! Sterba's proposal does not integrate, so much as assimilate, pacifism into just war theory. The conceptual kernel of both theories, in my view, cannot be reconciled—the one says warfare *can* be permissible, and then defines those conditions, whereas the other says, *regardless* of the conditions, war *cannot* be morally justified. Quite literally and straightforwardly, a pacifist rejects war in favor of peace.

It is not violence in all its forms which the most challenging kind of pacifist objects to; rather, it is the specific *kind and degree of violence that war involves* to which the pacifist objects. A pacifist objects to killing (not just violence) in general and, in particular, he objects to the mass killing, for political reasons, which is part and parcel of the wartime experience. So, a pacifist rejects war; he believes that there are no moral grounds which can justify resorting to war. War, for the pacifist, is always wrong.[3]

Having come to a working definition of pacifism as anti-war-ism, we can now consider some of the reasons offered in its favor. Many such reasons have been offered but not all of them are appropriate to our concern. For example, many pacifists are so for religious reasons. Christians and Buddhists, in particular, have vibrant pacifist sects, such as the Quakers. They base their beliefs on sacred scriptures and a drive to be more like The Divine, whom they view as essentially peaceful. Christians, e.g., point to Jesus' life and teachings as disclosed in the New Testament. These do indeed, at first glance, seem to recommend something very much like pacifism. Consider the quote above, and the other important imperative to love even your enemies.[4] Jesus also says that he is "gentle and humble in heart" and he refuses to use force to resist his arrest, commanding his disciples: "Put your sword back into its place; for all who take the sword will perish by the sword."[5] But this—like much else in religion—is hotly contested. For example, we saw in Chapter 1 that just war theory has historically been associated with, and supported by, the Catholic Church—so, clearly, the Church doesn't think pacifism is mandated by the New Testament. I will not delve further into religious justifications for pacifism because they rest on beliefs—about God and Scripture, souls, and the afterlife—which simply are too personal, speculative, contentious, and even exclusionary. I direct the reader to the relevant, voluminous literature for more on the religious perspective.[6]

This book will stick to secular justifications for pacifism, which try to appeal to any rational person regardless of religious affiliation. The most relevant pro-pacifist arguments here include the following: 1) a "*virtue*" form of pacifism (VP), which asserts that war and killing are at odds with human excellence and flourishing; 2) a "*consequentialist*" form of pacifism (CP), which maintains that the benefits accruing from war can never outweigh the costs of fighting it; and 3) a "*deontological*" form of pacifism (DP), which contends that the very activity of war is intrinsically unjust, since it violates foremost duties of morality and justice, such as not killing other human beings. Most common and compelling amongst contemporary secular pacifists, such as Robert Holmes and Richard Norman, is a mixed doctrine which combines, in some way, all three.[7]

Before describing in detail VP, CP, and DP, mention should be made of a very popular criticism of pacifism which will not here be employed. This criticism is that pacifism amounts to an indefensible "clean hands policy." The pacifist, it's often said, refuses to take the brutal measures necessary for the defense of himself, or his nation, for the selfish sake of maintaining his own inner moral purity. It's argued that the pacifist is thus a kind of free-rider on the rest of us, gathering all the benefits of citizenship while not sharing all its burdens. The pacifist is not willing to fight, yet gains security from those who are. Not only is the pacifist ungrateful for this, he actually looks down his nose, morally, at those who have provided him with his security. The picture is of a rather un-likeable, holier-than-thou, selfish free-rider. A related inference drawn is that the pacifist can actually be an internal threat to the overall security of the state, because his non-participation and self-absorbed objection diminishes the state's resources and moral resolve in fighting.

This "clean hands" argument is easily, and frequently, over-stated. It is important to note that, to the extent to which *any* moral stance will commend a certain set of actions deemed morally worthy, and condemn others as being reprehensible, the "clean hands" criticism can be so malleable as to apply to any substantive moral and political doctrine. *Every* moral and political theory stipulates that one ought to do what it deems good or just, and to avoid what it deems bad or unjust. The very point of morality itself, we might say, is to help keep one's hands "clean." So this popular just war criticism of pacifism is not especially appealing. Besides, the very idea of a selfish pacifist simply does not ring true: many pacifists have, historically, paid a very high price for their pacifism during wartime (through severe ridicule, job loss, ostracism, and even jail time), and their pacifism seems less rooted in regard for inner moral purity than it is in regard for constructing a less violent and more humane world order.[8] So, this argument against pacifism fails; but others, now to be discussed, succeed in questioning the plausibility of its core principles, at least relative to those of just war theory.

1. Describing and Criticizing VP

Virtue ethicists, such as Aristotle, believe that human beings must live their lives trying to develop their innate capabilities to the fullest extent; this is the purpose of life. Of course, we have many capabilities to develop: intellectual; physical; social; moral; and so on. What does it mean to develop one's *moral* capacity to the fullest? It is to pursue ethical excellence, which is displayed by the virtues (hence "virtue ethics"). What are the virtues? They are freely-chosen character traits which we praise in others. We praise them because: 1) they are difficult to develop; 2) they are corrective of natural deficiencies (e.g., industriousness is corrective of our tendency to be lazy); and 3) they are beneficial both to self and society.[9]

There are many virtues, and a moral person is one who develops them and displays them consistently over time. In this sense, the virtues are like muscles in that they need habitual conditioning to be real, strong, and toned. The ancient Greeks listed four "cardinal virtues"—wisdom, courage, moderation, and justice—and Christian teaching is well-known for its recommendation of faith, hope, charity and love. Other prominent virtues include honesty, helpfulness, forgiveness, pleasantness, consistency, tolerance, modesty, thoughtfulness, and so on. For the human vices, simply negate the above. Such: are destructive of self and society; give in to easy instincts; and represent a triumph of the base and mediocre.

The essence of VP is this: when we think of warfare and war-fighting, we see that none of this is praise-worthy activity. Violence, killing, and blood-shed are not virtuous activities; they seem clearly at odds with the kind of ideal life—a fully realized and excellent human life—which is the focus of virtue ethics. War is not part of any sane person's idea of a flourishing or excellent life. Warfare causes terrible pain and suffering, and the infliction of violence brutalizes the victim and causes a corruption of character—a hardening and insensitivity—even to the inflictor. A VP pacifist would also suggest that, although some aspects of courage might (admittedly) be called upon in war, just as common is the experience of post-traumatic stress disorder, which reduces the formerly strong soldier down to a broken shell. Moreover, which is truly more courageous: fighting, or refusing to fight in spite of the danger? There are a number of sharp questions here: is war truly a wise choice? A moderate and humane one? One expressive of hope and charity, or rather of hatred and malice? Doesn't war, as a destroyer, seem the opposite of creativity and life? How can war be consistent with love? Indeed, doesn't all this show that *peace itself is a virtue*—part of the human ideal—and that, although it might be very difficult, it is in pursuit of peace that we nevertheless must always orient our thoughts and actions?

There *is* something to VP, just as there is something in every major doctrine on the ethics of war and peace. But there are problems. The major one is whether the commitments of the pacifist are utopian—i.e., excessively unrealistic. War might be a nasty business which, ultimately, calls forth more vice than virtue. But it might also simply be needed to defeat an aggressor who is not moved by pacifist ideals. A world where aggressors are allowed to triumph, and then to inflict rights-violating brutality, is not part of any sane person's idea of the best life, either. And there is something to be said, in the case of a just war, for: the virtues of defending one's people (or fellow citizens) from aggression; the courage it takes to confront an aggressor; the self-discipline it takes to fight justly; and of the strength, team-spiritedness, and ingenuity it takes to formulate and execute a successful war plan. (Indeed, for a long time, the US Army's recruiting slogan has had a distinctly Aristotelian tone about it: "Be all that you can be!")[10] More generally, acting in accord with the demands of justice is also a virtue, and a major one at that. Much of the dispute has to do with different perspectives on what to do when the world puts us in situations where the virtues of peace and justice are in conflict, and cannot both be realized. Where just war theorists differ from pacifists is that they suspect that there can be cases where justice does not include peace or, more precisely, where peace includes or creates injustice. Consider that just war theorists, like Michael Walzer, argue that, by failing to resist international aggression with effective means, pacifists end up rewarding aggression and failing to protect people—fellow citizens—who need it.[11]

Pacifists reply to these just war arguments by contending that we do not need to resort to war in order to protect people and to punish aggression effectively. In the event of an armed invasion by an aggressor state, an organized and committed campaign of non-violent civil disobedience—perhaps combined with international diplomatic and economic sanctions—would be just as effective as war in expelling the aggressor, with much less destruction of lives and property. After all, the pacifist might say, no invader could possibly maintain its grip on the conquered nation in light of such systematic isolation, non-cooperation, and non-violent resistance. How could it work the factories, harvest the fields, run the transportation network, man the stores and banks, when everyone would be striking, refusing to comply, or quietly sabotaging orders? How could it maintain the will to keep the country in the face of crippling economic sanctions and diplomatic censure from the international community? And so on. Jack DuVall and Peter Ackerman have detailed many actual, historical cases of non-violent resistance around the world; Robert Holmes and Gene Sharp, amongst others, have developed the abstract non-violent tactics which pacifists might rely on.[12] Consider the following list of tactics offered by Sharp:

> general strike, sit-down strike, industry strike, go-slow and work to rule ... economic boycotts, consumers' boycott, traders boycott, rent refusal, international economic embargo and social boycott ... boycott of government employment, boycott of elections, revenue refusal, civil disobedience and mutiny ... sit-ins, reverse strikes, non-violent obstruction, non-violent invasion and parallel government.[13]

There are powerful reasons to agree with John Rawls that to view these tactics as universally reliable is "unworldly." For the effectiveness of these campaigns of civil disobedience depends on the standards and scruples of the invading aggressor. But what if the aggressor is utterly brutal, ruthless? What if, faced with civil disobedience, the invader "cleanses" the area of the native population, and then imports its own people from back home? It's hard to strike, or sabotage orders, if one is dead. And what if, faced with economic sanctions and diplomatic censure from a neighboring country, the invader decides to invade *it*, too? We have some indication from history—particularly that of Nazi Germany—that such pitiless tactics are effective at breaking the will of even very principled people to resist. The defense of our lives and rights may well, against such heartless invaders, require the use of political violence. Indeed, under such conditions, as Walzer says, adherence to pacifism might even amount to a "disguised form of surrender." He thinks that, in such instances, if one truly believes in values like "resisting aggression effectively" and "protecting oneself and fellow citizens from aggression," then one should be willing to fight for them—because, in such cases, fighting holds the only realistic prospect of actually defending these values. Unwillingness to fight here translates into non-support for these values. But how can you not want to protect people, and resist aggression effectively?[14]

Pacifists respond to this accusation of "unworldliness" by citing what they believe are real-world examples of successful non-violent resistance to aggression. Examples most often mentioned include: 1) Mahatma Gandhi's campaign to drive the British Imperial regime out of India in the late 1940s, leading to the independence of modern India; and 2) Martin Luther King Jr.'s civil rights crusade in the 1960s on behalf of African-Americans.[15] Walzer replies curtly that there is no evidence that non-violent resistance has ever, *of itself*, succeeded. This may be a bit rash on his part, though it is clear for example that Britain's own exhaustion—financial and otherwise—after World War II had much to do with the evaporation of its empire and the eventual independence of India. Walzer's main counter-argument, against these so-called counter-examples, is that they only illustrate his point: that effective non-violent resistance depends upon the scruples of those it is aimed against. It was only because the British and the Americans had some scruples and standards, and were in the end moved morally by the determined idealism of the non-violent protesters, that they acquiesced to their demands. But aggressors will not always be so moved. It might seem unthinkable to us, but a tyrant like Hitler, for example, might interpret non-violent resistance as disgusting weakness, deserving contemptuous crushing. "Non-violent defense," Walzer suggests, "is no defense at all against tyrants or conquerors ready to adopt such measures."[16]

To those pacifists who retort that even Hitler was faced with his own non-violent resistance—namely in Scandinavia after he conquered those lands in 1940—the point must be made that the problems that the Swedes, Norwegians, and Danes put in his way because of their strikes, sabotage and protest cannot really, in my view, be considered successful acts of pacifist resistance to aggression. They happened, after all, *after* Hitler had already conquered those lands—so how were they helpful in resisting the aggressive take-over of their territory and political systems? Second, perhaps the reasons why the Nazis didn't crush these Scandinavian protest movements were that they had already conquered Scandinavia, and didn't consider these protests a serious threat to their control; and that they now had bigger fish to fry, like England, Russia, and America. Thirdly, and speaking of the major powers, *they* were the ones who beat Hitler—*with force*—resulting among other things in the liberation of Scandinavia. It was not home-grown pacifist protest which got the Nazis out of Stockholm, Oslo, and Copenhagen; it was the decisive military defeat of Nazi Germany by the remaining Allies. This is not to deny the fact that Scandinavian resistance did cause problems for the Nazis, that it did boost the spirits of the locals, and that the co-ordination required was impressive and the acts often brave and ingenious. It is, rather, to put them into their proper perspective as smart and bracing tools of resistance but not, ultimately, as tools successful in rolling back aggression.[17]

Walzer puts the whole issue persuasively when he says that the idea of an effective "war without weapons," much less a world without war, is (for now) a "messianic dream." For the foreseeable future, and in the real world we all inhabit, it is better to follow just war theory, which is committed to an effective yet principled use of defensive armed force in the face of aggression. The constraints on violence established by just war theory are, in fact, the necessary conditions for the more peaceful world which pacifists mistakenly believe is already within sight. "The restraint of war," Walzer concludes, "is the beginning of peace."[18]

Another way philosophers have of making this point is this: there's an important difference between "ideal theory" and "non-ideal theory." Ideal theory is what is true, or best, under ideal conditions: i.e., a world with endless resources, nothing but wise people, and with everyone wanting to be morally good. Under such conditions, I suggest that everyone would probably agree that the only permissible attitude on these issues would be pacifism. But the world is not ideal. In particular, there are bad people and nasty regimes who indulge in violence and seek out rights-violating domination over others. It is this sub-optimal fact about the world which gives rise and plausibility to the use of defensive force. Just war theory is a piece of non-ideal theory: a set of ideas and values designed to guide us in the here and now, in the real world, until deeper and deeply better transformations can be found and generated.[19]

2. Describing and Criticizing CP

Consequentialism is another fundamental world-view regarding ethics. As the name indicates, the core focus of consequentialism is on the concrete results of one's actions. This tradition is skeptical of the value of focusing on personal character traits, as virtue theory does, or on abstract universal rules (as we'll see deontology does). The key, ethically, is whether the world ends up better as a result of one's actions. The proof is in the pudding: the right thing to do, in every instance, is to perform that action which is going to have the best contribution to the world's overall welfare. So, consequentialism involves a serious attempt to predict the costs and benefits of one's options, and then a mandate to act in accord with the one promising the highest "payoff"—in terms of pleasure, happiness, or welfare—to the world at large.[20] The CP element of contemporary pacifism, accordingly, is the notion that the costs of war always outweigh the benefits from undertaking war. One does not need to be a military historian to get the point, namely, that war is incredibly destructive, brutal, and often deeply inhumane. And the benefits, if any, of wars are often seriously unclear and are soon overtaken, in any case, by the flow of historical events. As the famous song asks: "War, what is it good for?" The CP pacifist agrees with the next line, "Absolutely nothing!" (And says it again.)

The first critical question to raise here, by way of response, is: what kind of costs and benefits are being appealed to here? Short-term or long-term costs and benefits, or both? Prudential or moral costs and benefits, or both? And costs from whose point of view? And so on. There is a lack, in the literature, of a detailed breakdown of war's costs and benefits; pacifists prefer instead to gesture towards very general—almost clichéd—understandings of war's destructiveness, such as those just offered last paragraph. Could this tendency towards sweeping generality and abstraction exist due to a lack of confidence in the results of a more finely grained analysis?

One important element to note, in this regard, is that we have to consider not only the explicit costs of war action (i.e., both military and civilian casualties, the costs of deployment, and the destruction of property), but also the implicit costs of war inaction: not resorting to war, to defend political sovereignty and territorial integrity, may well be tantamount to rewarding aggression in international relations. The lack of armed resistance and forceful punishment allows the aggressor state to keep the fruits of its campaign, thereby augmenting the incentives in favor of future aggression. To what extent can we have a well-functioning and stable—much less a just—international system in which aggression between nations is thusly rewarded? Call this the "macro-cost of war inaction": the rewarding of interstate aggression, which leads to the long-term weakening of the international system of peaceful dispute-resolution. The thought experiment becomes grimmer for pacifism when we think not just of classical cross-border wars but for potential armed humanitarian interventions (AHI). How the costs of inaction here—as we tragically witnessed in Rwanda in 1994—are not simply sovereignty and land but literally hundreds of thousands of lives.

We must also talk of the "micro-costs" of not resorting to war to defend one's own people from an aggressive invader. Such a pacifist strategy seems, at the very least, to run enormous risks with the safety and well-being of one's citizens, not to mention their right to be self-governing and not subject to a conquering regime. In light of this, we should ask: does pacifism make sense at the level of collective agents, like states, especially if those collective agents are charged with the responsibility of protecting and serving their citizen members? Is there too great a reliance, by the pacifist, on the intuitive appeal of the inter-personal case (of not killing another individual), as opposed to the analogous, yet different, inter-national case?

In other words, pacifism at the level of the individual—the conscientious objector, for instance—seems much more plausible and principled than advocating that an entire state be geared along pacifist lines, especially given the sub-optimal status quo of the international arena (as the realist would remind us). Again, the risks to one's people would be huge, and so it is deeply unclear whether a prudent, or moral, government ought to adhere to such a view. Just war theorists believe that it should not do so: one of the core functions of the state, after all, is to provide reliable protection from serious, standard threats to our human rights, one of which is armed invasion by an aggressor regime. It is compelling to conclude that states ought to be prepared to enforce that protection, through armed force if necessary.[21]

The combination of both the macro- and the micro-costs of failing to resort to war (in situations otherwise well-defined by just war criteria) are sufficient at least to cast doubt on whether war-fighting can only result in greater negative, than positive, consequences. It's very simple to cluck one's tongue and shake one's head at the destruction of warfare—"War is bad!"—and quite another to think through the costs of pacifism and what they might involve relative to just war theory. Being against war, after all, can be like being in favor of motherhood—a "no-brainer" that no one in her right mind would disagree with. But it's different for those with responsibility to protect their people, especially when threatened by a terrible aggressor who relishes warfare and conquest.

We might also, in our consideration of CP, consider the historical record. I am fully prepared to concede that many—perhaps even most—historical wars can be objected to, very forcefully, by the CP aspect of contemporary pacifism. World War I seems a fitting example of the futility, waste, and sheer human tragedy of many wars our ancestors fought.[22] But not all wars seem to fall neatly under this objection. World War II, for instance, is much more debatable. Many thoughtful people, including participants who actually made the sacrifices, have argued—appealing to both prudential and moral costs—that defeating ultra-aggressive regimes like Nazi Germany, Fascist Italy, and Imperial Japan was worth the costs of the war-fighting, as enormous as those admittedly were. Can we, they ask, imagine and endorse what our world would currently look like had the Nazis been allowed to conquer Europe and rule it, had Mussolini spread his "New Roman Empire" beyond Ethiopia, and had Imperial Japan been allowed to subdue most of East Asia? George Orwell's searing image of a soldier's boot "stomping on a human face forever" comes to mind. World War II didn't create a wonderful world—the world of our dreams—but it did prevent a truly terrible world from coming into being. It also ushered in many international improvements—the spread of democracy, the creation of the United Nations, the growth of international law and respect for human rights—which have made the modern world a more humane place.[23]

A third issue to raise, with regard to CP, focuses on the relationship between consequentialism and the denial of killing, especially on the level which is endemic to warfare. Pacifism places great, perhaps overriding, value on respecting human life, notably through its usual injunction against killing. But this core pacifist value seems to rest uneasily with the appeal to consequentialism in CP. For there is nothing to a consequentialist approach to the ethics of war and peace which would always outlaw killing. There is here no firm principle that one must never kill another person, or that nations ought not to launch military campaigns which kill thousands of enemy soldiers. With consequentialism, it's always a matter of considering the latest costs, benefits, and circumstances. Consequentialism was actually first designed, quite explicitly, to be flexible in a way in which virtue ethics and deontology aren't. (Note the difference between consequentialism and realism: while both appeal to cost-benefit utilities, consequentialism remains an ethical doctrine focused on the world's overall improvement whereas realism is a doctrine skeptical of ethics and thus featuring strong commitments only to one's own selfish benefit.)

When considering whether or not one should kill another human being, consequentialism will typically appeal to the pain and suffering such killing will cause both the victim and her friends and family—not just in terms of the loss of life but also in terms of the loss of further, future life experiences. Appeal will also be made to a more universal (or legislative) point of view, and contention made that permitting or mandating killing is a bad precedent which might lead to loss of respect for human life, and thus to serious insecurities within the community, and so on. These are all excellent and powerful points to be made against killing another human being. The remaining problem, though, is that a consequentialist approach to the injunction against killing and war does not seem to come with the kind of firmness which the pacifist needs to ground his categorical contentions. The pacifist isn't just committed to saying that, *usually*, killing and warfare are a bad idea; he wants to say, much more strongly, that killing—or least war—is *always* wrong. Can consequentialism deliver that kind of absoluteness?[24]

Since it is always a matter of choosing the best option amongst feasible alternatives, consequentialism clearly leaves conceptual space open to the claim that, under these conditions, at this time and place, and given these possible alternatives, killing and/or war seem(s) permissible. There can be particular counter-examples, some offered above, wherein the calculations may well come out the other way. After all, what if killing 3,000 people (say, some members of an invading army) seems necessary to save the lives of 9,000 people (say, people of one's nation who would die from the rights-violative activities of the unchecked invader, as it sought to consolidate its rule)? It is at least possible to conceive that a quick and decisive resort to war could be employed effectively to prevent even greater suffering, killing, and devastation in the future. Indeed, military and political historians often engage in this thinking, and sometimes claim things like "Had the Allies confronted Hitler after Austria, it wouldn't have taken so long, later, to defeat Germany. Appeasement made the war longer and more destructive." To put it plainly, it seems rather bizarre for the consequentialist pacifist, whose principles exhibit a profound abhorrence for killing people, to be willing in such a scenario to allow an even greater number of people to be killed by acquiescing to the violence of others less scrupulous. Two related points are being made here: 1) the general point that the CP element of pacifism does not, of itself, seem to ground the categorical rejection of killing and war which is the very essence of pacifism; and 2) the particular point that CP seems open to counter-examples (like World War II) which question whether consequentialism would even reject killing and war at all in certain conditions. Consequentialism might actually recommend warfare, if the circumstances were dark enough and the other options sufficiently limited.[25]

3. Describing and Criticizing DP

Deontology is yet another major world-view regarding morality. We discussed it, without using the word, when we spoke in Chapter 5 of supreme emergencies and Kant's "strict respect for the rules" option. Deontology has, as its core intuition, the notion that the concept of duty is at the foundation of morality. Ideas like duty, obligation, and responsibility are uniquely moral ones—indeed, the most uniquely and clearly moral ones. There might be confusion between morality and mere personal prudence when we talk, like virtue ethicists, about beneficial character traits or when we speak, like consequentialists, about costs and benefits. But there is no mistaking that we are talking about morality when we consider duty and obligation. So these ideas, and not the others, must be the very essence of ethics. Doing one's duty is what is central in ethics. And by "duty," deontologists usually mean that one's behavior is permitted, or demanded, by a first principle or general rule regarding morality, such as "Thou shall not lie," or "Honor your father and mother." How does deontology get used by pacifists? The exact nature of the DP element varies from thinker to thinker, but the core notion is that *the very activity of war-fighting violates a foremost duty of morality*. Thus, undertaking such activity can never be justified by appealing to the aims or consequences of the war action in question. War, as a means to an end, is thought to be intrinsically unjust. The supposed "justice" of the goal sought, through war, does not redeem the injustice of the means used to pursue it. There must be consistency between means and ends. War ought never to be resorted to: there is always some vastly superior option with regard to international dispute-resolution, such as diplomacy, sanctions, or organized campaigns of non-violence.

3.1. NOT KILLING PEOPLE

Much has been left unsaid in this terse characterization of DP. Depth and detail must be added: which foremost duty of morality is war-fighting supposed to violate? Why? In my view, the best pacifist consideration of these matters has been offered by Robert Holmes. Holmes deals with this consideration, at first cut, by stating that the foremost duty of morality violated by war-fighting is *the duty not to kill other human beings*.[26] But the obvious objection to this claim is that such a duty—though crucially important under normal conditions of life—does not seem to override all other considerations under special, very threatening circumstances. Consider the most obvious example: A brutally attacks B, thereby posing a severe threat to B's life. Provided that A attacks without justification, many people would respond that B may retaliate against A in self-defense, with lethal force if needed. Consider another example: are we not to kill a dangerous terrorist who is credibly threatening the lives of many innocent civilians? Say, one of the 9/11 hijackers while he was in the act? It seems defensible to assert that we may, so that we protect the lives of the innocent.[27]

The essence of this objection has been stated very forcefully by G.E.M. Anscombe, who lambastes pacifism for not distinguishing between "the blood of the innocent" and "the blood of the guilty." The question, as Anscombe would pose it, is: why should we respect the duty not to kill the terrorist when he is guilty of a seriously immoral act, namely, credibly threatening and endangering the lives of many innocent civilians? Do we not also owe the duty of protection, by lethal force if necessary, to those who are being so seriously threatened? After all, if we do nothing, then severe harm, or even death, will befall all these innocents. The terrorist will get his way, even though his way is the morally wrong one. In short, Anscombe's claim is that we have weightier moral reasons to side with the civilians instead of the terrorist, even if that means killing him.[28]

There is a raft of complex issues, addressed in the rhetorical questions above, which requires a much fuller development. The first concerns the permissibility, perhaps even the right, to kill a person who presents a severe threat either to oneself or to others. Why exactly is this permissible? Does it not, for instance, violate the human rights of the person presenting the threat?

The employment of lethal force against an aggressor is permissible because the victim of the aggression would lose too much if she were not permitted to kill the aggressor. Indeed, the victim could literally lose everything. But perhaps it will be objected that the aggressor, if killed in response to his attack, would also lose everything. So, why may the victim kill the aggressor? The answer seems to be that the aggressor is responsible for forcing the victim to choose between her life and that of the aggressor, and it would be not only unreasonable but unfair to bar the victim from choosing her own life.

An agent A is an aggressor, we've seen, when A uses force to violate the human rights of another person, victim V. In violating the human rights of V, A reveals himself to be a severe threat to V, since human rights serve to protect vital human needs. It is an important claim of this book, defended throughout, that the commission of aggression by A against V: 1) justifies V in responding to A with lethal force, if needed; and 2) justifies any third party, T, in employing needed lethal force to A in order to protect V. The key principle at work here—dubbed the "Core Principle on Aggression" (or CPA) in Chapter 2—is thus the following: *the commission of aggression by A against V entitles V, and/or any third party T acting on behalf of V, to employ all necessary means to stop A, including lethal force, provided such means do not themselves violate human rights.* Let us briefly remind ourselves of the elements of this complex principle.

Consider the first element, namely, the entitlement of either V or T to respond with the required force against aggressor A. Jan Narveson seems to put this point well when he notes that it is a matter of moral logic that if V has a human right HR to X (say, personal security), then V also has title to employ those means necessary to secure X from serious, standard threats, such as the violent aggression of others. This is required for us to speak of V's truly having HR at all.[29] Thus, if the employment of lethal force against A reasonably seems required to make A desist from aggressing against, or even killing, V, it follows that V is at least permitted to do so. But how does this first-person permission get extended to the third person?

The extension proceeds on the basis of the wrongness of the aggression and the intent of the third party to protect the victim from the wrongful aggression. Sometimes victims, for whatever reason, lack the wherewithal to defend themselves effectively from aggression. In such cases, are we to say that their factual deficiency undermines their normative claim that the aggressor either stop or be stopped? The answer, clearly, is no. It is crucial to stress that the normative essence of the victim's claim is that the aggressor stop or be stopped, and not more narrowly that only she (the victim) be allowed to stop him. This moral reality grounds a third party's intervention in the case, and we applied this reasoning to AHI in Chapter 3. It is clear, however, that to be justified, the third party's intent can only be protection of V from A.

Consider now more precisely the second element of the principle, namely, the permission to employ lethal force against A if required. Many thinkers will be quick to pronounce on the need for a proportionality of force in response to a threat from an aggressor. And this claim is undeniable. But it may be worth stressing how we ought not to succumb readily to pious delusions about first trying to disarm the aggressor and then, only if that fails, ought "the ante to be upped," perhaps to the point of killing. In situations where such a measured escalation of violent defense is reasonable, obviously it must be employed. But many situations wherein violent aggression is occurring are ones which practically require a very swift and effective response. We cannot hold victims to excessively stringent interpretations of proportionality in such cases: they are, after all, under an immediate, grievous threat to their lives and rights.

3.2. NOT VIOLATING RIGHTS

Let us now turn to the crucial third element of our principle, namely, that the violent response of V to A's aggression violate no human rights. The obvious, and important, question here is: why would V's killing A, in response to A's aggression, not violate A's human rights? As the DP pacifist would say: doesn't the above principle CPA actually compound the wrongness of the tragic situation by permitting V to kill A if required? Isn't this all just the notion that "two wrongs make a right"? Gandhi had a reply: "An eye for an eye leaves us all blind." The contemporary just war response is *no*: V does no wrong whatsoever—violates no rights—by responding to A's aggression with lethal force if required.

The reason grounding this just war claim is that the commission of aggression by A causes A to forfeit his human right not to be dealt with violently, or even killed. It must be understood that rights are reasons. They are not properties of persons, rather, they are reasons to treat persons in certain ways. From this conception, it marks no great conceptual leap to point out that reasons to treat persons in certain ways can change, depending on the circumstances and what they are doing. Provided that one has a non-absolutist, and thus reasonable, conception of human rights as claims no stronger than their justifying reasons,[30] forfeiture appears to pose no considerable difficulties. It amounts to nothing more than the claim that the weight of reasons in the situation informs us that V does nothing wrong in responding to A's aggression with lethal force if necessary.

Why does V do nothing wrong? What exactly constitutes "the weight of reasons" in this regard? We have already mentioned this, in Chapter 2, while defining aggression, but let's do a quick reminder, since it's vital for our encounter with DP pacifism. First, it is A who is responsible for forcing V to choose between her own life and rights and those of A. We can hardly blame V for choosing her own. For, if she does not choose her own, she loses an enormous amount, perhaps everything. It is simply not reasonable to expect creatures like us to intentionally suffer catastrophic loss. Also, consider the question of fairness: if V is not allowed to use lethal force, if necessary, against A in the event of A's aggression, then V loses everything while A loses nothing. Indeed, A gains whatever object he desired in violating or killing V. Such is a patently unfair reward of deeply objectionable behavior. Finally, V's having rights at all provides V with an implicit entitlement to those means and measures necessary to secure her rights, such as the use of force in the face of a severe threat. These four powerful considerations of *responsibility, reasonableness, fairness,* and *implicit entitlement* all unite together in supporting the just war claims that: 1) V may respond with lethal force to A's aggression; 2) V does no wrong in doing so; 3) it would be wrong to prohibit V's doing so; and 4) A bears all of the blame in the situation.

Once A has stopped his aggression, and poses no imminent threat of renewed aggression, his full set of rights spring forth intact, save for those still deemed forfeit for legitimate reasons of appropriate punishment for his act of aggression. The notion of "springing forth" is nothing more puzzling or magical than the claim that now the weight of reasons with regard to how we should treat this person has changed. Since he is no longer a clear and present danger to another's vital needs, for example, he may no longer be killed—though he may, perhaps, still be jailed, fined, and/or rehabilitated as appropriate punishment.

3.3. INNOCENT AGGRESSORS?

One related topic, which gets mentioned in conjunction with these issues, is that of the so-called "innocent aggressor." Say, for instance, that C and D are in an elevator together. Unbeknownst to C, D suffers from a very serious mental disorder, which suddenly causes him to attack C. Is C thereby justified in employing lethal force against D? A number of thinkers have denied this, claiming that at best C has an excuse. This is to say that C has done something which is not morally permitted (namely, killing an innocent) yet C ought not to be punished for it because he has an excuse. This excuse is the fact that C could in no way be expected to know what was wrong inside of D's head which caused him to attack C.[31]

These abstract thoughts, on this curious figure of the innocent aggressor, should be applied to a more relevant case. Sometimes pacifists will contend that soldiers are innocent aggressors—they are not to blame for the wars they fight, and many are conscripts in any event—and go further and deny even the excusability of intentionally killing them.[32] At the very least, they will assert, there is no moral permission to kill them: the just war theorist still does not have morality on his side.

The first thing to be crystal clear about, in response, is the uncontested fact that soldiers are aggressors, regardless of whether they are conscripts and regardless of their own personal attitude regarding the justice of the war they are fighting. They do indeed present themselves as severe threats against the lives and rights of those to whom they are opposed. They are armed with deadly force, and trained to kill for political reasons.

This first fact establishes, at least, a strong *prima facie* (or initial) case in favor of the notion that targeting soldiers with lethal force is morally justified and not merely excusable. After all, it is not as though soldiers can be thought of as being no different from unarmed civilians who do not present themselves as lethal threats.

The only plausible objection to this *prima facie* case is that there can be times when soldiers do disagree profoundly with the cause of their own state in fighting and yet still fight on its behalf for reasons which are outside of their control. But there are complicated issues to be resolved in this regard: if the soldier in question does have these personal objections, why does he continue to fight? Is the raw fact of his conscription (assuming that were the case) sufficient to exonerate him from his culpability as an aggressor? Or does some further story have to be told about what punishments he would have risked by resisting conscription? I do not pretend to have ready answers to these questions, only to insist that the realities at play in this case are considerably more complex than those in the highly contrived case of C and D in the elevator. The burden of proof is on those who would insist that soldiers are innocent aggressors. "Innocent" in what salient sense? It seems a category mistake to say combatants can be innocent, since just war theory and international law define innocence precisely as noncombatancy.

My view is that only rarely, if ever, do we come across a genuinely "innocent aggressor" in the heat of battle. Many soldiers are only too glad to fight on behalf of their own country, for good or ill. Conscription does nothing, one way or the other, to shed evidential light on their interior innocence or guilt. And the external fact remains that they are aggressors. Thus, states possess an on-the-whole justification in responding to aggressive armed forces with forces of their own, for reasons of reasonableness, fairness, and implicit entitlement described above. There may well be exceptional cases where this will mean targeting an innocent aggressor—i.e., a soldier involved in the war, somehow, through no fault of his own—with lethal force. I think, as opined by Helen Brocklehurst, that the closest to an "innocent aggressor" in real life would be a child soldier, and we discussed such in Chapter 4.[33] Such remain aggressors because they are combatants deploying armed force, yet they are also innocent in the sense that they are grossly manipulated by cruel adults and have probably not developed intelligent free will and moral capacities. Now, I still think such child soldiers are legitimate targets—you can't ask them their age while they're shooting at you—even though the whole affair becomes imbued with tragedy. I understand the moral problem of child soldiers to boil down to this: they are not a case for pacifism, rather, they are a case for having created (and now needing to enforce) a new and important category of *jus in bello* war crime. Generals and officers caught using child soldiers should be up on severe charges for it after the war.

3.4. NEVER KILLING THE INNOCENT

DP pacifists, however, are not at this point out of options. Holmes, for instance, offers another argument which contends that the real foremost duty of morality which is violated by war-fighting is not the duty not to kill aggressive human beings, but rather the duty not to kill innocent, non-aggressive human beings. What is the relevant sense of "innocence" now being employed? To be innocent here means the regular sense of: to have done nothing which would justify being harmed or killed; in particular, it means not constituting a serious threat or harm to other people. It means not being an aggressor. It is primarily in this sense, we know, in which civilian populations are thought, by traditional just war theory, to be "innocent" of war and thus morally immune from direct attack during wartime. Even if civilians support the unjust war effort politically, or even simply in terms of their personal attitude towards the war effort, they clearly are not armed and dangerous aggressors. Only armed forces, and the political-industrial-technological complexes which guide them, constitute serious threats against which threatened people may respond in kind. Civilian populations are morally off-limits as targets.

Holmes contends that this just war criterion of discrimination, with its crucial corollary of non-combatant immunity, can never actually be satisfied. For all possible wars in this world—given the nature of military technology and tactics, the heat of battle, the proximity between legitimate and illegitimate targets, and the limits of human knowledge and self-discipline—involve the killing of innocents, thus defined. We know this to be true from history, and have no good reason for thinking otherwise. There simply has never been a war, nor will there ever be a war, without at least some civilian casualties. But the killing of innocent non-aggressive civilians, Holmes says, is always unjust. Therefore, just war theory's claim that resort to war can be mandated, or at least permitted, by justice conflicts with the supposed moral fact that the very acts constitutive of war in our world are unjust. So, for a pacifist like Holmes, no war can ever be fought justly, regardless of the ends (such as self- or other-defense) supposedly aimed for. This is a strong pacifist argument because it does not contest the ends in question: it does not argue whether self-defense, or the defeat of the Nazis, might be morally legitimate causes for killing. It says that, even if the cause or goal of the war is worthy and just, consistency demands that it only be pursued through just means. But there are no just means, since they all involve killing at least some civilians who are innocent and non-aggressive. How is a just war theorist to respond to this pointed pacifist challenge, in my view probably the sharpest out there?[34]

A number of thinkers have sought to defeat this pacifist argument by casting doubt on the utility of employing the concept of innocence in wartime. But a just war theorist subscribing to the *jus in bello* rule of discrimination, with its corollary of non-combatant immunity, will neither want, nor logically be at liberty, to argue in this fashion. It seems that, despite all the residual ambiguities which remain regarding who exactly is "innocent" during wartime, just war theorists are correct to maintain this concept. It is hard to see, e.g., how infants could be anything other than innocent during a war (indeed, in general) and, as such, entitled not to be made the object of direct and intentional lethal attack. It is only those who are involved in harming us—i.e., those who are committing aggression against us—that we can justly target in a direct and intentional fashion during wartime.

We know, from Chapter 4, that the way in which traditional just war theory has dealt with this pacifist objection has been through the doctrine of double effect (or DDE). The DDE, recall, is based on the following scenario: assume agent X is considering performing an action A, which will have both good effects G and bad effects B. X is permitted to perform A only if: 1) A is otherwise permissible; 2) X only intends G and not B; 3) B is not a means to G; and 4) the goodness of G is worth, or is proportionate to, the badness of B.[35] Assume now that X is a country and A is war. The government of X, which is contemplating war in response to an unjustified armed invasion by country Y, knows that, should it embark on war, such activity will result in civilian casualties (both in X and Y), even if X manages to vindicate its rights of political sovereignty and territorial integrity. The DDE stipulates that X may still launch into such a justified war provided that: 1) this war is an otherwise permissible one of resisting aggression; 2) X does not intend any resulting civilian casualties (but, rather, aims only at vindicating its rights); 3) such casualties are not themselves the means whereby X's end (namely, vindicating its rights) is achieved; and 4) the importance of vindicating X's rights is proportionately greater than—or, at least, equal to—the badness of the resulting civilian casualties.

The key just war notion, we saw in the *jus in bello* chapters, is that civilians are not entitled to some kind of absolute, or fail-safe, immunity from attack; rather, they are owed neither more nor less than what Walzer has called "due care" from the belligerent government(s) that they not be made casualties of the war activity in question. Civilians are not entitled to such absolute immunity because the effect of allowing for such absolute immunity would be, essentially, to outlaw warfare altogether—and it is neither reasonable nor fair to require a political community to stand down in the face of an aggressive invasion which threatens the lives and rights of its member citizens.[36]

But this is precisely the nub of the DP pacifist's argument. The DP pacifist wants to say that the moral principle of never killing innocents throws a true blanket of immunity over the civilian population. Since just war theory doesn't likewise throw this blanket—but, rather, the thinner, threadbare fabric of "due care"—it does not really believe in civilian immunity. This is true: just war theory endorses due care only, and not complete immunity. Due care means the belligerents must fight in accord with *jus in bello* rules as we've previously defined them and, if indirect and unintended civilian casualties still result, they are justifiable provided that *jus ad bellum* is also met. Here we see that, ultimately, the moral difference between DP pacifism and just war theory remains the "big picture" difference of opinion whether war can ever be justly begun. Just war theory says that, since some causes of war—like resisting aggression—are morally just, this means that some civilian casualties must be permitted (provided they happen unintentionally after *jus in bello* gets satisfied). DP pacifism, by contrast, says that because civilian casualties can't ever be permitted—because of the wrongness of killing innocents—this shows that no causes of war can be sufficiently moral to start the murderous process. Here, just war theory moves from the top-down, whereas pacifism moves from the bottom-up. How can we adjudicate this vital, central debate?

I believe this is the strongest pacifist challenge to just war theory—war can't be justly fought, therefore the cause doesn't matter. The injustice of the conduct corrupts the cause and infects the entire war and, indeed, all wars. The only thing for the just war theorist to do is: 1) stress the importance of the cause as providing the moral context for the conduct issues; and 2) argue that due care for civilians is morally enough, given the stringency with which it is defined by just war theory, and the remaining need to defeat aggression. In other words, the cause does matter, and it affects our evaluation of fair conduct. My perspective is: how else are minimally just states, in our world, to defend themselves, to protect their people, and to vindicate the international system of law and order, save through armed force and the resort to war? And why should states capitulate their rights to political sovereignty and territorial integrity? Above all, why should they fail to protect their own people from aggression? Provided that the other criteria of just war are fulfilled, then the defense of rights, the protection of people, and the punishment of aggression seem worth the cost of incidental, indirect civilian casualties. It is worth it because, as contended above, it is unreasonable and unfair either to require or expect people not to resist an aggressive invasion of their country by force if required. They would lose too much, perhaps everything, if they capitulated. And it is not morally compelling for a government to fail to perform one of its core functions: to protect its citizens, by force if necessary, from severe threats to their lives and their human rights.

Whereas the DP pacifist wants to insist on the absolute duty never to kill innocent human beings, the just war theorist must disagree—because otherwise the pacifist will win. But how to disagree, since the principle seems so strong? By substituting for the pacifist's simplistic rule another one more responsive to war's complexity, namely, that we must never kill innocent human beings unless: 1) we have just cause to do so; and 2) the killing is unintentional and indirect. This is a more complex rule, but we can't side with simplicity for simplicity's sake. This new rule does preserve a serious prohibition on killing the innocent, which is very important for any plausible system of ethics. But it can allow genuinely unintended and indirect killing. (We know the DDE and *jus in bello* define indirection and non-intent for us much more specifically, as discussed in Chapter 4.) Moreover, this new rule does bring in the reference to the larger context and the issue of the justice of cause, whereas the pacifist principle refuses to do so (perhaps out of concern for what it might introduce). Having more information informing one's rules and principles clearly seems better than less. So, I argue that even DP ultimately isn't good enough to overthrow just war theory because: 1) it is too simple in comparison; 2) it is inflexible and absolute; 3) it ignores the issue of just cause; and 4) it deliberately and irresponsibly prefers less to more information. What DP gains in clarity, it loses in plausibility upon analysis. The operative rule should not be "never kill innocent people" but, rather, "never kill innocent people directly, deliberately, and without just cause."

A notable consequence of these reflections is that they support the theoretical point made throughout this book, namely, that the categories of just war theory must ultimately be tied together into a coherent whole. Here we see another strong reason why: if they're not so tied, they cannot fend off the strongest pacifist challenge. That challenge, we've just seen, focuses on *jus in bello* and—to be overcome—the connection between *jus in bello* and *jus ad bellum must* be made, and held fast. Those denying this connection are thus seriously vulnerable to pacifist overthrow.

This has been a difficult and challenging section, raising some of the most profound issues of moral theory itself. That's why it was saved until the end of the book. To summarize this section, DP raised a number of important duties, and alleged that just war theory violates them all. But:

1. The duty not to kill another person seems questionable, in light of compelling cases of self- and other-defense.

2. The duty not to violate rights is not broken by just war theory, which stipulates that war may be fought only in response to aggression. Once aggression has been committed by a state, it forfeits its state rights not to be attacked, for reasons of responsibility, reasonableness, fairness, and implicit entitlement. Although the people in the aggressor state retain their human rights, these will not be violated, provided that the victim state fights its just war in accord with the laws of war.

3. The duty not to kill innocent human beings is likewise not violated by just war theory, owing to its appeal to the doctrine of double effect (DDE). The foremost duty just war theory should seek to substitute and enshrine, in this regard, is the duty never to kill innocent human beings directly, deliberately, and without just cause.

4. Summary

The goal of this chapter was to discuss and evaluate the pacifist alternative to just war theory. We described various pacifist arguments with considerable care and charity. But the arguments for VP, CP, and DP are, in the final analysis, not as strong as those of just war theory. Pacifism, while well-intentioned, seems, in effect, to reward aggression and to fail to take measures needed to protect people from aggression. Pacifism is also premised on an excessively optimistic view of the world. It does offer an alternative to armed resistance, but the success of this method historically seems deeply questionable. The method of systematic civil disobedience in the face of aggression remains essentially untried, but what has been tried seems to have worked only in cases where the target was morally sensitive to begin with. When the target or aggressor is not sensitive, the result of this method is pure speculation. Pacifists hope it will work—and hope is a virtue—but this ultimately makes me wonder very seriously whether pacifism can actually be divorced from religion. It would seem that only under the warm blanket of religious faith could pacifism's prospects, in our rough-and-tumble world, seem promising.

Perhaps that's too quick. As in the previous chapter, we should remind ourselves not just of pacifism's weaknesses but also of its strengths. Even though I believe pacifism too optimistic to be practical in the realities of our world, I do agree that it's still important to hold on to ideals and do what you can to work towards them. It seems persuasive to say that, ultimately, we'd like to see the world to be peaceful and for disputes to be resolved peacefully—without violence and, certainly, without war. Who could disagree with that, at the level of pure ideal? Having that as a long-term (or end-point?) ideal can help shape our judgments and guide our actions in the present. While it probably does not trump just war theory—so long as the world remains so insecure and violent—it helps us resist realist pessimism that it's all a hopeless cycle of violent power-seeking. This is one reason why just war theory seems so attractive as a middle-ground option: it is not so optimistic that it's utopian and unresponsive to aggression yet it's not so pessimistic that it refuses to hold communities to a standard higher than their own national interests. In my own efforts at improving just war theory—notably through trying to articulate a rehabilitative *jus post bellum*—I must confess to having been motivated by pacifism's insistences that we shouldn't take war for granted and that we must do something to make the international system more peaceful, such as pro-rights post-war transformation and the evolution of better global governance.

So pacifism can be incorporated into just war theory, just as parts of realism were. Pacifism and *jus post bellum* can find many common causes and supports for reform, and pacifism reminds us of ultimate ideals most reasonable people would like to see one day realized. The other thing pacifism provides, in the meantime, is a very rich source of material regarding the last resort rule in *jus ad bellum*. The traditional interpretation of last resort, we saw in Chapter 2, is that after you've tried diplomacy and sanctions, force remains as the final option. Pacifism calls that small triad into question, and offers us many more tools within the anti-aggression toolbox. Some of these tools and tactics of non-violent resistance (general strikes, mass protest, systematic un-cooperation, etc.) may well be smartly deployed in several instances, even though we can't count on them working against the most ferocious aggressors, like the Nazis. Non-violent tactics, in some instances, hindered the Nazis but they didn't defeat them. What did was armed force. I see this illustrating the main conclusion here: that pacifism (like realism) does substantially contribute to the ethics of war and peace but it does not—at least, not yet—dislodge just war theory from its central position. Since just war theory incorporates the best from both extreme views, while sporting neither of their substantial flaws, it remains both rationally and morally the most choice-worthy position.

Notes

1 Jenny Teichman, *Pacifism and the Just War* (Oxford: Basil Blackwell, 1986), 3.

2 James P. Sterba, "Reconciling Pacifists and Just War Theorists," *Social Theory and Practice* (1992): 21–38. But see: Michael Neu, "Why There Is No Such Thing as Just-War Pacifism," *Social Theory and Practice* (2011): 44–68.

3 For more on defining pacifism, see: Robert L. Holmes, *On War and Morality* (Princeton, NJ: Princeton UP, 1989), 19–49; Jan Narveson, "Pacifism: A Philosophical Analysis," in Richard A. Wasserstrom, ed., *Morality and War* (Belmont, CA: Wadsworth, 1970), 63–77; Jan Narveson, "Violence and War," in Tom Regan, ed. *Matters of Life and Death* (Philadelphia, PA: Temple UP, 1980), 109–47.

4 Matthew 6:44.

5 Matthew 11:29 and 26:52.

6 The works of John Howard Yoder (e.g., *When War Is Unjust: Being Honest in Just-War Thinking* (Minneapolis, MN: Augsburg, 1984)) offer a good example of a religious justification for pacifism. See also: J. Patout Burns, *War and Its Discontents: Pacifism and Quietism in the Abrahamic Traditions* (Washington, DC: Georgetown UP, 1986); Lisa Sowle Cahill, *Love Your Enemies: Discipleship, Pacifism and Just War Theory* (Minneapolis, MN: Fortress, 1994); Michael G. Cartwright, "Conflicting Interpretations of Christian Pacifism," 197–213, and Theodore J. Koontz, "Christian Nonviolence: An Interpretation," 169–96, both in Terry Nardin, ed., *The Ethics of War and Peace: Religious and Secular Perspectives* (Princeton, NJ: Princeton UP, 1996); Daniel A. Dombrowski, *Christian Pacifism* (Philadelphia, PA: Temple UP, 1991); and Stanley Hauerwas, *Should War be Eliminated? Philosophical and Theological Investigations* (Milwaukee, WI: Marquette UP, 1984). On just war theory as part of official Catholic catechism, see <www.vatican.va/archive/catechism> as well as the works of Augustine and Aquinas cited in Chapter 1.

7 Robert L. Holmes, *On War and Morality* (Princeton, NJ: Princeton UP, 1989); Richard Norman, *Ethics, Killing and War* (Cambridge: Cambridge UP, 1995).

8 Peter Brock, *A Brief History of Pacifism from Jesus to Tolstoy* (Syracuse, NY: Syracuse UP, 1993); Peter Brock and Nigel Young, *Pacifism in the 20th Century* (Syracuse, NY: Syracuse UP, 1999).

9 Aristotle, *Nicomachean Ethics*, trans. by William David Ross (Oxford: Oxford UP, 1998); Philippa Foot, *Virtues and Vices* (Berkeley, CA: U of California P, 1978); Alasdair MacIntyre, *After Virtue* (Notre Dame, IN: U of Notre Dame P, 1984).

10 Thanks to Bob Martin for suggesting this slogan be mentioned. And he raises a deeper point: this contrasting set of virtues raises a more difficult problem for virtue ethics in general: what's the authoritative or best way for determining which of a clashing set of virtues—here, the clash between pacifist virtues and "soldierly" virtues—is the best one?

11 Michael Walzer, *Just and Unjust Wars*, 3rd ed. (New York: Basic Books, 2000), xvi.

12 Walzer, *Wars*, 329–36; Holmes, *War*, 260–96; Norman, *Ethics*, 210–15; Peter Ackerman and Jack DuVall, *A Force More Powerful* (New York: St. Martin's, 2000). This last book was also turned into part of an extended PBS documentary special by the same title.

13 Gene Sharp, "The Technique of Nonviolent Action," in Robert L. Holmes and Barry Gan, eds., *Nonviolence in Theory and Practice*, 2nd ed. (Long Grove, IL: Waveland, 2005), 254.

14 John Rawls, *A Theory of Justice* (Cambridge, MA: Harvard UP, 1971), 370–82; Walzer, *Wars*, 329–36.

15 Judith M. Brown, *Gandhi and Civil Disobedience* (Cambridge: Cambridge UP, 1977); Dennis Dalton, *Mahatma Gandhi: Nonviolent Power in Action* (New York: Columbia UP, 1993); Adam Fairclough, *To Redeem the Soul of America* (Athens, GA: U of Georgia P, 1987); Aldon D. Morris, *The Origins of the Civil Rights Movement* (New York: Free, 1984); Ackerman and DuVall, *Force*, 61–113 and 305–35.

16 Walzer, *Wars*, 330–35.

17 Ackerman and DuVall, *Force*, 207–41; Ernst Schwarz, *Paths to Freedom Through Nonviolence* (Vienna: Sensen-Verlag, 1959); Richard Petrow, *The Bitter Years* (New York: Morrow, 1974); Lennart Bergfelt, *Experiences of Civilian Resistance* (Uppsala, Sweden: U of Uppsala P, 1993); John Oram Thomas, *The Giant Killers* (New York: Taplinger, 1976).

18 Walzer, *Wars*, xxii, 330–35.

19 Rawls is usually credited with the ideal/non-ideal theory distinction. See his *Theory*, passim.

20 Jeremy Bentham, *The Principles of Morals and Legislation* (Indianapolis, IN: Hackett, 1981); John Stuart Mill, *Utilitarianism* (Indianapolis, IN: Hackett, 1987).

21 Michael Walzer, "The Moral Standing of States: A Response to Four Critics," *Philosophy and Public Affairs* (1979/80): 209–29; Thomas Nagel, "Ruthlessness in Public Life" in his *Mortal Questions* (Cambridge: Cambridge UP, 1979), 75–90.

22 John Keegan, *The First World War* (New York: Vintage, 1992).

23 John Keegan, *The Second World War* (New York: Vintage, 1990); Michael Walzer, "World War II: Why Was this War Different?" *Philosophy and Public Affairs* (1970/71): 3–21; William V. O'Brien, *The Conduct of Just and Limited War* (New York: Praeger, 1981), 35–65; George Orwell, *1984* (Harmondsworth: Penguin, 1989).

24 Norman, *Ethics*, 80–93.

25 Narveson, "Pacifism," 62–77.

26 Holmes, *War*, 146–213, esp. 183–213.

27 Relatedly, if it's true that, during 9/11, the pilot of the final plane deliberately flew it into the ground in Pennsylvania—once apprised of the aim of the hijackers—in order to save many more lives elsewhere (apparently in Washington, DC, as either Congress or the White House was thought to be the next target), then here too we have a complex case where it would seem permissible to intentionally take some lives for the sake of saving many more. Thanks to Bob Martin for the reference.

28 Gertrude Elizabeth Margaret Anscombe, "War and Murder," in Richard A. Wasserstrom, ed., *War and Morality* (Belmont, CA: Wadsworth, 1970), 41–53.

29 Narveson, "Pacifism," 63–78; Narveson, "Violence and War," 109–47; Henry Shue, *Basic Rights*, 2nd ed. (Princeton, NJ: Princeton UP, 1996); Alan Gewirth, *Human Rights: Essays in Justification and Application* (Chicago: U of Chicago P, 1982), passim.

30 Brian Orend, *Human Rights: Concept and Context* (Peterborough, ON: Broadview, 2002).

31 George P. Fletcher, "Proportionality and the Psychotic Aggressor," *Israel Law Review* (1973): 367–90.

32 Michael Otsuka appears to support this claim in his "Killing the Innocent in Self-Defense," *Philosophy and Public Affairs* (1992): 74–94. It is also present in Holmes, *War*, passim.

33 Helen Brocklehurst, "Kids 'R' Us? Children as Political Bodies," *International Journal of Politics and Ethics* (2003): 79–92.

34 Holmes, *War*, 146–213.

35 The DDE, thus defined, can't solve the innocent aggressor/child soldier problem discussed above. Say soldier S is considering shooting soldier T, who under some description is an innocent aggressor. S cannot appeal to the DDE here because, while he might say that he intends only to defeat the aggression and not kill an innocent, and while he might contend that the defeat of the aggression is worth the price, he cannot plausibly contend that killing the innocent is not means to his end of defeating the aggression, since the innocent and the aggressor are (by hypothesis) one and the same person. Innocent aggressors, if such there be, must thus be dealt with differently than innocent non-aggressors. Hence my further arguments above.

36 Walzer, *Wars*, 152–59, 257, 277–83, 317–21; Norman, *Killing*, 73–118 and 159–200.

CONCLUSION

"The virtue of justice consists in moderation, as regulated by wisdom." —ARISTOTLE[1]

Reflecting on the ethics of war and peace can be tough, and is fraught with dangers both conceptual and moral. We've seen this, in spades, throughout this book. Yet reflect on war's morality we must, as responsible individuals actively engaged in our world.

Active engagement, the press of events, and the weight of the stakes all make wartime decision-making doubly difficult. We thus appreciate, in its full force, the observation that rigorous contemplation of the justice of war—in all its phases—must be given *before* the decision to go to war is made. As decent people, citizens, and decision-makers, we must examine all the aspects we can, and formulate firm, sensible, and humane policies which can't and won't be dislodged during someone's rush to war. Quick action may indeed be necessary, but it can't be informed by rash decisions based on shoddy evidence, superficial values, and temporary fears.

I have argued, throughout this text, that the best aid to contemplation of these issues is just war theory and, to a somewhat lesser extent, international law. (Instead of summarizing all the main points again here, I remind the reader of the summaries at the end of each chapter.) My conviction now, at book's end, remains the same (in spite of the substantial contributions of realism and pacifism). Just war theory is more detailed and comprehensive than either of its rivals, and it is neither too pessimistic nor too optimistic. Just war theory is less extreme and sweeping in its conclusions; and it bases its views on deep, reasonable, and sincerely considered values, such as those of human rights, minimally just communities, and the need to protect both from aggression. Aggression, sadly, is a common failing in human beings and the societies they form. Lots of people love telling other people what to do. When that desire for dominance becomes coupled with physical violence, it must be resisted—for the sake of our lives, our rights, and the integrity and quality of our very humanity. Just war theory realizes this, and recognizes its profound moral importance. It is for all these reasons that just war theory is already so deeply ingrained in international law, as well as in our daily discourse and debate about the ethics of war and peace. Just war theory is, on these issues, "The Big Middle"—the common sense common ground, the expansive majority viewpoint—whereas its rivals occupy small (yet strident) positions on the edges of thought and opinion. Hence the above quote from Aristotle, on the virtue of moderation.

Today, those who we should, perhaps, be most suspicious about are those who argue that "a new age has dawned"—whether with the events of 9/11, the invention of drones, or the start of cyber-warfare—and that we must now do without time-tested values and fight with an unprecedented ferocity and lack of restraint. These self-appointed gurus of "a brand new era" are, all too often, wrong. And what they are here suggesting, proposing, and allowing is too extreme, far too dangerous, and verging at times even on savagery. Life is not a bare-knuckled fight to the death; it is our most precious gift—one we must strive to protect with rights, with decent conduct, and with shared institutions designed to afford us all our measure of security, freedom, and happiness.

Just war theory and international law remain hugely useful and insightful—indeed, unparalleled—aids to reflection and decision-making in connection with war, including the very latest and even future challenges. Until the advent of a genuinely more peaceful world, they will be—in one form or another—truly irreplaceable.

Note

1 Aristotle, *Nicomachean Ethics,* trans. by William David Ross (Oxford: Oxford UP, 1998), Book V.

Appendix A

SOURCES ON THE LAWS OF WAR

1. Primary Sources:

The best web-sites are below, where many of the major international laws and treaties on war can be down-loaded for free and in full. Go to:

The Avalon Project at Yale Law School:
<www.yale.edu/lawweb/avalon/lawofwar/lawwar.htm>

University of Minnesota Law of Armed Conflict:
<www1.umn.edu/humanrts/instree/auoy.htm>

Air War College:
<www.au.af.mil/au/awc/awcgate/awc-law.htm>

2. Thematic and Chronological Organization of the Primary Sources:

JUS AD BELLUM

Hague Convention I & III (1907)
The Kellogg-Briand Pact (1928)
Charter of the United Nations (1945), especially Articles 1, 2, 5, 6, 23-27 and 33-54
United Nations General Assembly Definition of Aggression (1974)
Decision of the International Court of Justice on Nicaragua vs. The United States of America (1986)
(Chapters 1 and 3 of Reisman and Antoniou, eds., *Laws* (see below Section 3))

JUS IN BELLO

United States' Field Army Manual (or "Lieber's Code") (1863)
Hague Conventions (1899-1907)
Convention Regulating Poisonous Gases (1925)
Convention Regulating Genocide (1948)

Geneva Conventions (1949)
Additional Protocols to the Geneva Convention (1977 and 1996)
Convention Regulating Cultural Property and Sites during Wartime (1954)
United Nations General Assembly Resolutions Prohibiting Nuclear Weapons (1961) and (1973)
Convention Regulating Aircraft Offenses (1963), including Aircraft Seizure (1970) and Civil Aviation Safety (1971)
Convention Regulating Biological Weapons (1972)
Convention Regulating Diplomatic Agents during Wartime (1973)
Convention Regulating Weapons Which Modify the Environment (1976)
Convention Regulating Hostages during Wartime (1979)
Convention Regulating Excessively Injurious or Indiscriminate Weapons (1980)
(Chapters 2, 4, and 6 of Reisman and Antoniou, eds., *Laws* (see below Section 3))

JUS POST BELLUM

Hague Convention IV (1907) (Articles 32-50)
United Nations Charter (1945) (Articles 73-85 and 92-96)
Nuremberg Judgments (1946)
Tokyo Judgments (1946)
Geneva Conventions (1949)
Treaty of Rome Establishing the International Criminal Court (1998)
(Chapters 5 and 7 of Reisman and Antoniou, eds., *Laws* (see below Section 3))

3. Compilations (often including editing and commentary):

I prefer, and have used extensively, W. Michael Reisman and Chris T. Antoniou, eds. *The Laws of War: A Comprehensive Collection of Primary Documents Governing Armed Conflict* (New York: Vintage, 1994). See also:

Best, Geoffrey. *War and Law Since 1945* (Oxford: Clarendon, 1994).
Byers, Michael. *War Law* (Washington, DC: Atlantic, 2009).
Gillespie, Alexander. *History of the Laws of War* 3rd ed., (New York: Hart, 2011).
Howard, Michael. *The Laws of War: Constraints on Warfare in the Western World* (New Haven, CT: Yale UP, 1994).
Kennedy, David W. *Of War and Law* (Princeton, NJ: Princeton UP, 2006).
Neff, Stephen. *War and the Law of Nations* (Cambridge: Cambridge UP, 2008).
Roberts, Adam and Richard Guelff, eds. *Documents on the Laws of War* 3rd ed., (Oxford: Oxford UP, 2000).
Simpson, Gerry J. *Law, War and Crime* (Oxford: Polity, 2007).
Solis, Gary D. *The Law of Armed Conflict* (Cambridge: Cambridge UP, 2010).

Appendix B

CONCEPTUAL OVERVIEW OF JUST WAR THEORY

War has three phases: start, middle, and end; and so just war theory requires three sets of rules to regulate the choices and behavior of decision-makers and actors: *jus ad bellum* (start of war); *jus in bello* (conduct in war); and *jus post bellum* (ending phase of war). But these three categories are *inter-connected, not separate*. And *jus ad bellum* sets the tone for everything else which follows:

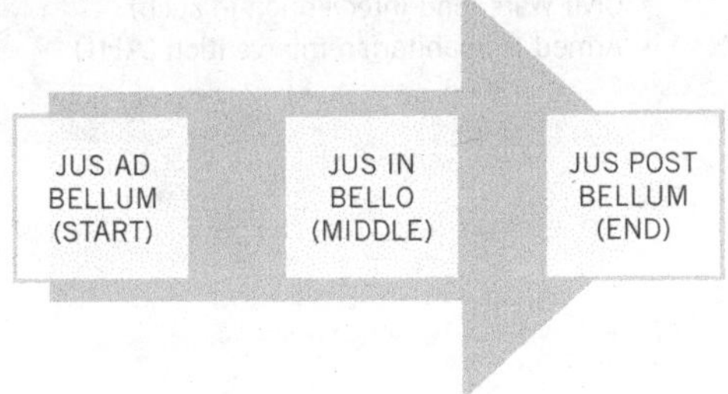

1) **Jus ad Bellum** *Rules (Classical, Inter-state, Responding to Prior Aggression):*

- Just Cause
- Right Intention
- Public Declaration of War by a Proper Authority
- Proportionality
- Probability of Success
- Last Resort

*(**N.B.** how the first 3 rules are expressive of **first principles**—notably, respect for rights—and are concerned with correct and fair process, whereas the last 3 are expressive of concern for **consequences** and are concerned with ensuring certain results are achieved.)*

Just Cause

(the most important rule, from which everything else flows):

CLASSICAL

- Resisting Prior, Inter-State Agression
- "Strict Defence Purism"
- Justified as; reasonable; fair; respectful of responsibility; and an entitlement implied by the need to secure all other rights

NON-CLASSICAL

- Punishing/Thwarting Terrorism & Any State Sponsorship Thereof
- Well-Grounded Anticipatory Attacks
- Civil Wars (and intervention in such)
- Armed Humanitarian Intervention (AHI)

2) Jus in Bello *Rules*

EXTERNAL (vis à vis The Enemy)

- Discrimination/ Non-Combatant Immunity
- Benevolent Quarantine for Prisoners-of-War (POWs)
- Follow the Doctrine of Double Effect (DDE)
- Proportionality
- No Illegal Weapons (esp. Weapons of Mass Destruction (WMD))
- No Means "*Mala in Se*"
- No Reprisals
- Follow Just War Values re: Emerging Military Technologies (EMTs), like drones or cyber-war

INTERNAL (vis à vis One's Own Citizens)

- Respect the Human Rights Claims of One's Own Soldiers, and Civilians, as Best One Can Amidst War

*(**N.B.**: A "Supreme Emergency" is an extremely rare and tragic threat of (near-) genocide and utter destruction, wherein the violation of these rules might be excused (though never justified). A Supreme Emergency cries out for international AHI, so that no violations would be required.)*

3) Jus post Bellum *Rules*

Substantially (and sadly) un-regulated by international law, we can only speak of different theories of post-war justice. There are 2 major rival theories in this regard—Retribution and Rehabilitation—though they do share some common ground:

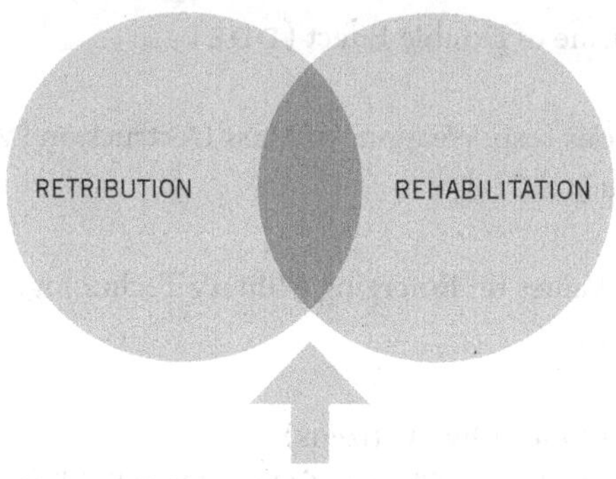

THE OVERLAPPING CONSENSUS

A. OVERLAPPING CONSENSUS: THE THIN THEORY

- GOAL: vindicating the rights whose violation triggered the war, forcing the defeated Aggressor to accept a proportionate policy on surrender which includes:
- Public Terms of Settlement
- Mutual Exchange of POWs
- Aggressor to Apologize
- Aggressor to Give Up Unjust Gains
- Aggressor to Demilitarize
- War Crimes Trials (*Jus ad Bellum* trials for Aggressor; *Jus in Bello* trials for all sides)

B. THICK THEORY #1: RETRIBUTION

- GOAL: to make the defeated Aggressor *worse-off* than prior to the war (as backward-looking punishment). MEANS: all of the thin theory above, plus:
- Compensation Payments from Aggressor to Victim, and possibly to International Community more broadly
- Sanctions put on Aggressor, to hamper its future economic growth
- No aid or assistance with post-war reconstruction. Such is left up to the locals, with no forcible regime change imposed on Aggressor

C. THICK THEORY #2: REHABILITATION

- GOAL: to make the defeated Aggressor *better-off* than prior to the war (as forward-looking reconstruction). MEANS: all of the thin theory above, plus:
- No Compensation Payments
- No Sanctions
- Aid and Assistance with post-war reconstruction, including Forcible Regime Change imposed on defeated Aggressor
- Follow 10-step "Rehabilitation Recipe" (Chapter 7), with best efforts over 10-15 years post-war, to realize in the defeated former Aggressor a new, and minimally just, society

* For a PowerPoint version of this appendix, visit: <http://sites.broadviewpress.com/moralityofwar>.

INDEX

A

B

D

H

J

K

N

Q

R

T

U

V

From the Publisher

A name never says it all, but the word "Broadview" expresses a good deal of the philosophy behind our company. We are open to a broad range of academic approaches and political viewpoints. We pay attention to the broad impact book publishing and book printing has in the wider world; for some years now we have used 100% recycled paper for most titles. Our publishing program is internationally oriented and broad-ranging. Our individual titles often appeal to a broad readership too; many are of interest as much to general readers as to academics and students.

Founded in 1985, Broadview remains a fully independent company owned by its shareholders—not an imprint or subsidiary of a larger multinational.

For the most accurate information on our books (including information on pricing, editions, and formats) please visit our website at www.broadviewpress.com. Our print books and ebooks are also available for sale on our site.

broadview press
www.broadviewpress.com

This book is made of paper from well-managed FSC® - certified forests, recycled materials, and other controlled sources.

PERMANENT